PUBLIC SPEAKING

The Lively Art

PUBLIC SPEAKING

The Lively Art

JOHN H. POWERS

Texas A&M University

Wadsworth Publishing Company
Belmont, California
A Division of Wadsworth, Inc.

Communications Editor: Kristine Clerkin

Editorial Assistant: Naomi Brown

Production Editor: Gary Mcdonald

Print Buyer: Karen Hunt

Designer: MaryEllen Podgorski

Copy Editor: Jennifer Gordon

Technical Illustrator: Valerie Felts

Signing Representative: Ragu Raghavan

Printed in the United States of America   34

  2 3 4 5 6 7 8 9 10—91 90 89 88

Library of Congress Cataloging-in-Publication Data

Powers, John H. (John Henry), 1947–
   Public speaking.

   Includes bibliographies and index.
   1. Public speaking.   I. Title
PN4121.P647   1987   808.51   86-30766
ISBN 0-534-07296-8

TO FRANK DANCE

*who first introduced me to the power
of the spoken word*

Brief Contents

Detailed Contents

Preface

*O*n first opening this book, readers may be tempted to ask why another public speaking textbook should be added to an already long list. After all, literally hundreds of books have been written about the art of public speaking. Everyone from famous actors (Valenti, 1984) to famous philosophers (Adler, 1983), from noted businessmen (Carnegie, 1977) to aspiring businesswomen (Sarnoff, 1970), has written a book on how to present a speech in public. Why is there all this interest in public speaking?

The vast quantity of books about public speaking is easy to explain. Speaking in public is an exceptionally important skill, and yet, most people feel a little overwhelmed and inadequate when they first try to do it. As beginnners, nearly everyone needs guidance in the art, and every profession that requires much public speaking has also produced gifted practitioners who write books to help its newcomers succeed. That explains why there are so many books about public speaking already. But why add yet another to the list?

There are really two traditions in the teaching of public speaking. The first is the purely practical tradition. This tradition recognizes that speaking is a skill that can be taught and learned through guided instruction and regular practice. Most of the popular books written by gifted practitioners of the art are working in this first tradition. The second tradition is both *theoretical* and *practical*, recognizing that public speaking is not only a skill to be practiced but also an art to be studied and understood. This second tradition views public speaking as a complex human activity that fits into a larger picture of human communication. It holds that students should attempt to uncover the underlying principles of public speaking and seek to understand their operation.

*T*his Book's Approach

Public Speaking: The Lively Art has its roots in both traditions. On the one hand, I regularly teach public speaking to students who are required to take the course and whose primary interest is the practical advantages that public speaking can provide them in college and their professional careers. Keeping their needs firmly in mind, I have written this book for practical day-to-day use with students like my own. Its goal is to present a clear and straightforward approach to the practice of effective public speaking.

On the other hand, I am also a speech communication theorist deeply committed to understanding human communication, including how practical public speaking reflects more general principles of speech communication and human nature. To provide a conceptual framework for understanding the principles of public speaking, *Public Speaking: The Lively Art* draws upon recent writings of philosopher Susanne Langer (1967, 1972, 1982). In particular, a set of five principles based on Langer's ideas is developed in Chapter 3 ("Public Speaking As 'Organic': The Power of a Metaphor"). These five principles should help students understand how all the specific public speaking skills they are about to develop fit together as one unified process. Working from these principles, the book attempts to engage students' minds and imaginations in the art of public speaking at the same time that it guides them through the practical skills that will produce effective public speeches.

For the most part, the conceptual framework that generates the five principles remains discreetly invisible, like a good skeleton. With the exception of Chapter 3, which explicitly presents some of Langer's ideas, the conceptual framework underlying this book expresses itself in more subtle ways. Even so, it is my hope that the explanations of key terms and the discussion of important traditional topics will hold together better because of the underlying framework of ideas. To help ensure student understanding, I have been careful to define new terms and to present examples in the most straightforward, accessible manner possible.

*T*he Plan of the Book

The organization of the book has also been planned to be of maximum help to students learning to speak in public. For example, since most instructors require a first speech assignment early in the course, long before students have worked all the way through the text, Chapter 1 presents a quick introduction to the essential steps of public speaking. Chapters 2 and 3 then present the conceptual foundations of human communication and public speaking, laying out the framework that is employed in developing subsequent chapters by presenting a general model of the speech communication process and outlining a set of principles that apply to all aspects of effective public speaking. Chapters 4 and 5 close out Part One of the book by focusing on two audience-related questions: What expectations do audiences have concerning the public speakers they hear? and How can you be a more effective listener whenever you are an audience member rather than a speaker?

Part Two presents the principles of general and informative speaking in the order students most frequently encounter them. Accordingly, Chapter 6 tackles the problem of selecting a topic for classroom speeches and shows how to prepare a specific purpose statement that can guide subsequent speech preparation most efficiently. Chapter 7 explains why effective speakers need to understand their audiences and provides guidance in how to analyze the audience to determine how to adapt one's speech content, language, and delivery. Because speeches are constructed out of a wide variety of supporting materials, which must then be organized into a unified and coherent whole, Chapters 8, 9, and 10 treat the types of supporting materials that typically compose a speech, the methods of organizing those materials into a readily understandable pattern of main points, and how to prepare introductions, conclusions, and transitions that will make your speeches seem to come alive in an audience's imagination.

With this basic material completed, Part Two continues with four chapters that can help you refine your speech skills to a higher degree. Chapter 11 discusses the types of visual aids that can enhance your speech, as well as how to integrate them into your speech. Chapter 12 explains how to use a diagnostic outline to analyze the adequacy of your speech preparation and how to modify your diagnostic outline for use in presenting the final version of your speech. Since a speech is a fabric of words, Chapter 13 emphasizes the choices speakers have in encoding their ideas into words and presents a large number of easy to use language techniques that can enhance the vividness of any speech. Chapter 14 concludes Part Two by focusing on the principles of effective speech delivery.

Part Three covers the principles of persuasive speaking. Persuasive speaking is given its own part because, even though it uses many of the principles of general and informative speaking, persuasive speaking also requires some very special adaptations of these principles. Furthermore, some aspects of persuasive speaking are not relevant to other types of public speaking. Chapter 15 introduces persuasive speaking and discusses the following topics: the nature of the impulse to persuade, topic selection for persuasive speech assignments, the types of persuasive purposes, how to formulate fact, value, policy, and definitional claims for persuasive speeches, and what issues are involved in arguing each of these four types of claims. Chapter 16 addresses the role of reasoning in persuasive speaking (including both inductive and deductive reasoning), how to organize a persuasive speech in the most effective manner, and how to marshal all of one's personal resources to support an analytical, well-reasoned speech when attempting to persuade an audience.

*U*sing the Book

Beyond its organization and step-by-step development of principles, *Public Speaking: The Lively Art* contains several additional elements to help students learn to become better speakers.

1. Many *examples*, of varying types and lengths, taken from real speeches, are distributed throughout the text.

2. *Questions for Review* and *Questions for Discussion* are provided at the end of each chapter to help students review for examinations and prepare for class discussions.

3. *Things to Try* at the end of each chapter provide activities that should enhance and deepen students' understanding of the material.

4. *Photographs* have been carefully selected to help students develop topic ideas for speeches. In each case, a photograph of an interesting event or situation is accompanied by a caption that should help students develop speeches in response to the personal or social implications of the subject of the photograph.

5. Two *appendixes* supplement the basic instruction presented in the main chapters of the book. Appendix A provides some guidelines for researching a speech and includes a step-by-step process for conducting a systematic search for information. Appendix B explains how to prepare a speech on a process, especially emphasizing how-to speeches.

6. Three *appendixes* present sample speeches for use in discussing the principles developed in the main body of the text: Appendix C presents a sample informative speech by a student, Appendix D provides a sample persuasive speech by a student, and Appendix E presents a sample persuasive speech by a professional speaker.

*A*cknowledgments

In closing, thanks go to all the people who have shown faith in this project, from its preliminary proposal over nine years ago to its final writing in the present version: friends who have discussed the ideas with me, colleagues who have class-tested the book in its developmental stages, and my department head, Kurt Ritter, who has allowed me the time necessary to work out the theoretical ideas and to develop them for a practical area of application such as public speaking. Thanks must also go to the score or more reviewers, mostly anonymous, who have over the years given their time and critical attention to making this a better book. I'd like to thank the following reviewers of this book who *are* known to me: Phil Backlund, Central Washington University; Leslie Di Mare, California State University, Los Angeles; Cynthia P. Flowers, University of Alabama; Sonja K. Foss, University of Oregon; Kathy German, Miami University of Ohio; Carol Jablonski, Indiana University; John Masterson, University of Miami; Beth Waggenspack, Virginia Tech University; and Barbara Warnick, University of Washington. Although I have not always been able to incorporate their advice into the final text, I have always appreciated the counsel and care they have lavished on this book. Thanks are also due to Gary Mcdonald and MaryEllen Podgorski for their generous work in producing the book and proposing the photographs that grace its pages.

But most of all thanks are due to Tom Gornick, at one time an editor in the speech communication area, who urged me to do what I had merely *talked* about doing, and to Kristine Clerkin of Wadsworth Publishing Company, who enthusiastically brought the project to fruition once the manuscript was finally completed. Without their timely encouragement and generous help, *Public Speaking: The Lively Art* would have remained merely another "interesting idea," presented vigorously by an ardent advocate, but never really tested where it counts—in the classroom and in the marketplace of scholarly discussion. It is to the faith these friends have shown that this work is dedicated.

*B*ibliography

Adler, Mortimer J. *How to Speak, How to Listen.* New York: Macmillan, 1983.

Carnegie, Dale. *The Quick and Easy Way to Effective Speaking.* New York: Pocket Books, 1977.

Langer, Susanne K. *Mind: An Essay on Human Feeling,* 3 vols. Baltimore: Johns Hopkins University Press, 1967, 1972, 1982.

Powers, John H. "An Act-Based Theory of Communication: First Principles." *Journal of Applied Communication Research* 10 (Spring 1982), 9–20.

Sarnoff, Dorothy. *Speech Can Change Your Life: Tips on Speech, Conversation and Speechmaking.* New York: Dell Publishing Company, 1970.

Valenti, Jack. *Speak Up with Confidence.* New York: William Morrow, 1984.

PUBLIC SPEAKING

The Lively Art

Orientation
and
Overview

CHAPTER 1

Getting Started: Preparing Your First Speech

Introduction

For more than 2400 years now—since at least the era of classical Greece—generation after generation of students has been systematically mastering the principles of effective public speaking. Step by step, they have learned how to better organize their thoughts, more forcefully develop their ideas, and more thoughtfully select the most appropriate modes of expressing what they want to say. And they have been more effectively standing up and presenting those ideas to others in a public setting. By enrolling in a course in public speaking you have committed yourself to joining these generations of students in mastering the skills of articulate public self-expression. You, too, will be following a systematic program of study designed to help you learn to effectively organize, develop, phrase, and publicly present your ideas to others.

Spontaneous versus Prepared Speech

People, of course, speak to one another all the time. We chat with our friends, answer questions in classes, transact business in banks and stores. Speaking, in fact, is so much a mark of the human species that Dennis Fry has dubbed us *Homo loquens*—the talking animal (1977), and Jean Aitchison has called us *The Articulate Mammal* (1978). Most of the time we don't give much prior thought to our speech. We don't need to—we just talk, someone responds, inspiring our next thought, and we talk again. Speech comes as naturally to most of us as mooing does to cows and meowing does to cats.

But speech is not always as spontaneous as thought nor as casual as conversation. In numerous situations speech may not seem to come naturally at all—situations where speech must be thought out and prepared in advance, where purely spontaneous conversational speech simply does not seem good enough for the occasion. Your employer selects *you* to make a report before the Board of Directors; the City Council calls a public hearing on a proposed zoning change that directly affects your neighborhood and *you* want to speak out against it; the local scout troop invites *you* to talk about your job or special hobby. In all these situations, and countless others, you will be called upon to prepare your speech ahead of time, and to stand up before an audience that expects you to "hold the floor." No longer will you be able to depend on the rhythmic give and take of spontaneous conversation to inspire your thoughts and words. The purpose of your course in public speaking is to teach you how to prepare your speech for such occasions, and to give you ample opportunities to practice presenting your ideas when you are expected to continue talking for a sustained, uninterrupted period of time.

Learn to Speak? Why Bother?

Some students (especially those who are required to take a course in public speaking) wonder why they should bother to learn to prepare speech for others. After all, they may think, they will never have to give speeches. In fact, nobody they know *ever* gives speeches. If spontaneous speech isn't good enough, then why speak at all?

Several traditional reasons help explain why public speaking is such a widely required course. First, the study of speech (under the name of **rhetoric**) is one of the traditional liberal arts. As such, speech has always played a significant role in Western education. The study of speech aims to free you to be able to express yourself in public situations so that your ideas may be heard. Second, speech is a democratic skill, required of all citizens of a modern democracy. We are said to be a "government by talk." According to this viewpoint, public speaking is necessary for democracy to function at its optimum. The citizens of classical Greece, from whom we inherit our modern public speaking tradition (as well as our democratic ideals), had to know personally how to speak on the legislative floor or at the judicial bar. All citizens were expected to participate freely in the life of the democracy. Although we may not be expected to be able to speak in Congress or to represent ourselves in court (as we might have been in classical Athens), in this country we still believe that if we are to participate effectively in the decision making that affects our lives—decision making that is inherent in the democratic form of government—we must learn to present our opinions on public issues as well as we possibly can.

Both of these are good reasons for requiring students to take speech as part of their liberal arts curricula. Being able to confidently speak one's mind in the public forum is indeed a liberating experience. But many students in the sciences and business are also required to take courses in public speaking. There are reasons for requiring public speaking in highly technical curricula, such as computer science, petroleum engineering, mechanized agriculture, and accounting, but they are not necessarily limited to the traditional liberal arts and democratic reasons. Thus, you might still legitimately ask why.

We may safely eliminate three reasons. Public speaking is not a snap course designed to help students who are in highly competitive professional fields raise their grade-point averages. Preparing and delivering good speeches requires as much work as any other skill you may be learning. On the other hand, academic departments are not so flooded with qualified applicants that they have tried to design the most difficult and terrifying course they could in order to weed out as many students as possible. Speaking is something you do spontaneously every day. The goal in a public speaking class is to help you enhance your effectiveness in doing something you already do, but on a less formal basis. Finally, your major departments have no interest in your becoming great orators—in the grand tradition of Demosthenes, Daniel Webster, William Jennings Bryan, Martin Luther King, Jr., or John F. Kennedy—swaying the crowds with your words.

The real reason college departments require you to take a course in public speaking is that, as college graduated professionals, you are quite likely to have to explain what you know both to other professionals and to interested laypersons. As professionals in whatever field you may be pursuing, you will not only have to know your subject matter, you will also have to publicly present that knowledge to professionally significant others. Through many short speeches and informal talks, perhaps to supervisees, perhaps to those higher up, you will have to be able to tell others what you know and to convince them of what you believe. A course in public speaking offers you an opportunity to practice the essential public communication skills and techniques in a situation where only a grade is at stake—not a job you want, or advanced professional standing.

Your course in public speaking is designed, then, to do two things for you. First, it is designed to help you learn techniques for structuring what you know and believe so that you can select the most effective way of communicating your knowledge and beliefs to others. Second, it is designed to give you actual practice in telling others what you know or believe, so that you won't be afraid to speak up when the situation arises in your community or professional lives.

So, although you may never have to speak in front of 500 people at a Chamber of Commerce meeting, never have to deliver a speech to the City Council advocating some important legislation, or never even be a guest speaker for some club or organization, you *will* be called on to structure what you know for oral presentation in important professional settings. You will be called on to argue for what you believe in many forums relating to your professional expertise. And that is why numerous academic departments require a course in public speaking. They recognize that no matter how much you may know about your professional subject matter—if you do not also know how to publicly communicate that subject matter, you are not a fully trained, fully functioning professional.

This book, then, is about speech communication in the public setting; it is about the demands made upon you when you prepare your speech for others; and it is about the techniques you can use to fulfill those increased demands more effectively.

What Will You Be Learning?

Now that you know more about why it is important to have a course in public speaking, it is time to look more closely at what you will be learning during your public speaking course. First, and perhaps foremost, you will be learning how to give speeches before a variety of audiences—learning such things as (1) how to select and narrow a speech topic to match a particular audience and occasion, (2) how to divide your subject into manageable subdivisions, (3) how to organize your ideas into an order of presentation that is easy for an audience to follow, (4) how to cast your ideas into memorable words and phrases so that your audience can more readily remember them, and, of course, (5) how to effectively stand up and deliver your speech.

In addition to these immediately practical aspects of public speaking training, you will also be learning about the theory underlying effective public speaking—the theory that both guides the practices you will use on a day-to-day basis and that helps explain why those practices work the way they do. An important part of this public speaking text will be dedicated to helping you understand why the things you are taught work the way they do, and why you are encouraged to prepare speeches the way the textbooks recommend.

Preparing Your First Speech

The theory in this book is both as ancient as Aristotle and as contemporary as I myself can make it. Public speaking theory has continued to grow new branches and leaves in the twentieth century at the very same time that it has preserved its roots in the fertile soil of the 5th and 4th centuries B.C. in Greece. Since most public speaking classes require you to begin giving speeches before you have had much opportunity to study either the theory or the practice of effective public speaking, this section will survey the major steps in preparing your first public speech. Most of the topics touched on here will receive extended treatment later in the book, after the first portion of the theory has been explained in the rest of Part One. This introductory section is a little bit like a tennis coach telling you during your first lesson, "Hit the ball over the net." Both of you know there is much more to tennis than that, but until you can successfully "hit the ball over the net," nothing else makes much sense—especially such things as theories, tactics, and strategies of the game. So consider this next portion of the chapter as basic, pretheoretical instruction in "hitting the ball over the net."

The basic process of speech preparation can be divided into seven component processes, usually done in about this order. But it is important to recognize that the order given here merely suggests how to plan your speech preparation; it cannot legislate how you will actually order the steps in your own work on any particular speech. The basic processes are as follows:

1. Deciding on a *topic*

2. Deciding on your central *purpose* or *idea*

3. Deciding how you will make your topic *relevant* and *interesting* to your specific audience

4. Preparing your speech's *body*
   a. Deciding what your *main points* will be
   b. Deciding what *developmental material* you will use

5. Preparing your *introduction*

6. Preparing your *conclusion*

7. Preparing your *delivery*

You will probably notice that speech preparation is divided into two types of processes—deciding and preparing. You begin by making several preliminary decisions about your speech and then follow up with preparation based on those preliminary decisions. Let's take a look at each of these steps in turn.

Deciding on a Topic

The first step in speech preparation is deciding on a topic to talk about. What should you talk about in your first few speeches? Usually something you already know quite a bit about—a serious hobby, an important or unusual aspect of your major, or some other area of special interest to you. Failing that, select something you are willing to find out more about. The point is, your first speeches should probably be composed of ideas you are thoroughly familiar with, ideas coming from your own direct, personal experience or background—because you will have enough to be concerned about in simply organizing your ideas for presentation and controlling your anxiety about speaking, without having to deal with strange or unfamiliar ideas and materials as well. So, unless your instructor assigns a specific topic, choose your topic from areas you already know well and feel relatively comfortable talking about. Besides, there is ample time later on to do a fully researched and documented speech—and plenty of reason for doing so as well. But not here at the beginning of your speech training. Select a topic you can manage comfortably.

Deciding on Your Central Purpose or Idea

Having decided upon your topic, you must next decide on your purpose in giving the speech. Are you going to try to inform the audience? Persuade them? Entertain them? Each of these purposes places different demands on you and on how you will handle your topic. What are you trying to accomplish with your speech to this audience? What main idea do you want them to take away from your speech?

Let's imagine that you're a computer science major and that you've chosen to give a five to seven minute informative speech on the topic of computers. Since you cannot tell your audience everything you know about computers, you must decide what major key idea you want to share with them. Will you explain who made the scientific breakthroughs that made the modern computer age possible? What a microprocessor is? When the first computers were commercially produced? Where the research was done that made the computer age possible? Why the computer is so fast? How to use a computer to help ourselves in school or work? Each of these specific approaches to the topic places different demands on you, demands that will be talked about in a later chapter. At this point, it is important to decide which aspect of the vast topic of computers you will talk about and to formulate that idea into a single key statement of purpose. For example:

Specific Purpose: To explain the three most significant recent breakthroughs in computer technology

Formulate this statement of purpose as fully and explicitly as you can because it will guide the rest of your preparation.

Deciding How You Will Make Your Topic Relevant and Interesting to Your Specific Audience

Suppose your topic is hunting. Do your classmates hunt for sport? You don't know? Then you must find out a little about them. Your next task is to decide how you will make your topic interesting and relevant to your specific audience. That is, you must try to understand your audience well enough to be able to connect your topic with their known or anticipated interests. Suppose, for example, you find out that none of them hunts. Does that mean you automatically have to eliminate your favorite topic? No, definitely not! It just means that a speech with a central purpose of telling your audience what to do with their birds after a successful day of hunting will probably fall on deaf ears. But this topic has many other angles of interest for you to choose from, angles that might work quite well: the human interest angle of knowing what one of their classmates does, the angle of possible sources of income available to an enterprising college student, the angle of satisfying natural curiosity about an unusual process they may never have seen before. Any of these might serve as a way of marshaling your audience's attention—which is required for the sustained act of listening they must perform during your speech. And any of these angles might help you focus your speech—so your angle of interest might read:

To explain the five steps in mounting a duck so the audience can see how easy it is to make some money in their spare time

Preparing Your Speech's Body

Having considered your audience's needs and interests, you will begin planning the main body of your speech. This involves two substeps. First, you must decide what your main points will be and the order in which you wish to present those points. Second, you must decide what developmental material you will use to give those points adequate substance and impact on your particular audience. Some topics and specific purposes strongly dictate the order in which you will present your points (how-to speeches, for example) and what kinds of developmental material will be most effective. Other topics allow quite a bit of free choice in both organizational and developmental matters. But whatever the situation, you must next prepare the body of the speech, weaving your pattern of points together into an organic whole with your supporting material.

Deciding What Your Main Points Will Be A speech is composed not only of a topic and a specific purpose (germinating idea) to accomplish, but also of a pattern of main points that you are hoping to communicate to your audience. So the next step is to select your major points and to word them as carefully as you did your central idea. If your topic was drawn from your hobby as a part-time taxidermist, you might have as your topic:

Mounting Ducks for Fun and Profit

Your specific purpose might be:

To explain the five key steps in preparing a mallard for the trophy-room showcase

And your five main points might be:

1. The first step in preparing your prize bird for showing is gathering the materials you will need to complete the process.

2. The next step is preparing the bird for wiring.

3. The third step is wiring the duck for posing.

4. The fourth step is posing the bird as you want it to look in the final display.

5. The final step is adding the finishing touches to the display.

Deciding What Developmental Materials You Will Use A speech is more than a skeleton of ideas; it is also a full-bodied organism. What gives the speech its bodily substance are the materials you choose to develop your main points with. Your audience will need to have *definitions* of key terms, *examples*, *anecdotes*, *statistics*, *visual aids*, *quotations* from others, *comparisons* and *contrasts* of the unknown material with the known (something that is familiar to them), and *descriptions* of people, places, and things if they are to fully understand the skeleton of main points you are trying to communicate to them. At this point you really have an opportunity to target your speech for your particular audience—by planning your specific developmental material for them. Talking about the coming teacher shortage? Then here are some examples of the types of materials you might use:

1. A *definition* of what you mean by teacher "shortage"

2. *Statistics* concerning:
   the number of teachers presently available
   the number of school-age children expected by the 1990s
   the number of students in the schools at present
   the number of teacher-trainees now working toward degrees

3. An *anecdote* from a teacher-friend of yours describing how underpaid grade school teachers presently are

4. *Quotes* from leading educators describing what will happen if the trend toward fewer college students choosing teaching careers continues into the nineties

5. A *visual aid* charting such trends as cost of living and teachers' salaries and the need for new teachers

Many more examples could be given; but the point is that you should look for as many of these forms of supporting material as you can during your speech class in order to get a good sense of the available options as you prepare your speeches.

Preparing Your Introduction

Although the purpose of your speech is to communicate your main idea, audiences are not usually completely prepared to consider that idea from the minute you begin your speech. You must help them get ready for the task of considering your idea. So every speech must have an introduction as well as a body. The function of the introduction is to prepare your audience for the main portion of your speech. In it you will probably reveal your subject matter, overview the structure of your speech, mention the source of your expertise on the topic, and try to make the audience feel that the topic is important to them.

Preparing Your Conclusion

Once you are finished presenting the main body of your idea, you must let the audience know you are finished by presenting a conclusion: a special portion of the speech that gives it a feeling of completion. Speeches may end

This father has assumed some aspects of his daughter's day-to-day care. Have you seen changes in gender roles in your lifetime? Do you plan to have children? Do you know any single parents?

with a summary or restatement of your main points, a quote that captures your theme in a memorable way, a call to audience action based on what they've heard. Whatever approach you decide to take, your conclusion should be clearly marked, and the audience should know that you have definitely concluded.

Preparing Your Delivery

Preparing the delivery of your speech does not mean that you will be practicing specific gestures, postures, and platform movements—although at one time it meant exactly that to many students of public speaking. It is not that such aspects of delivery cannot be practiced, but that certain types of practice tend to lead to a feeling of artificiality in your final speech delivery. More will be said about practicing specific aspects of speech delivery later, after the theory of public speaking has been explained, since the theory can help us distinguish between practice that leads to greater personal expressiveness and practice that leads to a stilted and artificial presentation. For the present, preparing your speech delivery will involve two steps: (1) selecting the manner of delivery, and (2) rehearsing the speech for fluency.

Selecting the Manner of Delivery What will you have in front of you when you actually speak? Nothing? A few hastily sketched notes? A formal outline, or an entire manuscript of the text, word for word? In most circumstances, the **extemporaneous** mode of delivery seems to be the most desirable. In the extemporaneous mode you are expected to be quite comfortable with your speech by the time you give it—because you are familiar with your chosen topic, because you have carefully planned the structure or pattern of ideas you intend to talk about, and because you have worked hard in rehearsing the speech you have prepared. You should be familiar enough with your speech so that a topical outline is all you need in front of you. And even that is only to remind you of the sequence of ideas you intend to present in case you happen to forget. Using the extemporaneous mode of delivery, you normally have the best chance of being truly spontaneous and natural-looking in front of your audience, because you have not memorized a sequence of words, but rather, a sequence of ideas.

But there are also times when you must resort to nonextemporaneous deliveries: **memorizing** a previously prepared speech word for word, preparing a complete manuscript to **read** word for word, or speaking with almost no prior formal preparation, that is, **impromptu.** Memorized speeches are rare, occurring only when the speech must appear to be spontaneous but when the exact wording of your ideas is crucial. More frequently, when exact wording of ideas is critical, speakers will resort to developing a word-for-word manuscript that is used to read from. To try to achieve a sense of spontaneity, such manuscripts must be rehearsed aloud several times and adapted, wherever possible, to an oral rhythm. Since written vocabulary and sentence structure is typically more complex than is spoken, the manuscript speaker must consciously use the general rehearsal process (described below) to try to adapt the written draft to a more natural spoken style.

Although most speeches allow for some prior preparation, you may also be called upon to "say a few words," to speak impromptu. In these circumstances, you must quickly adapt the speech preparation process by giving yourself a moment to organize an appropriate response. Especially important in the impromptu speaking situation is deciding what your main point or points will be and clearly announcing them as you begin. Doing so will not only get you started in a positive manner, but will also give you additional time to consider the details of your response.

Rehearsing the Speech Practicing your speech is especially important for the beginner; but you will probably find that you still want to rehearse your speeches even as you gain more and more public speaking experience. In order to profit most from your rehearsal sessions, there are at least six principles to remember.

1. *Practice Aloud.*

The first thing you need to remember is to practice your speech aloud rather than silently. You need to hear what the speech sounds like to your own ears before you try it out on the ears of your audience. Strange things sometimes happen when you step up on the platform, and you do not want one of those things to be a sense of amazement at what you hear coming out (or *not* coming out) of your own mouth as you listen to the speech for the first time. Even though the extemporaneous mode does not require that you memorize the words of your speech exactly, you do expect to deliver the same ideas in essentially the same way every time you work through your speech. Practicing aloud should also help you choose from among possible alternative phrasings of your ideas. And it should get you used to trying to present them aloud in the first place, no matter how you finally decide to phrase them in front of your actual audience.

2. *Practice While Standing.*

Not only will you want to practice your speech aloud, you will also want to practice your speech while standing up. And the reason is the same: Standing up is how you will actually be delivering your speech. You need to get a sense of what it feels like to be on your feet talking without interruption (or help) from others for several minutes. Furthermore, you need to get used to the fact that your body will want to move around and your arms will want to gesture as a natural accompaniment to your speaking. Since the question "What do I do with my hands?" is a common one for beginning speakers, it is important to see for yourself just what your hands are naturally inclined to do—which is to move in spontaneous synchrony with your speech. The answer to the question of what to do with your hands is simple: Gesture as spontaneously as you do in conversation. Although nervousness may cause you to develop distracting mannerisms (such as playing with a pen, your hair, glasses, buttons, or change in your pockets), your instructor will call these to your attention and help you eliminate them. But it is better to forget about your hands and feet, especially during the rehearsals, and concentrate on your ideas. Your natural inhibition during the actual speech will normally prevent you from distracting, excessive movement.

3. *Practice Without Stopping.*

The suggestion that you practice without stopping is different from saying "practice without ceasing." The latter means that you would practice your speech continuously from the time you finish preparing your speech text to the time you actually give it. Aside from being impractical, such an approach to rehearsal would probably also be counterproductive, especially if you finish preparing your speech text reasonably far ahead of the time you actually plan to present it. Rehearsals are most productive when they occur over several different sessions rather than carried out back to back, since the distributed pattern of rehearsal allows you to incorporate what you learned from earlier sessions into your later practices.

What practicing without stopping really emphasizes is that, within any particular run through of your speech, you do not stop every time you make a mistake (or think of something new) and correct the speech. It is too easy to get in the habit of stopping, when, during the actual speech, this will be impossible (or at least highly undesirable). Can you imagine making a mistake, stopping your speech, and asking your instructor if you can start over? It happens, but it is rarely a better idea to stop and start over than it is to simply cover your mistakes and go on. Get used to the idea of practicing without stopping. This will also help you get used to the order of the ideas in your speech as you intend to present them. Too much stopping during your rehearsals defeats one of the real benefits of rehearsal: getting the feel of the overall flow of your speech from beginning to end.

4. *Practice in a Classroom-sized Room.*

Another important element of your rehearsals is to practice in a room as close to the size of your classroom as you can, since part of your task as a speaker is to fill the entire room with your speech. Many students, living in a dorm or an apartment with one or more roommates, go into a small room to get away from everyone else so they won't be embarrassed or interrupted. The danger of this choice is that you will get used to being too "small" when, in your actual speech, you will have to project yourself much larger than you typically do in conversations. So it is important to try to rehearse in a room that invites you to make yourself as large as you will need to be for your class. If the situation permits, practice your first speech in the classroom itself, to get a feeling for what it looks like to speak from the front of the room.

5. *Practice from Your Outline.*

One dangerous thing you should not do is practice using notes other than the ones you actually intend to take with you to the lectern. Some instructors emphasize using a minimum of notes; others may want you to use nearly a full manuscript. Whatever you plan to take with you, though, should also be what you practice with. You want to gain experience in quickly finding what you need in your notes so that you do not lose contact with your audience for very long. Every look down at your notes is an opportunity to lose your audience's attention. To practice with a manuscript and then to utilize only a topic outline for the speech itself (because you know that is what your instructor wants you to use) can cause you real headaches when you look down for the friendly reminder-word you had been practicing with and you can't find it. If you are going to work with only a few notes during your speech, gradually wean yourself from extensive notes during your rehearsals.

One further suggestion concerning notes: Don't be afraid to mark your notes with reminders and underlinings of key terms—in a strongly contrasting color—to help you quickly pick up what you need from the page. Your notes are a tool for your speech, not a sacred document for eternal preservation. During your rehearsal sessions you should mark your notes as you discover what you need in order to make them as useful as possible.

6. *Talk through Your Speech—Don't Memorize It.*

This advice is really the converse of the previous one. It is meant to remind you that your speech, under most circumstances, will work best if it is extemporaneous rather than memorized. Only special circumstances require a text to be delivered word for word from memory. So, unless absolutely exact wording is required, get used to talking through the speech, using whatever wording comes to you under the impulse of the moment. After several rehearsals, some wordings will come to you more often than others, and you will find that you want to preserve them. Consideration of exact wordings for special effects will be discussed in the chapter on language choices. For the time being, it is more important to work for what is called a "conversational" quality. The predominant image of a speech, since James Winans introduced it in 1915, is that a speech is an "enlarged conversation." Since conversations are spontaneous and interpersonally involving rather than memorized and distant, a speech viewed as an enlarged conversation means that you should seek to involve your audience with your natural enthusiasm for your topic. You will have more difficulty doing this if you are continually searching your mind for the exact wordings you have memorized.

*H*andling Stage Fright

Perhaps the hardest part of giving your first speeches will be the anxiety you feel about being in front of your audience. That's normal and to be expected.

According to one widely reported survey, having to give a speech is the number one fear among Americans. Furthermore, even experienced performers and speakers will tell you that they continue to experience some degree of stage fright before nearly every performance or presentation. So don't expect to rid yourself of stage fright entirely; that is not a realistic goal. But, if you have done a thorough job of preparing your speech and have rehearsed it adequately, then you need not be excessively concerned about the natural anxiety you will feel. You may even begin to look forward to the "butterflies" as a sign that you are readying yourself for your presentation.

What Stage Fright Is

Why do you feel the symptoms of stage fright you experience—such things as shallow breathing, sweaty palms, shaking hands, heart palpitations, dry mouth, and cracking voice? Stage fright is a normal physiological response brought on by anxiety in a potentially threatening situation—part of the body's so-called fight-or-flight response. It is actually your body's way of preparing for action. Since we experience these ready-for-action symptoms in a potentially threatening situation, we call them fright—and thus the term *stage fright.* But the symptoms themselves are actually the result of an overflow of energy in a body that is prepared for immediate action.

Controlling Stage Fright

Since stage fright is a physiological ready reaction, the problem is not how to avoid it, but rather how to best utilize the adrenalin/glycogen reserves that have already been generously dumped into your circulatory system. The first thing you can do is to recognize that the symptoms of stage fright are really a positive sign that your body is readying itself for the sustained act of speaking you are about to perform. Continuous speaking requires vast amounts of energy. Recognizing the positive value of what is happening inside you, rather than emphasizing the negative symptoms you feel, can help you not only to be bothered less by those feelings (which only makes things worse anyway), but also to anticipate them as a good sign. They are really signs that—as an otherwise fully prepared speaker—you will now also have the benefit of extra reserves of energy to see you through. Failure to have any butterflies will eventually worry you more, since it may mean that you don't care enough about the success or failure of your speech to present it well.

Whether or not you ever begin looking forward to the symptoms of stage fright, there are two more general things you can do before you begin to speak that will minimize paralyzing levels of stage fright: (1) *Select an interesting topic.* Having confidence in your topic can give you greater confidence in yourself as a speaker. Confidence in your topic eliminates one source of worry. (2) *Be well prepared*. Don't invite strong speech anxiety by giving your-self a legitimate reason to be frightened. If you have taken the time to work through the phases of speech preparation and have rehearsed your speech, the most realistic sources of harm to you or your reputation have already been eliminated.

In addition to these general suggestions, there are several quite specific suggestions for handling stage fright, all of which involve the use of physical action. Since stage fright is the result of your body's preparation for physical action, take advantage of that fact by using physical activity to use up the ex-cess adrenalin/glycogen surging through your body. There are two types of physical action that you may find helpful: (1) physical action *before* you speak, and (2) physical action *while* you speak. Let's look at each of these in turn.

There are four key suggestions for using physical action before you speak. First, sit upright in your chair and start breathing deeply and regularly. One of the characteristic bodily changes produced by stage fright, which is not captured very well by the phrase fight-or-flight is short, shallow, irregular breathing. For not all animals in all situations are able to either fight or flee. Many animals respond to potential threats with yet a third response. They try to make themselves as small, motionless, or inconspicuous as possible. Shal-low breathing minimizes eye-catching movement that might induce a preda-tor's attack. Since as public speakers both fight and flight responses are almost always out of the question (who would you fight, where would you run?), your body quite naturally takes another option it *does* have available: it shrinks as much as it possibly can toward invisibility, through, among other things, very shallow breathing. But have you ever tried to talk like that? Since shallow breathing is counterproductive to you as a speaker, you must attempt to overcome the tendency to shrink by consciously forcing deeper and more expansive breathing.

Second, you should try to relax your hands and arms, which have stiff-ened up and become more rigid as your body has tried to make itself as invisible and inanimate as possible. This can be done by flexing your arms and fingers as unobtrusively as you can, or by pressing your fingertips to-gether firmly. Besides, how can you gesture conversationally if your hands and arms are locked tight?

Third, the facial muscles can be relaxed by unobtrusive flexing and re-laxing. It is pretty tough to talk when your face won't move.

Finally, if you can do it without calling attention to yourself, yawn. Yawn-ing is one of the best exercises for prespeech relaxation of the face, since it involves virtually all of the muscles of the face, jaws, and throat simulta-neously. Since it is not always possible to yawn before your speech without being noticed, use this relaxation device before you are in front of your au-dience, or before attention has been focused on you.

There are three suggestions for physical action while you speak. First, you must get set before you speak. All organic activities begin with a preparation phase, and delivering your speech is no exception. To get set (1) walk confidently to the lectern, (2) set your notes or text on the lectern and arrange them the way you want them, (3) place your feet squarely on the floor, about shoulder's width apart, with your knees slightly bent, (4) stand up straight, neither drooping over the lectern nor standing rigidly at attention, (5) look at your audience for a second or two to get set, (6) take one last deep breath, and (7) begin with a well-prepared and rehearsed introduction.

Second, use natural gestures while you speak; they help use up excess tension while at the same time contributing to the overall impact of your speech.

Third, if the room and circumstances permit, move around as you talk. Again, this uses up the excess energy that contributes to the symptoms of stage fright, and it helps your audience attend to the structure and content of your speech by marking transitions and points of emphasis.

On Cookbooks and Masterpieces

This chapter began speculatively, asking why you should bother to learn to speak in public, and why it is important to understand the principles of effective public speaking. But it has ended practically, prescriptively, outlining specific speech skills that are to be learned in some order, as if they were ingredients for a recipe, along with instructions for mixing them, as you might find in a cookbook. That is how the entire book will develop—theory and practice constantly interwoven from chapter to chapter. So, is public speaking essentially a skill, requiring primarily practice, learnable from a cookbook? Or is it an art, an area of human knowledge permitting a theoretical treatment? It is both.

During the past 2400 years a vast wealth of commonsense observation and conventional wisdom has been developed concerning the elements of successful public speaking. In addition to this extensive tradition based on thoughtful observation of marketplace public communication, the modern scientific era has begun to add to and refine what we know about speech in the public setting. Since we know a good deal about actual speech in the public setting, there is much to tell you in a straightforward manner, prescriptively, in cookbook fashion: "Mix a little supporting material with some organization, add a dash of vivid language, and spice it up with an appropriate anecdote; bake it for a while in a temperate mind, and you will come out with a very passable speech." Where we know such things, this book presents principles directly, with the hope of making them as accessible as possible for you to learn, and as interesting as possible for your instructor to teach.

But speech making also has an intangible, artistic element that goes beyond the skills that can be formally taught, an element that needs to be experienced more directly. Even so, the artistic aspect *can* be understood. Thus, this book attempts to set public speaking within a larger theoretical approach to human speech communication in general. In that way, the artistic element of speaking can be understood and practiced. This book not only seeks to tell you clearly what has been discovered about public speaking by patient observation and experimental test, but also to provide you with a unified explanation for why those practices work as they do.

Cookbooks and masterpieces? What a masterpiece adds to mere technical skill is imagination. No book can teach you imagination. What a book can give you are the materials to help you structure your natural imagination into its most powerfully expressive form. Having given you those skills, as well as an understanding of how and why they work, it is hoped that you will eventually give speeches that are more than simply competently informative or persuasive, but also significant, interesting, and artfully crafted. If you learn only the practical skills of public speaking during your public speaking course, you will have accomplished much. Even so, there is more to public speaking than mere cookery, and you can aspire to master it.

Conclusion

Application of these steps in your actual speech preparation is a continuous process composed of adding new skills to your repertoire, and of refining those skills you have already acquired. Eventually, these skills will become second nature to you. Eventually. With practice. But at first you must work on them deliberately, self-consciously, even at times, awkwardly. For, like all complex skills—such as playing a musical instrument, using a microcomputer, or driving a car—preparing a speech seems to require that you know everything at once before you can do it at all, and certainly before you can do it well. Yet, as a practical matter, you can only concentrate on improving isolated skills that you work on one at a time—skills that you will eventually do simultaneously and almost unconsciously. Since the goal of knowing everything at once is impossible, you must be patient with yourself and give your speech preparation ample time. The skills will accumulate, and you will become much more efficient at accomplishing them, if you work at them conscientiously and vigorously in the order your instructor thinks is best for you. For the time being, you will at least be able to "hit the ball over the net."

Questions for Review

1. Why should college-educated students have formal instruction in public speaking as part of their requirements or electives?

2. What are the main steps in preparing a speech?

3. What are the extemporaneous, impromptu, and memorized manners of delivery?

4. What are the six basic principles guiding how you should practice delivering your speech?

5. What is stage fright? How can you best control the major symptoms of stage fright?

6. Why is a little stage fright helpful for giving an effective speech?

7. Is giving a speech primarily a "skill" or is it primarily an "art"? What is the difference? What difference does it make to you as a novice speaker?

Questions for Discussion

1. List the reasons you are taking a course in public speaking. Was it a required course or an elective? What do you hope to learn from it? What do you expect to be able to do after your course that you couldn't do before?

2. Make a list of some of the occasions that might require you to speak during the next 12 months. For example, does a course you will be taking require an oral report? Are you thinking about running for an office in a club or organization? Is there a campus or local problem that you might want to speak out about?

3. When was the last time you had to speak publicly? What were the circumstances? How did you feel about the event? How did you prepare for the speech? Were you satisfied with the results? What would you do differently to get ready for a similar occasion?

4. Who are some of your favorite speakers in public life? What do you especially like about their speeches? Why are these speakers typically more effective than others you have heard? Are their ideas more clearly presented? Delivered with greater animation or enthusiasm? Worded in more colorful language?

5. If you have heard a speaker who did a particularly weak or ineffective job, identify what went wrong. Why didn't you like the speaker's presentation? What specific recommendations would you make to help the speaker improve?

Things to Try

1. If your major department requires a course in public speaking, find out why they considered the course important enough to require. Did they take a written survey of recent graduates' opinions?

2. Interview someone whose college major was the same as yours and find out what public speaking requirements the person has had in the past five years. What advice would the person give concerning your own public speaking class?

3. There are many famous orators, including Demosthenes, Daniel Webster, William Jennings Bryan, Martin Luther King, Jr., and John F. Kennedy. Select a famous orator and find out more about that speaker. Your instructor can give you the names of several others, both past and present, who may interest you.

4. Prepare and deliver a brief (one to two minute) speech about yourself. Make sure you plan and rehearse it. Try to avoid just listing random details about yourself. Instead, select a central theme that runs through your life and illustrate the theme with examples, anecdotes, visual aids, and so on. Make sure you have a definite introduction and conclusion as well. Some themes that may apply are the good or bad effects of being an only child, being left-handed, being from a small town, having blond hair, and so forth.

5. As a variation, instead of talking about yourself, select a classmate to interview. Find out enough details so that you can present a speech introducing the student to the class. Again, select a central theme that runs through the student's life to present to the class.

Bibliography

Aitchison, Jean. *The Articulate Mammal: An Introduction to Psycholinguistics*. New York: McGraw-Hill Paperbacks, 1978.

Fry, Dennis. *Homo Loquens: Man as a Talking Animal*. Cambridge: Cambridge University Press, 1977.

Winans, James A. *Public Speaking,* rev. ed. New York: The Century Company, 1917 (first published 1915).

CHAPTER 2

Public Speaking As a Communication Process

*T*o present a speech is to try to communicate your ideas to your audience. In this chapter we will look at the elements and processes of communication that underlie the act of public speaking. Understanding the general processes underlying speech communication can help you better understand the details about public speaking that are presented in later chapters of this book. Although there are several new words and concepts to master in this chapter, learning them well now should help make your subsequent learning about public speaking much easier, since they provide an important vocabulary for later discussions. This chapter is divided into two major sections: a definition of communication and a model of the communication process.

Communication: A Definition

Many scholars have tried to define the word *communication*.[1] Some definitions are very broad and inclusive; others are quite narrow and limited in the scope of what phenomena they include under the term.[2] Each type of definition serves a different research, theoretical, or practical goal. Although it is currently popular to use broader rather than narrower definitions of *communication,* lumping everything a person does under the single term, the precise approach seems more useful in understanding the role communication plays in effective public speaking. This is because much of your effort in a public speaking class will be directed toward improving your specific verbal communication skills—the transmission of your ideas to an audience through the spoken word. You will be trying to put your ideas into words, to organize your word-formulated ideas into easy-to-understand patterns, and to support your word-encoded main ideas with a variety of supporting materials, themselves also encoded into carefully considered words. The notion of specific, improvable communication skills seems to require a fairly narrow, and even relatively traditional, definition of communication—one placing words and ideas at its center.

---

[1] It is customary to italicize a word when you are talking about the word itself rather than using the word to talk about the thing or phenomenon it names. Thus, in the sentence, "Communication is an important human activity," the word *communication* is not italicized since it is being used to make a statement about the act of communicating. But in the sentence "*Communication* is an important word to know how to define," the word is italicized because the word itself is being mentioned as the subject that is being talked about.

[2] Two representative efforts to define the word *communication* are helpful in pointing out just how difficult and yet important such a definition is: Thomas R. Nilsen, "On Defining Communication," *The Speech Teacher* 6 (1957), 10–17: and Frank E. X. Dance, "The 'Concept' of Communication," *Journal of Communication* 20 (1970), 201–210.

Accordingly, for the purposes of this book, a rather precise definition of communication will be adopted: *Communication is the intentional transmission of ideas from one individual to one or more others* (Langer, 1972, p. 201).[3] This means that whenever you are literally communicating—rather than merely observing, silently interacting with, or nonverbally influencing someone else—you will be consciously trying to express your ideas in a way that makes those ideas comprehensible to others. Communication will be said to occur only when someone else understands your ideas as you intended those ideas to be understood. Although several very important non-verbal elements of the total speech situation obviously affect your success as a public speaker, and must be taken into account if you are to do your best, these are not literally forms of communication, and do not constitute the central goal of instruction in public speaking. Non-verbal expression works on such intrinsically different principles from verbal expression that it is simply confusing to call them both by the same name. Although the non-verbal elements of public speaking are not left to chance, the fact is, instruction in public speaking is strongly dominated by the goal of making your ideas clearer to your audience through the spoken word.

A *Model of Communication*

Broad or narrow, any definition of communication has implications that must be taken seriously. One way to identify those implications and to help make them more memorable is to create a model of the communication process. A **model** is a verbal or physical representation of some thing or process—as in a model of an airplane or a blueprint for building a house. All models must contain at least two parts: a representation of the components or **elements** that make up the thing or process being modeled, and a representation of the **relations** that exist among the various elements. In a model of an airplane, for example, the *elements* are such things as the wings, fuselage, tail pieces, nose, cockpit, and engine housings. The *relations* among these elements are the order or the pattern among them that makes them into an airplane rather than just random pieces of plastic in a box. All models—whether of a material object, such as an airplane, or a temporal process, such as com-

---

[3]I adopt a narrow definition of *communication* in this book on strictly practical grounds. This definition has been defended elsewhere on theoretical grounds. For the present purpose, I will simply state the definition I use and develop its implication for public speaking. For those interested in the supporting rationale for this definition, see John H. Powers, "An 'Act' Based Theory of Communication: First Principles," *Journal of Applied Communication Research* 10 (1982), 9–20.

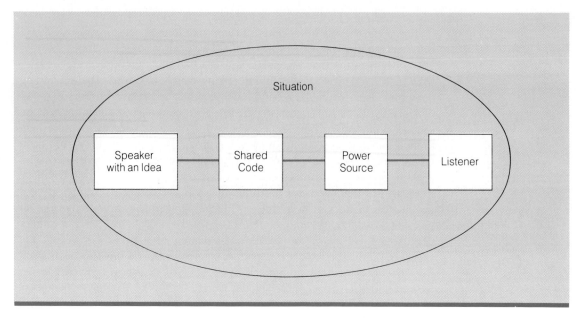

Figure 2-1   The Elements of Communication

munication—attempt to represent both the elements and the relations that go together to make something what it is.

Communication models are usually two-dimensional drawings of the elements and relations involved in communication. The elements are typically illustrated by boxes or circles, and the relations among these elements are illustrated by lines and arrows. The following section of the chapter identifies the major elements of communication as it has been defined in this chapter, and the final section explores some of the most important relations among the elements of communication that you as a public speaker need to consider as you begin preparing your speeches.

Elements of Communication

Embedded in the definition of *communication* as the intentional transmission of ideas from one person to one or more others are at least six major elements we need to look at: a speaker, a listener, an idea to be transmitted, a code for use in transmitting the idea, some physical means for carrying the coded idea from one place to another, and a situation or set of circumstances in which the communication process occurs. These six elements may be visually modeled with a simple drawing, as in Figure 2-1.

Two more elements that often influence the course of communication but that are not strictly intrinsic to it are also usually included in most com-

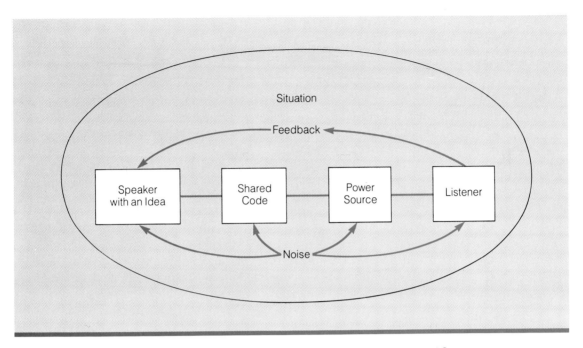

Figure 2-2   The Elements of Communication in Their Broader Interactional Context

munication models: the listener's overt response to the ideas communicated (as contrasted with the covert act of understanding, which *is* intrinsic to the complete act of communicating) and various sources of interference with the successful completion of the communication process. The listener's overt response to a speaker's presentation is usually called **feedback;** the sources of interference, **noise.** These two additional elements may be added to the model in the way shown in Figure 2-2.

We will look at each of these elements of the speech communication process to see what is involved when someone is literally communicating an idea to someone else.

Speaker and Listener If communication is the intentional transmission of ideas from one individual to one or more others, then the communication process requires at least two different individuals to accomplish it—one to encode and send the idea and another to receive and understand it. Thinking silently to oneself, even in words, is not communication—nor is speaking aloud to an empty room. Communication is an activity that requires one person to initiate it and someone else to complete it. In spoken communication, the person who initiates a round of communication is the speaker; the person who joins in and tries to complete the communication act is the listener. In conversational communication the speaker and listener roles switch back and forth frequently, like playing catch with a ball in the backyard; in public speaking, the roles of speaker and listener remain stable for long periods of time. But, in either case, if no one tries to transmit an idea, or if the listener fails to comprehend what the speaker is trying to say, no communication occurs. As Susanne Langer says, concerning the speaker's intention to transmit a particular idea, "If the intention miscarries, i.e., no idea 'goes across,' the individuals fail to communicate, though they may interact closely, elaborately, even violently" (1972, p. 201). Communication requires active participation from both the speaker and the listener.

The cooperative nature of communication may be seen in another analogy. Communication is a jointly completed act, like playing tennis. Although one can hit a ball against a practice wall or smash serves over the net into an empty court, this is clearly practice; it is not literally "playing tennis" if there is no opponent to share cooperatively in the game. Similarly, if you are being observed by someone else who is trying to figure out what is going on inside of you, this is not communication. Talking to someone who does not understand you is no more communication than is hitting tennis balls at someone without a racquet playing tennis. Communication requires two people to enact it; it requires an active, effective effort on the part of both persons to consummate the act of communicating.

Ideas to Be Transmitted We humans are capable of producing a constant stream of ideas about nearly everything under the sun. We produce ideas about the nature of the universe, about how people should behave, about how a beautiful lawn or painting should look, and about how a government should be run.

Not only do we produce an abundance of ideas, we also have a strong desire to share our ideas with others. We can hardly keep still, our ideas are so intensely exciting to us. In fact, the world is aroar with talk about ideas—ideas about computer technology, improving crop yields, methods of eradicating diseases, overthrowing despotic governments, excelling in athletic contests, going faster and doing more. Communication is the conscious attempt by one person to share the ideas constantly formulating in his or her head with others. Although there is much controversy about the nature of the process of producing ideas—that is, about what is going on within a person who is formulating ideas—there is little doubt that communication is the presentation of the fruit of that process for the understanding and consideration of others. A public speech is just one among hundreds of occasions in which people try to express ideas for others to share.

Logical Projection Communication is the intentional *transmission* of ideas. If the idea fails to "go across," no communication takes place, even though significant interaction may have taken place. **Interaction** may be defined as all joint actions occurring between two or more people; communication is the very special type of interaction that occurs only when an idea is transmitted from one person to one or more others. But how do you get your ideas across to another person? To understand what it means to get an idea to go across, we need to look at the means by which we accomplish this feat: the projection of an idea via the **verbal code** we use.

What's going on when you are communicating? The complex process by which you make your ideas available to others is called **logical projection,** and it involves two major steps: (1) putting your ideas into a perceptible "coded" form (usually words and sentences), and (2) making the coded forms accessible to others (usually via speech or writing). The act of logical projection gets its name from two important features of the process. First, it is called *projection* because you must actively project your ideas outward from yourself in a pattern of symbols. This process is similar to a slide projector, which must actively send out a pattern of light and color across a room to a screen. Your means for projecting your ideas is most often the act of speaking; the slide projector's means is a powerful light. Second, the process is called *logical* projection because the process involves a change of **form** from unencoded thoughts to encoded words, and logic is the discipline that deals in pure forms as such (Langer, 1937). Thus, the process of projecting your ideas to others is composed of two subprocesses, which we may call *encoding* and *empowering*.

Encoding. The process of putting your ideas into words is called **encoding.** To see why encoding your ideas into a verbal form is a major component of the communication process, consider what is going on when you are *not* communicating ideas in a coded message. As you sit in your easy chair, quietly reading your speech assignment or thinking about your next speech, you are not communicating your specific thoughts to anyone else, although your quietness, the detached look on your face, and your position in the chair may all express the fact that you are "lost in thought." But, if anyone wants to know *what* you are thinking, they will have to ask. Or, if you want to share your thoughts with them, you will have to put those thoughts into words and begin to talk. That is, you will have to put your ideas into a form other than the one they are in while you are sitting there quietly thinking. And you will have to actively send the words outward, away from yourself—because your silent thoughts are not available to anyone else. In order for you to share your thoughts with another person, you have to first put them into a form that (1) gets them outside of yourself, and (2) makes them available for others to perceive. That new form into which you put your thoughts is the **verbal code.**

Your goal as a speaker is to select words and sentences that encode your ideas in ways that make it possible for your audience to receive the ideas you intended to communicate. When your audience decodes the message as you intended it, the audience understands. Understanding your ideas as intended is the final necessary component of the act of communication. If your audience understands your idea as you intended to encode it, then the idea has gone across and communication has occurred. If the audience fails to decode

This is a high school football coach. What sports interest you? Has any coach been a big influence on you? Should athletes be required to keep up their grades?

the message as you have intended, then communication has not occurred, only mutual interaction among people.

Empowering. Once you have encoded your ideas into a form that is capable of expressing them accurately—that is into a pattern of words and sentences—you must physically send them from yourself to others through the instrumentality of the verbal code. The act of stating your ideas in words is called **assertion.** To assert an idea is to state that some situation is the case. "Jack ate the cake" is an assertion. So, too, are "If I were you, I wouldn't go to the party," and "e = mc²." Even "yes" in answer to a question is a highly abbreviated form of assertion.

Assertion, then, is the second component of the projection process required for true communication. In this phase of the process, you must make the coded idea available to your listeners. This is where the actual act of speaking comes prominently into play. To accomplish the act of assertion, you must physically transmit the coded message, adding power from your lungs and vocal cords to the words you wish to express. This lung and vocal power is physically transmitted to the air molecules surrounding you and your listener, which then carry your word-encoded ideas to the listener. The listener then takes over and begins the reverse process of taking the sound wave into which you have encoded your idea and interpreting it. Some people are better than others at understanding someone else's ideas—just as some people are better than others at catching a ball. Communication can break down either because you do not adequately encode your ideas or because your listener is not able to adequately "catch your meaning."

The fact that your ideas must be empowered by bodily means introduces some fascinating complications into the communication process. For speaking is a total bodily act in which your posture, gestures, facial expression, vocal color, and countless other nonverbal elements are either spontaneously or consciously added to the verbally encoded signal you intend to send. Although these nonverbal elements are not themselves a part of the coded *ideas* you intend to communicate, they are the inevitable concomitants of the transmittal process and can affect your communication either adversely or beneficially. Since good listening is also a total bodily act—not restricted to the ears alone—these nonverbal artifacts of the empowering process often profoundly affect the listener's ability to attend carefully to the specific ideas you intend to communicate. Speech delivery is the act of empowering your ideas and is the physical means by which your encoded ideas are sent forth from yourself to one or more others. Much is known about how audiences typically respond to various elements of the empowering process, as you will learn in Chapter 14 on delivering your speech.

A Situation Speech communication always occurs at a certain place, at a certain time, with a particular set of people in attendance, and with a particular prevailing pattern of social circumstances. This unique pattern of people, places, times, and circumstances is the **situation** within which a specific act of speech communication occurs. Because it usually matters who is being spoken to, where and when the speech is occurring, and what the social circumstances are that have induced the speaker to speak, Chapters 4 and 7 each treat more fully some facet of these aspects of the speech communication process.

Listener's Response Because speech communication is a jointly shared activity, both the speaker and the listener must actively participate if the communication act is to be successfully completed. At any time during the communication event, the listener's changing responses may influence, alter, or modify the subsequent course of the speaker's communication activity. The listener may even induce the speaker to suspend communication altogether under some circumstances. If, for example, a look expressing the listener's rapt attention subtly or suddenly changes to express momentary confusion, the speaker may abruptly be induced to stop and to elaborate or reformulate the idea being expressed. The look of confusion does not *assert* that the speaker should stop and elaborate; no such idea is directly communicated. By a means other than verbally encoded communication, the speaker has been, at least temporarily, inhibited from continuing the presentation of the idea. Cooperation has been temporarily suspended because the listener is no longer understanding; he or she is no longer able to participate in the communication act. Due to the temporary inability of the listener to participate, the forward motion of the communication act has been suspended while a bridge to the listener's understanding is rebuilt. Whenever we communicate, listener response continuously influences the flow of the speaker's communication. The listener is as important in shaping the actual course of communication as a road is in shaping the course of a motorist's driving.

Sources of Interference Communication acts rarely run smoothly from beginning to end. More typically, they are encumbered by many sources of interference that either slow down communication or prevent it from happening altogether. For example, other people may interrupt you while you are talking, airplanes may pass overhead and drown out your voice, codes may fail to be shared between the two participants, or the listener's mind may drift away for a period of time and thereby stop being engaged in the communicative interaction. Although interference is clearly not an inherent element of the communication process itself, it is such an ever-present companion of communication that it deserves to be included in our model. Furthermore, you can plan your speeches with enough repetition and reinforcement of your ideas so that you can overcome these interferences.

Relations among the Elements of Communication

A complete discussion of all the possible relations among the various elements of the communication process would require a book of its own; but several of these relations hold special importance for the public speaker. In the discussion that follows, a few of the most important relations affecting successful public speech will be mentioned; others have already been mentioned in the discussion of the elements themselves, and still others will be treated throughout the following chapters.

The Speaker and the Audience Your goal as a communicator is to transmit your ideas to a listener. Because audiences must actively participate with you if you are to communicate successfully, developing positive relations between yourself and your listener is critical to the communication process. As a public speaker you will need to find out as much as you can about your audience before you speak—who they are, what they are interested in, why they will have gathered to hear you speak, and what they will already know about you and your topic before you speak. Communication occurs most easily when there is a relationship of rapport, similarity, or identification between the speaker and listener. By finding out as much as you can about your audience beforehand, you can adapt your speech's content to enhance your sense of shared commonality with them. Thus, the first relation for you to consider is that between yourself and your audience. Because this relationship is so important, Chapter 7 is devoted to explaining how to do a basic audience analysis.

The Speaker/Audience and the Idea In addition to considering the relation between yourself and your listener, you must also consider the relation of both you and your audience to your idea. Is the idea worth transmitting? Does the audience need the idea you have chosen to transmit? Can you interest the audience in what you have to say? These, and a host of other questions concerning the audience's relationship to your idea, must be asked as you prepare your speech. For example, if you were a meteorology student who has been asked to talk to a sixth grade science class about how the weather changes, you would want to find out such things as what other units the class has previously studied, how motivated the class has typically been, how much scientific vocabulary and detail are expected, and what the class will be expected to do with the information you will be giving them (taking a test, doing an experiment, and so on). Only then would you be able to adapt your college-level training to the level of ideas needed by a sixth grade class.

The Speaker/Audience, the Idea, and the Code Communication only succeeds when the audience and the speaker share the code in which your idea is encoded. So, you must also consider whether or not your audience shares the vocabulary and sentence structure you are employing. If, for example, the topic is technical and the audience is a group of interested laypersons, brought together because they are all members of a local club, you must adapt your customary professional code to the code available to the listener. Special supporting materials such as definitions, analogies, and examples become especially important if you suspect that the coding of your ideas may be a problem for members of your audience. Chapter 8 discusses the forms of supporting material available to you as you prepare to speak on any particular occasion. For the present, it is sufficient to point out that you must make an effort to match your verbal code to the background and knowledge of the audience.

The Speaker/Audience and the Delivery Style There are many ways to deliver your speech—from the formal to the informal. Different audiences and occasions may require you to be more or less chatty, more or less animated, more or less stationary, and so on. A major address to a large audience generally requires larger gestures and wider vocal variety, more dramatic pauses and a relatively stationary position behind a microphone. A speech to a class of 25 students can probably be more informal and relaxed. So you must give some special thought to how you will empower your ideas. Chapter 14 treats the processes and options related to empowering your speech.

Conclusion

Public speaking is an interactive process in which communication plays a central role. Throughout your speech preparation you are constantly encoding your ideas into words, trying out different ways of expressing your thoughts, organizing your verbally coded ideas into larger units—all with the hope that your audience will eventually join you in completing the communicative act by understanding what you intended to say. Moreover, because communication requires you to physically empower your verbally encoded ideas, new complications enter the process of sharing your ideas with others. Although this non-verbal expression may not literally be communication, it can profoundly affect your ability to be understood and therefore to communicate effectively. By becoming more aware of the elements of communication as presented in this chapter, you should be on your way to accomplishing the goal of becoming a better communicator, as well as a better public speaker.

Questions for Review

1. How does the author define *communication*?

2. How do broad definitions of communication differ from narrow ones?

3. What criteria must an act fulfill to be an instance of communication proper?

4. What two types of components of any thing or process must a good model try to capture?

5. What are the key elements of the process of communication?

6. What is the relation between communication and interaction?

7. How does verbally encoded communication differ from non-verbal forms of expression such as smiles or yawns or grimaces? List as many examples as you can, including ones not mentioned in the chapter.

Questions for Discussion

1. Many alternative definitions of *communication* are available, each with different practical and theoretical implications. For example, Thomas Nilsen (1957) argues that the broadest possible definition of communication should be adopted and offers S. S. Stevens's statement that "Communication is the discriminatory response of an organism to a stimulus" as a positive example. Similarly, Shannon and Weaver (1949) say that communication should be defined as "all of the procedures by which one mind may affect another" (p. 13).
   a. What does each of these definitions mean? That is, what criteria are involved in deciding whether or not a particular phenomenon should be classified as an instance of communication? Be as precise as you can.
   b. How does each of these definitions differ from the other and from the definition presented in the chapter? That is, what seems to be implied beyond the literal terms of the definition about the nature of communication?
   c. What are the advantages and disadvantages of each of the three definitions?
   d. Based on the considerations above, which definition of *communication* do you prefer and why?

2. If everyone is unique, how is it possible that we communicate at all? Conversely, if everyone is basically the same, why is communication necessary?

3. As a speaker's audience grows larger (from 20 people in a classroom to 150 in a lecture hall, for example), what changes are likely to occur in such elements of the communication process as encoding ideas, feedback, and the relations among the elements?

4. What difference does it make to your encoding process whether you are speaking to an audience that is already somewhat familiar with your topic or one that has had little prior experience with it?

5. What non-verbal feedback from your audience would signal that your ideas had failed to go across and be understood? What signs would you notice if the audience were especially interested in your ideas?

6. If you noticed that your audience seemed restless, what aspects of your presentation might you try to change? Using the model as a guide, list as many possibilities as you can.

7. Consider speakers you have heard. What aspects of their encoding and empowering processes did you find especially helpful or interesting? Were there any features you especially disliked?

8. What are some of the most typical sources of interference public speakers encounter? How can the encoding and empowering processes be modified to help overcome them?

Things to Try

1. Write a definition of *communication* that employs whatever criteria you need in order to be able to include the things you believe should be called communication and that allows you to exclude anything you think should be excluded.

2. Select your favorite definition of *communication* and draw a model of its elements and relations. Compare and contrast your model with the one presented in the chapter.

3. Analyze the implications of your definition of *communication* (and the derivative model) for public speaking. What advice would your definition involve for the public speaker? How would the chapter have to be re-written according to your definition?

4. Using a tape recorder for precision, tell a friend a brief story about some incident in your life and then ask your friend to repeat it back to you. Compare how similar the two versions are and discuss the reasons for any discrepencies you may find. Note, for example, any differences you find in how the story was encoded and empowered. Look for any sources of interference, and so forth, that account for the differences between the two versions.

Bibliography

Arnold, Carroll C., and Kenneth D. Frandsen. "Conceptions of Rhetoric and Communication." In: *Handbook of Rhetorical and Communication Theory*. Boston: Allyn & Bacon, 1984, 3–50.

Frentz, Thomas S., and Thomas B. Farrell. "Language-Action: A Paradigm for Communication." *Quarterly Journal of Speech* 62 (December 1976), 333–349.

Langer, Susanne K. *Mind: An Essay on Human Feeling,* Vol. II. Baltimore: Johns Hopkins University Press, 1972.

Langer, Susanne K. *An Introduction to Symbolic Logic,* 3rd ed. New York: Dover, 1967 [original ed., 1937].

Nilsen, Thomas R. "On Defining Communication," *The Speech Teacher* 6 (1957), 10–17.

Shannon, Claude E., and Warren Weaver. *The Mathematical Theory of Communication.* Champaign, IL: University of Illinois Press, 1949.

Chapter 2 presents a basic model of the communication process. Although all elements of the communication process are important to your success as a speaker, the components over which you have the most control are how you encode and empower your message for your audience. Since you yourself choose the words that carry your ideas from yourself to your audience, the part of the communication model that has traditionally received the most theoretical and practical attention is the careful construction of your message. Accordingly, we will be primarily concerned in this book with the principles of effective message preparation and presentation.

If the goal of a course in public speaking is to have you understand the principles of effective public speaking, as well as to produce effective public speeches, then an important question becomes: *How do we get started understanding the principles of effective public speaking?* Where do we begin in our attempts to understand how a public speech should be constructed and delivered? As a recent book by George Lakoff and Mark Johnson, entitled *Metaphors We Live By* (1980), makes clear, we often use our understanding of one thing as a tool to help us understand something else that seems similar to it. That is, we attempt to understand the unknown by means of a series of comparisons or analogies with something we feel we understand better. Thus, for example, if we are trying to understand the principles of the brain's operation, we might use our understanding of computers to help us understand how the brain processes information. Or, we might make comparisons between the heart and a water pump and pipes to understand the principles of the circulatory system (Miller, 1979). To build our understanding of one thing by comparing it with something else is to use a metaphorical process.

In using metaphors to help us understand something, the question is always one of "What is *X* LIKE?" In terms of the principles of effective public speaking, we can ask, "What is an effective public speech *like?*" Fortunately, a very fertile explanatory metaphor has been available for millennia: Plato's "organic" metaphor. A speech must seem to be "alive," "vivid," "living." For nearly 2400 years Plato's organic metaphor has been interpreted and reinterpreted to help teach the principles of public speaking (Orsini, 1975; Rousseau, 1972). The purpose of the present chapter is to give Plato's organic metaphor a contemporary, *process* interpretation as a way of gaining new insights into the principles of effective public speaking. The rest of the book will then apply what we learn from the organic metaphor to understanding each of the specific skills and principles that are required for effective public speaking. The theme of this book is that effective public speaking must seem "organic" in the special way explained in this chapter. Each of the specific principles of public speaking can help contribute to making your own speeches seem more organic if they are properly applied. The fact is, the principles of effective public speaking work as they do because they contribute to the apparent "organicness," "livingness," or "vividness" of the speeches that employ them.

Toward a Theory of Public Speaking: Plato's Organic Metaphor

In an attempt to explain what a good speech should be like, the philosopher Plato hit upon a metaphor that has continued to be used in one form or another ever since: *A speech should be like a living organism.* What does the organic metaphor imply for our understanding of effective public speaking? In his dialogue *Phaedrus,* Plato writes:

> Well, there is one point at least which I think you will admit, namely that any discourse ought to be constructed like a living creature, with its own body, as it were; it must not lack either head or feet; it must have a middle and extremities so composed as to suit each other and the whole work (246C).

According to this passage Plato seems to believe that a speech must be like our *material* bodies—having clearly separated parts (head, body, feet)—and that these parts must all relate to one another in an orderly way (a middle and extremities so composed as to suit each other and the whole work). Living creatures are the most highly organized physical things we know of and, following the traditional interpretation of Plato's metaphor, a speech must be organized as skillfully as is a living creature's physical body (Wimsatt, 1972).

Plato's metaphor is generally taken to be a *material* metaphor—a speech must be like a creature's physical body (head, body, and feet). Only secondarily is the metaphor taken as a *temporal* metaphor—that is, as implying that a speech must be like a creature's temporal life, having a beginning, middle, and end. When the temporal aspect of living is emphasized, we see that a speech's material parts relate to one another in *time* as well as in space. A speech must have at least three material parts that must also follow one another in time: an introduction, a body, and a conclusion, in just that temporal order.

These insights into effective public speaking are important, and, simple as they may seem, many beginning public speakers fail because they neglect to take seriously the notion that effective speeches have functionally separate parts, and that these parts must be clearly organized to follow one another smoothly in time. But, can the organic metaphor be mined for any greater insights than these?

During the 20th century a conceptual revolution has been gradually taking place that has the potential for giving us important new insights into effective public speaking based on a new understanding of the organic metaphor. The modern perspective sees the world as a process rather than as static material. For example, atoms are high energy physical processes, not merely self-contained chunks of elemental material. Living creatures are intricately organized temporal processes; they aren't just material bodies that happen to move. If a speech is like a living creature, it is like a creature as a *temporally organized process,* not just as a *materially organized form.* Our new insights into the nature of effective public speaking come from exploring the ways a speech is like a living process rather than the ways it is like a material body.

The Concept of Acts

What kind of a process or activity is the one that underlies all living organisms?

Philosopher Susanne Langer (1967) has given considerable thought to this problem of imagining living beings as temporal processes. Furthermore, she has stated her conclusions in a way that has many important implications for how we interpret Plato's organic metaphor in process rather than material terms. In this and the following section we will explore Langer's concept of *the "act" as the natural unit of all organically based processes,* and see what implications this "act concept" of process has for mining Plato's organic metaphor for insights into the principles of effective public speaking. We will begin by looking at what Langer means by saying that living processes take the form of acts.

Langer's basic theory of organic processes may be stated in deceptively simple terms: *All organically based processes take the form of acts.* The **act form** that all such processes take may also be quite simply stated: "Every act ... has an initial phase, a phase of acceleration and sometimes increasing complexity, a turning point, or consummation, and a closing phase or cadence" (1967, p. 291). This sentence captures the essence of the nature of organic processes and will become the basis of our process interpretation of Plato's organic metaphor in the pages and chapters to follow.

What Langer claims is that *all* organically based processes, at any level of observation—from the most microscopic, such as a neuron's discharge or a muscle's twitch, to the most macroscopic, such as the wave of a hand or a person's life as a whole—exemplify a typical four-phase **act form.** The four phases of all organic processes are:

1. **Impulse:** an initial period of relatively quiet *preparation* during which an organized tension or store of energy is built up that will be spent during the subsequent phases of the act

2. **Rise** or **Development:** a period of increasing or *accelerating* activity during which the act progressively unfolds in accordance with the tensions built up during the impulse phase

3. **Climax:** a turning point of maximum energy expenditure or activity

4. **Fall** or **Cadence:** a period of decline and exhaustion of the impulse's

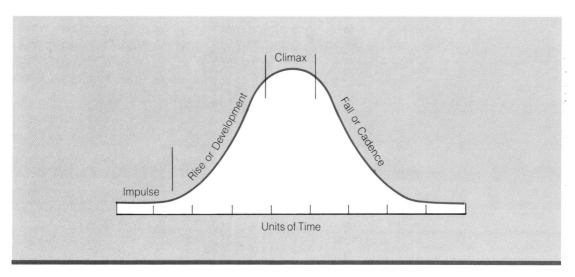

Figure 3-1   The Four Phases of the Act Form

initial energy, resulting in *decreasing* or *decelerating* activity and a return to relative inactivity—the impulse is spent.

Figure 3-1 illustrates the four phases of the act form.

Impulse, development, climax, and fall—these four successive phases of the act form underlie all organically based processes. Whether you look at a plant or a person, a heartbeat or a headache, the story is the same. Each begins with a period of **preparation** from which the rest of the act develops; each passes through a **developmental** phase of increasing growth, strength, and possible complexity; each reaches full maturity with a peak or **climax** of vigor and vitality; and then each fades back, **falling** toward inactivity, exhaustion, and finally extinction. It is this four-phase act form—and all of the organic principles that it yields—that is the essence of *livingness* or organic form in the world of living creatures. And it is these four phases, and the natural principles that derive from them, that *a speech must imitate* if it is to seem alive and "like a living creature." From your own first *impulse* to give a speech, to the *consummation* of that impulse with the speech's actual delivery, every step of your work must seek to utilize the form and principles of acts if the final outcome—the speech itself— is to seem alive, vivid, and organically whole to your audience.

*Y*our Speech As a "Living Creature"

We will next outline the most prominent organic principles that you should apply in your speeches. Figure 3-2 illustrates the relationship between the

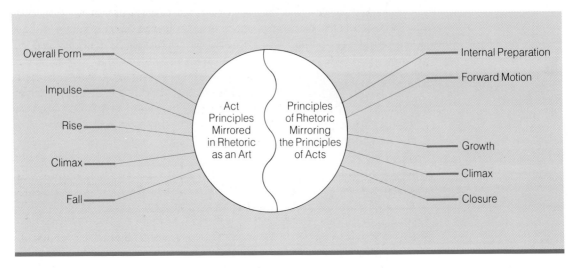

Overall Form ——————— Internal Preparation

Impulse ——————— Forward Motion

Rise ———————

Act Principles Mirrored in Rhetoric as an Art | Principles of Rhetoric Mirroring the Principles of Acts

——————— Growth

Climax ———————

——————— Climax

Fall ———————

——————— Closure

Figure 3-2   Principles of Acts and Rhetoric

principles of actual organic acts and the corresponding principles of rhetoric as an art that may be derived from these principles of acts. On the left-hand side are listed each of the four phases of the basic act form, which all organic processes display; on the right-hand side are five principles of organic speech construction, which correspond to significant features of the act's four phases. These five principles derive from the characteristics of each of the four phases of natural organic processes. Although there are many principles of acts other than the ones shown in the figure, and many more applications to the theory of rhetoric than the figure illustrates, we will look at five of the most useful principles in this chapter.

Create a Sense of Internal Preparation

Organic acts always begin with a period of preparation during which the tension or energy that will be used during the course of the rest of the act is built up. You can experience this preparatory period by merely monitoring your own behavioral acts. For example, if you are presently seated, stand up. What preparatory steps did you have to go through in order to actually perform the act of standing up? Did you have to shift position in your chair? Push yourself away from your desk or table? Move your feet apart to form a platform upon which to stand? Tense your muscles in order to spring upward from your seated position? As simple as standing up is, it requires numerous preparatory subacts in order to accomplish it. Only after the preparation period is completed, with all of your preparatory activity poised at a critical threshold, can you actually complete the act of standing up.

The act of speaking occurs in the same way. Whenever you talk you must literally "get ready" to talk. Try it and see. If you have been quietly reading, or even actively listening, becoming a talker requires a period of preparatory actions. You may have to shift your posture; you will certainly have to take a quick breath and hold it while you set all of your vocalizing organs into their starting positions. Thus, whether we are looking at a large and easily visible act such as standing up, or at smaller and less readily visible acts such as vocalizing, the act begins with a period of preparation during which all the elements needed for the act are moved into a ready position, anticipating the rest of the act.

From this fundamental fact about actual organic processes comes the first principle concerning what effective public speeches must be *like.* An organic, living speech, a speech that the audience will experience as being well crafted and alive with feeling, will create a sense of internal preparation. If you do your work properly as a speaker, you will make the audience feel a sense of *anticipation* concerning what is to come. You will evoke a feeling of *expectation.* The audience will be prepared for something specific to follow. This feeling of expectation is a major part of what effective, organic speech making is all about—and it can be accomplished with a few carefully chosen, properly used speech techniques.

To see just how strongly a few thoughtfully chosen words can prepare an audience to anticipate something later in a speech, try the following little experiment. What acts do you expect to follow when someone says the phrase: "Knock, knock"? Do you feel a powerful urge to say "Who's there?" For most English-speaking people, the phrase "knock, knock" prepares a powerful expectation that a joke of a very particular type will follow. If you say "knock, knock" and then do not follow the natural course of the act you have prepared your audience for, they will be disappointed, and even somewhat frustrated. After all, you have promised them a little game and have not fulfilled your promise—leaving them with a charge of energy to use up and no effective way to complete the act on their own.

Similarly, what do you expect to follow when someone says:

There once was a lady from Dread

Who liked to stand on her. . .

Or,

Did you hear the one about the traveling salesman?

In each case, the words you say not only prepare the listener for something more to follow (and usually something quite specific), but also create an expectation that the prepared-for something *will* come, and usually fairly soon. Because of the need to use up the prepared-for energy, the listener strongly desires that you fulfill the expectation you have created.

Preparing expectations and creating audience anticipation is absolutely fundamental to effective, organic speech making. As a whole, your speech

A student archaeologist restores a 2,000-year-old mural at ancient Herculaneum in Italy. What educational experiences have you been involved in outside the classroom? Have you ever visited the site of an archaeological dig? What local restoration projects do you know about?

must imitate the act form by preparing your audience for what is to come during the main body of the speech. If, for example, you say, "Today my main three points will be . . ." you are both preparing the audience to listen for a three-point speech and also creating an anticipation of each of those three points. The audience will listen specifically for each of those three main points. If you do not talk about each of those announced points, or if you subsequently talk about a fourth point for which you failed to prepare your audience, they will think your speech was poorly constructed (and definitely *not* like a living creature). An organically effective speech prepares the way for only those expectations that it can actually fulfill. Chapter 10 explains how to create audience anticipation in the introduction to your speech, and thereby give it a feeling of internal preparation.

Your speech's introduction is, of course, an obvious place to prepare your audience for whatever is to follow. But it is not the only place. Just as a living organism is comprised of numerous hierarchical levels of acts within acts, a living speech has many interlocking levels of organization—from large to small. Each of these levels must fulfill the organic principles if the speech is to seem fully alive. For a public speech, the largest actlike unit of organization is the entire speech as a whole, and the largest preparatory period is the speech's introduction. The speech as a whole is the level at which Plato's organic metaphor was originally meant to apply.

But we can move progressively downward, unit by unit, from the speech as a whole, all the way to the individual sentence, and even smaller—to the individual word or, smaller yet, to the individual speech sound. At every such level you can prepare your audience for some special speech effect that contributes to your speech's total living qualities. Let us look at a few examples of the many ways you can prepare your audience for some of the smaller units of speech process that can occur within your overall speech as a whole.

First, you can prepare your audience for movements within your speech from one section to the next—from introduction to body ("Let's look now at that first main point") and from body to conclusion ("In conclusion" or "In summary"). These are major passages within the speech and should be prepared for with phrases called **transitions** (see Chapter 10). Within the main body of the speech, you can also prepare the audience for smaller moves from one major point to the next major point. For example, you might say, "Now that we've examined *why* we must act this month, let's look at *how* we should proceed." This sentence prepares the audience to change from thinking about *why* to thinking about *how*. On a smaller level, yet within a particular main point, you can prepare your audience to consider a specific situation by using a phrase such as "for example," and for an unexpected side trip away from your main point by saying, "let me add parenthetically." If you want to prepare the audience for an added thought, you might say "in addition," or "moreover."

Another way to prepare your audience for something you are about to do or say is to ask a question. For example, you might ask: "Why should you ask a question during the course of your speech?" The reason you ask questions during the course of your speech is because questions create a strong sense of anticipation that you will subsequently answer the question. Having developed the expectation that an answer that will satisfy their curiosity will soon follow, your audience will listen attentively until you answer the question.

Expectations can also be created at the sentence level by carefully preparing sentences that have a sense of incompletion about them. When John F. Kennedy began his now-famous sentence "Ask not what your country can do for you," he said it in a way that prepared an expectation that something more was to follow—something that would satisfy the anticipation he had planned: "Ask what you can do for your country." The temporary incompletion of the first part of the sentence creates an expectation of future completion, which the audience eagerly awaits.

You can even prepare for special effects at the level of individual speech sounds, since any repeated sound pattern sets up an expectation that the pattern will be continued for some period of time. Even if we did not know that the next word was *peck* in the sentence "Peter Piper picked a . . ." we would have a strong anticipation that the next word would begin with a *p*. Spiro Agnew's declaration that the students of the Vietnam era were the "*n*attering *n*abobs of *n*egativism" depends for its effect upon the expectation prepared for by the repeated sounds of the first two words.

Thus, as you can see, there are numerous levels at which thoughtful speakers can prepare the audience for elements that are to come and thereby enhance the organic qualities of their speeches. Because acts begin with a period of preparation, the first principle of effective, organic speeches is to create anticipation by preparing your audience for what is to follow.

Create a Sense of Forward Motion

Just as actual acts proceed from phase to phase, your speech must seem to move forward from subunit to subunit toward its final conclusion. The impulse phase of an act always prepares for *something*—the rest of the act—so the subunits of your speech must also prepare the way for something that is to follow. In your speech, you must seem to fulfill the expectations for which you have previously prepared your audience. Creating and then fulfilling expectations throughout your speech brings about the organic sense of forward motion that is common to all living processes, which your speech must imitate if it is to seem like a living creature.

Of course, whenever you speak your speech *literally* moves forward, sentence by sentence, through time. After all, one sentence must follow another. But more is involved in the organic principle of forward motion than mere sequence. Your speech isn't merely an actual organically based event; it is also a consciously constructed, complex *symbol* for your ideas. This symbol of your ideas is what actually gets projected from yourself to your audience during a speech (see Chapter 2). And it is the speech *as a symbol for your ideas* that must consciously be made to seem like it is advancing forward. What is important, then, is not that the individual sentences actually *be* moving forward in time, but rather that the idea as projected in your symbols must *seem* to be moving forward. So you must consciously craft your speech as a symbol of your ideas so that it *seems* to have forward motion. For example, if you have prepared your audience to receive some specific information by asking a question, when you answer that question you give your speech a little life-like motion.

How can you create a sense of forward motion? How can you help your audience feel the movement of your ideas through a speech text? Although any technique that prepares an expectation (transitional words, internal summaries, rhetorical questions, and so forth) can be used to create forward motion, the single most useful device for giving your speech a feeling of forward motion is the strategic use of **repetition**. Repetition sets up a pattern and automatically creates an expectation of something to follow. Completing the pattern fulfills the expectation and moves your speech forcefully along to the next actlike subunit. Repetition may be used in numerous ways in speech construction, and it will be employed at virtually every level of speech preparation—from the overall structural organization of the speech, to the formulation of specific sentences, and even to the choice of individual words. To preview just a few of the types of repetition you might use in a speech to produce forward motion, look at the use of repetition in the following phrase:

from plants to persons, from heartbeats to headaches

The phrase uses at least the following types of repetition:

Repetition of a sound: from *p*lants to *p*ersons, from *h*eartbeats, to *h*eadaches

Repetition of a word: from plants to persons, *from* heartbeats to headaches

Repetition of a grammatical structure: from . . . to, from . . . to

Can you find others? How about repetition of the plural marker?

from plant*s* to person*s*, from heartbeat*s* to headache*s*

Are there still more types of repetition?

These, and many more uses of repetition, will be treated in the pages to follow. (How many times has the word *repetition* been used in the preceding paragraph? Was it too many? If not, why not? How many types of repetition can you find in that paragraph? Count them and see.) Chapters 9 and 13 will give you many more ideas concerning how to use repetition to induce audience expectations and, therefore, to help give your speech a sense of organic forward motion.

Create a Sense of Growth

Acts do not merely pass quietly from one phase to another throughout time; they *grow*. The impulse phase is merely a beginning, a gathering together of the energy or tension needed for the act to proceed. Under fertile circumstances, the act does not cease with the impulse, nor does it stay the same size, strength, or intensity throughout its successive phases. It takes off, accelerates, and grows. The impulse of an act contains all the potential for growth of the fully developed act. But the impulse is not the entire act. As the act proceeds to use up its store of potential energy, the act develops, it grows—in scope, intensity, and complexity—drawing many other organic elements into its sphere. To seem organic, your speech must also seem to grow and develop from its basic idea, drawing many other conceptual elements into its basic symbolic structure.

In order to seem organic, your speech, as a symbolic expression of the idea you have grown from your original impulse, must have the appearance of growth. What resources do you have to create the feeling of growth in your speech? In addition to repetition and the other devices already mentioned, your most useful tool will be what is quite appropriately called developmental material—definitions, examples, anecdotes, and statistics, among others. For a speech is not merely a loose collection of sentences, like bones lined up end to end, with no particular orderly relation to one another. Instead, a speech is a *structure* of various types of sentences, some abstract, others concrete; some general, others specific. All are needed to give your speech a sense of growth.

The sense of growth in a speech comes from the interweaving of the general, structural statements ("My three main points today . . .") with the details that fill in and develop those statements. The abstract and general sentences serve as impulses to growth because they invite development with ever more specific and concrete details. Growth is a process of differentiation and expansion. The specific details suggest organic growth because, like bodily organs, they cannot stand alone outside the structure provided by the whole. They need a context to give them meaning; without their relationship to the structuring elements of the speech, they would fall apart. Your speech will seem to grow in an actlike manner when it weaves together both your general and specific ideas, and your abstract and concrete vocabulary. The chapters on speech development and speech structure (Chapters 8, 9, and 10) will help you accomplish the task of "growing" your speech in this manner.

Create a Sense of Climax

Growth (whether of an individual act, or of a complete organism) is not a never-ending process. Creatures do not become infinitely large; acts do not become infinitely powerful; speeches cannot become infinitely long and developed. At a point in the development of every act, it reaches the limits of its potential for growth, uses up its reservoir of energy, and begins its period of decline. That phase in the progress of an act—when it turns from increasing growth, power, or acceleration and toward increasing deterioration, debilitation, and deceleration—is its **climax.** An act first builds up, moving toward its climax, and then turns from its climax toward final closure.

To seem organic, your speech must not only seem to move forward and to grow; it must also seem to move to a climax; it must seem to build, as Kenneth Burke calls it, to a "crescendo" (1931, p. 45). The forward motion you create during your speech must seem like movement toward something, which is its climax. Just as you can create many levels of forward motion in your speech, so you can create many levels of consummation or climax. Certainly the speech as a whole should seem to have an overall sense of movement from its beginning to a highest point—often, but not necessarily, just before the actual conclusion. In addition, within the speech each greater and lesser component unit can be organized so that the speech seems to move to greater and lesser consummations. In fact, every expectation you subsequently fulfill helps provide a minor climax to your speech. This sense of minor but multiple climaxes is much like what happens within a three act play. The play as a whole will have one overall climax—the moment toward which the entire drama has been leading. But the play will also have many little climaxes—some corresponding to the ends of each of the individual acts (Act I, Act II, Act III), others to what are called "French scenes," within each act: the periods between entrances and exits of characters. Your speech will need to build to a series of little climaxes if it is to seem like a living creature. These minor climaxes are one of the natural results of fulfilling the expectations you have been creating throughout your speech.

Create a Sense of Closure

An act has *four* phases, and your speech must imitate all four phases—including the phase of closure—if it is to seem as fully organic as it can. Although each subunit of the speech must achieve its own sense of impulse, rise, climax, and closure, the concept of closure will be most fully discussed in the section on speech conclusions (Chapter 10), since it is the conclusion that most strongly establishes a sense of final closure. By now it should also be clear that the satisfaction of each expectation will also create a corresponding sense of closure within that unit. For example, if you have asked a rhetorical question, answering it climaxes the tension you created by asking the question in the first place. Furthermore, answering the question also provides closure to the overall act represented by a question-answer sequence. With the completion of the answer, nothing more is expected relative to the specific question you have raised. Closure has been achieved.

*C*onclusion

To be effective, a speech must seem to be alive. Metaphorically, it must be like a living creature. In this chapter we have applied a contemporary process interpretation to Plato's ancient metaphor. We have used Susanne Langer's act theory of organic processes to explain five key principles of "livingness" in public speaking: internal preparation, forward motion, growth, climax, and closure. Each of the five organic principles of speech developed in this chapter represents some aspect of the four phases of the act form itself. To seem like a living creature, your speech must seem to exemplify the form of acts. The five principles that have been developed are the most fundamental and useful for the beginning public speaker. All five will play a prominent role in the chapters to follow, as the principles of effective organic public speaking are developed in detail.

Questions for Review

1. What is a metaphor?

2. How do we use metaphors to aid our understanding of things and processes around us?

3. What is Plato's organic metaphor? What is the difference between a "material" reading of the metaphor and a "process" reading?

4. What is an act? Is there anything a person does that is *not* structured in the form of an act?

5. What are *internal preparation, forward motion, growth, climax,* and *closure* as these terms relate to public speaking?

Questions for Discussion

1. Five similarities are developed here between the act-based approach to living processes and the principles of public speaking. List any other similarities you can think of.

2. Metaphors are rarely exactly applicable to the objects of their comparisons. List any ways in which the process interpretation of the organic metaphor might be misleading or might fail to be adequate in explaining the principles of public speaking.

3. Describe one or more metaphors that others have used to explain some principle, process, or device.

Things to Try

1. Below are five popular American aphorisms. Each uses one or more devices to enhance its living qualities and make it more memorable. In each case determine what techniques were employed to add more life.
   a. Waste not, want not.
   b. A bird in the hand is worth two in the bush.
   c. A friend in need is a friend indeed.

d. Nothing ventured nothing gained.

e. A penny saved is a penny earned.

2. Below are dead versions of five famous quotes. See if you can reconstruct the five well-known originals and explain why the originals are more vivid or alive than the moribund versions given here.

a. I would sacrifice my entire kingdom for a horse. (Hint: "A horse, a . . .")

b. Crimes should be punished commensurate with acts done. (Hint: "An eye . . .")

c. Requests will be granted. (Hint: "Ask, and it shall . . .")

d. Fear of acting is our only problem. (Hint: "The only thing . . .")

e. Everyone is equal, almost. (Hint: "All animals are equal, but . . .")

3. Select a speech to analyze from a recent issue of *Vital Speeches of the Day*. Identify the features of the speech that make it either seem to be especially alive or dead.

Bibliography

Aristotle. *Rhetoric*. W. Rhys Roberts (tr.). New York: Modern Library, 1954.

Burke, Kenneth. *Counter-Statement*. Berkeley: University of California Press, 1968 [1931].

Cicero. *Cicero on Oratory and Orators*. J. S. Watson (tr.). Carbondale: Southern Illinois Press, 1970.

Lakoff, George, and Mark Johnson. *Metaphors We Live By*. Chicago: University of Chicago Press, 1980.

Langer, Susanne K. *Mind: An Essay on Human Feeling*, Vol. 1. Baltimore: Johns Hopkins University Press, 1967.

Miller, Jonathon. *The Body in Question*. New York: Random House, 1978.

Orsini, G. N. G. *Organic Unity in Ancient and Later Poetics*. Carbondale: Southern Illinois University Press, 1975.

Plato. *Phaedrus*. R. Hackforth (tr.). Indianapolis: Bobbs-Merrill, 1952.

Rousseau, G. S., ed. *Organic Form: The Life of an Idea*. London: Routledge and Kegan Paul, 1972.

Smith, Barbara Herrnstein. *Poetic Closure: A Study of How Poems End*. Chicago: University of Chicago Press, 1968.

Wimsatt, William K. "Organic Form: Some Questions about a Metaphor." In: *Organic Form: The Life of an Idea*. (Ed.) G. S. Rousseau. London: Routledge and Kegan Paul, 1972, pp. 61–81.

Expectations and Fulfillments: The Audience's Impulse to Listen

*I*n Chapter 1 we noted that preparing your speech for a public audience is more demanding than simply producing spontaneous speech for casual conversation. One reason premeditated speech is more demanding is that whenever people believe you have specially prepared your speech, they listen with a special set of expectations. As a speaker you are strongly obliged to fulfill these expectations; not to do so is to court disaster.

Thus far the emphasis has been primarily on your own impulse to speak. After all, that is where most speeches actually do begin. But normally you prepare your speech for delivery to someone else. Without an audience it is difficult to satisfactorily implement your impulse to speak out on some topic. However, just as you prepare your speech for a reason, so too does your audience attend your speech for a reason. Sometimes they are required to attend your speech—like your classmates in your speech class or your subordinates in an organization. Sometimes they come to hear you voluntarily—because they expect to learn something new or are curious about your views on some important controversy. Whatever their reasons for being there, each member of your audience has his or her own impulses for listening, impulses that await for your speech to implement them.

This chapter presents an overview of some typical impulses your audience brings along with them when they come to hear you speak. These audience impulses may be called their **expectations.** Your implementation of the audience's impulses will be called **fulfillments.** Failure to fulfill their expectation leads to **frustrations** of their impulses for listening and can result in the subsequent frustration of your own impulse for speaking.

Audience expectations can be divided into two types: *situation-generated* expectations and *speaker-generated* expectations. Situation-generated expectations are those expectations that audiences bring with them as they prepare to attend your speech, that is, expectations they bring to *any* situation in which they anticipate hearing a speech. In contrast, speaker-generated expectations are the expectations you yourself induce as you speak on a particular occasion.

Since the creation and satisfaction of expectations plays a major role in your success as a speaker, much of this book discusses how you create expectations in general, how you can control which expectations you actually do create, and finally, how you can fulfill the expectations created when you present your speech. In this chapter, we will first survey the situation-generated expectations you can anticipate your audience will have as they prepare to listen to your speech; next, we will briefly overview the speaker-generated expectations that are addressed in the following chapters.

Situation-Generated Expectations

As the communication model in Chapter 2 makes clear (Figure 2-1), speeches always occur in a *situation*. That is, they occur in the midst of a host of other personal, social, cultural, and community activities that are constantly going on around you. Furthermore, speeches usually occur for reasons that are linked to the ongoing social and political life of the community in which you live. Speaking—or not speaking—can make a difference in people's immediate lives.

More often than not, audiences know ahead of time that they are going to hear a speech, and so they have time to build up a specific set of expectations concerning the speech. This is not always the case, of course. It could be that you are strolling in the park on a fine Sunday afternoon and you happen upon a group holding a rally. One of its members is giving a speech. In such a situation you probably had no *prior* expectations about the speech you are hearing. But, as soon as you recognize that a speech is being delivered and decide to listen in for a few minutes, you will bring to bear your expectations of what a speech fundamentally must do. Even as you move closer to hear what is going on, you will be building up your impulse to listen, developing many general expectations about what you are likely to hear. Let's look at some of the expectations that people typically generate whenever they know they are going to hear a speech.

Expectations about You As a Speaker

If you are speaking, your audience is listening. Audiences assume there must be a reason for that relationship. Accordingly, they expect that they will hear someone who is qualified to speak about whatever the topic is, someone who has some special kind of experience of knowledge related to the topic, or some special kind of competence. These are minimum expectations and every audience will have them about you as a speaker. Therefore, it is important that you speak on topics about which you *do* have a reasonable level of expertise—such as long-time interests, your professional knowledge, or personal experiences you have had.

In addition to knowing what you are talking about, you must also *show* that you know what you are talking about. The audience will expect you to give evidence that you do indeed know what you are talking about. Your subject matter knowledge and personal trustworthiness must quietly shine through your speech. This expectation may be fulfilled by such things as the confidence you exhibit as you speak, your skillful use of established or recognized authorities to support your ideas, and by the references and allusions you make to your sources of expertise during the course of your speech. Chapter 10 on speech introductions and Chapter 8 on supporting materials will help you learn how to reveal your personal expertise on your subject matter, thereby satisfying this particular audience expectation.

Furthermore, an audience expects you to be a person of good will—someone who not only knows, but also who will present the information in a responsible manner. This means that you must seem to be someone who will not distort information or withhold relevant facts that may be needed to assess your case. Often this feeling is carried more by your manner of delivery than by any specific thing you say. Chapter 14 on delivering your speeches will be helpful as you try to convey your basic personal integrity. More will be said about your good will as a speaker when we consider the audience's expectations concerning your personal ethics.

Expectations about Your Topic

Sometimes your audience will know ahead of time what your topic is going to be and sometimes they won't. But once they do know, they will have expectations about the type of content they will hear, depending upon the general situation in which the speech takes place. Different types of situations induce different types of audience expectations about the same topic as a result of factors other than the topic itself. The Travel Club that arrives prepared to hear a speech on "Africa" will probably not expect to hear a speech on African political or economic strife. More likely, they will expect to hear about some aspect of touring Africa. On the other hand, the Public Policy Forum *will* expect to hear a speech about current political activities. If you have doubts about what your audience may expect, ask someone. Don't try to prepare a speech without attempting to do some serious **audience analysis** (see Chapter 7) to find out what your audience might expect concerning your topic.

Expectations about Your Purpose

Every speech must have a fundamental purpose: a reason for being given. Without such a purpose, the speech can drift aimlessly from point to point, filling up the available time without accomplishing anything in particular. Audiences expect your speech to have an identifiable purpose, and they will expect to be able to determine what that purpose is very early in their listening activity. Once they feel they have found your purpose they will have a much easier time listening to and understanding your speech. Because your audience depends upon finding your overall purpose as a way of guiding their listening activity, they expect you to reveal it early. Your audience will be restless and ill at ease until they understand what is going on within your speech. To fulfill their expectation, reveal your central purpose early in your speech, and be sure to adhere to it as the speech progresses. To help avoid upsetting your audience's expectations, announce any "side trips" you plan to take away from your central theme.

Your speech should emphasize one of the three major general purposes for speaking in public: to inform, to persuade, or to entertain. It is especially important that one or another of these three general purposes predominate in your speech. A speech entitled "Why We Should Legalize Marijuana" creates the expectation that you have a specific point of view to express, whereas one entitled "Marijuana: The Pros and Cons" creates an expectation of dispassionate neutrality. If you do not intend to be neutral, there are dangers in inducing an audience to expect such a speech. They may respond more unfavorably to your proposal when they discover they have been deceived than they would have if you had been more honest with them. If you believe that being too direct in stating your purpose may be a disadvantage, then it is better to create a situation that induces fewer expectations of any kind than to create expectations that you know in advance you will not fulfill.

Expectations about the Occasion

Is the situation an after-dinner speech? Then the audience will expect a lighter treatment of your topic—whatever it is—than they would if the speech were given at a business meeting. Is the community up in arms about a new zoning ordinance? Are you angry? Then those who hear you will expect to feel your involvement. Is the speech for a special occasion, to mark an event such as Memorial Day, or accepting an award? Then there are special speech forms for such occasions that you must fulfill because special occasions create their own special patterns of expectations about your speech. Thus, you must assess the specific demands of the situation and make sure you fulfill the expectations appropriate to the occasion.

Expectations about Your Preparation

You may be an expert in aerospace engineering, but have you prepared for this particular speech? What difference does it make whether you are talking to the High School Science Club or to graduate students in aerospace technology? Each audience requires a separately prepared speech. Even in politics, where a candidate for national office must present the same essential ideas dozens of times to nearly identical audiences all over the country, adaptations must be made from place to place. Communities differ in how they personally experience national issues. Audiences expect you to prepare your speech especially for them, and they will be disappointed if it looks as if you have not.

Most fundamentally, though, audiences will have general expectations about your preparation for giving a particular speech. They will expect you to have put together a speech, not merely to have strung together a series of random thoughts. Specifically, your audience will have expectations about the following four aspects of your speech preparation:

1. *Your speech's content, organization, or structure.* A speech is not a series of randomly selected ideas; it is a patterned fabric of ideas woven into a whole cloth. Audiences expect your speech to be coherently constructed and thoughtfully developed with them in mind.

2. *Your preparedness as a speaker.* Audiences expect the delivery of your speech to be skillful and competent, that you will have rehearsed your speech in preparation for this occasion. Don't disappoint them on this or all else may be lost.

3. *Your fairness.* Having given you their attention, audiences expect you to repay them by treating them fairly. You must not only be fair by being well prepared, you must also be fair by treating the topic as even-handedly as the situation permits.

4. *Your understanding of your audience.* Audiences expect that you will have taken some care in understanding them and their needs. What do they know about your topic already and what are their specific interests in the topic? If you do not make an effort to learn these things, you may find yourself either talking above or beneath your audience and losing them as if they were not there at all. Audiences expect that you will adapt your speech to them. Because of the crucial importance of this particular expectation, Chapter 7 will consider the goal of adequately understanding your audience and adapting your speech to them.

Expectations about Themselves As Listeners

Not only do audiences have expectations about you and your preparation, they also have expectations about themselves as listeners. They expect that they will be able to understand what a speaker says if the speaker has made a conscientious effort to adapt the speech to their level of knowledge. They also expect that they will become involved in the topic if the speaker has made an effort to present it interestingly. Listeners bring to the speech situation a reservoir of interest that you can either build upon or fritter away. Your audience typically expects that they are intelligent enough to follow what you are saying and interested enough to try. Do not disappoint this expectation by failing to plan your speech in terms of the audience's known interests and levels of knowledge. Your audience's good will is one of your most important speech resources.

Expectations about Your Personal Ethics

From almost as early as we have had manuals and handbooks teaching principles of public speaking, there have also been critics of the art—critics who challenge both the ethics of the speaker and the moral character of the rhetorical art. Learning the principles of effective speaking, these critics argue, means having power over others, and the temptation to use that power unfairly is too great. "To make the worse case seem the better," critics have worried. The concern is not entirely unfounded. There have been many instances in the past where the gift of effective speech has been used to mislead, befuddle, and confuse. But the misuse of speech cannot prevent people from talking and listening to one another; nor can it prevent people from being strongly influenced by what others say. *Homo loquens* is our nature and worrying extensively over whether or not we should try to use speech to influence others is nearly as futile as wondering if we should breathe because the carbon dioxide we exhale might pollute the air. However polluted the air might accidentally become, we still must breathe. Similarly, we must talk to express the fullness of our humanity. And our words will have an impact on others; this cannot be avoided. But, just as we have developed standards, codes, and even laws concerning the kinds of pollutants that can be put into the air others must breathe, we have also developed standards for the words that can be put into the air for others to hear. We believe, and often enforce by laws, such standards as the following:

1. No one should knowingly promote something as true that they honestly believe to be false.

2. No one should suggest a greater degree of certainty about their beliefs than their evidence will actually support.

3. No one should misuse the available facts to support their cause.

4. No one should withhold relevant information that might bear on the issues under discussion.

5. No one should distort information to make it conform to their own position.

These are among the most important ethical standards that apply to speakers, both public and private. Such standards all constitute expectations your audience has about your speech. Your audience will assume—in absence of evidence to the contrary—that you are adhering to these standards. Furthermore, audience members have ways of finding out—in time if not immediately—the falseness of your words. Unless you are already known to be a fraud, your audience expects you to be ethical and will quickly turn on you if they discover otherwise.

This family is hiking along the Pt. Reyes National Seashore in northern California. Have you done any hiking or backpacking? Should more land be preserved for parks even at the expense of economic development?

Thus far, we have discussed the expectations virtually all audiences typically bring to all public speaking situations. But as the speaking event begins and develops, many new and more specific expectations will also be generated, expectations that are either fulfilled or frustrated by what you subsequently say and do.

*S*peaker-Generated Expectations

As a speaker, your behavior will generate expectations from the moment you appear. If you seem nervous, they will expect a weak and hesitant speech from you. As soon as you start speaking, the expectations build quickly and powerfully: "This is going to be dull, I can tell it already." "Doesn't look like he knows too much—did you hear how he pronounced the chairman's name?" "Oh. That's what the speech is about. I thought the program said . . ." "Four main points to the speech, huh?"

As with the expectations the audience brings with them, those expectations you inspire from the first moment you come to the audience's attention are impulses with which you must deal—fulfilling or frustrating—again, at your own peril if you ignore them. One way of thinking of the speech situation is as a complex series of promises that you either implicitly or explicitly make to your audience and that you either systematically fulfill or fail to fulfill. A speech is a constant rhythmic interplay between promises made and promises kept or broken—expectations generated and expectations fulfilled or frustrated.

Expectations Generated While You Wait to Speak

As the speech event begins, the audience receives new information upon which to base its expectations. Are you being introduced warmly by someone who extols your virtues? Are you seated in an awkward or nervous posture that suggests discomfort? Do you fidget or seem withdrawn? Are you dressed appropriately for the occasion? Do you walk enthusiastically or timidly to the lectern? Your audience's expectations are influenced by these behaviors over which you have some measure of control. Sometimes called "impression management," or "the presentation of self," these factors have a greater impact on your effectiveness than you might think. The lengths to which one may go in consciously trying to influence the expectations of an audience are illustrated, for example, by the teacher's credo that an instructor must be very tough during the first two weeks of school before allowing more informal patterns of student-teacher interaction to take over. This is an attempt to establish expectations for one's students in much the same way that a speaker tries to establish expectations for the audience by the way he or she dresses, sits, and behaves while waiting to speak.

Expectations Generated by the Introduction

Perhaps the most powerful generator of expectations in the speech situation is the introduction. Not only does the introduction prepare the audience for the content and structure of the speech, but also for its **tone**. Do you begin with humor? With quiet seriousness? With dramatic flair? With a personal anecdote? Do you ramble, trying to find a way to get started? Do you mumble, trying to get the courage to speak? Or do you begin directly and forcefully, exuding confidence? However you begin—and there are many different ways, depending upon the occasion—your audience can reasonably assume that you will maintain elements of your opening tone throughout the speech. If that is not desirable, then the transition from one tone to another should at least be prepared for, so that you do not throw the audience's expectations off the track.

Student speakers often try to capture attention in their introductions through dramatic activities that are unrelated to the overall mood of their speeches. They will try, for example, to be humorous even when their intent is solemn or somber. Or they will have lots of volume and enthusiasm in the first 30 seconds of the speech, only to run out of steam when they get to the body. This energy letdown frustrates the audience, which has been prepared by the introduction for an upbeat, energetic performance only to be disappointed by what subsequently happens. The audience has empathically joined in with the enthusiastic opening, building up a high energy impulse for listening, only to have the speaker let them down. Emotionally, they are "all dressed up with no place to go." Accordingly, plan your introduction so that it creates an expectation about its tone as well as about its content and structure.

Expectations Generated by the Body

The body of your speech is the fulfillment (or frustration) of the impulses prepared for in the introduction. In addition, the body of your speech is composed of numerous subacts that have their own phases of impulse, rise, climax, and fall. And each of these smaller units within the speech's body creates its own expectations to fulfill. For example, if your overall speech has three main points, each of these points may be thought of as a speech within the speech; each creates an expectation of its own with its own period of preparation. Similarly, the subunits within a point must be prepared for. The phrase "for example" prepares an expectation that an example will follow; it is a way of setting up an expectation. Similarly, the phrase "let me illustrate this with a story" prepares your audience to expect a narrative with plot, characters, and punchline. Thus, even within the body of your speech you have many opportunities to establish expectations and to fulfill them.

Expectations Generated by the Conclusion

Even the conclusion of your speech creates its own expectations. The most obvious source of expectations is the **conclusion marker**, a phrase that indicates that the conclusion is coming and tells what type of conclusion to expect. A common conclusion marker is simply to say, "In conclusion." "In summary" leads the audience to expect an overview or summation of the speech. But your conclusion can create other types of expectations as well. Perhaps other speeches are on the program for the evening, and your conclusion serves not only to finish your own speech, but also to prepare transitionally for another. Or perhaps your speech is only a part of a large campaign you plan to develop in the weeks and years ahead. Or perhaps you expect your audience to take a specific action following your speech, and part of your conclusion will be designed to prepare your audience for such activity. In a church service, for example, the sermon might be followed by a call for an offering. A speech at a political rally might conclude with a call for contributions or volunteer help.

Conclusion

Chapter 4 has shifted the emphasis away from your impulse to speak and toward your audience's impulse to listen—an impulse signified by their becoming members of an audience. The points made in this chapter are general ones that apply almost without exception to all audiences. But different occasions and different speeches bring different audiences together—audiences that have special characteristics and special impulses to be fulfilled. Thus, Chapter 7 explains how you can try to systematically understand the specific audience you are going to address. Keeping in mind these general audience expectations, as well as those of particular audiences, will help you become a more effective speaker.

Questions for Review

1. In terms of public speaking, what is an expectation?

2. Why are audience expectations important to a public speaker?

3. What is the difference between a speaker-generated and a situation-generated expectation?

4. What is a fulfillment in public speaking terms?

5. How does an audience generate expectations about you prior to hearing you speak on a particular occasion?

6. What ethical standards does your audience expect you to fulfill?

Questions for Discussion

1. What difference does it make whether or not you try to understand your audience's expectations concerning your speech? Can a speech be relatively successful even if audience expectations are given little or no prior thought?

2. What typically happens when a speaker fails to adequately take into account an audience's expectations in planning a speech? Can you think of an example of a speaker you have heard who missed the mark because of inadequate consideration of the audience's impulses for listening?

3. Assuming that your speech topic comes from your college major or profession, how might you go about satisfying the audience's expectation that you have sufficient knowledge about your topic? Specifically, what types of things could you do or say during your speech's introduction? During the body of the speech? Is there anything you might do during the conclusion to reinforce the audience's confidence in your expertise?

4. How would the audience expectations differ on a topic like "The Needs of Our Community" if the speech were delivered to both the Downtown Businesspersons Luncheon Club and to the evening meeting of the local City Council?

5. What might you do during the introduction to subtly suggest that your speech was specially prepared for the present occasion and not just a stock speech that could have been delivered to any audience in general?

Things to Try

1. Before your next speech, analyze the specific expectations you can anticipate your audience to have before hearing your speech. Use the following checklist of expectations to guide your analysis.

   a. Expectations about you as a speaker

   b. Expectations about your topic

   c. Expectations about your purpose

   d. Expectations about the occasion

   e. Expectations about your preparation

   f. Expectations about themselves as listeners

   g. Expectations about your personal ethics

2. Having analyzed your audience's anticipated expectations, prepare a plan for how you will try to fulfill those expectations during the course of your speech. Account for each specific expectation you included in your previous analysis of audience expectations.

CHAPTER 5

The Process of Listening Well

*I*n Chapter 4 we discussed the expectations audiences have as they prepare to listen to your speech. But what about you yourself as a listener, listening to the speeches of others? In a typical public speaking class you will listen to about 20 to 25 speeches for every speech you actually present. That listening time can either be wasted (treated as if it were merely one of the costs of learning to speak in public), or it can be seized as an opportunity to learn about new subjects you may never have thought about and to examine different approaches to speaking you may want to consider trying. Since there is little point in wasting your time while others are speaking, the purpose of this chapter is to introduce you to the process of listening well to the speeches of others. We will begin by explaining three principles that serve as background to the study of listening, and we will conclude by describing a systematic procedure for listening more effectively.

*L*istening Is the Reciprocal of Speaking

Communication, by definition, requires at least two people: one to encode and project a message and one to intercept and decode the message. In spoken communication, listening is the necessary counterpart of speaking. It requires you to actively reach out to the speaker's ideas and try to take them in. Using the tennis metaphor mentioned in Chapter 2, communication requires that one person serve up a message; but it also requires that another person, ready and waiting, try to receive the message. At first, the server has the more active role—both in tennis and in communication. The server must toss the ball up in the air, then wind up like a windmill, bringing the racquet to strike the ball at its highest point and empowering it toward the receiver. Having struck the ball, the server completes the act by coming back to earth and getting into a ready position in case the receiver returns the ball. In the meantime, the receiver is not just passively standing around. Rather, the receiver warily watches the server, preparing to receive the serve. Typically, the receiver takes an active stance with knees bent, body well balanced, racquet in a ready position, prepared to spring into action depending upon whether the shot is to the left, to the right, or head on. As the ball arrives, the receiver moves to intercept it.

Listening is quite similar, in that the speaker at first appears to be doing all the work. But listeners must reciprocate; they must be prepared to mentally leap to the left or the right in order to catch a speaker's idea. They must actively watch the speaker to anticipate when the idea is coming and to anticipate what type of idea to expect. If a speaker's "idea-serves" are a little wild and hard to anticipate, then listening can be a very tiring activity. Listening is that active a process. The suggestions in this chapter are designed to help you be a better receiver of ideas.

Listening Differs from Hearing

Listening is sometimes confused with hearing—as if the physical act of hearing a speaker were the only thing involved in the process of effective listening. But, the processes differ in important ways. Hearing is a relatively mechanical act of translating sound waves pulsing in the air into neurochemical impulses that the brain can deal with. The ability to hear adequately depends primarily upon having healthy ears and functioning neural connections leading from your inner ear to your brain. Listening, on the other hand, is a mental process of understanding and thoughtfully considering what you have heard. Thus, although listening depends upon the ability to hear at a minimal functional level, it also requires considerable mental activity. We will discuss this mental activity through our analysis of listening as an organically based process.

Listening Is an Organically Based Process

In Chapter 3 we developed the theory that presenting a speech is a very special type of process: a four-phase, act-based process. Because listening is the active counterpart of speaking, it too follows a four-phase, act-based developmental form. Thus, in the sections that follow we will examine the component activities that make up each of the four phases of listening: preparing for the listening act, developing the listening act, culminating the listening act, and concluding the listening act.

Preparing for the Listening Act

The act of listening begins with a preparatory phase. Listening actively requires that you get ready to listen. Preparing to listen effectively involves both a long-term and a short-term component. Long-term preparation for listening well is like the general conditioning an athlete undergoes before any thought is given to preparing for a specific partner or opponent. You must get your listening skills in shape. As a listener, your long-term preparation includes at least three components: (1) reading widely on a variety of topics, (2) building your vocabulary, and (3) breaking any long-term bad listening habits.

Read Widely One of the best ways to improve your listening effectiveness is to read widely—both on a variety of topics and, if possible, on the particular topic of the speech you are preparing to listen to. The more you know in general the easier it is to understand what a speaker is trying to communicate on a particular topic. This is because you will have a fund of knowledge to which you can relate the speaker's ideas. At least four types of useful background can be gleaned from your reading and put to use in your listening.

First, whenever you read you will be adding to your reservoir of factual knowledge. This type of knowledge allows you to evaluate the facts presented by the speaker. Second, you will develop a richer bank of concepts. The more complete your own base of ideas, the more you bring to the task of understanding another person's ideas. Third, wide general reading will help you practice understanding complex presentations of ideas. Speeches can be complex in their arguments, but rarely as complex and detailed as a written essay or article. Although speeches are typically somewhat simpler than written essays, you only hear them once. So you must analyze them quickly and understand them in the ongoing present, even as the words fade one after another into silence. The more you read, the more practice you will have in thoughtfully considering complex arguments and ideas as they occur in the ongoing flow of the listening situation. Finally, wide reading will permit you to understand allusions to the writings of others. Many speakers assume a well-read audience and save many unnecessary words by alluding to the works of others (especially literary and Biblical writings). As a listener, you will miss the subtlety of a speaker's presentation if you do not understand indirect references to famous or important writings.

Build Your Vocabulary Effective speakers use a precise and varied vocabulary to capture and express the nuances of their points. If you are to understand anything beyond the vague or general ideas conveyable by vague or general words, you will have to actively prepare yourself for the demands of serious listening by adding to your vocabulary. Reading widely will naturally help. But you must be willing to do some self-conscious vocabulary building as well. While stopping to look up every word you don't know is an inefficient way to read, keeping a note pad handy to write down new words to look up later can help you immensely in future listening.

Break Any Long-Term Bad Listening Habits Since you have been listening all of your life, you have probably not only developed some proficiency at it, but some bad habits as well. These bad habits are probably rather deeply ingrained in your listening behaviors and will require long-term practice to undo. Two of the most damaging listening habits you should try to correct if you have them are: (1) mistaking the messenger for the message and (2) evaluating ideas early.

While it is difficult to separate your evaluation of what is said from the personality or mannerisms of the person who says it, effective listening depends on your ability to focus your attention on the ideas the speaker is trying to convey. The speaker may be unattractive, nervous, or have a questionable reputation and still have something meaningful to say on this particular occasion. Prejudging the speaker risks causing you to miss important information. Conversely, being an attractive, polished speaker with a good reputation does not guarantee that the ideas presented on this particular occasion will be valuable, true, or worthwhile. Each occasion for listening must be treated on its own merits. So, do not harm your listening ability by mistaking the messenger for the message.

Even if you do not prejudge a speaker, effective listening can be short-circuited by a tendency to prematurely judge the speaker's message. While no listener should accept messages uncritically, there is a proper time in the listening process for evaluating the message on its own merits. Listeners evaluate ideas early by reacting negatively or positively to such things as how an idea is worded or how the speaker presents his or her delivery. Most people have certain land mine ideas or key words to which they are supersensitive and to which they overreact. Poor listeners have many such land mines waiting for the innocent speaker to set them off. When this happens, the listening process comes to an abrupt halt. As you work to improve your long-term listening ability, you must try to make yourself aware of the conceptual land mines to which you react and practice disarming them so that they do not explode the listening process.

If you work on your long-term preparation for listening by reading widely, building your vocabulary, and breaking any bad listening habits, you should be ready for the short-term preparation for listening that starts immediately before the speaker begins. As already noted, listening is an active process that requires you to be as flexible as possible in order to reach out and catch the speaker's ideas. Short-term preparation includes, then, all the steps you take as you get ready to listen to a particular speaker on a specific occasion. As with any act, the impulse or preparatory phase of listening is the most important for determining the success or failure of the act. Although good preparation cannot guarantee your success, bad preparation almost invariably condemns you to failure. So the advice on improving your listening is richest right here at the beginning. Much of the rest of the listening act depends upon and develops the preparatory work you do in the impulse phase of listening. Preparing to listen effectively entails at least four substeps:

1. Sitting in an efficient listening posture

2. Clearing your mind of competing impulses

3. Selecting an appropriate purpose for listening

4. Suspending prespeech judgments about the speaker

We will look at each of these and how they contribute to the process of effective listening.

Sit in an Effective Listening Posture Because listening is an active process, it cannot be accomplished from just any posture you happen to adopt. You must be prepared to do what listeners do, just as an athlete must be posturally prepared for whatever the contingencies of the sport demand. Generally speaking, the most useful posture for listening to speeches is seated erectly with moderate muscle tone and slight forward lean, face pointed toward the speaker. A slouched, limp posture leaning away from the speaker leads to poor listening because you lack any focus on the speaker. Since the absence of muscle tone is a better preparation for sleep than for listening, the first thing you should do as you prepare to listen is sit upright in your chair and focus your attention on the speaker.

Clear Your Mind of Competing Impulses Before you begin listening your mind may be drifting to a thousand other topics. Perhaps you are visiting with someone seated near you, or perhaps you are worried about some problem. Every such thought represents an impulse that competes with your ability to listen well to the speaker. Although it is impossible to completely rid yourself of such competitors for your listening attention, you should try to temporarily suspend all other thoughts competing for your attention and clear room for the speaker's ideas. Listening effectively means taking in completely and considering adequately the speaker's ideas. Since you cannot do this if your mind is wandering, you must try to clear your mind of competing impulses as a part of your preparation for listening.

Select an Appropriate Purpose for Listening We listen for many different reasons, and because we have different purposes for listening, there are different types of listening. Our purpose for listening determines how we will approach any particular opportunity for listening—even influencing what we will be listening for. As you prepare to listen on any particular occasion, it is useful to select an appropriate purpose for listening.

In general, the purposes for listening roughly parallel the reasons for speaking. Accordingly, you might listen for pleasure or leisure, for understanding or information, and for reasons or arguments. Leisure listening is the least demanding and occurs when you attend a speech merely because you feel like it. Perhaps a famous person is on campus and you want to be able to say you saw and heard the person. Listening for understanding or information is considerably more demanding. Here you must determine the speaker's central theme, follow the pattern of main points, and take note of the supporting material. You are required to give much more attention since you must try to remember the significant information in the speech. Listening for reasons or arguments implies that you attend the speech not merely to understand but also to make a decision about some issue or controversy. In this case you must listen for how the speaker's ideas cohere to form a rational case in support of one side or the other.

Suspend Any Prespeech Judgments about the Speaker Even though good listeners develop a less judgmental attitude in general, the immediacy of the speech situation itself can touch off specific biases and judgments about the speaker that must be controlled if you are to adequately listen to the speech as presented. Before the speech begins try to inventory any personal judgments you may have made about the speaker that may adversely affect your listening ability so that you can consciously suspend them for the course of the speech.

Developing the Listening Act

If you have prepared well, you are primed and waiting for the speaker to begin. Now the listening impulse can move forward and begin to develop as well. As the speaker begins your listening act develops. The developmental phase of the listening act focuses heavily on the opening portions of the speech, when you must do the following six tasks:

1. Internalize the introduction
2. Determine the speaker's purpose for speaking
3. Determine the structure of main points
4. Discover the supporting details
5. Reach out to catch poorly projected ideas
6. Take notes selectively

Internalize the Introduction Since virtually all speakers begin with an introduction designed to prepare the audience for the theme and structure of the speech, you must take in this introduction and use it to guide your listening for the rest of the speech. If the speaker has carefully crafted the speech, the introduction should be a tremendous help as you develop your listening act. The introduction should establish your expectations and make it easier for you to listen as these expectations are subsequently fulfilled. Listen especially carefully to the speaker's introduction and internalize it for your subsequent use.

Determine the Speaker's Purpose for Speaking Once the speaker begins, you should listen for the speaker's overall purpose for speaking. In a well-prepared speech the speaker's purpose provides a key to understanding everything else that is said. The speaker's purpose should dictate both what is said and how it is organized. Thus, as soon as you have determined the speaker's purpose you can more easily anticipate what ideas the speaker is likely to project your way, and therefore you can listen more effectively.

Determine the Structure of Main Points Since a speaker must break ideas down into a set of smaller points so that the ideas can be projected as a sequence of words, listen for any preview of the speaker's intended pattern, structure, or arrangement of the speech materials. How will the ideas be divided into units? What are the speaker's main points?

This is a violin maker in New York City. What crafts do you enjoy? Contrast traditional handwork crafts with white-collar or high tech jobs. Would you rather be self-employed or work for a large organization?

Discover the Supporting Details Speeches develop ever finer webs of ideas as they progress. Speakers typically begin with a general position and a structure of main points and then present the developmental details that support their theme and each of their main points. Although you cannot retain in memory all the supporting materials and details a speaker employs, it is nevertheless important to try to discover the relationship of the supporting materials to the pattern of main points. Such details give meaning to the structural frame.

Reach Out to Catch Poorly Projected Ideas Good listening requires a sympathetic attempt on the part of the listener to meet the speaker halfway. Speakers do not always project their ideas as carefully as you would like. You will have to do the extra work of reaching out for those "poorly pitched" ideas and try to catch them in spite of the errant way they were encoded, empowered, or transmitted. Ideas may be poorly pitched for several reasons. Perhaps, for example, the speaker has an articulation problem that prevents him or her from clearly saying the sounds of the words. More typically, a speaker's vocabulary, sentence structure, organization, or delivery mannerisms will make the speech difficult to catch. Although even the best listener cannot fully compensate for an errant speech, being willing to reach out for a speaker's ideas, rather than demanding that the speaker make a direct hit, is the best policy for effective listening.

Take Notes Selectively Speeches worth listening to are often worth taking written notes about. That is, you should supplement your oral memory with written notes that allow you to reconstruct what you want to take away from the speech. But not just any notes will do. If your goal is to capture the essence of the speech, a more systematic approach to note taking should be used. Typically, there are three types of information you will want to place in your notes for later reference, and they are exactly the three things you have been listening for in the developmental phase of the listening process. Whenever you take written notes, you should write down a clear statement of the speaker's main theme—for not only is this the key to understanding the speech as you hear it, but also to reconstructing the speech as you try to recollect it from memory. Second, carefully write out the speaker's main points. If they are truly main points, the speaker will probably repeat them often enough that you can take them down in a reasonably precise fashion. Finally, jot down brief notes about supporting details. Since it is virtually impossible to write as rapidly as a speaker speaks, don't try to write in complete sentences; instead use critical words and phrases.

Culminating the Listening Act

The culmination of the listening act is an understanding of the speaker's ideas. Listening during this phase is at its most intense. In the culmination phase of listening you have now heard most of the speech and are getting ready to consider the merits of what you have heard. Accordingly, the culmination phase of listening involves two components: (1) summarizing the speaker's message and (2) re-engaging your critical faculties.

Summarize the Speaker's Message Because you have now heard the majority of the speech, you should be prepared to summarize in your own words what you have heard. Up to this point in the listening process you have been taking the speaker's own words and using them as a basis for understanding the ideas being presented. Now you must put those ideas into your own words to test how well you can relate them to ideas you already have and to test how effectively you have made the speaker's ideas (at least for the sake of argument) your own. For it is unfair to move to the final phase of the listening process—evaluation of what you have heard—until you have accurately understood what the speaker intended to say. The best way to test your overall understanding of the speaker's message is to try to reformulate it into one or more summary statements, which you can then check against the details of the speech, such as those you have jotted down in your notes.

Re-engage Your Critical Faculties The early phases of effective listening require you to temporarily suspend your critical judgment so that you can give both the speaker and the speech a fair chance to be heard. Premature judgments about the speaker's character, delivery, ideas, or speech craftsmanship interfere with your ability to fully consider what the speaker is trying to say. But, effective listeners do not merely drink in a speaker's ideas, accepting them with little or no further thought. Listening is an active mental process, one of whose major components is critical judgment. Thus, as the speaker concludes a speech (or, in a longer speech, a major subportion of the speech), you must re-engage the critical faculties you previously suspended and begin considering the merits of what you have heard. As these critical faculties are re-engaged and you begin to raise probative questions, you are moving toward the final phase of the listening process: evaluating the speech.

Concluding the Listening Act

As you now realize, listening is more than hearing and taking in the speaker's words: It is a mental act of considering *what* you have heard. The concluding phase of serious critical listening occurs after the flow of the speaker's words has ended. Your role now becomes that of an evaluator of the ideas that you have been taking in and processing. Although a speaker's purpose, combined with your own purpose for listening, determines the type of evaluative issues that are most appropriate to raise on a particular occasion, the following questions will help you launch your initial evaluation.

1. Was the speech clearly focused in presenting its ideas?

2. Did the main points really support the major theme or purpose?

3. Was the supporting material appropriate to the points being made?

4. Was the speech adequately adapted to the actual audience?

5. Did the manner of delivery contribute to the overall effectiveness of the speech?

6. Is the speaker right about the position being taken?

7. What action, if any, should be taken in light of the speech?

We will now explore each of these questions just a little bit further.

Was the speech clearly focused in presenting its ideas? Every adequate speech has a central theme to develop and an overall purpose to accomplish.

The theme and purpose guide its growth and development. Accordingly, one of the first evaluative questions to raise concerns how clearly that purpose came through and how well it served to guide the speaker's choices throughout the construction of the speech. Did the speaker stay on the topic? Or did the speaker drift away from the theme, perhaps with material that seemed only marginally related to the speech's central purpose?

Did the main points really support the major theme or purpose? One common way for a speech to lose focus is for the speaker's main points to be off target in their relation to the speaker's announced theme. Although this may happen in informative speeches, it is considerably more likely in persuasive speeches. Persuasive speeches have a definite proposition to defend, but speakers do not always show precisely how the reasons given to support the claim directly relate to the proposition being defended. As a listener, it is vital that you determine whether or not the speaker's reasoning actually supported the claim being made.

Was the supporting material appropriate to the points being made? Since the framework of reasons used to structure a speech is merely that—a skeleton of main ideas that are intended to subdivide an overall main theme— speakers must flesh out that skeleton with a variety of supporting materials in order to develop it and fully bring it to life. But those materials must be appropriate to the specific points being made, not just to some general point of view being developed. So you should evaluate just how directly the detailed material offered to support the speaker's framework of ideas actually fits the points being made.

Was the speech adequately adapted to the actual audience? Speeches are presented to specific audiences on definite occasions. A speaker who prepares a speech without thinking about the nature of the specific audience to whom it will be presented, or who fails to adapt the speech to any known characteristics of the audience, invites trouble and perhaps failure. You, as a listener, can assess how effectively the speaker targeted the speech to the audience, of which you are perhaps a representative member. For example, you might notice whether or not there are examples the speaker could have employed but failed to. Or, perhaps there were characteristics of the audience the speaker failed to take into account that limited the speech's overall appeal.

Did the manner of delivery contribute to the overall effectiveness of the speech? Delivery can range from the casually informal to the stiffly formal, and from the skillfully prepared to the carelessly inept. It can range from quietly controlled to explosively bombastic, and from self-consciously nervous to spontaneously abandoned. Although there is not a single best way to deliver a speech on all occasions, there are degrees of appropriateness that apply to particular occasions. From a listener's point of view, the evaluative issue is whether or not the speaker's manner of delivery was the best choice that could have been selected given the nature of the speech's subject matter, the occasion, and the audience before whom the speech was being presented.

Is the speaker right about the position being taken? With this question we turn from the more descriptive aspects of the critical-evaluative process toward the more overtly judgmental. Now you must ask whether what you have heard is worth believing and remembering or should be dismissed as untrue or valueless. Here the critical faculties are fully at work because you must relate what you have been hearing to everything else you know and believe, everything that might be relevant to assessing the truth or rightness of what has been said. This question invites a no-holds-barred critique of the worth of the ideas that have been presented.

What action, if any, should be taken in light of the speech? Most speeches, even informative ones, invite or imply that the listener take some action. The action may be anything from simply remembering what was said to joining a political movement to which you commit yourself. Accordingly, the final evaluative act of the listening process is to determine what action you will take based on the speech. This is your final judgment concerning the value of the speech and your most important one as well.

Conclusion

Speeches require listeners if they are to accomplish their purposes. But listening is an active mental process that involves far more than merely hearing the speech in a mechanical or passive manner. Good listening begins long before the speaker starts to speak. It begins with practice and long-term preparation, and it progresses through short-term preparation as you prepare to attend a specific speech on a particular occasion. Listening develops as the speaker begins and the listener does the work of trying to understand the speaker's ideas on the speaker's own terms. The listening act culminates as you fully understand the speaker's message and re-engage your critical abilities—now understanding the speech on your own terms. Listening comes to an end only after the speech has concluded, as you critically evaluate the characteristics of the speech and the quality of the ideas that have been presented. Listening actively is hard work, but there is no other way to learn from the speech of others than by careful, effective listening.

Questions for Review

1. In what ways is listening the reciprocal of speaking? Name at least three.

2. What are the phases of the listening act? What are the subprocesses comprising each of these phases? Why are the phases treated in the order they are?

3. Where does hearing fit into the listening act? Why are *hearing* and *listening* not synonymous terms?

Questions for Discussion

1. As an active listener, what skills are involved in accurately decoding a speaker's message? Use the model of communication presented in Chapter 2 to help you generate some possibilities.

2. When you are listening to a speaker, what typical expectations (see Chapter 4) are most beneficial to the listening process? Are there any listener expectations that can hinder your ability to listen effectively? If so, how might you lessen the potentially harmful effects of such expectations?

Things to Try

1. List any bad listening habits you may have developed. Devise a strategy for overcoming each of them.

2. As you listen to the speeches in your class, try outlining the speaker's central theme, pattern of main points, and major supporting material.

3. Based on recent experience with your classmates, list any judgments you may have already made about three of your classmates that might harm your ability to listen to them effectively. Determine what you can do to help yourself suspend those judgments as you prepare to listen to their speeches.

4. Prepare a written critique of a speech you have recently listened to. Evaluate both the quality of the speech's content and the effectiveness of the speaker's delivery.

Bibliography

Adler, Mortimer J. *How to Speak, How to Listen*. New York: Macmillan, 1983.

Barbara, Dominick A. *The Art of Listening*. Springfield, IL: Charles C. Thomas, 1958.

Colburn, C. William, and Sanford B. Weinberg. *An Orientation to Listening and Audience Analysis*. Chicago: SRA, 1976.

Floyd, James J. *Listening: A Practical Approach*. Glenview, IL: Scott, Foresman, 1985.

Glatthorn, Allan A., and Herbert R. Adams. *Listening Your Way to Management Success*. Glenview, IL: Scott, Foresman, 1983.

Hunt, Gary T., and Louis P. Cusella. "A Field Study of Listening Needs in Organizations," *Communication Education* 32 (1983), 393–401.

Steil, Lyman K., Larry L. Barker, and Kittie W. Watson. *Effective Listening: Key to Your Success*. Reading, MA: Addison-Wesley, 1983.

Wolff, Florence I., Nadine C. Marsnik, William C. Tracey, and Ralph G. Nichols. *Perceptive Listening*. New York: Holt, Rinehart & Winston, 1983.

Wolvin, Andrew D., and Carolyn Gwynn Coakley. *Listening Instruction*. Urbana, IL: ERIC Clearinghouse, 1979.

Principles of General and Informative Speaking

Topic Selection and Specific Purposes: Formulating the Impulse to Speak

*P*ublic speaking is an extended act that, like all other speech acts, begins with an impulse to speak. The impulse to speak in public comes from many sources. Sometimes you are asked to speak by some club or organization; sometimes your job or professional responsibilities require you to give a speech; and sometimes circumstances in your local community seem to demand an oral response. Whatever circumstances motivate them, your speeches always begin with some sort of impulse to speak.

Speech preparation extends from your first impulse to speak to the final consummation of that impulse—your actual presentation before your intended audience. Since the act of speaking in public is a large one, requiring a substantial commitment of time and energy, it must be sustained by a rather large and complex initial impulse. Speech preparation is made up of numerous component processes. Among the earliest phases of the speech preparation process are selecting, evaluating, and refining your topic. These acts are immediately followed by decisions concerning your general and specific purpose. During these early phases of the speech preparation process you will select a subject to talk about and prepare a carefully worded specific purpose statement to guide your subsequent preparation. This chapter considers the various components comprising the typical impulse to speak in public: it is divided into two portions: (1) an overview of topic selection, evaluation, and refinement, and (2) an overview of how you prepare a specific purpose statement to guide your subsequent speech preparation.

*T*opic Selection

Although the impulse to speak always actually comes from within you yourself, it sometimes *seems* to come from the outside (as when you are assigned to prepare a speech for a class, or a group invites you to speak for its monthly meeting, or your employer says that you are to give this week's sales report). At other times, the impulse may seem to be generated internally ("I'm going to march right down to that council meeting tonight and give them a piece of my mind!"). When the impulse seems to spontaneously arise from within yourself—as is most often the case outside the classroom—then topic selection and specific purpose statements present no particular problem. Both your topic and your purpose arise simultaneously with the very impulse to speak. Although you still may have to face problems of narrowing your topic and focusing your specific purpose (after all, the City Council will not give you unlimited time to air your views), this situation does not require you to "come up with" a topic merely because you have to give a speech. You experience an impulse to speak, and with that impulse also comes a topic and a purpose for speaking. The impulse, topic, and purpose almost seem to be one and the same.

But, since the first steps in speech preparation are essentially the same—whether the impulse seems to come from the outside or seems to be internally generated—we will assume the more difficult situation in the discussion that follows: the one in which you are assigned a speech and invited to pick a topic. This occurs both in a speech class and in some common situations calling for a speaker, such as a ceremonial occasion or an organization's monthly social or business meeting. Therefore, Chapter 6 begins with the problem of how to find, evaluate, and refine a topic for your speech.

Selecting Your Topic

Most of us have little trouble finding topics to talk about with our friends. We simply strike up a conversation and begin talking. Topics come to us spontaneously and unbidden. Somehow the situation changes when someone—like a teacher—pronounces the sentence: "Everyone select a topic for your first speech and bring it to our next class session." The mind freezes over, the fingers lock up, and all the thoughts that flowed between our friends and ourselves 10 minutes before class suddenly either evaporate or seem inferior and inadequate. Why? The reason seems to be that, in almost stimulus-response fashion, the sentence "pick a topic" is followed by one of three responses: (1) "I don't *know* anything about anything." (2) Nobody will be interested in anything *I* have to say." Or (3) "There aren't any good topics." "Pick a topic" has just about the opposite effect upon you as does the typical speaking situation affecting spontaneous conversations. "Pick a topic" seems to inhibit rather than induce new conversational options.

Well, the fact is, you know more than you think, you are more interesting than you ever imagined, and there are mountains of good topics from which you can choose. Students have been finding and mining such topics for years—as you were doing just before you came to class! The real difficulty in picking a topic for a classrooom speech is to **select,** from among the many good topics available to you, one that has the best chance of making a good speech—for you. We'll talk about evaluating your possible topics in a moment. But now let's see just how many topics are available to you.

The first step in topic selection is to inventory your own interests. This is a form of brainstorming, a technique in which you try to generate as many ideas as you can, in order to give yourself the opportunity to select from among several options the one that is best for you. So, where do good topics come from? From many places. For example, from your college major:

▲ Computer Science majors might talk about:

Becoming Friends with Your "User Friendly" Computer

Computer Speak: How Your Car Knows What to Say to You

From Laser Beam to Itemized Grocery List: The Computerized Checkout Counter

Warfare and Double Agentry in the Modern Computer Industry

▲ Business Administration majors might talk about:

Starting Your Own Business after Graduation

The Laffer Curve or the Last Laugh? The Theory behind Your Taxes

How the Cost-Benefit Ratio Helps Determine the Products You Can Buy

The Role of Labor Unions in Inflation and Unemployment Trends

▲ Horticulture majors might talk about:

Poinsettia Production for a Profit

Killing Your Plants by Over- and Underwatering

Propagating New Plants from Old Ones

Making a Terrarium for a Living Room Display

▲ Animal Science majors might talk about:

Artificial Insemination of Beef Cattle—More Meat for Your Money

The Special Characteristics of Horses' Eyes

The Free Market System in Farming and Ranching

Cardboard Boxes as Cattle Feed

▲ Education majors might talk about:

Child Abuse

How to Recognize the Abused Child

How to Report Child Abuse Cases

How to Prevent Child Abuse

Psychological Portraits of Abusive Parents

Accountability in Education—Strengths and Weaknesses

New Approaches to Grading—Performance Objectives

The Effects of Television Advertising on Children

▲ Marketing majors might talk about:

The Nature of Industrial Distribution

The Role of the Middleman in American Business

▲ Science majors of various types—from biochemistry to meteorology and zoology—might talk about:

Cyclic AMP Research in Your Daily Life

Shifting Patterns of Weather and a Possible New Ice Age

How Tornadoes and Hurricanes Form

Strange Facts about Salt

The Role of Protein and Cholesterol in Your Diet

The Physics of Soap Bubbles

Genetic Engineering: The Process of Cloning

▲ Psychology, sociology, and anthropology majors might talk about:

"To Sleep, Perchance to Dream": Recent Advances in Sleep and Dream Research

Slips of the Tongue—What Do They Reveal about Your Inner Nature?

Color Choices and Your Personality

What Does Your Gait Tell a Potential Mugger about You?

▲ Humanities majors might talk about:

Understanding the Great Chain of Being in the Existential Era

The Unique Character of American Humorous Fiction

Is Poetry Still Relevant in the Computer Age?

Is a Company's Business Philosophy a Philosophy of Business?

But good topics do not come exclusively from your academic major; they may also come from jobs you have had. For example:

▲ A grocery store checker might talk about the Universal Product Code.

▲ A carpenter might explain the advantages of earth-sheltered housing, or how to evaluate the qualities of a house.

▲ A bar worker might discuss what it's like to work at a popular campus pub, or how to get more and better drinks simply by the way you order.

▲ A musician might discuss how disco affected the fate of the live musician.

▲ A mechanic might talk about the costs or advantages of changing to the metric system.

Good topics may also come from your hobbies or interests. The following are just a few of the many topics about which students have given speeches that came from their hobbies and interests:

Methods of Bird Hunting

Hunting for Sand Dollars along the Gulf Coast

The Bermuda Triangle/Pyramid Power/Astrology

Bathing Habits Old and New around the World

Types of Human Superstition

Bottle Collecting for Fun and Profit

Birth Order and Your Personality

Art Exhibits on Campus

How to Travel Better by Air

Body Building/Yoga/Slimnastics/Jazzercise

Finally, an excellent source of speech topics is your personal experiences. Try to imagine the personal experiences that provided the impulse for speeches with these titles:

Chainsaw Safety

College Rodeo—You Too Can Join the Fun

Anorexia Nervosa/Diabetes/"Iron Deficiency Anemia"

Wart Removal by Mental Suggestion

Taming the Alaskan Wilderness

The Drugstore Cowboy

Operating a Legal Fireworks Store

Legislative Aides—Our Real Legislators

How to Appeal a Traffic Ticket

If inventorying topics from your major, jobs, hobbies, interests, and personal experiences still does not produce a satisfactory topic, you may want to visit with your instructor to see if his or her experience with such matters can't help spark your brainstorming processes. Assuming that you now have some good possibilities for speech topics, you next need to evaluate the topics you are considering.

Evaluating Your Topic

You have now generated several potentially good topics for your speech, and the time has come to evaluate them to see which is the best one for your speech. The questions to be answered now shift from what are the available topics to what is the best topic for you on this occasion.

A good topic must fulfill several requirements. Among these are the following:

1. You must be interested in the topic yourself. If you are not truly interested in the topic, how can you expect your audience to become interested in it?

2. You must know something about the topic already, or be willing to spend the time to find out about it. If you don't know the topic already and aren't willing to find out much about it, how can you hope to inform or persuade your audience?

3. You must be able to induce others to become interested in your topic on this particular occasion.

4. You must be able to fit the topic to the total situation in which the speech will actually be given.

Thus, in evaluating your topic there are at least four basic considerations: your own interests, your audience's present or potential interests, your audience's prior knowledge, and the occasion or situation within which the speech will be delivered. These concerns can be formulated as four questions. You should be able to answer each of these positively if the topic is to be a good one on a particular occasion.

Do I know enough about the topic to make a speech on it? Although you need not be an expert on your topic when you begin your speech preparation, your topic should be one upon which you either have some prior knowledge or are willing to spend considerable time researching. Your audience expects to learn something new from you, and they expect you to know what you are talking about. Thus, it is important that there be enough material available for you to do a thorough presentation of your subject and that you be willing to put forth the effort to seek out those materials. You might want to talk about subjects with which you are already quite familiar because that makes managing yourself and your ideas easier when you are speaking in public for the first time. Besides, too much research immediately before your speech condemns you to dependency upon extensive notes or memorizing. Developing a good speech involves allowing enough time to internalize your materials, to make them yours.

Do I care that others know about the topic? No matter how much research you may have done in preparing it, a speech is a personal statement you yourself make about some subject. It is *you* who put the speech together. It is *you* who selected the developmental materials. And, most importantly, it is *you* who are up there saying it. Thus, selecting a subject for a speech is really a question of whether or not you care enough to talk about it. Because a speech is really a personal statement about your topic, the problem of topic selection is one of "What do I really *want* to talk about?"

Can I limit the topic adequately? Sometimes the problem with a topic is not that you have too little material available to you, or too little interest in the subject, but that you have too much. If this is the case, you must select a more narrow aspect of the topic rather than trying to cover the whole subject area in a single speech. If you have enough material for two speeches, then divide it into two. But don't try to cram everything you know into a single speech, "just to be on the safe side."

Can I interest my audience in the topic? This is perhaps the toughest question of all. It requires that you project yourself into your audience's mind and decide whether or not what you have to say will seem interesting and worthwhile to your audience. You may have been involved with your hobby for years and have thereby gained such expertise that finding materials to talk about is no problem. Then your problem is to find a point of entry that does not require that your audience know a great deal about your topic before they can understand the point of your speech. For example, you may be fascinated with the physics of flight and may know numerous formulas that explain why airplanes can fly. But can you translate your specialized knowledge into a form that makes the information accessible and interesting to your audience? Audience analysis (treated in Chapter 7) should help you determine your audience's level of background preparation and interest related to your chosen topic.

To determine whether you can interest your audience in your topic you can also ask: Is the topic worth my audience's time? Does my audience have a prior reason to be interested in this topic? Is the topic appropriate for the occasion? Does the age, sex, and social background of my audience influence how likely they are to be interested? Again, using your audience analysis will help you determine the answers to these questions.

If the answer to each of these questions is yes, then you are ready to go on to the task of formulating your general and specific purpose. If no, then you must next work on refining your topic.

Refining and Narrowing Your Topic

Often, you will like a particular topic very much but find that you cannot answer with an unequivocal yes to all the questions involved in evaluating the topic. If this is the case you may want to refine your topic. Most commonly, you will find that you have to narrow your topic in order to bring it within the time limits for a particular speech—especially if the time limit is the five to eight minutes usually allowed in a speech class. You know too much, not too little; you care too much about the subject, rather than caring too little. Under these circumstances, you must find a way to limit your subject matter to the time available, and that demands that you refine your topic by narrowing it.

The process of narrowing a topic usually involves taking a more specific aspect of your topic than your first wording of it suggested. For instance, examples A through E are all good topics, but they are worded in a general way that neither focuses your preparation nor helps you keep the topic to a manageable length.

A. New Advertising Techniques

B. Recent Advances in Animal Reproduction

    C. Aspects of Energy Conservation

    D. Being a Better Consumer

    E. Some Aspects of Beauty Care

A too general topic forces you to become vague or rushed in your supporting materials in order to remain within the time limits. In contrast, A_1 through E_1 narrows each of the same topics. At the same time, the revised topics are worded so as to make them more specific. In this way they also give your speech preparation more guidance.

A_1. *New Advertising Techniques* might become:

    Subliminal Seduction in Recent News Magazine Ads

B_1. *Recent Advances in Animal Reproduction* might become:

    Ova Transfer in Beef Cattle

C_1. *Aspects of Energy Conservation* might become:

    Motor Sports and Energy Consumption

D_1. *Being a Better Consumer* might become:

    How to Get Your Money's Worth in Shopping for a Used Car

E_1. *Some Aspects of Beauty Care* might become:

    The Chemical Effects of Herb-Scented Shampoos on Your Hair

*F*ormulating Your General and Specific Purposes

Selecting a topic gets your speech preparation started. But as a guide to subsequent preparation, a topic alone is not very complete. Like a sculptor's block of marble, the topic must be given more specific form. Accordingly, the next step in speech preparation is to refine your topic by shaping it with a precise specific purpose statement. The specific purpose guides the subsequent growth of the speech, and helps you make more efficient choices concerning which research materials will be most helpful to you and which can be safely ignored for this speech. The specific purpose statement is designed to guide your subsequent preparation and help you narrow the focus of your speech. The importance of formulating the impulse to the speech in a carefully worded specific purpose statement is captured in the maxim: "As the twig is bent, so grows the tree." Once you have formed the speech's driving impulse in a specific purpose statement, you will be in a better position to accomplish the subsequent phases of speech preparation.

This is a museum of twentieth-century art. What kinds of art do you enjoy? Do you know any artists? Should the government be involved in supporting music, theater, dance, painting, and other arts?

Types of General Purposes

Normally your first attempt at topic selection will be too broad, and you will have to narrow your topic in some way. One of the best ways of doing this is to consider what your general and specific purposes are *for this speech*. That is, what are you trying to accomplish in this speech with this particular audience? For, if communication is the *intentional* transmission of ideas, then you must have some purpose for engaging in this particular instance of communication. You must have some idea you intend to communicate. Getting up in front of an audience is not usually an accidental happening.

The Purposes of Public Speaking Traditionally, teachers of public speaking have recognized three major purposes for speaking in public: to **inform,** to **persuade,** and to **entertain.** The first two purposes arise from the fact that speech may be used to formulate (give verbal form to) one's unique ideas and to express those word-formulated ideas to others. That is, the first two purposes occur because speech may be used to communicate your individual thoughts. The third purpose arises from the fact that during the process of speaking, the spoken word serves to bind the community together and helps us remember what we have in common. Let's look at each of these three purposes more closely.

We are constantly using speech to formulate new ideas into words for the purpose of sharing those ideas with others. The **informative** purpose of speech is served when you intend to tell your listeners something they do not already know (for example, how to macrame or what the theory of relativity really says). From the audience's point of view your goal is to help them *understand* your ideas. The main communicative tool for informative speaking is the declarative sentence, which expresses the informational propositions you wish to transmit. These propositions are chained together to present your ideas for another's understanding.

Even where our experiences overlap, we may not all formulate exactly the same ideas about them. In fact, we commonly formulate opposing ideas based on what seem like quite similar experiences. The **persuasive** purpose is served when you speak to change another person's ideas. In some cases, you merely intend to persuade the listeners to act upon ideas they already have; in other cases, you intend to change the ideas that serve as the basis for the listener's present actions (sometimes called "the speech to actuate"). In any case, the persuasive purpose is distinguished by the fact that you intend to change the other person's ideas in some specific way. You may accomplish this change simply by the addition of new information to the listener's store of ideas, but persuasion is more often accomplished by changing the audience's interpretation—that is, their understanding, their meaning—of the facts and ideas they already have. The main communicative tool for persuasion is **argumentation**—the public presentation of your serial reasoning about the conclusions you have arrived at. Argumentation usually occurs when the truth of your communicative assertions is in doubt. We will discuss it in detail in Chapter 16.

But what of the speech to **entertain**? How does it relate to ideas? The phrase "speech to entertain" is really a catchall term for a wide variety of speaking situations in which the central purpose is neither real informing nor persuading: one speaker introducing another, giving and receiving awards, and especially after-dinner speeches. Rather than adding new ideas to our previous stock, or changing ideas we already have, the speech to entertain often *uses* ideas to promote community unity—by promoting a uniquely human form of psychological contact: symbolic contact. Such contact is always created through speech—as you project your personality outward to your audience through your speech. Thus, even though ideas are formulated and expressed in the speech to entertain, the contact function of speech serves as the central motivating impulse for this type of speaking. The speech to entertain is not (in its idealized, pure form) focused upon communication at all; it merely uses communication in order to serve the contact function of speech, by bringing individuals into mental contact with one another in an artistic fashion. Since speeches to entertain are used infrequently by most people, they will not be treated further in this text.

Formulating Your Specific Purpose

Having decided whether your general purpose is to inform or persuade, you should next formulate as detailed a specific purpose statement as you can. A specific purpose statement is a single, declarative sentence that presents the essence of what you intend to accomplish in your speech. The sentence is usually modified so as to begin with an infinitive phrase, such as the following:

Specific Purpose: To explain the five basic steps in running a short program in FORTRAN computer language

Specific Purpose: To persuade the class that legislative aides should be considered our real legislators because of their actual legislative actions and the constituency requirements of their job

Using the infinitive phrase construction (*to* plus a verb) allows you to formulate both your general purpose ("to persuade," "to inform") and your specific purpose within a single overall purpose statement and also tells what kind of an act you intend to perform. Other wordings of your speech's purpose fail to emphasize the fact that you are going to *act* to accomplish a goal during your speech. For example, the statement below does not formulate the speaker's *purpose* for preparing the speech; it merely declares a particular fact.

Specific Purpose: There are four major criteria to use when shopping for jogging shoes.

If you revise it to read like the specific purpose below, you give verbal form to your purpose.

Specific Purpose: To explain the four major criteria audience members should use when they are shopping for jogging shoes

The second statement contains not only the same information, but also emphasizes your role as a speaker in the act of explaining. In addition, it emphasizes your audience's role as an active respondent to the speech. The second statement tells what you hope the audience will take away from the speech.

Why should you try to formulate a precise specific purpose statement early in your speech preparation? Because this statement can serve as your guiding impulse as you continue to grow and develop your speech. Putting your ideas into words gives form to those ideas; the phrasing of your purpose gives form to the goal you are trying to accomplish. A clear statement of your specific purpose can serve as a guide to the rest of your preparation for any particular speech by formulating the ideational impulse of the speech. It does this by establishing the limits and directions of the speech's possible avenues of growth.

Formulating a precise specific purpose statement begins to give both direction and shape to your speech preparation. You are beginning to decide which of your options you will develop and which you will let drop for this particular speech. Virtually any topic you pick for your speech has the potential for growing in many different and mutually exclusive directions. Since you cannot possibly cover all of these directions in a single speech, you must try to decide as early as you reasonably can which options you will actually exercise and which you will ignore. Your subsequent speech preparation will be a continuous process of deciding among ever narrowing options, until you reach the point where the speech has actually been delivered and all the options have therefore been decided; but what you actually say during your speech will be determined in large degree by the lines of growth you have previously formulated in your specific purpose statement.

We will now look at an example of how careful formulation of your specific purpose into a single, declarative sentence can help you narrow and focus your topic, as well as guide your subsequent speech preparation. Let's say you are a dairy science major, and last semester you took an interesting class about dairy products. So you decide to do your speech on the topic of milk. At this point, the options for your speech's potential growth directions seem almost limitless. So your first step in the process of narrowing your topic might be deciding that your general purpose will be *to inform your classmates about the common dairy product, milk*. But you took an entire course on the subject, and now you have only 5 to 10 minutes to present your speech. The topic is too broad, even when stated in the form of a general purpose statement: "To inform the class about milk." You still have too many options; such a statement does not yet give you much guidance. Since you need more focus, you need to decide upon your specific purpose for this particular speech.

How do you go about deciding upon your specific purpose for a particular speech? Just as you did when you selected your topic in the first place, you will probably need to brainstorm by inventorying the possibilities. That is, within the large general topic of milk, what *might* you talk about? Without criticizing the possibilities as you generate them, quickly jot down as many things as you can about milk:

1. Milk pricing policies

2. How to milk a cow

3. Increasing milk production yields

4. Preparing milk for consumer sales

5. The protein structure of milk

6. Milk's nutrient characteristics

7. Products made from milk: cheese, butter, ice cream, and so on

Having compiled this list, you now know what you yourself are interested in relative to the subject of milk. Next you should probably inventory what you know about your audience's interests based on any audience analysis you may already have done. Is there anything on your list that you think you could make especially interesting or valuable to them? Every topic on your list is potentially a good one if you find the appropriate angle of interest for your audience.

Suppose you decide that milk products would be interesting to both you and your audience. By making this one decision, you have automatically decided numerous other options as well. There are now countless subtopics you do not have to research because they are unrelated to this particular speech. You are well on your way to developing a manageable specific purpose. But even having made this decision, you still have too many options for you to be able to cover them all in a single speech. Will you talk about whole milk, butter, cheese, or ice cream? Will you give a speech about the wide variety of products made from milk, explaining the types of milk products available? Then your specific purpose might look something like this:

Specific Purpose: To describe four of the major types of food products processed from raw milk

If you decided to focus more narrowly on one particular product, your purpose might read:

Specific Purpose: To explain the four major steps in producing chocolate ice cream

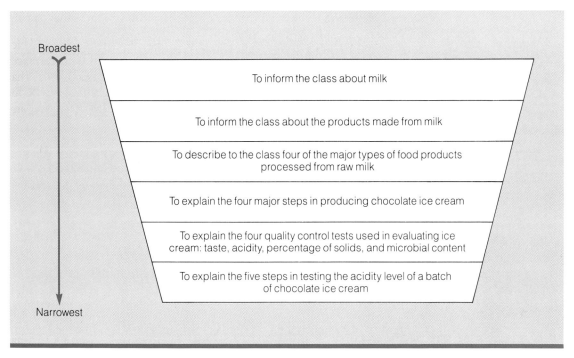

Figure 6-1   Narrowing Down a Specific Purpose to a Manageable Size

Or, if your interests are in one particular aspect of the production of a single product, you might have as your specific purpose:

Specific Purpose: To explain the four quality control tests used in evaluating ice cream: taste, acidity, percentage of solids, and microbial content

This last specific purpose is perhaps the best formulated because it clearly identifies the main points of the speech—as well as the general purpose of the speech, the act to be performed by the speaker (inform, persuade, or entertain), and the specific purpose to be accomplished with the audience. Figure 6-1 illustrates the process of narrowing the specific purpose.

It is, of course, possible that you might find yourself unable to formulate a highly detailed specific purpose early in your speech preparation. If you are stalled and cannot narrow your topic at first, and therefore cannot yet formulate your specific purpose, then go ahead and begin your research. Perhaps your investigations will help you focus on your specific topic. Even so, the sooner you can narrow your topic and formulate it into its final form the better. Although it doesn't always pay to force the issue too quickly, and you may wish to keep your options open a little longer, life is characterized by the inexorable and inevitable process of having to choose your actual course from among a sea of options. Similarly, your speech cannot ultimately preserve *all* of your options. Eventually you must decide the course you will take, and the earlier the better.

Evaluating and Refining Your Specific Purpose

Having now formulated one or more specific purpose statements, you are ready to evaluate them. Some of the criteria used for evaluating your specific purpose statement have already been mentioned. To summarize, the specific purpose statement should:

1. Be a single, declarative sentence

2. Be modified so as to use the infinitive form

3. Emphasize the act you are to perform (whether to inform, persuade, or entertain), the topic of speech, and, if possible, the specific pattern of main points the speech will have

4. Ensure that the general purpose is clearly indicated and that the general purpose corresponds with the specific purpose as stated

These criteria can be checked in a rather mechanical fashion. But there are some additional criteria you may wish to apply that are more organic in their emphasis. These may be worded as a set of questions, all of which derive from the major question:

Does the specific purpose statement serve as an adequate impulse for the rest of the speech and its preparation?

Some specific questions you may want to ask include the following:

1. Does the specific purpose have organic potential—that is, fertility? Does it invite growth and development with ample examples, anecdotes, statistics, and visual aids? Or does it fail to motivate you to think in terms of such development?

2. Does the specific purpose statement give direction to subsequent speech preparation? Or does it allow you to wander aimlessly in your search for things to say?

3. Does the specific purpose statement give form to the actual speech by suggesting a particular structure? Or does it leave you with no guidance concerning the possible structure of your speech?

Once you have evaluated your specific purpose against these criteria, you are in a position to refine its final formulation. Having reformulated it so that it satisfactorily fulfills its intended purposes, you are ready to advance to the next stage of speech preparation: analyzing the audience for whom the speech is intended to see what special modifications must be made as you continue developing your speech from this initial impulse phase of your speech preparation.

*C*onclusion

In this chapter you have learned how to select a topic for your speeches, how to evaluate the available topics, and how to refine your own understanding of the nature of the topic you have chosen. You have also learned how to formulate a clear specific purpose statement that can serve as a guide for the rest of your speech preparation. Finally, you have learned how to evaluate and refine your specific purpose statements so that they fulfill their purpose as the generating impulse of your speech. Once you have a clear idea concerning what you want your speech to accomplish, you are then ready to gather together the materials you will need in order to "grow" a good speech. Chapter 7 will explain the audience factors you must consider as you gather the developmental materials you will want to use in developing your speeches.

Questions for Review

1. Why is it important to select a topic as early as possible for your speech? What reasons does the organic metaphor suggest?

2. What role does the specific purpose statement play in your speech preparation? Is formulating a clear specific purpose statement really necessary in guiding your speech preparation, or is it just a useful step if you happen to have the time? Why?

3. What criteria are most useful in evaluating a speech topic for a specific occasion and audience?

Questions for Discussion

1. In a highly regarded essay on "The Rhetorical Situation," Lloyd Bitzer suggests that the impulse for speeches come essentially from conditions in the speaker's environment rather than from within the speaker, as pre-

sented in this chapter. Are these two positions in complete opposition to one another? If so, which do you agree with? If there is truth to both positions, how may the apparent contradiction be resolved so that we can more fully understand the impulse to speak?

2. Characterize the major differences between persuasive and informative speaking as you presently understand these two speech purposes. Then consider the following: According to some authors (Richard Weaver, Richard Cherwitz, and James Hikens), even quite straightforward informative speeches have an inherently persuasive character to them. On what basis do you think such a claim might be made? If you cannot think of any supporting reasons, look at Weaver's book, *Language is Sermonic.*

Things to Try

1. To give you practice in evaluating and refining specific purposes, this exercise provides samples of specific purposes that are all in need of refining for various reasons. Decide which criterion or criteria fail to be met in each case and rewrite the purpose statement to improve it.

   a. To describe the physical characteristics of the sun and the fate that awaits it

   b. To give reasons why a military career isn't as bad as people tend to believe

   c. To encourage increased agricultural prosperity through irrigation

   d. To explain some aggressive driving techniques that are useful in specific situations

   e. To explain why women should be drafted

   f. To explain the process of fish filleting, the materials necessary to fillet a fish, and the advantages of filleting over conventional fish cleaning

   g. To give four major ideas to be used when shopping for jogging shoes

   h. To explain how running can make you a healthier and happier person only if you prepare properly

   i. To describe the problem of overpopulation in white-tailed deer herds, and to persuade the audience of the purpose of deer management

   j. To explain the controversy of the grading system, leading the audience away from its usage to a more effective system

2. You have been asked to speak to a fraternity meeting about some aspect of your major. The choice is yours. Develop five possible topics and specific purposes related to your academic major that might be effective with such an audience.

Bibliography

Bitzer, Lloyd F. "The Rhetorical Situation," *Philosophy and Rhetoric* 1 (1968), 1–14.

Cherwitz, Richard A., and James W. Hikens. *Communication and Knowledge: An Investigation in Rhetorical Epistemology.* Columbia: University of South Carolina Press, 1986.

Weaver, Richard. *Language Is Sermonic.* Baton Rouge: Louisiana State University Press, 1970.

C H A P T E R   7

Audience Analysis

*T*he impulse to speak typically springs from some purpose you hope to accomplish. Normally, you won't speak publicly merely to be speaking. You expect to accomplish some specific goal: explaining a new idea or changing some belief. Whatever goal you may have for speaking, your goal cannot be accomplished by yourself alone. Communication is a jointly engendered act. It is your audience who must complete the communication act that you initiate. It is your audience who must come to understand your idea or be persuaded by your reasoning. If your audience fails to understand or be persuaded, your speech's purpose has gone unfulfilled.

As a public speaker you must be thoughtfully aware of your audience's prior knowledge, attitudes, and beliefs if you are to succeed in accomplishing your goals. Their positive or negative reception of your ideas ultimately determines the success or failure of your speech. But, audiences are never merely passively "stimulated" into "responding" as you would like them to respond. Even though your audience may be sitting quietly, listening as you speak, they are still highly active persons whose minds are abuzz with their own thoughts—considering what you have said, disputing your arguments, and even daydreaming about being elsewhere. While you as a speaker determine what message is *given* (projected) during your speech, it is the audience who determines what ideas will be *taken away* from your message—that is, what they will do with the ideas you have projected. Your speech cannot *make* them understand, believe, or enjoy anything. All you can reasonably do is put together the best speech you can, taking into account everything you know about your audience and adapting your presentation to whatever facts you have previously gathered about them.

Because audiences are not all identical in their knowledge, attitudes, and values, you must try to find out as much as you can about your particular audience before you speak. The purpose of this chapter is to introduce the problem of audience analysis, to present some of the factors you should consider as you think about the people to whom you are talking, and to recommend some things you can do in order to find out more about your audience. Armed with adequate information about your audience, you can adapt your speech's content (Chapter 8) and organizational structure (Chapter 9) to take advantage of the forces already at work in the audience's mind.

*S*pontaneous Audience Analysis

To see just how much audience analysis you already perform as you speak throughout a typical day, let's explore a commonplace speaking situation in which a person like yourself constantly *spontaneously* analyzes an audience and adapts to it. In the example below, notice the different ways the same person answers the same basic question, depending upon who is asking it.

In our imaginary situation, it's the end of a typical fall semester and Jack is headed home for a well-deserved vacation. To welcome him, Jack's parents have invited a few of his relatives over for a big family dinner.

Jack pulls into the driveway just in time to meet his father on his way to get some last-minute groceries. After a preliminary "Welcome home" and "How are you?" Jack's father inquires, *"How's school?"*

"Not bad," Jack replies, a little tiredly. After all, it's been a long drive and his father will understand. "But I'll sure be glad when May gets here and I can get a full-time job. Sure will be nice to get away from the books and earn some money for a while."

Next, Jack pops his head into the kitchen to find his mother. "Well, helllllOoooooo there," she says. "Glad to have you back home. *How's school?*"

"Just great," Jack enthuses. "Couldn't be better. I've been working hard, my grades are up (I got an *A* in my speech class), I've attended all my classes. Yeah. Things are going just great—I even like the roommate I got this year!"

Since dinner's not ready yet, and none of the guests have arrived, Jack changes clothes and goes over to his best friend's house. On the way, Jack meets the kid who used to idolize him when he was in high school. *"How's school?"* the kid asks.

"Terrific," Jack answers, summoning up his most macho, heroic voice. "The social life is great. There's the Chicken Oil Company for a drink with the guys on Monday, Duddley's Draw on Tuesday, the University Movie on Wednesday (for culture, you know), the Lakeview Dance Club on Thursday, and best of all, on Friday night, there's the Dixie Chicken. If I'm bored on Saturday, I can go to the game. College sure is a lot of fun!"

Finally, when Jack gets to his friend's house, his friend wonders, *"How's school?"*

"Really rough, this semester. You see, I've just started dating this new girl, and, uh, well, you know, we spend a lot of time together. And it may get serious. And I . . . I just don't know what to do. I didn't really want to come home this time. And, besides . . . she's kind of the serious type—spends a lot of time in the library studying, and, well, I've spent more time in the library this last few weeks than in all the rest of my time at school put together. My grades have come up, but I haven't been to the Lakeview Club in weeks!"

In every case Jack was asked the same question, "How's school?" And in every case he gave a different answer. Why? Is it that Jack is basically dishonest? Is it that he really doesn't know how school is? Which is the real and honest answer to the question "How's school?"

The truth is, of course, these are *all* real and honest answers to the question. For, at one time or another, school is all of those wonderful, social, distressing, confusing things Jack mentioned in his various conversations. Why then all the different answers to all those different people? Jack was adapting spontaneously to his audience. Since there is simply no way Jack could ever tell someone else everything he knows or feels or believes about a subject as complex as "school," he spontaneously selected from his wealth of ideas the ones he thought this or that person (his immediate audience) would be most interested in hearing about, or could best handle given the person's own convictions, or could best understand given the person's history with him or knowledge about him. Other things he simply left out on this particular speech occasion.

This same principle—audience **analysis** and **adaptation**—applies to the more formal public speaking situation as well. What you actually say about your topic should not exhaust what you actually know about that topic. You will need to do some judicious selecting for your particular audience. If it *does* exhaust your knowledge, then your speech is probably headed for trouble anyway. But assuming that what you will say does not exhaust your knowledge, how do you select what you want to present to this particular audience, on this particular occasion?

In order to make the most appropriate choices from among the many organizational and developmental options you have as you plan your speech, you need to analyze your anticipated audience carefully and consciously, just as Jack spontaneously analyzed his audience of family members and friends based on his years of experience with them. To do this, there are three basic questions to ask about your public speaking audience. Answering these questions early should help guide your speech preparation from the beginning, as the impulse to speak takes shape and gathers force:

1. What are my audience's relevant **demographic involvements?**

2. What are my audience's relevant **social involvements?**

3. What are my audience's relevant **conceptual involvements?**

To help you understand what these three questions entail, we will look at two important natural processes that relate rather directly to the task of audience analysis: individuation and involvement. We will then return to explore these three types of audience involvements in detail.

Individuation and Involvement

"Birds of a feather flock together."

"Opposites attract."

These two popular sayings each capture one component of a paradoxical aspect of human nature: Not only are we likely to be found in the company of people who are similar to ourselves, but we also frequently seek out people who are dissimilar. Why is this so, and what does this have to do with the problem of audience analysis? The act theory presented in Chapter 3 yields a pair of concepts that can help us understand not only these paradoxical maxims, but also many of the most important aspects of audience analysis. These two concepts are **individuation** and **involvement.**

Individuation is the tendency for a group of closely related organic activities to become progressively more separate from the larger organic system they are part of. As they do this, they begin taking on an identity of their own. The process of individuation may be illustrated in the prenatal growth of a human being. From the single cell from which you started life, the original cell divided several times, forming a cluster of identical cells, all clinging to one another. This is the beginning of your personal individuation. Then, something almost miraculous happened. When the cluster reached a certain size, various portions of the cluster began to differentiate (that is, to further individuate) into what have become your various organs—arms, legs, and head externally; heart, lungs, and liver internally. Thus, each of these little groups of cells began to separate from the larger cluster and to take on their own identities, which distinguished each of them from all your other organs. This increasing separation constitutes the process of individuation.

But the little pockets of individuating cells did not completely separate from one another and become a new organism (which is what happens, for example, in the process of identical twinning). Instead, each pocket of individuating cells became functional parts of a more complex single organism— you! They were inhibited in their process of individuation by an opposite and equally natural organic process, involvement.

Involvement is the tendency for separate organic activities to progressively join together to form larger, usually more complex, wholes. It is a natural counter tendency to the process of individuation. Like individuation, involvement is a natural outcome of the ebb and flow of organic acts (Langer, 1967). These reciprocal processes occur at all levels of living activity, including the level of human psychology. Thus, throughout the organically based world, at every level of observation, there exists a rhythmic competition between the push of the process of individuation toward greater separation and the pull of involvement toward greater integration. The processes of individuation and involvement apply to your audience as well.

Individuation, Involvement, and Public Speaking

The dual processes of individuation and involvement play a significant role in making symbolically projected speech communication possible and also in making it necessary. Because we are each separate persons with our own private experiences and thoughts, our minds have strong impulses to individuate and to become progressively more separate from one another. But because we are able to project our ideas back and forth to one another by way of spoken symbolic communication, we also have a means of overcoming our individual separateness—consequently slowing down the natural tendency toward individuation and thereby producing greater mutual involvement and mental similarity with one another.

The ever-present tension between the development of an idiosyncratic private mental life (individuation) and the similarity produced by our shared symbolic communication (involvement) has implications for analyzing your audience. Every audience member has developed somewhat differently from every other and is therefore unique. But every audience member has also developed, through spoken symbolic communication, numerous social involvements with all the other people to whom they might talk. Accordingly, individual audience members share many common conceptual attributes with members of the same language community—shared ideas, beliefs, and attitudes toward life and its daily problems and activities. Although we are each unique, human individuality is not total. Otherwise, human communication would be impossible.

What has this to do with public speaking? Whenever you hope to communicate your ideas to another, you must overcome human individuation, and the separateness it produces, by some sort of symbolic means. You must find the ways you and your audience are already similar (involved) so that you can use that similarity as a starting point for communicating your ideas in the most appropriate way—a way that allows the audience to understand those ideas and to become more fully involved with them. Your task as a speaker is to employ your spoken symbolic strategies (methods of organization, types of supporting materials, and so forth) so that your words involve your audience with your own individuated way of seeing things. To do this, you must discover the ways you and your audience are already mentally involved with each other. By doing so, you can induce further involvements through your use of speech. Failure to take your audience's prior individuations and involvements into account as you prepare your speech may lead you to fail to accomplish your goals.

In informative speaking such involvements are the bridge to maintaining your audience's interest in your topic; you will try to relate your topic to some aspect of the audience's prior interests, their previous involvements. The more successful you are in relating your topic to the audience's prior involvements, the more successful your speech is likely to be.

But in persuasive speaking, increasing the audience's sense of involvement with your idea is not merely important; it is the lifeblood of the entire process. *Persuasion is the attempt to bring another person's individuated thinking into line with your own.* Persuasion is necessary for maintaining the human community because it counteracts the natural tendency for our minds to spontaneously go their separate ways if they do not come into periodic symbolic contact with one another (Berger and Luckman, 1966; Langer, 1982). Accordingly, persuasion is the natural, necessary, and inevitable result of our mental activity. Just as we need a measure of separateness from others for our individual minds to grow, so do we need mental contact and continual mutual persuasion if we are to create and maintain our social community. Without constant efforts at mutual persuasion, the human community would fragment into its ultimate units—the isolated individual.

Because you need to make mental contact with your audience in order to be able to inform or persuade them, you need to know your audience's current mental situation before they hear your speech. Hence, the need for audience analysis. Audience analysis provides an opportunity for you to find potential starting points and developmental resources for involving your audience with your ideas. The advice that follows concerning audience analysis is designed to help you understand your audience's prior, generally long-term, involvements.

To understand your audience, you will want to know as much as you can about your audience's demographic, social, and conceptual involvements. In each case, you are looking for what binds this "flock" together so that you can determine the best way of bridging the separateness between yourself and them. But, remember that the factors that follow are exceedingly general; there are literally thousands of topics for speeches and thousands of different patterns of audience members before whom you might actually speak. Every such combination of topic and audience will require some very specific adaptation that cannot be covered in a general survey of audience factors. Thus, all we can realistically do here is to develop a list of general types of audience involvements to consider as you prepare your speech. Some of these involvements may make a critical difference in how you plan a particular speech on a particular occasion; others may not. In any case, the types of involvements listed below represent significant audience factors for you to consider. Choose the ones that make a difference for your particular speech and plan accordingly.

Demographic Involvements

Demography is the statistical study of the characteristics of a population. When we fill out census forms every 10 years, we attempt to establish a demographic profile of the people of the United States. Everything from the number of children we have to the number of televisions we own is charted to try to understand who we are, what we like, and what we *are* like as a people. You do not need a complete demographic profile of your audience— even if it were possible to get one—in order to give an effective speech, but you can enhance the effectiveness of your speech by adapting it to several key demographic factors. This is so because people tend to be involved psychologically with people with whom they are involved demographically. Three particular demographic factors are among the most general and useful of the audience involvements you can assess: (1) age, (2) sex, and (3) ethnic, cultural, or national background. We will examine each of these broad demographic involvements to show its possible influence on your speech preparation.

Age As people grow older they change in many predictable, physical ways. The ancient riddle of the sphinx acknowledges this fact in its question: "What is it that goes on four legs when it is young, two legs when it is mature, and on three legs when it is old?" The answer is, of course, humans—who crawl on all fours as children, walk upright on two legs during the middle years of life, and use the support of a cane in old age. Such physical changes are fairly predictable and can be taken into account as you prepare your speech. But we change psychologically as well as physically during the course of our lives. Gail Sheehy's book entitled *Passages* is only one among many recent works that take note of the predictable changes we undergo. And Aristotle's 2400-year-old description of the phases of a person's life rings as true today as the day it was written. He writes, for example, that the "youthful type of character [has] . . . strong passions and tends to gratify them indiscriminately."

In addition to these individual psychological changes due to the personal aging process, there are *generational* changes that apply to most persons of the same age, as generations of age-mates go through life together. This means that people of the same relative age tend to share in certain unifying national experiences that characterize the decade in which they grew up and developed. For example, the generation growing up in the 1930s is bound together by experiences and memories of the Great Depression; those growing up in the 1940s are bound together by their experience of World War II. The 1950s generation is involved as a group by their experience of such things as the early days of television—with its introduction of the great TV comedians and programs like "The Mickey Mouse Club" and "Leave It to Beaver." Also affecting this generation's memories are the McCarthy hearings, the Cold War, Sputnik, and the birth of Rock and Roll. The 1960s generation was inextricably bound together by the war in Vietnam, assassinations of the Kennedys and Martin Luther King, Jr., racial strife, and the Beatles. The generation of the 1970s will probably forever be involved together by the Watergate hearings, the resignation of a president, and a crisis of faith in American political values. The 1980s generation will probably be characterized by Yuppies, the candidacies of the first woman and first black for a national office, and by the rise of the computer era. Knowing the relative age of your audience—at least in relation to such age-specific, generationally involving experiences as those listed above—should give you many ideas for how to relate the subject of your own contemporary speech to the shared experiences of your audience as generational age-mates.

Remember that however we might describe the ages a person passes through, we speak differently to those who are older than ourselves than we do to those who are younger or to those who are in our own age range. In addition to factors such as Aristotle analyzed, it is important to assess the relative age of your audience because those who are older than yourself may need more proof of your expertise; those who are younger may not respond to examples drawn from a different historical era, and so forth.

Sex Because of the rapid transition in traditional sex roles in the last two decades, it is difficult to generalize about differences between the sexes. But it is still important to know whether your audience may be primarily of one sex or the other, or equally mixed, as you select your topic, collect supporting material, and begin shaping and organizing your speech into final form. Then you can determine whether or not your topic appeals to audience members of both sexes and whether or not your supporting examples will be meaningful in the light of everyone's experience. If, for example, your topic for a classroom speech is your gun collecting hobby, but your classroom audience is primarily female, you might decide to focus on the aesthetics of the various guns rather than on their relative qualities as hunting tools since women traditionally have shown a greater interest in beauty than in sport hunting. Similarly, if your topic were developing a home exercise fitness plan, and the audience represented both sexes equally, you would want to be sure to include exercises that appealed to the fitness needs of both sexes or to alternate with exercises that were specialized for the needs of one sex and then the other. Even these two examples might be seen as sexist, since they are based on traditional values that might already be dated. In any case, the point is the same. The sexual makeup of your audience should be considered as you construct your speech.

Ethnic and Cultural Background and/or Nationality Whatever truth is in the image of America as the great melting pot, the United States is not composed of a culturally homogeneous population. To a greater or lesser degree, many communities have groups of people with long-preserved aspects of their cultural, ethnic, and national heritages—in spite of the overall trend toward a typically American cultural formula shared by the majority. For this reason, it is wise to know if your audience has any cultural and ethnic involvements that set them off from the "Standard American Average." The success of your speech may depend upon your awareness of any systematic differences between yourself and your audience based on their cultural involvements with a particular national or ethnic heritage. To inadvertently insult some ethnic or national constituency within your audience not only characterizes you as insensitive, but also jeopardizes your chances of success. For example, a careless remark during a speech by James Watt, the former Secretary of the Interior, eventually cost him not only his effectiveness in a particular speech, but also his job.

Furthermore, by failing to realize that such a constituency is in your audience, you do not get to take advantage of the opportunity to relate your

These California farmers are harvesting oysters grown with aquaculture methods. What other shellfish are raised with aquaculture? How might local water pollution problems affect fish and shellfish?

topic meaningfully to your audience's commonly shared and deeply involving national pride or experience. To see how effective adapting a message to the ethnic, cultural, or national involvements of an audience can be, read the speeches of politicians as they move from community to community, speaking among the electorate. What you will find is specific references to each community's cultural values and an attempt to identify the general political message with the specific values of the community in which the speech is being given. Identifying your message with the ethnic or other demographic involvements of the audience can play an important role in determining whether or not your ideas get a favorable hearing.

Social Involvements

People are more similar to those with whom they fraternize frequently than to those with whom they have only occasional social contact. Social contact typically breeds shared involvement in basic values, beliefs, interests, and experiences. Unlike the demographic involvements, which are based primarily on the facts and accidents of one's birth—when one was born (age), whether one has an XX or an XY chromosome pattern (sex), who one's parents are (race and ethnic background)—social involvements are determined by the choices one makes concerning whom to spend time with. These choices include such things as the following: place and type of employment, club and organizational memberships, socioeconomic class, and educational and religious affiliations.

Social involvements are not as broad and general as are demographic involvements, but they are equally important for you to understand and adapt to. Anything you can find out about your particular audience that individuates them from the general demographic involvements they may share with many audiences is a potential source for individualizing your speech for them in particular. Let's look at some of the social involvements you may wish to consider as you prepare to adapt your speech to a particular audience.

Employment: Place and Type The phrases "white collar worker" and "blue collar worker" are familiar to most of us, and we can easily imagine the general type of person with whom we associate each type of label. We can also imagine the values we presume people under each label to share. The type of work we choose is both a reflection of who we are and a major influence upon who we will become as we grow older. Since the involvements people develop at work have an influence on their beliefs, attitudes, interests, and values, try to determine what lines of work your audience engages in and try to use this knowledge to adapt your speech based on their commonly shared work experiences or on the values typically shared by those particular workers. What changes, for example, would you make on the topic of White Collar Crime for each of the following two audiences: line workers in a factory and a new crop of management trainees?

Club and Organizational Memberships We work and we play. Our club and organizational memberships indicate with whom we socialize in our leisure time. Is this the Lions or the Optimists Club you are speaking to? If so, what do you know about these organizations? What shared values lead people to involve themselves in such organizations? Is it a job-related club or completely social? Does the club do some sort of community service? Different clubs and organizations each have their own reasons for existing, and each have their own values that tend to bind their members together. When speaking before a club or social organization, try to find out what values the group professes and adapt your message in order to take advantage of those values in your speech.

Social or Economic Class Although the economic and social class structure in the United States is generally more fluid than in most other countries, Americans still make distinctions concerning social class that can influence your audience's responsiveness to your speeches. Those people who have ample money will have a different outlook on many government policies than will those who are barely able to make ends meet. Since public speaking frequently concerns public policy issues, the appeals one uses are potentially quite different as the socioeconomic level changes. Accordingly, you must vary the appeals and examples you use as the socioeconomic status of your audience varies. Sociologists are able to distinguish numerous socioeconomic gradations in our population, but even as rough a set of levels as "lower," "middle," and "upper" may be of some help to you as you seek to adapt your message to the ears you most want it to reach.

Educational Level Closely related to considerations of socioeconomic class are those of general educational level. A college education not only entails a body of academic knowledge, but also a particular way of thinking. Typically, those people going to college may be expected to value such things as "being educated" and "getting ahead." But the involvements among college-educated people may go even deeper. Sociolinguist William Labov has even found that college-educated people tell stories about "close calls" in their lives in a very different way from those who had a high school education or less. It is not that each group merely had different stories to tell, but that the entire structure of the story was different. According to a lecture by Labov (1983), college-educated persons told their stories from an impersonal distance and evaluated the feelings they felt during the incident at the same time as they retold the events. In contrast, the people with less than a college education tended to recreate the incidents in the ongoing present, dramatizing the story almost as if they were currently reliving it. Thus, whatever its liberating, individuating influences on our general thinking ability, a college education also involves us with all those others who are college educated and makes us more alike in certain important ways.

To know the general educational level of your audience is to have a better idea about what kinds of supporting material might help your speech's cause. The more highly educated the audience, the more likely that they will understand technical vocabulary and be able to follow sophisticated reasoning.

Such an audience is also more able to entertain counterfactual speculation, such as "If the Soviets had landed on the moon first, what might have been the implications for the subsequent development of our own space program?" Accordingly, try to determine the general educational level of your audience so that you can determine the level at which you may safely pitch your speech.

Religious Preference Few social involvements are as powerful an influence on a person's attitudes as one's religious preferences. Atheist, agnostic, or true believer—a person's religious preferences involve him or her with countless other people whom they have never met. Every religion and every denomination has its own central articles of faith that its adherents use as premises for action and as bases for developing derivative beliefs about more secular matters. Whether or not your speech concerns an overtly religious topic, your audience's religious preferences may still influence their receptiveness to your ideas. Accordingly, you must, if possible, take these preferences into account as you plan the strategies for your speech.

Conceptual Involvements

Typically, most audience members will come to your speech with at least some prior involvement with the topic. This is especially true in speaking situations outside the classroom. Usually, the reason the audience has come to hear you speak is because they already have some involvement with your topic. They attend your speech because they want to learn about your ideas or to understand your viewpoint concerning the topic. Your success as a speaker depends as much upon your ability to assess your audience's prior topical involvements as it does upon understanding their social and demographic involvements. To help you gauge your audience's prior involvements with your topic, you should try to answer three questions:

1. What are the audience's prior interests (expressed or implied) concerning the topic?

2. What is the audience's prior level of knowledge about the topic?

3. What are the audience's prior attitudes or values related to the topic?

Audience Interests Whenever you speak you will want to find out what the audience's prior interests are. Why? So that you can tell them "what they want to hear"? Emphatically not! Rather, it is so that you can tell them what you want to tell them in such a way that they *can* hear it at all. For, if you cannot link what you intend to talk about to your audience's own spontaneous interests, then the audience may simply tune you out and stop hearing you. You must know their interests in order to be able to link your topic to their thinking; you must take advantage of the impulses already going on within your audience's mind.

What are audiences interested in? While it may not be possible to determine an audience's interests specifically enough to know, for example, what individual audience members pursue as their hobbies, it is rarely necessary to be this precise either. General types of audience interests can be intuitively outlined and evaluated. The following is an inventory of the general sources of interest that can be applied to many audiences. Your specific goal as you research your particular audience will be to determine which of these interests apply most forcefully to your particular speech situation. Here, then, is a starter checklist to help you determine your audience's most likely types of interests.

Audiences are interested in those things that fulfill one or more of their basic needs. For as long as there have been speech textbooks, there have been inventories of the basic human needs to which speakers might appeal in trying to adapt their ideas to their audiences. Aristotle, the author of the earliest systematic textbook on the art of effective speaking, was also among the first to try to analyze human needs as they relate to the speaker's purpose. More recently, speech textbooks often present a list of human needs first generated by psychologist Abraham Maslow. Maslow ranked human needs in a hierarchy, ranging them from the most universally basic personal needs (physiological and safety needs), to social and esteem needs, and finally to the most uniquely individual need of all, self-actualization needs. Maslow's hierarchy of needs is illustrated in Figure 7-1.

Each of the needs Maslow identifies seems to be quite basic, and it would be a good idea to use one or more of them in gaining and holding your audience's attention. A speech about performing the Heimlich Maneuver (to assist a choking victim) would appeal to our safety needs. A speech on how to clean the air in our homes in order to reduce allergic reactions would appeal to our physiological needs. If you were giving a speech about weather modification—talking, for example, about the techniques scientists are using to try to steer hurricanes away from coastal areas—you might be hoping to appeal to our safety needs. Similarly, a speech on "How to Win Friends and Influence People," would be appealing to our esteem needs, and so forth.

But, we are also interested in many things that have very little to do with true need fulfillment in any direct way. So, we can continue our inventory of things people usually find interesting as we continue to look for additional sources of audience interest in our topics.

Audiences are interested in what other people are doing. We are very curious about our fellow human beings—as television programs such as "That's Incredible," "You Asked for It," "Candid Camera," and "Lifestyles of the Rich and Famous" all reveal. Magazines such as *People* tell the same story. We want to know what others are doing and how they live their lives. Because people

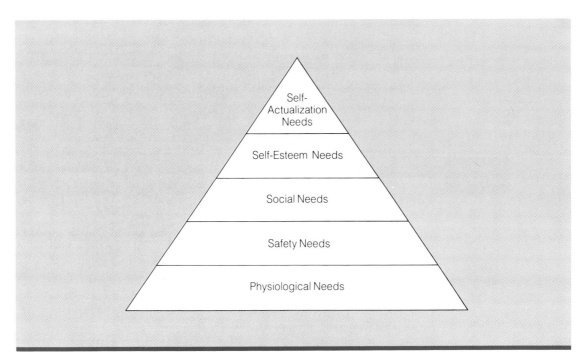

Figure 7-1   Abraham Maslow's Hierarchy of Human Needs

are interested in what others are doing, using personal anecdotes to support your main points should appeal to your audience.

Audiences are interested in things that improve their competence. Bookstores are filled with how-to books. We love to feel like we can do something well. One important way of maintaining your audience's interest is to show them how listening to your speech can improve their skills and competencies. Speech topics such as the following are aimed at this goal.

How to Improve Your Fly Fishing Technique

How to Invest Your Hard-Earned Money while Still in College

How to Choose the Best Time to Eat at Your Favorite Restaurant

Audiences are interested in things that give them new understandings or greater appreciations of commonplace things in their world. Americans not only love to *do,* they also seem to love to *understand.* If we let them, children will take things apart "to see how they work" and "what makes them tick." Your audience is probably very little different in this regard. A good approach to marshaling their natural impulses to listen is to explain new insights into your audience's everyday world. Subjects such as the following attempt to appeal to this inherent source of audience interest.

Why We Should Take a New Look at Old Museums

Why Macrame is Not for Women Only (here you could tell us that macrame was born among pirates and fishing fleets)

Audiences are interested in the unusual and the extraordinary. Audiences are eager to hear everything from adventure tales of the high seas to descriptions of how tiny creatures capture their food. People are interested in mysteries of every sort. Thus, if you can find and emphasize the mysterious, strange, or the unusual about your topic, you should have a ready fund of audience interest to draw upon. For example, most audiences know about basic pet care, but it would be unusual to learn about the effects of music on your choice of pets.

Audience Knowledge One of the audience interests you will want to take advantage of is their interest in learning something new. But first you must find out how much your particular audience already knows about your subject. It will do you no good if the audience either already knows everything you are going to say or if it cannot understand a word of what you say because it is too new. Your second audience analysis question must be about the audience's level of knowledge (a) about the topic itself and (b) about topics that might serve as comparisons as you explain new things to the audience. You can often explain the unknown in terms of the already known, but you must first have a good idea of what the audience already knows.

If, for example, your audience analysis turns up the fact that your audience knows very little about atomic energy production, and you want to give a speech criticizing a proposed nuclear power plant in your area, you might have to spend some portion of your speaking time giving your audience the needed background before the point you really wanted to support would make any sense to them.

Similarly, if you were going to give a talk about ham radio, you might want to develop a speech comparing and contrasting ham radio with CB (citizen's band)—since you might expect your audience to be more familiar with CB than ham radio. A speech about photography would require you to determine whether your audience already knows about such things as aperture, F-stops, and shutter speeds before you could tell them how to use these adjustable features of the modern SLR (single lens reflex) cameras to take creative pictures (Do they even know what an SLR is?). Similarly, if you are an expert in stereo hardware, plan a speech telling your audience how to get the most stereo for their money. But if you use terms like *infinite baffle, bass reflex, horn enclosure, combos,* and *woofers, tweeters,* and *midranges,* then you had better be prepared to spend a substantial portion of your time defining these terms and comparing these unfamiliar concepts (for most classroom audiences) to things with which they are already familiar. Whenever you can, you want to help your audience understand new concepts and ideas by employing definitions and comparisons that you have found by audience analysis that they *do* know, or at least things they might be expected to know.

Audience Attitudes You may have found some general audience interests, and you may have analyzed your audience's general level of knowledge. But you still leave yourself open to failure if you have not considered your audience's general attitudes toward topics like yours—and, whenever possible, what their attitude toward your particular topic happens to be.

For example, suppose that your town is struggling with the problem of inadequate parks due to a recent growth spurt in your area. You have determined that the Town Council is interested in the problem (they have scheduled a hearing) and that they are knowledgeable (basic research has been done concerning the alternatives). You are new to the area and decide to speak on behalf of a federal loan program designed to help small towns like yours. Your speech would probably fail if you were not aware that the Town Council members had publicly expressed negative attitudes concerning accepting federal money "because of the strings attached." This attitude against federal help would necessarily affect the strategies available to you as you plan your speech, since you would have to change this general negative attitude as well as advocate a specific proposal. It is important to discover whether or not your audience has any prejudices concerning your topic that might affect how you plan to handle it on a specific occasion.

But how do you find out about your audience's interests, level of prior knowledge, and attitudes? Most importantly, you can investigate.

Investigating Your Audience

In spite of the general audience interest factors developed here, not every topic will be of interest to every audience just because the topic happens to fall into one of these typical interest categories. Nor is topic selection the only, or even the most important, reason for learning as much as you can about your audience. Even after you have inventoried the possible sources of audience interest, you must next **investigate** your particular audience to find out as much as you can about them. Depending upon how you came to be giving your speech in the first place, there are several different ways you can find out what you need to know.

First, you can contact the person who is responsible for arranging the speech situation in which you will be speaking. If you have been invited, for example, to speak before a club or organization, the program chairperson should be able to supply you with information about the group, its values, its demographic characteristics, and most importantly, its expectations in asking you to speak. If you cannot get enough information in this way, you may then want to follow up what you learn from the program chairperson and contact other group, organization, or club members. Perhaps they will be able to give you more or different information about the audience. Third, you will want to review your own experiences, either with this particular audience or with audiences you consider to be similar in makeup to them. Fourth, if the occasion is particularly important or the speaking challenge difficult or urgent, you may also wish to read about the group—in the local newspaper, in the literature produced by the group itself, and in library resources. Finally, you may even feel that it is necessary to conduct a written survey of the group's interests and opinions before you can determine how to best adapt your speech to their prior needs and involvements. Some of these methods require more work than others, but the information you gain can be highly significant in terms of the success or failure of your speech. So the time spent is typically very worthwhile.

*C*onclusion

As we pointed out in Chapter 2, communication will always be initiated by someone who wants to express his or her ideas to one or more others. But merely expressing those ideas in a spoken form does not itself guarantee that communication will actually occur. Effective communication requires not only a sender of ideas, it also requires a receiver of those ideas: someone who is able and willing to understand them. To help you improve your chances of having your ideas understood you must learn as much as you can about your audience ahead of time. The goal is to find out how your audience members are involved with one another and how they may become involved with your topic. In that way you can adapt how you encode your ideas as you seek to make them available to your audience. Encoding your ideas in appropriate examples, anecdotes, statistics, and so on, which address your audience's prior involvements, will allow your speech to take advantage of the forces already at work within your audience, thereby giving those ideas an audience-based forward motion that enhances the drive and energy you have already put into encoding your speech. Knowing your audience, and adapting your speech to their needs and interests and motivations, is one of the important keys to successful public speaking.

Questions for Review

1. How are demographic, social, and ideational involvements different from one another? Is it possible to rank them generally from most important to least important? Why or why not? What difference does the topic you are talking about make to such a rank ordering?

2. What are some of the involvements that are significant in understanding your public speaking classmates? Are you all about the same age? From similar social, cultural, and racial backgrounds? What are the relevant involvements based upon the fact that you all chose to attend the same college? Analyze your classmates' relevant involvements related to your first major speech.

Questions for Discussion

1. Assuming that you have selected a topic for your speech and are now investigating your audience's involvements, what will you do with the information you discover? That is, what difference does it make whether your audience is involved in certain ways demographically, socially, or ideationally?

2. Using the concepts presented in the chapter, explain why two different people might observe the same event and still describe or evaluate it differently.

Things to Try

Imagine that you have been invited to speak to a local club or organization on some hobby or topic related to your college studies, and you wish to find out about the people who are likely to attend. Using the following checklist as a guide, prepare a set of questions you would try to ask during a phone call to the arrangements chairperson for the meeting.

Audience Analysis Checklist

Demographic Involvements
   1. Age of my audience
   2. Sexual makeup of my audience
   3. Ethnic, cultural, or national background of my audience

Social Involvements
   1. Employment: places/types
   2. Club or organizational memberships
   3. Social or economic class
   4. Educational level
   5. Religious preferences

Conceptual Involvements
   1. Audience's prior interest in the topic
   2. Audience's prior knowledge about the topic
   3. Audience's prior attitudes or values concerning the topic

Bibliography

Aristotle. *Rhetoric,* 1389a.

Berger, Peter L., and Thomas Luckman. *The Social Construction of Reality.* Garden City, NY: Doubleday, 1966.

Labov, William. Lecture, Texas A & M University, 1983.

Langer, Susanne K. *Mind: An Essay on Human Feeling,* Vols. 1–3. Baltimore: Johns Hopkins University Press, 1967, 1972, 1982.

Maslow, A. H. *Motivation and Personality.* New York: Harper and Row, 1954.

Sheehy, Gail. *Passages.* New York: Dutton, 1976.

Developmental Materials for Speeches

*I*n Chapter 6 you learned how to select a topic for your speech and how to formulate a specific purpose statement that can guide your subsequent speech preparation. But, your idea for a speech topic and a well-formulated specific purpose statement do not by themselves guarantee a good speech—any more than a well-formed embryo guarantees that a good person will develop. A well-formulated specific purpose statement is an important starting point, but many accidents and misfortunes may befall your "best laid plans" as your impulse to speak grows toward maturity. Poet T. S. Eliot (1962) put it succinctly when he wrote:

> Between the idea
> And the reality
> Between the motion
> And the act
> Falls the Shadow

To help ensure that the guiding impulse for your speech has a good opportunity to develop into a mature speech, you need to nourish it with an adequate supply and ample variety of developmental materials. Developing an idea into a mature speech is a very similar process to organic growth. Just as healthy organic growth requires you to take in ample nutrients, developing a good speech requires you to research your topic thoroughly, looking for an ample supply and wide variety of new ideas that you can assimilate and use in your speech. This chapter characterizes the seven major kinds of developmental materials you will want to gather and use. These developmental materials are somewhat like the basic food groups needed for good nutrition; your speeches cannot get along without each of them for very long. You may not need every one of them for every speech, but over a period of time they will all prove necessary for your best speeches. (Appendix A provides a brief overview of the research process and the resources available as you try to gather an ample supply of supporting material.)

Because there are many ways to project your ideas, there are many ways to develop a speech. Human minds have themselves individuated and subdivided into many different modes of thinking. And each form of supporting material described here represents a different way of projecting your ideas into verbal symbolism. As you try to project your ideas to another person, it is important to weave a wide variety of supporting materials into your speeches, since various audience members may not be responsive to one kind of material but may be responsive to another. The seven forms of supporting materials treated here all derive from the ways our minds work. They are:

1. Definitions

2. Examples

3. Anecdotes

4. Statistics

5. Quotations

6. Comparisons and contrasts

7. Descriptions

Let's now look at each of these to see what is involved in using them.

Definitions

A speech is a pattern of *words* used to project your ideas. If your audience fails to understand your words, everything else about your speech is merely academic. So your first responsibility is to build into your speech definitions of key terms that make your ideas readily available to your audience. Because of their central importance in speeches, and the difficulty of finding adequate treatments of definitions in other readily available sources, we will pay extra attention to helping you understand what definitions are and how various types of definitions work.

A **definition** *is an explanation of the meaning of a word.* It is used to help make your speech more comprehensible to your audience. In two situations, definitions are an especially important form of support. First, you should develop a definition whenever you are using a key word with which your audience is simply unfamiliar. For example, if you are giving a speech on the types of magic and you use the word *prestidigitation,* then you will want to tell your audience that *prestidigitation* means sleight of hand.

The second situation that routinely calls for a definition occurs whenever you are using a familiar word in an unfamiliar, technical, or restricted sense. For example, the word *charm* is a common enough English term, but nuclear physics in recent years has employed the term *charm* to label the properties of a particular subatomic particle, called a *charmed particle,* because of its special behavior. To begin talking about a particle's *charmed nature,* without defining this very special use of the term, risks audience confusion. In this context, a definition of the term *charm* would be necessary.

Intension versus Extension

Explaining the meaning of a word involves several important considerations. One of the most important considerations is the distinction between a word's *In*tension and its *Ex*tension. Whenever we use a word, such as *pen,* there are two things we usually know about the meaning of the word. First, we know the typical conditions or criteria that control the proper use of the word. That is, we know what specific characteristics something must display if it is to be properly labeled by the term *pen*. Furthermore, if we had to, we could make a list of these characteristics. A pen must be (a) a writing instrument (b) that uses ink. Similarly, with the word *cup*. It is a (a) small, (b) open-topped, (c) container, (d) with a handle, (e) used for drinking. A list of attributes that control the proper use of a word is called the word's **intension**. The ability to make such lists of attributes is the basis for our ability to compile dictionaries.

When we know the meaning of a word we usually also know how to use the word to refer to specific items in the world. That is, we not only know the proper conditions for using the word, but we also know how to use the word to mention particular instances of whatever the word names. The **extension** of a word is any actual instance or example of what the word refers to. Figures 8-1 and 8-2 illustrate the relationship between the intensions and the extensions of the words *pen* and *cup*. In each case, the list on the left side of the figure presents a list of attributes that constitute the intension of these words. The illustrations on the right present an instance of what the words can properly be used to name. Such objects are examples of the words' extensions.

Because knowing the meaning of a word involves two aspects—intension and extension—whenever you define a word you need to make sure that your audience knows the conditions that control how you are using it (intension) and also how they themselves would recognize an example of the word (extension) in their daily experience. To accomplish these goals, you might characterize the intension of the word, or you might show a typical example of the extension of the word and allow the audience to generate their own intensional meaning. Depending upon the speech's circumstances, the audience's needs, and the significance of the concept to your overall speech purpose, you may wish to use a variety of intensional and extensional definitions to build up a richer understanding of the word for your audience.

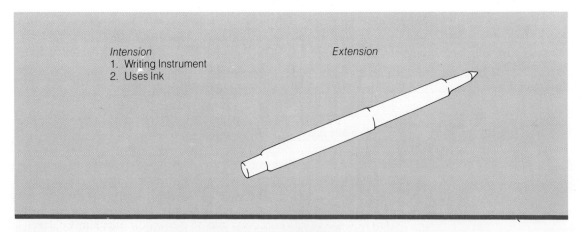

Intension
1. Writing Instrument
2. Uses Ink

Extension

Figure 8-1 Intension and Extension of the Word *Pen*

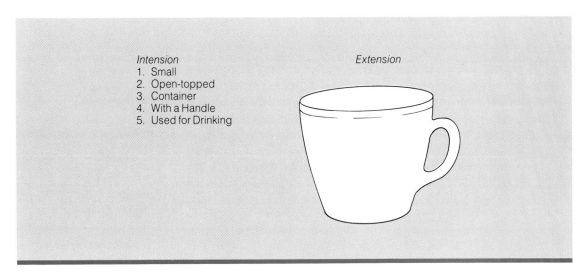

Figure 8-2   Intension and Extension of the Word *Cup*

Methods of Definition

How, then, do you go about defining a word? The following seven ways are perhaps the most commonly used and useful methods:

1. Classification and differentiation

2. Example

3. Enumeration

4. Comparison and contrast

5. Synonym and antonym

6. Etymology or historical origin

7. Negation

Classification and Differentiation Classification and differentiation is an important and widely used method for explaining the intension of a word. Defining by classification and differentiation is a process composed of three subacts, always done in the same order:

1. *Mention* the word you are going to define.

2. *Identify* the general class of concepts into which the word fits.

3. *Distinguish* the word's particular intension from the intensions of the other members of the class.

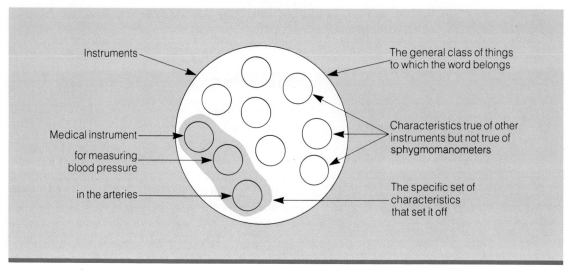

Figure 8-3   Definition by Classification and Differentiation of the Word *Sphygmomanometer*

For example, in a speech about taking someone's blood pressure, you might say:

> A (1) sphygmomanometer is (2) a medical instrument (3) used for measuring blood pressure (4) in the arteries.

This definition is a good one because it (1) mentions the word to be defined, (2) identifies the general class of concepts into which the word fits (for example, sphygmomanometer is an instrument not a process), and (3) clearly distinguishes it from all other members of the class of instruments. The relationship between the general classification into which the word fits and the differentiating attributes among related words is illustrated in Figure 8-3. In Figure 8-3, the outermost circle represents the general class of things to which the word being defined belongs. By identifying a class you are immediately both narrowing the possibilities of what a word can mean and also beginning to relate the new word to other words with which the audience may be familiar. The middle-sized shape encompasses a set of characteristics that, taken together, define the word; the smallest circles represent each of the individual attributes required to make something into a sphygmomanometer.

Although classification and differentiation definitions are the most commonly used, they are not always easy to create. To see if you have developed a good definition, check it against four common tests. These tests may be worded as four questions:

1. Have I unambiguously named the word to be defined?

2. Have I identified a useful class for my audience?

3. Have I clearly set off the word from other members of the class?

4. Have I made sure the definition includes all the members of the sub-class to which it may typically be extended?

Example Defining by example requires that you mention specific instances of the word's extension. Often a classification and differentiation definition (which defines by intension) is immediately followed by an example definition. For example, in a speech on biological cycles, you might define the term *circadian rhythm* as "a biological rhythm exhibiting approximately 24-hour periodicity." This classification and differentiation definition tells your audience how the word is used—that is, the conditions that control its proper application. But to what does the word apply? Now some specific examples would help: Sleeping and waking, mealtimes, body temperature, blood pressure, and waste removal all typically manifest 24-hour cycles. Each of these is properly designated by the term *circadian rhythm* and is, therefore, an example of its extension. Similarly, you might note that *palindromes* are words, phrases, or sentences whose letters read the same backward or forward, and then provide the example: "Madam, I'm Adam."

Ostensive definitions are a special case of definition by example in which you show the audience an actual instance or illustration of the term you are defining. For example, in delivering a speech on types of clouds and their weather effects, you might want to define the term *cirrus* with both a classification and differentiation definition and with a slide or enlarged photograph.

Illustrative definitions are extended examples in the form of a story. For example, if you wanted to provide an illustrative definition of the term *frustration,* you might say:

Frustration is being a Chicago Cubs fan. Year after frustrating year for the past 39 years, the Chicago Cubs have begun every new season with the highest of hopes—with new managers, new players, and loyal old fans earnestly believing that "this will be the year." And year after frustrating year, as April fades into October, the Chicago Cubs fold, fade and frustrate their way into the nearly numb psyches of their perennially loyal fans. Even as I speak the Cubs are threatening a new round of late-season frustration. Here on September 7th, the Cubs are in first place by seven full games—and they have just lost to the Mets 10 to zip—getting only *one* hit in the process! Will this be the year they finally end their frustrating ways and win a pennant? Or is this just the beginning of their annual fade—a fate always lurking just around the next clubhouse corner? Well, if history tells us anything about this coming October, it tells us that *frustration is being a Chicago Cubs fan*. But "wait'll *next* year." Will we have a team!

Enumeration Definition by enumeration may be thought of as a special form of definition by example. When you define by enumeration, you list *all* the members of the class to which the word refers, rather than including only representative examples. Thus, if you were to define the phrase *Southwest Conference* using enumeration, you would list the following universities:

Arkansas	Rice	Texas A&M
Baylor	Southern Methodist	Texas Christian
Houston	Texas	Texas Tech

Comparison and Contrast Examples are a way of sharpening an audience's understanding of the intension of a word by supplying specific instances of its extension. Comparison and contrast are ways of aiding the audience's understanding of a term by showing how the word's intension or extension is either similar to or different from that of some closely related term. Comparison and contrast are especially important when your audience is quite unfamiliar with your subject and therefore needs help in understanding similarities and/or differences with something with which they *are* familiar. Comparison and contrast allow you to point out resemblances or shades of differences between two terms. This process may be seen in the example that follows. While speaking about the difference between the words *continuous* and *continual,* the speaker pointed out that

> *continuous* means "without any interruption or stoppages of any sort," but *continual* means "to be repeated frequently and regularly." Thus, the two words differ from one another in that *continual* emphasizes intermittent repetition of some process or activity, while *continuous* emphasizes uninterrupted repetition of a process or activity.

The speaker then completed the definition by comparison and contrast by giving a pair of contrasting examples, pointing out that "time is continuous, but the ticks of a grandfather clock are continual."

Synonym and Antonym Many words have similar meanings to one another. Two words having the same essential meaning are called synonyms. Many times all you will have to do to adequately define a word is to provide a synonym for it. For example, a common synonym for *prestidigitation* is *magic* or *sleight of hand.* A person who performs prestidigitation performs feats of magic. By telling your audience that prestidigitation is a form of magic, an unfamiliar word is explained by using a more familiar word meaning approximately the same thing.

You may also find it useful to define a word by its opposite. Two words having opposite meanings are antonyms. Antonyms cannot usually be used alone to define a word, but they are nonetheless helpful in guiding your audience to a fuller understanding of the subtleties of a word's intension or extension. For example, after telling your listeners that *acme* means the highest point, and that it is a synonym for *zenith,* you might note that *acme* is the opposite of *nadir,* which is the lowest point. To be at the nadir of one's life is a bad thing; to be at the *zenith* or *acme* is good. In this way you are explaining the distinctions among several closely related terms at the same time.

Etymology or Historical Origin Like people and nations, words have histories. To define a word by its etymology is to explain its current meaning based on the historical meanings of its component parts. For example, the word *triskaidekaphobia* means fear of the number 13. You could have figured out its meaning if you knew that *phobia* comes from the Greek word meaning "fear of" (compare it with words like *claustrophobia* and its antonym *agoraphobia*), that *tris* means "three," *kai* means "and," and *deka* means "10."

Definitions by etymology are especially helpful when you want your audience to associate the new word with others with which they may be familiar. Because definition by etymology takes advantage of the systematic relations words bear to one another, this method utilizes the audience's present knowledge in order to add new knowledge. Definition by etymology is also useful when you wish to bring out nuances or shades of meaning in a familiar word. For example, the word *atonement* means to make amends, usually for some wrongdoing. But its etymology suggests a richer meaning. The word has three component parts, each with its own historical meaning: *at, one, ment.* Literally, these three parts might be translated to mean "at one with," and thus the word *atonement* suggests that the two persons (the wronged and the transgressor) are as *one.* Atonement is a process that makes the two of one mind. This kind of etymological treatment reveals additional meanings.

Negation To define by negation is to tell what a thing is not. "A speech is not an essay on its hind legs," W. N. Brigance once wrote (1961, p. 37). Although definition by negation cannot stand alone—there are millions of things a word does *not* mean—it is still a useful technique in many circumstances. Definition by negation is especially useful when (1) you want to stipulate a new or specialized meaning for an otherwise familiar word (such as a word like *democracy,* which has many possible meanings to different people), or (2) you want to define an unfamiliar word that sounds like or suggests meanings that are not in your usage. Definitions by negation are usually linked with some other method of definition, as in the following example: "An aglet is not a baby Aggie; it's the little plastic wrapper on the end of a shoelace." Here the speaker first uses a negative definition in order to tell the audience what a particular word does *not* mean; then the speaker follows this definition with a classification and differentiation definition to specify the exact intension of this otherwise unfamiliar word. You use definition by negation whenever you describe someone or something as "funny," and then add for clarification "funny strange, not funny ha ha." You are emphasizing which intension for the word *funny* you are not employing.

Special Supporting Techniques for Definitions

Sometimes a word plays such an important role in your speech that a simple definition is not enough. In such cases you may wish to give the word an extended treatment. Then you may employ two special supporting techniques: use of authorities and use of history.

Use of authorities is especially important when you are stipulating a meaning for a familiar term and you wish to show that your definition has significant support among other experts. Usually the use of an authority involves a classification and differentiation definition, followed by a citation of the authority who has formulated it. In actual practice, such a definition might sound like this: "According to Dr. So-and-So, pornography is 'written, graphic, or other forms of published material whose primary intent is to excite lustful, violent, or destructive feelings toward persons or property.'"

Use of history to support a definition involves presenting a narrative account of the circumstances that led to the coining of the term. For example, you might say:

> The word *bowdlerize* means "to edit someone else's writing for the purpose of removing any potentially offensive passages." The word comes from Thomas Bowdler (1754–1825), who is famous for publishing an edition of the works of Shakespeare in which he simply removed every passage he thought would be offensive in any way. The process of prudish deletion of passages from an author's work has been known by Bowdler's name ever since.

In summary, using these techniques for defining significant words will help your audience to understand your speech's content and make it far easier for you to accomplish your speech's short-term and long-term goals. So don't overlook the opportunity to help your audience understand your speech by explaining the meanings of your words. Use ample definitions throughout your speech, whenever you think there is a realistic possibility of confusion or lack of understanding.

Now let's look at each of the other major forms of verbal speech support.

*E*xamples

Speeches are not merely a succession of words. When we speak we usually chain our words together so as to create a higher level of organization called sentences. That is, we use our words to make statements about situations in our world. But not all statements are alike. Some are more general than others. These general statements are meant to encompass a larger number of situations, but in lesser detail. Other statements are quite specific to a particular situation but lack a general application. A speech must be composed of both types of statements—the general and the specific. The generalizing statement makes the speech's remarks applicable to a wide variety of instances. The specific statement helps your audience understand *how* the general statement applies to specific cases. A speech must contain both types of statements, and it must weave them together in a rhythmic interplay between the two types.

An **example** is an item or instance that is presented as a representative case of some more general group as a whole. Whenever you make a general statement that applies to a large number of instances, you will probably also want to immediately mention one or more concrete examples. Your audience's mind hungers for the specific example once it has been exposed to the general statement. The general statement typically establishes an expectation that a concrete example will follow to fill in the details. Where specific details have been left out to enable you to make a more general statement, the mind begins to search for a specific detail to fill in the gap.

For example, if you tell your audience to beware of many perfumes and lotions because they can be hazardous to your health, you will probably want to give them several examples of those hazards—noting that such lotions may be flammable, poisonous, allergenic, and nauseating. Here, the general point "dangerous to your health" is immediately given concrete embodiment with the four dangers: flammable, poisonous, allergenic, and nauseating. From this example, you can see that the general statement formulates the idea for your audience; the more specific statement of examples gives your general point greater memorability, comprehensibility, and impact.

*A*necdotes

Anecdotes are stories that embody a general point you are trying to make. What makes an example into an anecdote is that an anecdote has a plot that develops to a climax and resolution and also has characters who are involved in the action. The story portrays the characters in an action that serves to make the point you are trying to make. You use an anecdote when you wish to flesh out some main point to make it memorable, interesting, personal, and uniquely yours. Anecdotes formulate your points in a particularly powerful and memorable form: the narrative account. The anecdote adds variety and human interest to your speech.

We can see the powerful and long-term effects a well-told anecdote can have on an audience by looking at the Bible, which not only contains a relatively continuous narrative in its own right, but which also contains numerous anecdotes in the form of Jesus's parables. For example, when Jesus wanted to stress that it did not matter precisely how long one had been a follower of his ways, he drove the point home with an anecdote—the parable of the laborers in the vineyard (Matthew 20:1–16).

This fireman is using a high-powered stream of water to fight a fire. What should you do if you're caught in a fire? What kinds of training and testing do firefighters go through?

Children's stories and fairy tales also give narrative form to socially important points in order to give them greater impact on their intended audience. These stories formulate some significant general cultural or human value, giving it symbolic expression and making it more memorable. Aesop's tales serve this function and show the power of a brief narrative to vividly present a point you wish to make.

Anecdotes are generally more personal than Aesop's fables. They come from your own real or imagined experience or from the experiences of people you know. For example, if you have previously told your audience that one of the dangers of after-bath body lotions is their flammability, you might want to emphasize the point by telling the story of poor Alice in Denver, Colorado, who stepped out of the shower, splashed a new brand of after-bath oil all over herself, started to light a cigarette, and went up in a ball of fire. Poof! Such a story makes the danger of these products real, personal, vivid, and unforgettable.

You might wish to try telling at least five types of stories. The easiest, and often most compelling, is the first person **personal anecdote.** It is easiest and most compelling because *you* are the central character, and the story happened to you. In the following example, the speaker is presenting an informative speech concerning the governmental protection of exotic wildlife species in his home state.

> December 18, 1983, was a bitter cold day in the hill country of central Texas. A blue norther had ripped its way through the state the night before, leaving an ice-covered countryside. I was out hunting that morning, and as small droplets would run from my nose, I could feel them freeze to my upper lip. As I sat there freezing, little did I know that I was about to shoot the largest deer that I would probably ever see. Even more spectacular, it would be an imported deer from India—the Axis deer. The events of that morning led me to investigate the future of exotic wildlife in Texas, and more specifically, the future of Axis deer in Texas.

The **third person incident** is like the personal anecdote except that the central character is someone other than yourself—perhaps a friend, perhaps someone you heard about on the radio or television or read about in the newspaper, as in the following example:

> The Baltimore police found Patty Saunders, 9, in the 23-by-52 inch closet where she had been locked for nearly half of her life. Patty weighed only 20 pounds and stood less than 3 feet tall. Smeared with filth, scarred from parental beatings, Patty had become irreparably mentally retarded. Patty is typical of the many children each year who become the victims of child abuse.

The **fictional story** is made up for the purpose of your speech. Often it is intended as a composite sketch designed to be a typical story. One speaker began her speech with this fictional story.

> I'd like to tell you the story of "Mrs. Bradley." Mrs. Bradley is an 84-year-old resident of Leisure Lodge Nursing Home. She cleans her room at least 12 times a day because there is nothing else for her to do. She has no living relatives in the local area to visit her, and she

doesn't like to socialize with the other residents. She used to milk the cows and feed the chickens every day on her farm. But as her medical needs increased and she was forced to enter Leisure Lodge, she was also forced to give up her loving animal companions and all the responsibility that went with caring for them. Mrs. Bradley's situation is typical of a circumstance in our state that is hindering thousands of elderly people in our state's nursing homes. For, you see, Mrs. Bradley is forbidden to keep any sort of pet animals with her in the nursing home environment.

The **humorous story,** whether based on fact or made up for the occasion, has as its distinguishing characteristic the attempt to induce the audience to laugh. It has a punch line. Humor is especially effective in reducing barriers between a speaker and an audience and in binding the individual listeners together into a collective audience. Remember, though, that humor does not help your speech if the humor has little to do with the point you are trying to make. The audience may get the punch line but wonder what's the point.

Recounting a **historical event** may serve many purposes, especially in helping set up a context for a contemporary speech on a longstanding problem or in presenting the distant history of some modern topic. The following example, retelling the story of the discovery of the first terrarium, serves the latter purpose: telling the audience the unusual origins of a current informative topic.

In 1827, Dr. Nathaniel Ward, a London physician, was experimenting with caterpillars, putting them in glass jars so he could observe them as they emerged from the pupa stage. One day he noticed that one of the jars he had used and left stoppered on a shelf had something growing in it that was not a caterpillar! He looked more closely and saw it was a tiny fern. Somehow, a fern spore had found its way into the jar and had germinated in a spot of mold that had formed on the jar bottom. Dr. Ward was so excited about his discovery that he dropped his caterpillar research and started building larger versions of the jar for further experiments. To his surprise and delight, he discovered that he was able to grow ferns and other tropical plants in the enclosed soil for as long as 15 years. Ward called his glass gardens terrariums, and in the late 1830s, no self-respecting Victorian household was without one.

Statistics

Many of the subjects you will be talking about have important aspects that can be measured or counted. "Ralph Sampson is 7 feet 4 inches tall." "Inflation is down to 4 percent annually." "We've sold 20 percent more widgets this year than last." **Statistics** are numerically formulated facts. They are reports concerning the quantities of something measured in some appropriate unit. Statistics are especially useful when you want to make your point seem more precise and more impressive. Well-used statistics give your ideas more impact because they emphasize the magnitude of something. Statistics may be used in at least five ways:

To report **Absolute Magnitudes.** Sometimes you will simply wish to report how big something is or how many of something there are.

> The English language has nearly 700,000 words.

To make **Quantitative Comparisons.** Statistics may also be used to report quantitative comparisons of one thing with another. For example, if you were talking about the amount spent on state services in various regions of the country, you might need to make a comparison like this one:

> In 1976, Alabama spent $94.28 per capita on highway maintenance, but California spent only $53.88.

If you were trying to compare criminal activity in various major cities, you might present statistics such as the following:

> According to the FBI index on crime, New York City is by far the most dangerous city in America. Whereas Chicago reports 203,000 incidents annually, and Los Angeles reports about 217,000 incidents, New York City reports a whopping 610,000 incidents annually.

To **Chart Trends.** Often you will want to quantify changes that occur in some situation over time—from day to day, month to month, or year to year. To compare the magnitude of some thing, situation, or attribute at various periods of time is to use statistics to chart trends. In the example below, the speaker is charting trends in murder rates.

> During the years between 1968 and 1983, the murder rate in the United States has continued to increase at an alarming rate. In 1968/69 it jumped 7 percent over the previous year; in 1969/70, 8 percent; in 70/71, 11 percent. For the next three years, it grew at 5 percent per year. In only two of the years since 1968 has the murder rate either declined or held steady when compared with the previous year.

To **Suggest Relationships.** Statistics are also often used to suggest relations between magnitudes of two or more different phenomena. If your sales force increased by 20 percent last year, did this produce a corresponding rise in your actual sales? If so, is there a relationship? If the sales rates were flat, is there some other quantifiable factor that played a part? Perhaps these numbers may be used to suggest a causal relationship. In the example below, the speaker uses statistics to show that the increasing use of early discovery techniques and preventive measures is inversely related to the incidence of certain forms of cancer.

> Uterine cancer mortality has declined 65 percent during the last 40 years due to the wider application of the pap smear; 80 percent of all lung cancers would be prevented if no one smoked cigarettes.

To **Summarize.** Often your audience does not need to hear a rundown of each and every instance of something. What it needs is a summary of large amounts of quantitative data in a relatively brief form. For example, if you were talking about incomes in America, reading even a small sample of people's individual incomes would be impossible. Instead, you would probably want to deal with averages of some sort. Accordingly, you might report:

> According to the Bureau of Economic Analysis, the average annual income in 1976 in the U.S. was $6,399. But Alaska's per capita average was $10,415, the District of Columbia's was $8,067, and New Jersey's was $7,381.

As you can see, statistics allow you to summarize vast numbers of individual instances in a relatively brief set of figures.

Use Statistics Fairly A little knowledge of statistics is a dangerous thing. Statistics must be used carefully if you are to fairly represent the situation you are talking about. Statistics are one of the easiest supporting materials to misuse—so much so that Darrell Huff has written a famous book entitled *How to Lie with Statistics* (1954). Huff's point is not to teach you how use statistics to deceive; rather, it is about how to avoid being deceived when others use statistics and how to avoid inadvertently deceiving others by your own use of statistics. The book is well worth reading if you will be using statistics often and are concerned about whether or not you are using them fairly. Short of reading Huff's book, what is involved in using your statistics fairly? Over and above the general ethical considerations mentioned in Chapter 4, the following three aspects of fairness are especially important when you use statistics as a form of supporting material for your speeches.

Reveal who generated your statistics. Statistics are generated by many groups and organizations in order to support their points of view. It may make a difference, for example, whether a right-to-life or a pro-choice group generated the statistics you plan to use during your speech on abortion. Although you may firmly believe in the integrity of the group whose statistics you are citing, your audience has the right to know where the numbers came from. In that way they can make their own judgments concerning whether or not there is some potential for bias. Since it doesn't take but a second to do so, identify the source of your statistics.

Explain which type of "average" you are using. When you are using statistics to summarize large amounts of quantitative data in a relatively brief form, you are most likely reporting on averages. "The average income in

Texas in 1976 was $6,201." "The average state divorce rate in America in 1984 was 9.9 per thousand marriages." There are several ways to calculate an average, but they are not all alike. Calculating the *mean* average of some set of numbers involves simply adding up all the individual numbers and dividing the sum total by the number of members. The *median* average is calculated by arranging all the numbers in the set from lowest to highest and finding the one that is halfway in the list. The *modal* average identifies the number that appears most frequently in the set.

For example, suppose you want to find the average of the following set of numbers:

1	2	2	2	2	2	3	4	5	5	6	7	9
10	10	10										

To find the mean, you would add up all the numbers and divide by 16. The mean average would be 5. To find the median, you would simply count down eight numbers and take that number as the average. That number is 4. To discover the mode, you would look for the number that appears most often. The mode is 2.

As you can see, each method of calculating the average results in a different "average." When you can determine it, report which average was employed to develop the statistic you are reporting. Your report might sound something like this: "According to the *Farm Journal,* the median farm income for all wheat farms in Kansas was. . . ."

Extrapolate trends reasonably. In using statistics to chart trends, the goal is often to use the events of the past to predict what will happen in the future by projecting the course of the statistical trend. This process of projecting a trend is called extrapolation. Extrapolating in order to make predictions about the future is intrinsically dangerous because the extrapolation can be based on unreasonable assumptions. Mark Twain provides a clever example of just how far astray a careless extrapolator may go:

> In the space of one hundred and seventy-six years the Lower Mississippi has shortened itself two hundred and forty-two miles. That is an average of a trifle over one mile and a third per year. Therefore, any calm person, who is not blind or idiotic, can see that in the Old Oolitic Silurian Period, just a million years ago next November, the Lower Mississippi River was upwards of one million three hundred thousand miles long, and stuck out over the Gulf of Mexico like a fishing-rod. And by the same token any person can see that seven hundred and forty-two years from now the Lower Mississippi will be only a mile and three quarters long, and Cairo [Illinois] and New Orleans will have joined their streets together and be plodding comfortably along under a single mayor and a mutual board of aldermen. There is something fascinating about science. One gets such wholesale returns of conjecture out of such a trifling investment of fact.

In order to avoid being as humorously off-base as Twain was in the example above, be sure that the assumptions you are using as the basis for your extrapolations are reasonable—that is, that they take into account significant limiting forces that may alter the course or magnitude of the trend you are trying to extrapolate.

Interpret Statistics for Your Audience Statistics rarely "speak for themselves." Instead, you must speak for them, telling the audience what you believe their significance to be. If, for example, the per capita income in your state "has gone up 250 percent in the last 10-year period," that sounds impressive. But are your citizens better off? Is your purchasing power increasing or decreasing when general inflation is taken into account? The raw statistics do not tell us. So you must answer such questions, interpreting the significance of your numbers for your audience.

Such interpretation can be either of two types: *verbal elaboration* and *commonsense comparison.* To elaborate is simply to give a fuller explanation of something you have previously said. In a verbal elaboration, you seek to answer the important questions raised by the statistics: What do they mean? Why are they significant? You will be describing what you think the statistics indicate or suggest concerning the point you are trying to make.

In developing commonsense comparisons you try to give the raw statistics greater impact by comparing their absolute magnitude with some commonplace reference point that is more familiar to the audience. Such comparisons, when done well, are often very memorable. The following two examples attempt to interpret the significance of raw statistics into more personally meaningful terms by the use of a vivid commonsense comparison.

In a speech about the immensity of the sun's size, and the enormity of its thermal power, the speaker first observed that

> The sun is an incredibly immense controlled thermonuclear reactor. To sense the magnitude of the sun's physical size, consider the following: The diameter of the sun is about 1 million miles across, compared with the earth's puny 8000-mile girth. *Over 1 million earths* would fit comfortably inside the sun. Let the sun be an *orange* and the earth would then be a *grain of sand* circling in orbit around the sun at a distance of 30 feet.

The speaker then followed this statement with a second observation: "The sun generates tremendous physical forces every second." He elaborated with the following statistics and commonsense comparisons:

> The pressure at the center of the sun is a billion times as great as the atmospheric pressure on earth. The gravity at the sun's surface is 28 times as great as the gravity here on earth. Thus, if you were a 98-pound weakling here on earth, you'd weigh a whopping 2744 pounds on the sun—as much as a small circus elephant. The sun

radiates as much energy every second as would be released by several billion atomic bombs all exploding simultaneously. Even though the earth only receives two billionths of this energy, that's still over 4.5 million horsepower per square mile reaching the earth's atmosphere every second: more than enough to power every automobile in a city the size of Houston.

Visualize Your Statistics Another way to give your statistics more impact is to present them visually as well as verbally. The power of charts and graphs to emphasize statistical information is treated in Chapter 11.

Chain a Series of Statistics Together To help you project the overwhelming magnitude of some point you are making, you might try chaining together a series of statistics, one after another. The speaker cited above, talking about the magnitude of the sun's forces, used just such a technique—linking statistics to evoke an overwhelming feeling of the sun's immensity, enhancing and magnifying the effects the statistics might have had if presented individually. Reread the two selections, noticing how the speaker weaves together a series of quantitative facts about the sun to create a feeling about the sun that is greater than the facts alone might have evoked.

*Q*uotations

Quotations are statements made by others that you use to support the points you are making. Two circumstances in particular call for the use of quotations. First, you should plan to quote someone if the person you are quoting formulates the point you are trying to make in an especially clear, interesting, or memorable way. Second, a quotation can be used to help you demonstrate that someone else—usually someone having higher credibility with your audience than you do—shares your ideas on a particular topic. The functions of quotations, then, are to add emphasis, variety, and authority to your speech.

There are several types of quotations you may find useful in preparing your speeches, each having its own special role to play in developing your speech. First, you may quote an important expert on the subject of your speech. In addition to helping capture your audience's attention, this use of quotations also helps establish your own credibility—by subtly expressing the fact that you have done research on the topic and by lending the weight of the authority to your own. For example, you might say:

> Supreme Court Justice Louis Brandeis knew what he was talking about when he said: "Experience should teach us . . . the greatest dangers to liberty lurk in insidious encroachment by men of zeal, well meaning but without understanding."

"Like an insect version of Genghis Khan," writes *Time Magazine,* "the fierce Brazilian bees are coming. Millions of them are swarming northward from the Brazilian basin at the rate of 200 miles a year, liquidating passive colonies of native bees in their path, quick to sting—and sometimes kill—any unwary animal or person. At their present rate," *Time* continues, "they will conquer all of South America in the next ten years, and start to invade Central America. Unless stopped by man, the bees will eventually invade Mexico and the southern U.S." What can be done to stop these killer bees, so forcefully described by the writer in *Time?*

W. O. Greenwood raises the question I would like to address in my speech today when he asks: "Did these fortuitously prepared aggregations of molecules need the touch of the Master in order that they should live or did they just live because they had reached an appropriate complexity?" What Greenwood is talking about is . . .

Second, you may decide to quote from someone who has artistically captured your theme in a pithy phrase that epitomizes the point you would like to make, and therefore gets the speech or point started with some imaginative power. Your speech then develops the theme captured in the words of the quote.

Adlai Stevenson has been quoted as saying that Americans would rather "discuss a question without settling it, than to settle a question without discussing it." We are a government by talk and these words are as true in today's ever more complex world as they were when Stevenson uttered them.

Third, you may use a popular maxim, famous literary quote, or popular cultural expression to capture your audience's attention and direct it toward the point you are trying to make. Each of the following examples uses a quote in this way.

"When it rains, it pours." While that's a good description of our weather here recently, it is also one of the most famous advertising slogans around. For many of you it may conjure up the image of a round, blue box with the picture of a little girl carrying an umbrella on it. That is, to most of us, those words mean "salt."

"Star light, star bright, first star I see tonight. I wish I may, I wish I might, have the wish I wish tonight." These words are the words of a superstition we have all used or heard at one time or another.

"A rose by any other name would smell as sweet." Perhaps they would *smell* as sweet, but would they *sell* as sweet? As the daughter of a florist here in town, I . . .

"The trouble with START is to stop!" Do you remember that slogan for a once-popular orange drink? If you don't, perhaps it's because the slogan hasn't been in use for a long time now. If you do remember it . . .

Quotations are a significant resource for developing your speech. But it is important not to misuse them if they are to remain effective. Therefore, be aware of several cautions as you select quotations for use in your speeches.

Limit the number of quotations you use. Your speech must be *yours.* Quotations support points *you* wish to make. To quote too frequently or too extensively is to risk not only plagiarism, but also to lose your own ideas in the process. Speeches are not to be patchworks of quotations sewn together by a few comments of your own; they are your own ideas supported with the words of others.

Quote honestly. Give credit to the originator as fully as is reasonably possible. He or she said it first and, accordingly, deserves to be properly acknowledged.

Quote fairly. Although you will often need to edit quoted material to an appropriate length, make sure that you do not in the process distort what your source intended to say. Quote in context, supplying that context for your audience, if necessary.

Introduce your quotations unobtrusively. Quotations may be introduced into your speech in several ways. You might say: "According to . . ." or "Jack Smith says. . . ." Using formulas such as these makes it unnecessary to use the intrusive and distracting "quote . . . unquote" at the beginnings and endings of quoted material. Instead, use your voice to indicate that you've begun or completed quoting from someone else.

Comparisons and Contrasts

You cannot directly *cause* someone else to understand your ideas simply by presenting your message. All you can really hope to do is to structure and develop your message in a way that makes audience understanding possible. One way of helping induce audience understanding is to use comparisons and contrasts in order to take advantage of knowledge the audience already has. Comparisons and contrasts help build a mental bridge between ideas the audience already understands and the new ideas and information you are trying to explain.

Comparisons and contrasts are attempts to explain the unknown in terms of the known—the unfamiliar in terms of the familiar. **Comparisons** point out similarities between some concept, skill, object, or process that you are trying to explain and some other concept, skill, object, or process with which your audience is already familiar. For example, in a recent advertisement for Lockheed (*Science 84,* Jan./Feb.), which describes the precision with which a new space telescope can hold its position on a distant object, the technique of comparison is used to help the readers comprehend the degree of precision that has been achieved. The ad begins by giving the technical details first.

> And how precise is that lock-on? In angular measurement, there are 1,296,000 arc-seconds in a circle. For perhaps as long as 20 hours at a time, the telescope will hold onto a target with a stability accuracy of just *seven thousandths of one arc-second* in all directions.

Then, to help the reader understand just what this means in more common-sense terms, the ad uses the following comparison.

> That stability is 100 times greater than any ever achieved so far. It about equals standing in Boston and holding rifle sights steady on a dime suspended over Washington, D.C.!

Thus, to make your speech vivid and more readily understood, use comparisons to help your audience understand.

Contrasts point out dissimilarities between two such concepts, skills, objects, or processes. They are used to help audiences distinguish between things that may seem similar or to help them see subtle but significant differences. Comparisons and contrasts are especially important forms of supporting material when the idea you are trying to communicate is difficult but important to grasp. The effect of a well-used comparison or contrast is to help make your speech more vivid, more easily understood, and more memorable.

*D*escriptions

To **describe** is to create a mental picture of some place, object, or process through the use of words. Your goal in description is to help your audience imagine whatever you are describing. Painting a verbal picture requires you to focus upon specific, concrete details. Although the notion of a picture suggests the visual sense, good descriptions are not restricted to evoking visual images. In fact, descriptions may include details about such things as size, shape, weight, color, texture, internal structure, material composition, age and physical condition, function, and position relative to other objects in space.

When using description as a form of support, try to be *succinct, specific,* and *structured.* Descriptions must be structured in an organized pattern (see Chapter 9) rather than a random collection of facts. They should be as brief as the point you are making permits in order to allow you to move on to other aspects of your topic. And, most of all, descriptions must be specific in details.

To use descriptions more effectively to support your speech, there are three guidelines to follow to make the descriptions more alive:

Use more than one sensory mode if possible. Since most objects and places appeal to many senses, don't limit your descriptions to only one sense or dimension. Unless your purpose is best served by one-dimensional description, employ additional senses.

Create animation or motion if possible. Although it is possible to describe something by giving random details, it is far better to organize your description so that you create a sense of reasonable progression. If, as you describe something, you also emphasize the organizational principle you are using, you will create a sense of forward motion in your speech and give your description additional living qualities.

Use comparisons if possible. Whenever you describe something novel to an audience, it may be difficult for them to begin the process of getting a mental picture. You can help them begin imagining what you are describing if you compare whatever you are describing with something with which the audience is already familiar. This takes advantage of their prior knowledge, saving you descriptive work and furthering your ability to help them imagine and understand your description.

*C*onclusion

Human minds are complex and varied. Psychological individuation has seen to that. Because different audience members respond more positively to some kinds of supporting material than to others, it is important as you encode your ideas into words to cast those ideas in a variety of different forms of supporting material. Do not restrict yourself to only one or two kinds. Some audience members will be attuned to the quantitative impact that only precise statistics can provide; others will be moved by the personal anecdote that focuses attention on the situation of a single individual. Still others will understand best and be moved most by descriptions or by a series of brief examples. A single mode of projecting your ideas will not necessarily be best for everyone.

Speeches develop by the thoughtful use of a variety of types of supporting material. Examples, anecdotes, statistics, and all the others can add to the power and impact of your speeches. Using each of the types of developmental material discussed in this chapter can bring your speech to life, animate your ideas, and help your audience to better understand and longer remember what you have to say. If the goal is to make your speech as alive as possible, vivid and varied supporting material is vital. Using the seven types of developmental material described in this chapter will help bring your speech to life by fleshing out the skeleton of key ideas that your framework of main points represents.

Questions for Review

1. What are the seven forms of supporting material for speeches? When should each of them be used?

2. What is the difference between the intension and extension of a word? How does changing a word's intension typically affect the word's extension?

3. What is a parable? What is a personal anecdote? When is a fictional anecdote preferable to an actual first or third person incident?

Questions for Discussion

1. If you have a choice among an anecdote, a statistic, and a hypothetical example to support a point in your speech, what considerations would be relevant to deciding which form of support to use? For example, are there audience characteristics that would make a difference in the type of supporting materials you use (for example, demographic, social, or conceptual involvements)?

2. Where would you look to find each of the various forms of supporting material if you were preparing a speech on: (a) some aspect of your major, (b) a controversial topic, such as prayer in the schools or changing the abortion statutes?

Things to Try

Support the following claim with an instance of each of the seven forms of support:

"There are many unique benefits to living in our state."

Bibliography

Brigance, W. N. *Speech: Its Techniques and Disciplines in a Free Society.* 2nd ed. New York: Appleton-Century-Crofts, 1961.

Eliot, T. S. *Collected Poems.* New York: Harcourt, Brace and World, 1962, pp. 81–82.

Huff, Darrell. *How to Lie with Statistics.* New York: W. W. Norton, 1954.

Organizing the Body of Your Informative Speech

When Plato said that a speech must be like a living creature, more than anything else he meant that a speech must be *organized* like a living creature: "with its own body, as it were; it must not lack either head or feet; it must have a middle and extremities so composed as to suit each other and the whole work." Even the simplest single-celled organism is intricately organized in both space and time. So, too, must a speech be organically organized. Without a "lifelike" organization, a speech cannot be alive in any other sense.

What does it mean to say that a speech must have a lifelike organization? Traditionally, Plato's organic metaphor has always meant two things: (1) that the overall speech must be divided into functionally separate parts, known as the *introduction, body,* and *conclusion* (Plato's "head," "body," and "feet"), and (2) that each of these parts must be closely related to the others, so that they add up to a coherent and singular whole (Plato's "so composed as to suit each other and the whole work").

But by now it should be clear that the organic metaphor means much more than this. It also means that your speech must seem to exemplify the act form—both as a whole and in all of its parts. Your speech must always seem to be an organized progression from one phase to the next. Earlier phases of the speech must seem to prepare the way for later ones. Your speech must seem to exemplify the organic characteristics of **internal preparation, forward motion, growth, climax,** and **closure.**

The purpose of this chapter is to help you learn to organize your informative speeches so that they have a more lifelike quality. We will begin by describing the six major patterns for organizing an informative speech. These six patterns can be adapted for use with persuasive speeches, but they are far more typical in informative speeches. (Patterns of organization that are more appropriate to persuasive speeches will be described in Chapter 16.) The second part of the chapter will explain how to refine the organization of your speeches so that they have the necessary sense of progression to fulfill the five organic qualities discussed in Chapter 3.

*T*he Systems of a Speech

Just as a human being is composed of different systems (circulatory, digestive, respiratory, neural), each with its own functions to perform, so it is with your speech. Your speech has three main systems, each with its own primary functions and its own requirements for organization: the introduction, the body, and the conclusion. In addition to the three main systems of the speech, a fourth system binds them all together into a larger whole. This system we call

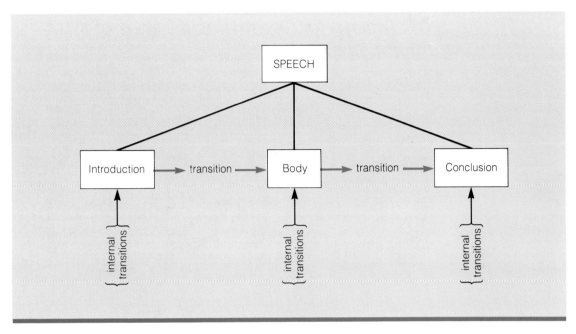

Figure 9-1   The Four Systems of a Speech

the transitions. Thus, the study of speech organization can be divided into four aspects, as diagrammed in Figure 9-1.

When thinking about your speech as a living organism, remember that the terms *introduction, body,* and *conclusion* do not simply mean "beginning," "middle," and "end." There's more to it than that. The reason each different phase of the speech has its own separate name is that each part has its own function to perform and its own pattern of organization to follow. The **introduction** is the speech's impulse phase and must prepare the way for what is to follow. Its major function is to create an appetite or expectation for the rest of the speech. The **body** must develop and systematically complete all the promises made in the introduction. It must also lead to a climax for the speech as a whole, a climax that leads smoothly to the cadence or **conclusion.** The conclusion wraps up the speech, giving the audience a feeling of satisfying completion.

What makes a speech seem organic and alive, then, is this sense of progression from phase to phase. Since the body of the speech is usually prepared first—because you usually have to decide what you are going to say before you can decide how you will introduce it—we will first discuss the arrangement of the speech's body. Chapter 10 will explain how to develop and organize the three other main speech systems: the introduction, conclusion, and transitions.

Six Patterns for Organizing the Body of the Informative Speech

The body of your informative speech is your main discussion. Its function is to present and develop your ideas concerning your topic. In preparing your speech's body you have three significant responsibilities:

1. You must divide your topic clearly into two to five main points.

2. You must arrange those main points into some definite **pattern** of organization.

3. You must develop each point adequately with a variety of supporting materials.

In a speech, you cannot present all aspects of your topic at once. The audience must be able to use your individual words to build up a conception of the ideas you are trying to communicate. To help guide your audience in understanding your ideas amid your sea of words, you will need to divide your topic into a number of smaller units. Although it is possible to have a brief, "one point" speech, speeches of any length will need at least two parallel major divisions. But what is the maximum number of main points a speech may have? Although three main points is probably the preferred number by most speakers, five is typically the most main points an audience can be expected to remember. In a clever set of articles, George Miller (1967) demonstrated that five to seven "chunks" of new information is about the limit of a person's immediate short-term memory at any one time. Since an audience must remember what you have said if they are to act on it, dividing your speech into no more than five major chunks should keep your speech's organizational plan within the immediate memory capability of most audience members.

Dividing your topic into a number of smaller chunks for rapid transmission involves selecting some organizing principle. These units help your audience to more easily understand your ideas. Having a definite principle for dividing your topic provides a key to understanding how the parts of the speech relate to one another and to the overall speech as a whole. The main **principle of division** you use for your speech determines which **pattern of organization** you will be using. For example, if your major principle of division is "the order in which things happen," then your pattern of organization is "chronological." If your principle of division is "where things are in relation to one another in space," then your pattern of organization will be "spatial." There are at least six common patterns of organization for informative speeches.

1. Chronological order

2. Spatial order

3. Topical order

4. Cause-to-Effect order

5. Simple-to-Complex order

6. Comparison and contrast order

Chronological Order

Chronological order organizes your speech according to the order in which events occur in a sequence of time. For example, in a speech on learning to fly an airplane, you might divide your speech into four major steps:

1. Ground school

2. Flight school

3. Flying with an instructor

4. The solo flight

In this case, the speaker has begun "at the beginning" and moved progressively from the earliest type of training to the final stage in the process. We can also reverse the order and move from the most recent period of time back to the most distant. This might be done when you want to systematically trace the precursors of some current phenomenon. For example, a speech on the history of flight might begin not with the Wright brothers but instead with Neil Armstrong's first step on the moon.

Chronological order is especially useful when you want to explain how to do something, how something works, how something is made, and how some current or historical situation came to be as it is today, or as it was at a particular moment in time. Here are a few examples of topics that are good candidates for organization by chronological order.

▲ How to do something
How to make a stained glass window
How to plan a sales call

▲ How something works
How black and white film produces a negative image
How a microprocessor handles computer data

▲ How something is made
How hot dogs are manufactured
How scrap iron is reprocessed

▲ How some current situation came to be as it is today
How the U. S. came to be militarily involved in Central America
How the American automobile industry lost its preeminent status in world production

▲ How something in the past happened

How the South American Indians lost control of their lands to the Spanish explorers

How the Great Pyramid came to be built

Using chronological order effectively involves at least two steps: dividing the continuum of temporal events you plan to talk about into from two to five major time periods, and ordering your telling of these major component events so that they seem to exhibit the qualities of internal preparation, forward motion, growth, climax, and closure.

Dividing the natural continuum of time into smaller chunks requires you to look for significant peaks of activity within the overall process. These peaks of activity serve as focuses for your main points. In general, most processes can be easily broken into four time periods, which follow the act form rather precisely: (1) preparatory events, (2) developmental events, (3) culminating events, and (4) concluding events. To see how this is so, let's look at a typical chronologically ordered speech—the how-to speech.

Whenever you explain how to do something—whether it is how to cook a soufflé, refinish a piece of furniture, or program a computer—the first step is almost always a *preparatory* one. Thus, you might find yourself saying something like: "The first step in the process of _____ is gathering together the materials you will need." For example, each of the three processes mentioned above begins with a preparatory period during which one must assemble the materials needed to accomplish the process:

I. Preparatory Events—Assembling the Materials

Soufflé	*Furniture Refinishing*	*Computer Programming*
Eggs	Stripper	Hardware
Cream	Sandpaper	Software
Salt	Rags	
	Brushes	
	New finish	

The second major step in the process is always *developmental*. This step takes the materials gathered together during the first step and begins to use them to accomplish the task that is the purpose of the process. The developmental phase ends at the point where you reach the actual purpose of the process and are ready to explain how to accomplish it. For example:

II. Developmental Events—Using the Materials

Soufflé	*Furniture Refinishing*	*Computer Programming*
Mixing the ingredients	Preparing the old surface	Planning and entering the program

The third step is always the climax or culmination of the process: the stage where you explain how to do that part of the process that actually yields the final desired result. In the three examples being developed here, the culminating phase might be labeled as follows:

III. Culminating Events—Accomplishing the Task

Soufflé	*Furniture Refinishing*	*Computer Programming*
Cooking the soufflé	Applying the new finish	Test running/debugging the program

The final step of the process tells your audience what happens after the main process itself is complete. Sometimes this explanation is fairly elaborate and detailed; at other times it is brief and swiftly accomplished. Either way, there is usually some postclimactic part of the process that needs comment to bring the process to a satisfying resolution.

IV. Concluding Events—Closing the Task Off

Soufflé	*Furniture Refinishing*	*Computer Programming*
Garnishing and serving the soufflé	Cleaning the brushes or displaying the furniture	Putting the program to work

Chronological processes may not always be neatly divisible into exactly four steps, but the four phases of the act form should nevertheless underlie all chronologically ordered speeches—whether you are telling how to do something, how something works, how something is made, or how something came to pass historically. Fewer or greater numbers of steps may be needed for particular speeches depending on how you choose to divide the substeps of the process. Often the rising phase is divided into two or more substeps of nearly equal importance. That is, two or more of the process's subacts are featured. At other times, you may decide to omit any reference to the postculmination events.

Before closing this section on chronological order, it is also important to note that this four-phase analysis of a process may be used with all types of processes, not just with how-to processes. For example, any historical event can be cast in the form of a dramatic narrative that has preparatory conditions, developmental events, culminating events, and declining events. Thus, if you were retelling the history of the Iranian revolution, there would likely be a section narrating the events that prepared the way for the revolution's start, a section telling how the revolution began to accelerate and develop from those beginnings, a portion explaining how the revolution culminated in Ayatollah Khomeini's rise to power, and a postscript describing what has happened in the time since. Virtually any process takes this form—at least when it is narrated using verbal symbolism (Fisher, 1984; 1985).

Spatial Order

Whenever you give directions for how to get somewhere, you are using spatial order. You are telling the listeners where their destination is, taking them from location to location in order to get them where they want to go. Although they would of course follow the steps in chronological order, what you are featuring when you give directions is the spatial order of the relative locations of things in comparison with one another. Spatial order is also used when you are describing a place—that is, when you are giving your audience an idea of how the place is organized geographically.

Spatial order requires that you divide the space to be described into from two to five significant subunits and that you arrange your presentation of those subunits in such a way that the order you choose suggests some definite pattern of movement from one subunit to the next. Spatially ordered speeches, like chronologically ordered ones, should not be static.

To see the importance of grouping your spatial organization into subunits, imagine how you typically give directions to someone. You start from here and say something like this: "Go to the third stoplight and turn right. Go all the way to the new shopping mall and turn left. The zoo will be about four blocks." What you have done in this "speech" is to divide the route to the zoo into three major landmarks and three directions for action. Thus, this set of directions was accomplished in three major steps.

Creating a sense of forward motion is easy enough when your goal is to tell someone how to get from here to there. But spatial organization has other uses, including description of a place. It is also used as a way of organizing nondescriptive speeches in which geographical locations are important but are not themselves the actual point of the speech. However, even when you are not telling someone how to get from one place to another, but are merely talking about items that are located at particular geographical places, it is important to order your points in a way that gives your speech a sense of progression. For example, a speech on your five favorite national parks could be ordered from north to south if the parks were Yellowstone, Rocky Mountain, the Grand Canyon, the Petrified Forest, and Big Bend. Emphasizing east to west would be possible if the parks were Yosemite, Carlsbad, Hot Springs, the Great Smoky Mountains, and the Everglades.

Depending upon your topic and the goals you've set for your speech, some of the principles of spatial progression you might employ include the following:

1. North to south; east to west, and so on

2. Right, center, left

3. Near to far; far to near

4. Front to back; back to front

5. Top, middle, bottom

6. Around a circle or semicircle

Whichever principle of spatial progression you choose, you should subtly re-emphasize the principle you are using by mentioning it occasionally at significant points during your speech. For example, you might say, "Now that we've seen the natural wonders offered by highland parks such as Yellowstone and Rocky Mountain, let's drive southward along Interstate 25 toward Carlsbad Caverns, where we will plunge nearly a half mile into the earth." This transitional mention of the direction you are traveling and the contrasts you will develop, help the audience to *feel* the sense of progression and forward motion you are trying to induce. Climax may be achieved by choosing a spatial order in which each unit of space not only moves in a direction, but also progresses in terms of interest value to the audience.

Topical Order

Topical order organizes your speech around a set of categories that are either relatively standard and/or natural for your subject or that you have created especially for the occasion. Topical order involves dividing the subject into a small set of significant categories or "topics," and ordering your presentation of the topics in a way that would be meaningful and memorable to your audience. For example, if you were to talk about the structure of your school's personnel, you might decide upon three topics: (1) the administration, (2) the faculty, and (3) the support staff. This would be a relatively natural and standard way of dividing the school's personnel.

Topical order is used when your speech's goal is to characterize or overview some subject. But topical order is not simply a catchall term inviting you to say whatever you want to say about a topic because "those are the topics I chose to talk about." Topical *order* is not an excuse for random selection. It is a definite *pattern* of organization. In fact, topical order rests upon carefully using a specific principle for dividing your topic: the principle of **analysis and classification.**

Analysis is the process of breaking a subject down into its component parts for closer scrutiny. **Classification** is the process of grouping the parts together into meaningful subsets or units for ease of understanding. If, for example, your speech were an introduction to antique collecting, you might decide that there were five major types of collectibles:

1. Furniture

2. Personal memorabilia

3. Clothing

4. Glassware

5. Household/kitchen devices

This list represents the results of your analysis and classification. You have divided the subject into its parts (all the things that might be collected) and grouped the parts together into a small number of categories (the types of collectibles). These categories would then each constitute one of your five major points or topics. Your speech would not necessarily have to cover all five topics, but your analysis and classification has given you a relatively complete breakdown of the total subject matter so that you have a better basis for choosing which topics you will actually speak about during a particular speech.

To test the quality of your analysis and classification before you begin arranging the individual topics into the pattern of organization, you should ask the following questions about your work:

1. *Is my analysis complete?* That is, have I broken the subject down and listed all the major parts of the subject matter I intend to talk about?

2. *Is my classification system appropriate?*
   a. Does it really fit the subject matter? That is, would most members of my audience consider it relevant and appropriate?
   b. Does each category exclude members of the other categories? Or are there some items that could fit relatively easily into more than one category? If many items could fit into several categories, the classes are not specific enough and need to be refined.
   c. Is the category system comprehensive? That is, is there an appropriate class for all the items discovered by the process of analysis? If there are a significant number of items that do not fit into any of the established classes, then the category system once again needs to be refined.

Once you have analyzed your subject matter thoroughly and have classified it appropriately, you must arrange it in a meaningful and memorable order. Again, you will look for ways to employ the principles of forward motion and climax if at all possible. Some subjects may suggest an order of presentation immediately—from least important to most important, for example. But, for the most part, analysis and classification does not in itself dictate a principle that determines a preferred order of presentation. Analysis and classification merely divides the topic and groups its component parts together.

For example, what intrinsic order is there in the items for the speech on antique collecting? They are just five types of collectibles. Since there is no obvious order of priority among the topics, you must create an order that allows you to evoke the feeling of forward motion and climax. Thus, you might decide to order the topics from large to small, or from relatively impersonal to more intimately personal items, as in the two examples below:

Large to Small	*Impersonal to Personal*
Furniture	Furniture
Household/kitchen devices	Household/kitchen devices
Clothing	Glassware
Glassware	Clothing
Personal memorabilia	Personal memorabilia

In each case the order is somewhat different, but the goal of creating forward motion and climax is the same. As long as you tell the audience the principle of movement and climax you are using (preferably during the introduction, to start the forward motion as early as possible) and remind your listeners of this principle at intervals throughout the speech (such as at the transitions between topics), the speech will seem to move, to pick up speed, and to reach a natural climax near the end. Without a principle of order underlying the "topics," the speech will seem randomly organized, far less interesting and lifeless.

Cause-to-Effect Order

Sometimes the goal of your informative speech is to explain *why* some important or interesting phenomenon occurs. If you gave a speech explaining why the swallows return to Capistrano on the same date each year or why consumer products seem to have life cycles similar to those of plants and animals, your speech would probably be best organized according to the cause-to-effect order of presentation.

The cause-to-effect order of presentation is used whenever you are trying to explain why something happened in the past, why it is happening in the present, or why it will happen in the future. Cause-to-effect order organizes the body of your speech around a series of causes or contributing causes that account for some observed effect. Each main point of the speech explores one of the causes of the effect you are trying to explain.

To use cause-to-effect order well involves developing a list of from two to five causes (or contributing causes) for the effect you are trying to explain and arranging them in an interesting order of presentation. Unlike topical order, cause-to-effect order suggests a natural organizational progression—*from* cause *to* effect. Overall, your speech's introduction will call attention to the effect you propose to explain, the body will present and develop the causes of that effect, and the conclusion will bring the audience's attention back to the effect itself. But since the body of your speech will probably develop several contributing causes rather than one grand cause, you still must decide upon the order in which you will present your list of contributing causes.

For some effects you might choose to talk about, there may be a direct chronological sequence of causes. X causes Y, which causes effect Z. You will then treat the causes in the order in which they occur. The simplest example of such a linear causal chain occurs in pool playing: The pool player A causes the pool cue B to strike the cue ball C, which strikes the 8-ball D, causing it to enter the side pocket E.

At other times the "causes" are not sequentially chained together but must all occur more or less simultaneously for the effect to occur: $A + B + C$ causes effect D. For example, in explaining the causes of a spontaneous murder in the neighborhood, you might note that crime in the neighborhood A had caused the murderer to buy a gun recently B; you might also note that the murderer had been drinking C on the night of the murder, and finally, that the murderer had come home early from work D to find his wife embracing another man E. Here there are five contributing causes, all of which needed to be in close temporal proximity for the spontaneous murder to occur.

Even in this second type of situation, where the contributing causes are all causally independent of one another, and yet must be present simultaneously, you must present the causes in a linear succession of words, and you must therefore decide upon an order of presentation that can suggest, if at all possible, movement and climax. In this case, the buying of the gun is chronologically first, but it is not the direct cause of either the drinking or the infidelity. But since it is a preliminary that is absolutely necessary for the other events to occur, it would probably be placed first in the sequence. Similarly, the bout of drinking is chronologically next in the causes, but it is neither the direct result of the gun purchase nor the direct cause of the wife's behavior. What this example illustrates is that you should find a reasonable method of ordering your presentation of causes, one that leads to some sense of building and forward motion. Whenever you use the cause-to-effect order, you should still attempt to find an organic principle for ordering the points.

Simple-to-Complex Order

When you are explaining some new or complex concept, principle, or device to your audience, you may wish to begin with a simpler concept, principle, or device and work by a series of incremental steps from the simpler to understand to the more complex. Each main point in the body of your speech then becomes a presentation of one of the increments between the simple starting place and the complex idea you are planning to explain.

When you use simple-to-complex order to arrange the points in your speech, you must select from two to five intervals between the simplest and most complex things you will treat and present them in a sequence that clearly moves progressively from simple to complex. The pattern itself helps create the sense of progression *from* simple *to* complex. The following example on scouting an opposing football team demonstrates a topic whose main points might be arranged from simple to complex.

SIMPLE

1. Watching the other team play a game.

2. Charting which plays they used.

3. Close analysis of films of their strategies and techniques

4. Computer breakdown of all the team's statistics and tendencies in certain situations.

COMPLEX

In this example, the simplest form of preparation that a scouting team might employ would be to go to the other team's game to watch how they play. This would give them a rough estimate of the other team's ability to pass and run the football, kick field goals, and defend against the pass and the rush. A more complex system of scouting would be to fill out a play-by-play chart of the plays the team ran during the course of a game. More complex yet is a close film analysis of the individual players' techniques, habits, tendencies, and weaknesses to see if those could be exploited by your team. Finally, you could use a computer to analyze all aspects of the other team's performance. This would also involve interpreting the statistical results and deciding how to use them to plan your own strategy. A speech explaining this sort of progression would be organized with simple-to-complex order.

Comparison and Contrast Order

We sometimes learn best by comparing and contrasting what we are learning with what we already know. How are two things, concepts, or principles similar or different from one another? Comparison and contrast order organizes a speech around a sequence of similarities and differences. Comparison and contrast order is used when the thing, concept, process, or principle you are trying to explain either is so new that your audience needs comparisons and contrasts with familiar things if they are even to begin to understand what you are explaining, or is so similar to something else that they need an emphasis on the differences so that they will not become confused between the old and the new.

A team of doctors and nurses performs major surgery. Have you ever been hospitalized? Should we have a system of national health care? Discuss an issue of medical ethics such as artificial organs, Living Wills, or euthanasia.

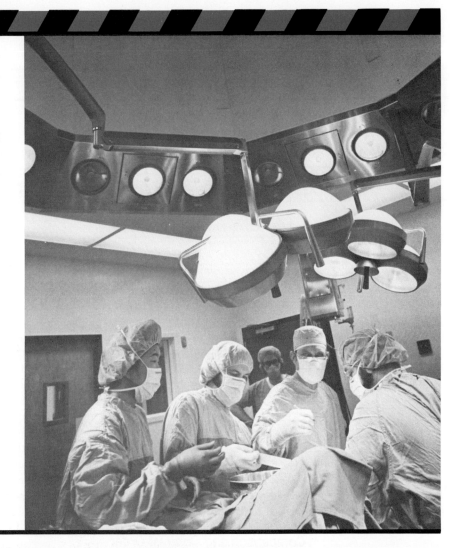

There are at least two ways to use comparison and contrast order to outline a speech. The first approach outlines the body of the speech into two major parts, as follows:

I. Similarities (Comparisons)
   A. Similarity #1
   B. Similarity #2
   C. Similarity #3

II. Differences (Contrasts)
   A. Difference #1

    B. Difference #2
    C. Difference #3

The second form outlines the body of the speech into two or more major parts, as follows:

I. Feature #1
    A. Similarities
    B. Differences

II. Feature #2
    A. Similarities
    B. Differences

III. Feature #3
    A. Similarities
    B. Differences

Thus, if you were presenting a speech on the similarities and/or differences between conventional medicine and chiropractic medicine, you might use the first pattern of organization if you wanted to emphasize similarities and differences *per se.* Under similarities, you might note that both attempt to heal the sick, both use modern technological equipment, and both perform detailed diagnostic checks prior to administering any kind of treatment. You would then develop a parallel list of differences. You would probably use the second pattern if you wanted to emphasize the areas of similarity and difference between the two approaches to medical practice—using as your features for comparison such areas as approaches to prevention of illness, use of drugs, and theories of the nature of illness.

Selecting a Pattern of Organization

Selecting a pattern of organization is not a matter of matching the ideal pattern to a particular topic or subject matter. Topics themselves do not usually dictate a particular pattern of organization. Your purpose on a particular occasion is the real force guiding the selection of a pattern of organization for your speech. Organizing a speech is a problem of strategic choice among options. Virtually all topics yield speeches that may be organized in several different ways. In fact, many topics could be organized using any of the six patterns of organization we have described.

    For example, if your general topic were "fishing," then any of the six patterns of organization might be useful to you, depending upon your specific purpose on a particular occasion. Take a look at some of the possible speeches that could be made about fishing and the pattern of organization that might best serve a speech on that particular aspect of fishing.

I. **Chronologically** ordered speeches on fishing
   A. The four steps in successful fly casting
   B. The best times to fish here in the local area
      1. The best times of day or night
      2. The best times of the month, year, and so on

II. **Spatially** ordered speeches on fishing
   A. The best places to fish within a 50-mile radius of our school
   B. The best places to fish along the local lakeshore or riverbed

III. **Topically** ordered speeches on fishing
   A. Common types of game fishing in our state
   B. The characteristics of the most popular sport fish locally

IV. **Cause-to-Effect** ordered speeches on fishing
   A. Causes for the seasonal fluctuations in fishing at the local lake (would include such things as temperature, light conditions, food, mating seasons, and so forth)
   B. Reasons why different types of lures work—with different types of fish, at different times of the day or year

V. **Simple-to-Complex** ordered speeches on fishing
   A. Equipment used to fish (from rod and string with a hook, to highly sophisticated electronic hardware, for example)
   B. Techniques used to fish (from simple casting with a worm to hand preparing all of your own bait and equipment)

VI. **Comparison and Contrast** ordered speeches on fishing
   A. Saltwater versus freshwater fishing
   B. Lake versus stream fishing
   C. Fishing versus crabbing
   D. Fishing alone versus fishing with a friend

Because most topics may be arranged using any of several patterns of organization, you might ask which pattern you should use for a particular speech. At least three factors can affect your choice of a pattern of organization.

The demands of the subject itself. The first question you should probably ask is "What are the demands of the subject matter itself?" That is, what choices or options does the subject matter permit you? If the topic is a general one such as fishing, then the options include all six patterns. But if your speech were "Computer Applications in the Modern Office," then you might immediately decide that topical order or simple-to-complex order, was the most appropriate. Thus, although the topic may not dictate a particular pattern of organization, it may place some fairly obvious restrictions on which patterns of organization are the most likely candidates for arranging the main points of your speech on a particular occasion. A how-to speech seems to demand chronological order, but a description of a place suggests a spatial pattern.

The demands of the audience. As you know from Chapter 7, audiences are not all identical to one another. Different audiences may have different needs—needs that may influence your choice of an organizational pattern. If, for example, your audience is already fairly knowledgeable about your topic, you may decide not to use simple-to-complex order, so as to avoid insulting your audience's intelligence. On the other hand, an uninformed audience might appreciate the gentle progression from simple to complex because it allows them to gradually build up the knowledge needed to understand your final points. Therefore, your audience's needs and expectations are important considerations as you plan your speech's organization. Take some time to analyze your audience in order to see if these needs and expectations place any special demands upon the pattern of organization you might choose to use on a particular occasion.

The demands of your purpose. Your purpose for giving the speech in the first place is probably the most important factor in your decision concerning which pattern of organization to choose for any particular speech. What are you trying to accomplish? By what division and progression of your ideas can you best hope to accomplish your goal? If, for example, your purpose is to explain the major steps in buying a new or used house, then either topical order (to emphasize the nature of the steps to be accomplished) or chronological order (to emphasize the order in which the steps need to be accomplished) would probably give your speech the best chance of success. Simple-to-complex order would probably be confusing since the appropriate chronology would be lost, and very little advantage would be gained in its place. Cause-to-effect order would seem to be completely useless for such a purpose. The point is, then, do not merely pick an order because it is *possible* to arrange your speech in that order. Consciously select an order of arrangement because it specifically serves your speech's purpose.

*R*efining Your Speech's Sense of Organization

Good speech organization should, of course, be clear and easy to follow. It should move from point to point, creating a definite sense of progression. If your speech organization did no more than create a sense of progression, it would animate your speech and give it a feeling of life. But you can do much more with your speech organization than merely arranging the main points in a progressive sequence; you can also build **layers** of organization into your speech so as to give it more and more living qualities. This section assumes that you have already prepared your basic speech and have arranged your main points into a definite pattern of organization that creates a sense of movement. As you read the following sections, remember that the organic qualities you are trying to create are internal preparation, forward motion, growth, climax, and closure.

Use Parallel Grammatical Form

One important way to emphasize the structure of your speech's organization and to create the desired organic qualities is to formulate each of your main points using the same grammatical pattern. In English, there are no more than a dozen or so basic ways to organize a sentence. The most common is

Subject—Transitive Verb—Object

Bill   *saw*   *Sally.*

Another is

Subject—Linking Verb—Adjective

Bill   *seems*   *upset.*

Selecting a single grammatical framework to formulate each of your main points sets up an expectation that helps your audience anticipate and more easily process your speech. It also creates organic qualities by the strategic use of repetition. For example, in a speech entitled "Pets: Good Therapy for the Elderly," the speaker had the following three main points:

I. Pets can help ease the transition from the home environment to the institutional setting.

II. The companionship animals provide would give the elderly more of a will to live.

III. Animals enable people to physically live longer.

Although these three points are each clear enough individually, together they have little cumulative impact. They create no forward motion and climax. By rewording points II and III to match the grammatical form of the first point, a more organic pattern is created:

I. Pets can help ease the elderly's transition from the home environment to the institutional setting.

II. Pets can help provide the elderly with a greater will to live.

III. Pets can help increase the elderly's actual life span.

Use Active Verbs

Whenever possible, use active rather than passive or linking verbs. Although the word "is" *is* often unavoidable, it creates no motion. In fact, it is static—

as you were taught in grammar school when you learned that verbs could show "state of being." In the sentence, "The ball is red," no motion is created by the verb *is*. It merely reports a static situation. In contrast, active verbs inherently help create a sense of motion. Your main points should be worded using active verbs since the main points are a key source of forward motion through your speech. For example, in a how-to speech on making stained glass windows, the speaker formulated her points in the following way:

I. All the material you need is available at the Student Center Craft Shop.

II. A pattern, very similar to a dress pattern, must be drawn.

III. The third step is cutting the glass.

IV. Sand the edges of the glass so that the pieces fit closely and then wrap copper foil along the sanded edge.

V. The final step is soldering the pieces together.

In this example, the main points not only fail to be worded in parallel grammatical form, but they also mix active, passive, and linking constructions. In the revised version, all the verbs have been converted to active forms, and the sentences have been reformulated to utilize parallel grammatical form. The active verbs have been italicized. Since this outline is for a how-to speech, the imperative mood is also used in wording each main point.

I. *Purchase* your materials from the Student Center Craft Shop.

II. *Draw* a pattern for your design.

III. *Cut* the glass into the correctly sized pieces.

IV. *Prepare* the pieces for final assembly.
    A. *Sand* the edges of the glass.
    B. *Wrap* copper foil along the sanded edge.

V. *Solder* the pieces together to form the final design.

Use Word Repetition

Parallel grammatical form is a type of repetition at the sentence level. But it is also possible to use repetition at the word level to help create the psychological sense of movement within your speech. In one of the previous examples, word repetition has been employed at the same time that parallel grammatical form has been employed. Look back at the example on "Pets: Good Therapy for the Elderly."

I. *Pets can help* ease . . .

II. *Pets can help* provide . . .

III. *Pets can help* increase . . .

Another, more subtle, way to use word repetition effectively requires you to foreshadow your next point by the way you word the previous one. In Chapter 1, we saw an example of this technique without calling attention to it at the time. Let's look at the sample outline from Chapter 1 to see this technique in operation.

I. The first step in PREPARING your prize bird for showing is gathering the materials you will need to complete the process.

II. The next step is PREPARING the bird for WIRING.

III. The third step is WIRING the duck for POSING.

IV. The fourth step is POSING the bird as you want it to look in the final DISPLAY.

V. The final step is adding the finishing touches to the DISPLAY.

Here, at least one key word carries over from the previous point and is used to foreshadow the point that is to come.

Use Key Words

Another technique that can help add life to your speech is to give brief key word names to each of your main points. Using key words helps your audience remember the points that go with the key words. If the key words are well chosen, they also set up an expectation and thereby propel your speech forward.

For example, a sociology major who had taken a field trip to a local pizzeria to observe the prevailing social structure in that setting, used the key word technique in a speech reporting on her results. After analyzing her data, she classified pizza eaters into the following five natural categories:

I. Those who pick off and eat the cheese and meat and mushrooms and leave the crust

II. Those who eat the pizza as rapidly as possible—acting totally starved

III. Those who eat pizza as an excuse to drink beer

IV. Those who eat pizza as an excuse to try to pick up a date

V. Those who go to savor the flavor, tasting every bite as if it were their last

To these she gave, respectively, the following key word names:

I. Nibblers

II. Gobblers

III. Guzzlers

IV. Shoppers

V. Connoisseurs

Notice the names that were given to the classes of pizza eaters in this topically organized speech. These are not just "topics." These are also catch words that set up a pattern of expectations about the type of character who will be described. They are not only single words, but are also planned so that each has a similar sounding ending (*ers*). This sets up a powerful anticipation of what to expect as the speaker lists the types. It only takes two key words in a row to establish a powerful expectational set.

Thus, if you decide to use key words, do not break the pattern with something like *nibblers, gobblers, guzzlers,* and *those who go to show off their new clothes.* This breach of form destroys the pattern you were establishing. Unless you were trying to create a humorous effect by breaking the expected pattern (itself a useful technique under some circumstances), then you should give this final group a one-word name, too: the *modelers,* perhaps.

Use Mnemonic Devices

Using mnemonic devices can also help create movement throughout the organizational pattern of your speech. Literally, a mnemonic device is a formula or jingle designed to help aid memory. Three types of mnemonic devices are especially useful in helping your audience remember your main points and in giving your speech structure a sense of forward motion, development, climax, and closure: **acronyms, alliteration,** and **alphabet soup.**

Use Acronyms An acronym is a word formed by putting together the first letters of each member of a series of words. SCUBA is an acronym for *s*elf contained *u*nderwater *b*reathing *a*pparatus. For years, students have used the acronym ROY G. BIV to help them remember the colors of the rainbow: *R*ed, *O*range, *Y*ellow, *G*reen, *B*lue, *I*ndigo, and *V*iolet. Similarly, students of music remember the space notes of the musical scale as FACE. Acronyms are also widely used in advertisements to help television audiences remember advertisers' phone numbers. For example, a local law enforcement program called Crimestoppers has as its phone number 775-TIPS to emphasize the purpose of the phone number, as well as to help viewers remember the actual number to be called.

When you use an acronym to emphasize your speech's organization, you are creating a new word from the first letters of each of the key words that name your speech's main points. This technique is especially useful for helping audiences remember the main points of your speech. For example, one student gave a speech on how to plan a dance for an organization, such as a club, sorority, or fraternity. Planning the dance has five parts: (1) deciding upon party decorations, (2) sending out invitations, (3) securing a place to hold the dance, (4) having the party catered, and (5) arranging for the musical entertainment. Because the speech was about how to plan a successful dance, the speaker reformulated her main points so that she could create an acronym based on the word *dance*. Her main points were named:

*D*ecorations

*A*nnouncements

*N*iche

*C*atering

*E*ntertainment

Reformulating her main points required a little additional work, but the effort paid off in both greater memorability and greater organic qualities within the speech.

Use Alliteration Another way to enhance your speech's memorability and to create additional forward motion is to use alliteration when you are naming the key words of your main points. Alliteration is the repetition of the initial sounds of immediately successive or nearby words. I used alliteration when I named the three subpoints under the heading Mnemonic Devices: *a*cronyms, *a*lliteration, and *a*lphabet soup. A speaker talking about how to obtain credit mentioned the "Three *C*'s of Credit":

*C*ash

*C*ollateral

*C*haracter

Use Alphabet Soup A final mnemonic device that can help enhance the organic qualities of your speech's organization might be called "alphabet soup," since it requires you to name the key words of your main points with words whose initial letters are consecutive letters of the alphabet. Usually this results in the ABC's of some topic or process. For example, the ABC's of the process of cardiopulmonary resuscitation are *A*irway, *B*reathing, and *C*irculation. The points to be remembered are (A) to clear the airway of any obstructions, (B) to reestablish breathing, and (C) to get the heart circulating blood again. Since these three subprocesses of CPR are done in just this order, the alphabet soup method is especially effective for enhancing the memorability of the speech.

As with acronyms, using alliteration and alphabet soup requires a little more thought about how you formulate your main ideas. But, if your goal is to have your speech be remembered and acted upon, then the thought that goes into structuring your main points will be worth the effort.

Conclusion

The purpose of this chapter has been to introduce the basic principles of speech organization. We have emphasized six patterns for arranging your ideas that are especially useful in structuring speeches to inform. Chapter 16 will discuss five more patterns of organization that are especially useful for persuasive speeches. This chapter has also pointed out several ways to make your speech's organization as full of life as possible. The key to vividness in any art is careful organization of its elements. By putting an extra hour or two of careful thought and revision into your speech's organization, you can expect to produce great dividends in audience understanding and response. Your speech will seem like a living creature. Systematically applying the five principles of internal preparation, forward motion, growth, climax, and closure to the overall organization of your speech, and thoughtfully using each of the techniques explained in this chapter for refining your organization, should make your audiences far more responsive to your speeches.

Questions for Review

1. What has the organic metaphor traditionally meant concerning speech organization? What changes are implied when an act-based interpretation is used instead?

2. How many main sections or systems does a speech have? How do these relate to one another?

3. Why does the main *principle* you use for dividing your overall topic into main points determine the *pattern* of organization you will be using?

4. When using chronological order to organize your speech, what major divisions should you break your topic into? Why? How do these divisions compare and contrast with those for spatial order or the so-called topical order?

Questions for Discussion

1. Since many topics lend themselves to being organized according to several different patterns, how would you decide which pattern to use on a particular occasion? For example, what role does your purpose play in the decision? And what role does the nature of the audience and its expectations play?

2. Can you think of any topics for which the patterns and principles of organization developed in the chapter are not well suited? What other options are available for organizing a speech?

Things to Try

1. Select a topic based on your college major and outline a speech using each of the six different patterns of organization.

2. Decide what type of audience each of the different outlines might be best suited for.

3. Reword the main points of your six outlines so that each uses parallel grammatical form, active verbs, word repetition, and/or key words.

4. Revise one or more of your outlines to employ each of the three types of mnemonic devices: acronyms, alliteration, and alphabet soup.

Bibliography

Fisher, Walter R. "Narration as a Human Communication Paradigm: The Case of Public Moral Argument." *Communication Monographs* 51 (1984), 1–22.

Fisher, Walter R. "The Narrative Paradigm: An Elaboration." *Communication Monographs* 52 (1985), 347–367.

Miller, George A. *The Psychology of Communication: Seven Essays.* Baltimore: Penguin, 1967.

CHAPTER 10

Introductions, Conclusions, and Transitions

*I*n Chapter 9 we introduced the functions and principles for structuring the body of your speech. There you learned techniques for organizing your speech's body so that its structural pattern imitates the overall form of the act, as well as exemplifies some of the other important principles of acts that make a speech seem like a living creature. The purpose of this chapter is to introduce you to the organic functions of the other three structural systems of a speech: the introduction, conclusion, and the transitions, which bring the entire speech together as a unified, lifelike whole. For not only must the body of the speech seem organic; the entire speech from beginning to end must seem to be an organic whole.

*I*ntroductions

Listening to a speech is a sustained audience act, and it follows the same act principles as does speaking itself. One important implication of this fact is that listening requires a preparatory period during which an impulse to listen is built up. Part of that impulse is developed prior to your speech, while the audience members decide whether or not to attend your speech or sit waiting for you to begin. This period of preparation produces a *general* impulse to listen and a set of general audience expectations to be fulfilled. But once your speech begins, the audience must also be prepared to listen to it *in particular.* The introductory part of your speech is designed to induce the audience's impulse to listen to your particular speech and to shape the audience's general listening act. The introduction organizes the audience's general impulse to listen, creating specific expectations for you to fulfill, and bonding the separate individuals into the collective entity properly called an "audience."

Functions of Introductions

An audience has assembled to listen to your speech. That represents a substantial commitment on their part—even in a classroom situation. But just because the audience has made such a commitment does not mean they are prepared to respond appropriately from the very moment you begin to speak. In most cases, you will need to prepare your audience for your particular speech. Preparing your audience for what they are about to hear—building up their impulse to listen, establishing their expectations for the speech— these are the guiding functions of the introduction.

Because it has many preparatory responsibilities, your speech's introduction—though relatively brief compared with the subsequent phases of the speech—is a complex, intricate little structure with many functions to fulfill. The most important of these preparatory functions are the following:

1. Capture and direct the audience's attention

2. Reveal the topic, purpose, or theme of the speech

3. Relate the subject to the audience's interests

4. Establish the speaker's credibility

5. Create a goodwill bond between speaker and audience

6. Overview any necessary background information

7. Preview the structure of the speech

8. Lead smoothly into the body of the speech

Let's look at each of these eight functions more closely before exploring how you can best fulfill them.

Capture and Direct the Audience's Attention The first major preparatory function of the introduction is to capture your audience's attention and to direct it toward your topic. Although your audience may have assembled for the expressed purpose of listening to your speech, there are also powerful competing impulses constantly going on in your audience's minds, vying for their current attention.

To see this, think about your audience for a moment. As they wait for you to speak, their minds may be wandering from thought to thought—the meal they missed in order to attend your speech, the new baby-sitter they may not yet trust, the discussion they were having with a friend while waiting for you to speak. All these, and a thousand more thoughts, may be playing back and forth across their minds as you step to the lectern. Into that melee of mental activity your speech must strike if it is to have any impact. Your opening must be powerful enough to win convincingly in the competition for your audience's attention. Your audience must be induced to suspend its ongoing mental activity and attend to your speech. Accordingly, the first function of your introduction is to capture their attention away from the other impulses to which it is being given, and to direct their attention toward your topic, purpose, or theme.

Reveal the Topic, Purpose, or Theme of the Speech Having successfully captured your audience's attention and directed it toward your topic, you must next reveal the topic more explicitly. Your audience needs to know what your speech will be about. So you should next state your purpose or theme in a clear and direct summary sentence. In stating your topic explicitly you are establishing your speech's motivating impulse in the audience's mind and building up their expectations about what they will hear. As you remember from previous discussions, listening is an active process; in fact, listening is an act. As such, it has not only a phase of preparation (being built up during your introduction), but also phases of acceleration and increasing power, climax, and decline. If you induce a powerful enough impulse to listen at the beginning of your speech, the audience itself, through its own rising and culminating phases of listening, will help do much of the work of maintaining attention during your speech. A major part of their impulse to listen depends upon a clear understanding of your topic, purpose, or theme; thus, this should be given a clear, pithy, and substantial statement during your introduction.

Relate the Subject to the Audience's Interests Even though attending your speech represents a major commitment on the part of your audience, there are no guarantees that your audience will remain mentally in tune with you for the duration of your speech. Once an audience knows what your topic or theme is going to be, they want to know how the topic relates to themselves. If your speech turns out to have little relationship to their interests, their minds will wander to their other priorities. Simply having captured their attention by your opening does not mean that you will retain their attention. Accordingly, the third preparatory function of your introduction is to involve your audience in your topic by linking the topic to their own prior interests. Your goal at this point is to enlist their own impulses (and the interests those impulses lead to) in the service of your speech.

This process is somewhat like the principle of inertia. Once moving, an object is much easier to *keep* moving. What you are seeking to do is to find the audience's ongoing mental activities, to link your topic to them to take advantage of these previous activities. Thus, although the audience may not appear to care about your topic prior to your speech, there are numerous aspects of your topic than can be used to tap into their already active interests. These angles of interest were treated in Chapter 7 on audience analysis. You will want to find some way of taking advantage of the audience's common interests as you seek to build a bridge of interest toward your topic.

Establish the Speaker's Credibility Having gotten the audience interested in your topic, you must next give them a reason for listening to *you* in particular. Do *you* know what you are talking about? What special experiences have *you* had that qualify *you* to talk about this subject? Although establishing your credibility may not seem like a part of preparing your audience for listening to your speech, you are actually clearing your path of one of the most dangerous *counter*impulses to the success of your speech—the feeling that you may be no more qualified on your subject than your audience is. Just as a building contractor must prepare the construction site by removing any potential obstructions, you must prepare your audience's mind by removing any potential objections to yourself as a speaker. In some subtle way, you must establish the feeling that you are qualified to speak on this subject.

Create a Goodwill Bond between the Speaker and the Audience The goal of establishing a positive relationship between yourself and your audience has been given a variety of names: goodwill bond, speaker-listener rapport, common ground, audience identification. Each name emphasizes a different aspect of this function of speech introductions. The *goodwill bond* phrasing emphasizes the positive nature of the feeling one seeks to create; *rapport* emphasizes the feeling of speaker-audience similarity a speaker tries to evoke; *common ground* emphasizes the search for a shared starting place between speaker and audience; and *identification* points out the need for developing a shared mindset or approach to thinking about the topic. What all of them have in common is the importance they place on establishing mental *contact* between speaker and audience.

Whatever term is employed to characterize this function, you must seek to establish audience contact and to induce a feeling of similarity between yourself and your audience. Sometimes this can be done directly, by pointing out the known similarities; sometimes indirectly, by alluding to commonly shared knowledge or beliefs; and sometimes simply by humor. People tend to feel a strong identification with persons with whom they can laugh. However you decide to accomplish it, you must make your audience feel comfortable with you as a person.

Overview any Necessary Background Information Although not every speech requires it, you may sometimes need to prepare your audience by giving them some specific items of background information concerning your topic. Is there a situation they need to know about that provides a context for understanding your remarks? If so, you will need to supply them with that information as part of your introduction.

Preview the Structure of the Speech Having prepared your audience for the subject matter of your speech, you must now prepare them for its structure. As you know from earlier chapters, a speech is not merely a random succession of your ideas upon a topic; it is a structured symbolic projection of those ideas in a patterned presentation. You must prepare your audience for the pattern you will use in projecting your ideas. Often this will consist of a simple announcement, somewhere in your introduction, of the major points of your speech, in the order you will present them. At other times this function will be accomplished merely by telling your audience how many points you will have. We will illustrate several methods in the section on techniques of introductions.

Lead Smoothly to the Body of the Speech When the introduction is nearly complete, you must close it off and lead smoothly to the body of the speech. Since an introduction is a subact of the larger speech, it has its own impulse, rise, climax, and period of closure. Like an hourglass each subact must *nearly* close off. But, also like an hourglass, the narrow waistline that closes off the upper portion is at the same time the opening of the lower portion. The introduction of the speech must not only clearly close off the introduction, it must also directly open up the body. The following examples both close off introductions and open up the body of the speech as well.

> So, how can you go about demonstrating that you have that first *C* of credit—collateral? Let's begin with a definition of collateral, and then I'll explain exactly what you need to do to show the bank that you qualify for that loan you need.

> Now that you know what the four *P*'s of manufacturing chocolate are, I'd like to talk first about the first *P*, Preprocessing.

Techniques for Introductions

There are many ways to open a speech and accomplish the major organic functions that a speech's introduction must fulfill. What follows is a description of the most common introductory techniques, and examples of how these sound in actual practice.

Ask a Question or a Series of Questions   Questions can be powerful opening devices because they immediately induce a desire for their own answer. Question/answer is a very common pattern in our daily conversation (Nofsinger, 1975). When a question is asked, attention is instantly marshaled. Audiences wait anxiously for an answer. Unanswered questions are incomplete acts—acts that build an increasing tension pushing for resolution until they are completed with an answer. Because well-formulated questions can have powerful effects on an audience, they are treated extensively in the following pages.

Questions may be used in several ways. The simplest way is to ask a single, direct question, which typically induces the need for a relatively immediate answer. For example, the speaker asks, "How many times were *you* seduced today?" and all the members of the audience blink to attention while the attractive young woman continues to develop her introduction to a speech about an advertising technique that has been called subliminal seduction.

Other instances of the single question used to capture and focus attention may be seen in the following examples:

> Have you ever paid 500 dollars for the privilege of doing three hours of back-breaking work so that you could get something that has absolutely no practical use? Some people look at bill fishing this way, but . . .

> When was the last time someone told you about an opportunity that sounded too good to be true?

Have you ever felt like a french fry—drenched in suntan oil, boiling away trying to get crispy, golden brown?

Do you remember the last purchase you made that cost you over ten dollars?

What do you think the chances are of breaking the 55 m.p.h. speed limit merely by pedaling a bicycle?

A second way to use questions is to ask a series of questions. This technique both heightens the natural tension induced by the question form and immediately establishes the speech's sense of forward motion by repeating the question form. We will look at two different ways to take advantage of the forward motion created by asking questions in a series.

In the first use of the series, each of the questions represents one of the main points to be presented later in the speech. That is, each question is formulated so that it establishes an expectation that it will subsequently be answered. The questions induce the desire for an answer, and the rest of the speech becomes the satisfaction of that desire (Burke, 1931). The following examples illustrate how a series of questions can be used to foreshadow the structure of main points:

What would you do if you saw a rattlesnake? What would you do if you were bitten by a rattlesnake? And why is the public so afraid of rattlesnakes?

What should you take on your next overnight camping trip to the mountains? Where should you go that's especially unusual? And what can you expect to learn when you go there?

The second use of a series of questions employs the series as a focusing device. In this case, the questions have a definite feeling of progression—either from general to specific, or from specific to general (Burke, 1931). In either case, the final question in the series leads to the main theme or purpose of your speech, but does not necessarily lead to any specific single point within the body of the speech. This use of a series of questions moves your audience's mind in a particular direction, propelling their attention forward to build an expectation that this pattern of movement will continue throughout the rest of your speech. The following examples use a series of questions to progressively focus attention and to give the speech a sense of forward motion and direction.

Would you consider paying nearly six times as much for a quart of motor oil as you do now? Have you ever thought about what other alternatives there might be for your engine lubrication?

When do you think life begins? Is it at the point when a baby takes its first breath and comes into a world of light rather than the world of darkness of its mother's womb? Or does life begin long before birth, nearer to the time of conception?

Are you tired of school? Are you tired of all the homework, the tests, the reports, and all the speeches? Do you need to get away from it all and just kick back and relax?

Are you planning for a family someday? Are you going to be concerned about the basic skills and activities your children need? Or are you going to be content to let your children entertain themselves in front of the television all day long?

Are you broke? Do you want to buy something right now? Will you need extra money? How are you going to get the credit you need?

All questions are not created equal. Some types of questions work much better than others in capturing attention and establishing forward motion for your speech. To help you make thoughtful choices about the types of questions you may want to use on a particular occasion, we can classify questions based upon the kind of response they typically elicit. A rough but serviceable classification can be made that divides questions into four types: (1) those requiring strictly a yes/no answer, (2) those inviting a physical show of hands, (3) those inviting a substantive but brief answer, and (4) those inviting some sort of extended, multisentence answer.

Examples of speech introductions that employ yes/no questions include:

Have you ever wondered what happens to the tons of scrap steel our society turns out each year? Or do you wonder how the steel used in the construction of buildings, like the new classroom building we're in, was produced?

Have you ever had the urge to go out and hit a little white ball as far as you can and then go looking for it?

Would you like to learn an art that is hundreds of years old?

Have you ever noticed how beautiful and warm houseplants make a home feel?

Although yes/no questions seem easy enough to ask, they are not so easy to phrase in ways that help advance the purposes of your speech. Unless they are carefully phrased, yes/no questions are likely to induce a *no* response rather than a *yes* response. If the question results in a *no* response, no forward motion will be created. You will then have negative inertia to overcome. Although you may have answered *yes* to a few of the questions above, you may have also found yourself quickly answering *no* to some of them, and only a vague *maybe* to others. What is almost as bad as inducing a *no* response is the fact that even a *yes* response often fails to induce much forward motion. Yes/no questions are too easy to answer. We answer *yes,* we answer *no,* but either way we quickly dispense with the question. Effectively using a yes/no question requires that the question arrest the listener's attention on its own merits, and that the listener remain a little curious and uncertain about how to answer. We must be caught between our *yes* and our *no* impulses, with the decision weighing in the balance for an instant if the yes/no question is to be effective.

Questions inviting a show of hands are especially tempting to use. These have the virtue of involving an audience immediately and actively. Furthermore, this is a method of questioning that most students have seen modeled countless times in classes. Teachers are forever asking for shows of hands and head counts. But, for all its familiarity, this technique is also fraught with high peril, as any experienced teacher can tell you. What if no one cooperates, refusing to respond? What if the response is the opposite of what you expected? Even more problematic, as we shall see in a moment, is the question of how you really expect your audience to respond to your question. Do you really *want* to see a show of hands? Let's look at how such speeches typically begin.

> How many of you have ever attended summer camp as a child?

> How many of you like to read? How many of you like to watch movies?

> How many of you have built a plastic model and when you were finished, it didn't look quite right?

The problem with such questions is that your audience doesn't know quite how to respond. They have just settled into a listening posture, and you unexpectedly ask them a question. Suddenly, they have to shift impulses and decide whether the question is a **rhetorical question**—a question requiring a mental response, but no overt response—or whether you really want them to raise their hands. Faced with two competing impulses, most classroom audiences vacillate indecisively, waiting sheepishly for someone to rescue them by resolving the ambivalence. In the meantime, both time and attention are wasted while the speaker repeats the question, adding "C'mon . . . How many of you . . ." or simply ignores the distracting dilemma that has been created by this question and completes what's left of the speech's introduction.

What is expected here? The "how many of you" question is confusing because although it appears to invite a hand count, it also resembles a more clearly rhetorical question that begins "how many times have you." Sometimes student speakers really want a show of hands, but more often than not, they don't and have simply failed to consider the possible consequences of a particular way of formulating their question. Since the "how many of you" wording can almost always be reformulated to avoid the ambiguity, don't use it unless you really want a hand count. Even then, you may want to preface your question with a comment that lets your audience know you will be asking for a hand count. That way, they can prepare for the act of answering your question with a physical action.

Many questions invite a search for substantive answers rather than either yes/no answers or shows of hands. Most of the so-called Wh-questions are of this type.

Who was the first man to set foot on the moon? The first to orbit the earth? The first pilot of the space shuttle?

What are the three most common causes of death among college students? What are your chances of being stricken down by one of these killers? And what can you do to help protect yourself and your friends from these killers?

When was the last time you went on a miracle diet hoping to shed a few pounds? When was the last time you were sorely disappointed by the results? When was the last time you vowed "Nevermore!" after you failed?

These questions invite the audience to try to fill in the blank with short answers and are especially helpful in capturing attention and overcoming mental inertia by starting the audience's mind along a train of thought.

Finally, you may ask questions that invite a longer, more reflective response, which in a sense, your speech becomes. The following are examples of such questions:

Why has the economy—and especially unemployment—been so difficult to deal with in the last five years?

Should individual communities have the right to control what kinds of research go on within their local colleges and universities? Should recombinant DNA research be "banned in Boston"? Or anyplace else, for that matter?

Has America begun to lose its will to support its friends and allies abroad? What should be our role in helping developing countries sustain their economic progress?

Why did you come to college? Are you here to meet the mate of your dreams, or did you come here to join the pursuit of knowledge? Is college just a place to train you for a job? Or do you want more from your college education?

The advantage of such questions is that they establish the agenda for your entire speech. Their disadvantage is that if you fail to answer them fully you leave your audience feeling a little unsatisfied; part of the listening act that you have induced has been left unconsummated.

You have just been introduced to four different types of questions and their advantages and disadvantages. Each type of question induces a slightly different type of response from your audience, and each induces a slightly different expectation about the type of speech you will be presenting—a different expectation for movement, growth, climax, and closure. These types of questions can be used to help your speech, but they must be used with thoughtful care. As long as you consider the potential problems, opening with a question can be an effective strategy.

One final word of caution: When you open with a question, allow time for it to work its effect. Don't rush immediately from the end of the question to the answer. Remember, the purpose of using the question in the first place is to induce a tension in your audience that marshals their attention—as they try to resolve the tension by answering the question. If you rush in to answer it, or to move to the next portion of your introduction without even a moment's hesitation, you lose much of the beneficial effect of a well-conceived question. On the other hand, do not wait too long, or the tension may backfire and work against you—either because it becomes too great and the audience becomes resentful, or because your audience's attention becomes absorbed in thinking about something else. Only a brief pause is needed to achieve the desired effect.

Make a Startling Statement The human mind is easily roused to attention by novelty. Someone taps you on the shoulder and you reflexively flinch in a startled reaction. A glass is dropped somewhere at a restaurant and all the patrons immediately look around to see what has happened. This response is called the orienting reflex. To begin a speech with an unusual, unexpected, novel statement or observation takes advantage of the fact that our attention is so easily drawn to the unusual. You've heard of "eye-catching" clothing? In your speech, you are trying to begin with an "ear-catching" fact or phrasing that helps capture the attention of the "mind's ear."

For example, you might begin a speech on a commonplace topic—proper watering of houseplants—by trying to startle your audience from its complacency on the topic:

> PLANTS KILLED BY WATERING! Although that's a headline you're unlikely to see in our local newspaper, murdering your houseplants by over- and underwatering them is one of the most commonly committed acts of vegicide by college students today. As a horticulture major, I've had numerous opportunities to see innocent plants executed by drowning—their loving owners protesting up to the end that this trial by water is good for their plants. Since plant abuse is not punishable by law, it is important for you to learn both the symptoms of this common form of abuse and how to prevent yourself from innocently blundering into this insidious college crime wave.

Here the speaker humorously tries to shock us into thinking about his topic in at least two ways. First, by the dramatically delivered headline, which comes unexpectedly at the beginning of his speech. Second, by the repeated use of the metaphor of murder throughout the initial portion of the introduction.

Another form of startling statement, perhaps more common and more versatile, simply uses a shocking fact or statistic to rouse the audience's attention. For example:

> There is a killer among us—a killer that takes more lives each year than tornadoes; a killer that causes property damage in excess of 100 million dollars per year; a killer that strikes several million times each day. That killer is lightning.

The date is August 5, 1970. Every male in this room is either facing military service in Vietnam, has returned from Vietnam with a multitude of emotional scars and stories, or worse . . . is dead. Can this happen to our nation again in the 1980s?

America, you're out of shape! The *Reader's Digest Almanac* says that over 60 million people in the United States are overweight. That is over one quarter of our entire population. If you are like most college students, you probably feel that you are in pretty good shape. Well, you're not! Although you are in better condition than the average American, you are still in pitiful shape. How many of you can run a mile in under six minutes, do 100 sit-ups, or 100 push-ups, for example?

Quote Someone Else Sometimes the most arresting way to begin your speech is with a brief, significant quote. There are several types of quotes you may use and each induces a slightly different feeling in your audience. Chapter 8 discusses the types and functions of quotes in detail and that discussion will not be repeated here.

Pose a Challenge Why do you want to climb Mt. Everest? "Because it is there," George Leigh Mallory is reputed to have said. Because it is there! America is a "can do" nation. We love a challenge, an invitation to try a task, to meet a need, to right a wrong. President Kennedy perhaps best expressed the American spirit in his Inaugural Address when he said: "Let every nation know, whether it wishes us well or ill, that we shall pay any price, bear any burden, meet any hardship, support any friend, oppose any foe, in order to assure the survival and the success of liberty." Our ancestors crossed vast oceans to get here, crossed a vast continent to forge a nation; and several of our fellow citizens have walked on the moon "because it was there." Surely there is nothing in the service of good that we Americans cannot accomplish if we are just challenged to do so.

Because of this "can do" spirit, one significant way to capture your audience's attention is to pose a challenge, show them a problem to solve, paint them a picture of a bad situation to be set right. Portrayed with concrete details to stir their imagination, the challenge can be used to build a powerful impulse to be constructively channeled. And your speech will help them to do so, setting their energy free to conquer the challenge.

Today, here in our country, there is an acute shortage of whole blood of all types, and you can help, if only you will. You can help save people who have been in accidents and people who need surgery, if only you will. You can walk to the bloodmobile after class—over by the student union—and with the investment of only a few minutes of your time and energy, help extend someone else's life by extending your arm. If only you will.

Tell a Story or Anecdote Not only do Americans love challenges, we also seem to love to tell stories about our exploits and experiences. Who could resist hearing about the time you got lost in the Great Salt Desert while looking for the Bonneville "Racetrack," and how your mother saved your life by walking out of the desert for help—not once, but *twice!* Everyone has a story to tell, a story that can be used to make a point. Telling a story to open a speech accomplishes many things. It **humanizes** your speech (a story has characters). It **activates** your speech (a story has plot: starting, rising, climaxing, and closing action). It **essentializes** your speech's content (a story has a central theme or point). To be effective, though, the story should be short and directly relevant to your subject. Although for some people telling a story is more difficult than the other methods described thus far, its rewards are great and the technique is worth trying if you can tell stories at all. (Chapter 8 also discusses types of anecdotes and should be referred to for more information.)

Imagine a Scenario, Scene, or Situation Closely related to the story or anecdote is the scenario, which requires your audience to imagine a scene or situation. The scenario differs from the story or anecdote in two ways: (1) the scenario is in the present or future tense, whereas a story is always told about the past, as something that has already happened; (2) the scenario can place the audience *into* some imaginary situation that is, will, or might be occurring, whereas a story is told *to* the audience and is about someone else to whom the situation occurred. When well used, the scenario is highly involving because it invites the audience to project themselves imaginatively into a situation in which they are the prime actors. That is, it creates narrative motion, with the audience playing the central role in the action. The following example illustrates the scenario technique.

> There you are, walking into the interview room, waiting for the questions that will either land you the job you've been studying in college for four years to get—or land you back in the street looking again. You sit down in your brand-new designer blue jeans and polo shirt waiting for the interviewer to ask you those important questions that will allow you to show how much you know and why you will be such an asset to the company. The interview begins, "I see you've just graduated from college?" "Yes sir," you sincerely reply, sensing that the job is already yours, "just last May." And then what does the interviewer ask? "Haven't had time to buy any new clothes, I see?" "What?" you say, thinking to yourself, "Clothes? What have my clothes got to do with anything?"
>
> Well, although clothes may not *make* the man or woman, they can certainly *break* your chances of landing the job you want if you don't give them any thought when you are preparing for your interview. Today . . .

Explore an Analogy or a Comparison and Contrast Two situations are analogous when they are of the same form, that is, when they have a similar pattern. A helpful way to open a speech on a difficult topic is to explore an analogy,

An older woman obtains a degree after a long absence from school. What percentage of students in your school are older? Do you have any friends who are much older than you? What kinds of career changes and retraining have you seen among people you know?

which is a way of pointing out similarities between the topic of your speech and something else with which your audience is presumably already familiar. For example, a speech on computer memory might begin with an analogy between how a computer organizes data and the Library of Congress numbering system, which assigns a unique "address" on the library shelves for every individual reference source. Another analogy frequently used for explaining computer operations is the "file folder," in which a document the operator is working on is treated as a file folder into which information is placed for storage. Such analogies, when used during the introduction of your speech, help make difficult topics more readily accessible to your audience.

Make a Personal Reference Sometimes the speaking situation calls for a preparatory reference to some aspect of the total speech situation that has occasioned the speech, or to something that has occurred since the speech was prepared and that must now be taken into account. Four types of such personal reference are typically employed: references (1) to the speaking occasion, (2) to a previous speaker, (3) to the audience itself, and (4) to yourself as a speaker.

References to the Occasion. References to the occasion are often needed if the speech is being delivered for a special event or ceremonial purpose: convention and conference addresses, eulogies, award receptions, and banquets. But these ceremonial occasions are not the only time a reference to the speech's occasion may be desirable. Any time the occasion has special significance to your topic, or to how your topic will be treated, a reference to the occasion may be helpful. Such references take advantage of the audience's impulse for attending the speech and help propel your speech forward. The following example illustrates how one might refer to the occasion that calls for the speech.

> Tonight we have gathered together to celebrate the 25th anniversary of the founding of our company, and to look forward to our next 25 years of service to our customers and the community.

References to a Previous Speaker. If others have spoken before you, you may need to mention some aspect of their speech before continuing with your own. Perhaps the speaker has inadvertently covered some aspect of your topic already, and thereby prepared the way for your speech or preempted the need for part of it. Perhaps the speaker has developed an opposing point of view. In either case, this should be treated as an opportunity. By mentioning the previous speech at the beginning of your own, and using it to prepare for your own remarks, you can create a sense of rhythm (the previous conclusion preparing for your introduction), internal preparation, forward motion, and even growth. Your speech can become the culmination of a larger act, which you treat as having been begun by the previous speaker. But to accomplish these things, and to incorporate (as well as subordinate) the previous speech to your own, you must make a conscious transitional reference to the previous speech within your own introduction. In the example below, the speaker found it necessary to disagree with the previous speaker, but was able to do so without appearing to be simply disagreeable.

> According to Mr. Jones, there were three reasons why we should vote against the proposal before us tonight. Those were thoughtful and significant reasons to consider and, if the issues he raised were the only ones involved, I would join Mr. Jones in calling for tonight's resolution to be voted down. But, in spite of the cogency of Mr. Jones's argument, and after looking into the matter myself, I believe that there are even more compelling reasons for supporting the proposal. Let me begin by summarizing the reasons I am in support of passing the proposition before us.

Reference to the Audience. Who are you talking to? Do they need to be acknowledged before you begin introducing your specific topic? Do they need to be complimented for being who or what they are or thanked for providing you with this opportunity to speak? On some occasions you will need to refer to the audience itself as a part of readying them for your speech. For example, you may need to remind them of the commonality that brings them together as an audience. So you will address them in a way that calls this to their attention and binds them together as a singular entity:

> As college students about to graduate, each of you will soon face . . .

Reference to the audience may also be used to establish a common mind set rather than to simply remind them of what brings them together as a group. In this use of the audience reference, you let your audience know how you want them to think of themselves for the purpose of this speech—what image of themselves you want them to bring to the act of listening. This image becomes part of their guiding impulse for listening to your speech.

> As members of the loyal opposition on this issue, and as fair-minded people, I want to address you tonight on the question of . . .

Reference to Yourself. Finally, you may decide to make some reference to yourself, your purposes, or your qualifications for this speech before you launch into your specific topic. This is often done, for example, when you want to use your qualifications as a part of your attention-getting strategy.

> As a paramedic and a fellow student, I have had ample opportunity to see the results of careless use of alcohol. In fact, several times I've had to go on emergency runs here on campus to aid someone who's had "one for the road."

Using the techniques described in this section, you should be able to create effective, functional, living introductions to your speeches. We will now look at some complete introductions, both bad and good.

Illustrations of Complete Introductions

Because it is possible to destroy your speech by beginning it with a poorly conceived introduction, you must give your introductions special care and attention. The two introductions that follow are examples of just how far wrong an ill-planned introduction can go. Using the list of functions and techniques for speech introductions, see if you can identify what these speakers were trying to do in their introductions, and exactly what kinds of things went wrong.

> To begin, uh . . . the, you know, uh . . . topic I want to talk about is law school admissions. Now there's probably not a whole lot of you who are interested in going to law school after you graduate from here, but I think the things I have to say will also be useful to any of you who may be going to any other kind of professional school or graduate school, or any place—I think it will be beneficial to you.
>
> I've wanted to go to law school since my senior year in high school, and I've kind of geared myself toward that here at school in my undergraduate courses, and so I kind of know a little bit about it, and I had to do some research on it in the past so it is something I do know a little something about. Uh . . . I want to break it down into three main points that I want to talk about today because there's just a whole lot of material on it.
>
> And, uh . . . first of all: Should you go to law school or should you go to graduate school?
>
> Second, what should you look for in a graduate school or law school?
>
> And thirdly, what procedures should you use in applying to that graduate school or law school?
>
> So, let me take this first point first: Should you go to law school?
>
> Well. The main thing, I think, to say about that is *attitude*. . . .

> I'd like for y'all just to imagine a little bit with me that you're walking down a . . . maybe a road, to grandma's house, or maybe over next to the railroad tracks, and maybe . . . uh . . . you're near your dorm and you see a bottle in the ditch and you say to yourself: That's a bottle. But, you know, why should I get down there and maybe get snake bit or muddy or dirty trying to pick up some old bottle?
>
> Well. . . . It might be worth money . . . to you and it might not. . . . It might be worth money to somebody else, and it might have value to you . . . that uh . . .
>
> Well. . . . It has a value to me because . . . uh . . . well. . . .
>
> It's like a link with the past; it's something old, it's something simple; it's something that . . . that's not around any more. It brings back a time of, well, when things were a little different. . . . People weren't so serious.
>
> And, uh . . . it's like . . . they had all these different bottles, like bitters and remedies and cheers and medicines and mange remedies and draughts and elixirs. And it . . .

Like right here (shows bottle) it says "medicine." I mean, this is *medicine*. If you're sick you can take this and it might not make you well, but you're going to feel well because it probably had 40 or 50 percent alcohol in it. And uh . . .

So, it just brings back a little different times.

So. You're standing in the ditch and you're saying "All right," with this bottle in your hand, and it's dirty and you're saying, "Well, I don't know anything about bottles."

So, I'm going to tell you a little bit about bottles. Generally, the older a bottle is . . .

Since each of these introductions has considerable potential for being effective, each has been rewritten to take advantage of its best qualities. Notice in each case how the principles of forward motion, growth, climax, and closure have been fulfilled at the same time that the essential functions of the introduction have also been accomplished.

For many of you, getting your bachelor's degree does not mean the end of your schooling—it may be only the beginning. There may be graduate school, medical school, veterinary school, or dental school in your futures. For me, it's law school.

Getting into the postundergraduate school of your choice is quite a long process, and it's not too soon to begin thinking about it. Because I've wanted to go to law school since my senior year in high school, I've researched the process of getting into such schools quite thoroughly and would like to share with you today the steps required for choosing and getting into the graduate school of your choice.

I've broken the process into three major steps: (1) deciding whether or not to go to graduate school, (2) selecting the graduate school that best suits your needs, and (3) preparing a fully documented application for the school of your choice.

Let's begin by looking at the most important question you must ask first: "Should you go to graduate school at all?"

I'd like for you to imagine that you're walking down the road to grandma's house, or even just taking a shortcut back to your dorm, and you see a bottle down in the ditch. Is it valuable? Or is it just a piece of trash?

It may be either! Some old bottles can be worth a lot of money to the right person; others should just be taken to the dump. But how do you know whether or not to get down there in the ditch and risk getting muddy or snake bitten trying to pick up some old bottle?

As an antique bottle collector for the past several years, I've had quite a lot of experience tracking down and evaluating old bottles. Old bottles are all around us, and some have monetary value. Today, I'd like to teach you some of the tricks of the trade of evaluating the worth of the old bottles you may happen to find in the ditches you cross in life.

Four factors influence the value of a bottle: its original purpose, its actual age, its relative rarity, and its present condition. Let's begin by looking first at the influence the original purpose of a bottle has on its long-term value.

Suggestions for Effective, Organic Introductions

As you develop your speech introduction, use the following practical suggestions.

Try writing several introductions to your speech; then select the one you like best. Since there are several different techniques for you to choose from in fulfilling your speech's introductory functions, the first introduction you put together may not be the best introduction you can produce. It is especially important while you are first learning to speak in public that you try preparing a variety of alternate introductions to your speeches and then select the one you think works best for a particular situation.

Chain several introductory techniques together. The introductory techniques presented in this chapter are not mutually exclusive. Many times they can be used one after another to very good effect. Look back over some of the previous samples, especially the two longer ones, and you will see instances of several types of introductory techniques being chained together in order to fulfill the various functions of the introduction.

Fulfill the introductory functions in whatever order and combinations you find necessary for a particular occasion. We have presented the most common functions of speech introductions in what is a typical order for fulfilling them. But there is no magic in the order given. You may find that a very different order better serves your speech. That should be no cause for concern since speech introductions do not require that a certain order of presentation be maintained—only that a certain set of functions be performed. So fulfill the functions in whatever order you think works best for your speech. Furthermore, sometimes a single sentence or technique can be used to fulfill several functions at once. This, too, is perfectly acceptable as long as all the functions are taken care of in some way or another. Look back at the examples in this section to see how several functions were fulfilled while using only a single technique or sentence.

*C*onclusions

Speeches should not come to abrupt halts as if you had simply run out of things to say. Speeches with organic integrity do not simply halt. They *conclude,* they come to *closure,* they achieve what Barbara Smith (1968) calls "appropriate cessation." For like any organic process, a speech achieves its major climax and then has a brief period of cadence, where the final energy of the speech's motivating impulse is used up. The conclusion is the final closure of the speech as an act.

Functions of Conclusions

Speech conclusions have at least two essential functions. First, they serve to summarize, capsulize, or distill the speech's main theme or key points. During the course of the speech, you have planted the seeds of your ideas and then developed them in substantial detail. The conclusion gives you an opportunity to bring them all together into some essentializing statement for the audience to carry away. Second, a conclusion gives your speech a sense of finality or completeness. It signals that the speech is over; the act is complete and has come to closure.

Techniques for Conclusions

Simple Summary of the Main Theme Perhaps the simplest means of concluding your speech is with a direct summary of the speech. This method is usually clearly marked with words like "In summary, then, today I have talked about why you should . . ." and continues to fill in a statement concerning what the speech was about. Below are two examples of concluding statements that primarily summarize the speech's theme.

> So, now you're an architectural historian! Well—maybe not quite. But I do hope that having heard the distinctions among the doric, ionic, and corinthian orders of columns, architecture in general will feel a little less foreign to you, and you will be better able to notice and appreciate the various types of architecture we have here on campus.

> In closing, then, let me remind you that the pro-handgun lobby is seriously mistaken: Guns *do* kill. We must eliminate small, inexpensive handguns before they eliminate us.

Simple Summary of the Main Points Once you have summarized your speech's main theme, you can often review your specific main points for the audience. This may be accomplished by either exactly repeating your main points or by restating your main points in different words.

Exact repetition of the main points involves simply saying your main points once again exactly as you formulated them during your speech. Thus, in exact repetition, your audience hears the main points, which have been distributed throughout the speech, brought together one last time without the developmental material you have used earlier. This gives the points greater final focus and aids the audience's long-term ability to remember them. The following conclusion employs this method of exact restatement following a summary of its main theme.

> There you have it. You now know how to raise your college grades by cultivating a high quality professional relationship with your instructors through appropriate personal contacts. So the next time you start a new course remember the following five steps in raising your grades through personal contact: (1) teach your teacher your name; (2) ask intelligent questions; (3) neutralize your negative personal qualities; (4) practice politeness in conferences; and (5) make your sob stories effective. If you systematically practice these five steps to effective student-teacher contact, you, too, should see your grade point average soar.

Restatement of your main points differs from repetition in that when you restate your main points, you provide your audience with an alternate formulation of them, which puts them in a slightly different light. That is, you project the same ideas using different words, or a different phrasing, giving your audience yet another way of recalling your key ideas. In the example below, the speaker uses less formal language to reformulate the points made earlier in the speech.

> Just remember, then, when you're learning to slalom ski, to try to stay confident, use good equipment, and, once you're in the water, to be sure to keep your ski tips out of the water, your knees in toward your chest, your arms bent, and the center of your body in line with your ski. By following these few basic tips, you can begin enjoying slalom skiing your first time out. Good luck and, oh yes, remember to hold on tight!

Appeal, Challenge, or Call to Action You have given a speech on some specific informative or persuasive topic. Is there some specific action you want your audience to perform as a result? If so, your conclusion is the time to invite them to act. Furthermore, because the appeal seeks to induce behavioral or conceptual movement following your speech, this form of conclusion creates rhythmic continuity between your speech and the audience's subsequent behavior. The cadence of your speech induces the impulse to their own subsequent acts.

> Now you know what is wrong with advertising on children's prime time television. You know who is harmed every time a preschooler sits through one of these misleading animated ads; you know what the financial impact is on the average family, and why it would be constitutional to federally subsidize television programming in the early weekday afternoon and Saturday morning time slots. Now it is your turn. You must begin to take action *before* you become parents and have to experience the problems you and your children will have as the result of this advertising. Currently, congressional hearings

on this problem have been suspended. Write today to your representatives in congress. Let them know how you feel and why *they* should be concerned. Remind them that your vote counts, and you will use it to elect someone who *is* concerned if they are not. Do it today, before it is too late. Do it for your children and for your own peace of mind.

End As You Began Just as a refrain in music signals that the music is either preparing to move on to a new phase or is coming to an end, so too does a return to your opening strategy strongly suggest that you are either making a major transition or are coming to the end of your speech. Thus, if you end your speech by asking once again the question: "So, how many times were you seduced today?" you would be bringing your audience back to your opening question, a question to which your entire speech has provided an answer.

End with Some Other Introductory Technique Because a conclusion is a complete subact within the overall speech, it has its own period of preparation, rise, climax, and final decline. And, because of this, you may close your speech with any of the techniques available to you for opening the speech. Thus, you may, after a transitional marking statement indicating that the conclusion is coming, close with a question or series of questions, a startling statement, a challenge, a quote, an anecdote, a scenario, an analogy, or a personal reference—even if you did not use these techniques to open your speech. Since these techniques were extensively described and illustrated in the section on introductions, they will not be described again here.

Suggestions for Effective, Organic Conclusions

As was the case with your introductions, there are several things to keep in mind as you move to the conclusion phase of your speech. Among the most important of these are the following:

Write several conclusions, and select from among them the one you like best. Since there are many techniques for concluding a speech, and no single technique is best for all occasions, prepare several alternative conclusions using different techniques each time. Then try them all out to see which you like best and which seems to suit the mood or feeling you want to leave your audience with. Preparing alternate conclusions is especially important while you are first learning to speak in public—both so that you will know how the different concluding techniques sound and so that you will not be tempted to limit yourself to only the simplest, safest, and shortest of the available methods.

Rehearse conclusions for dramatic impact. Audiences need to know you've finished. Rehearsing your conclusion is as important as rehearsing any other part of your speech—perhaps even more so. Your conclusion represents the final impression the audience has of your speech. Its function is to signal that the end of the speech is coming and to give the audience a strong feeling of satisfying, organic closure. So your voice must carry the sense of closure you have built into your conclusion. To recite your well-prepared final words without the required vocal and physical indicators of finality will leave your audience restless and dissatisfied. Practice your conclusion until you can deliver it with a strong sense of finality and resolution.

Don't apologize for your speech. Many student speakers sound apologetic as they conclude—because of what they could *not* do or tell during the course of their speeches. If your speech was well planned for your particular audience, there is no need to apologize for what you did *not* talk about. No one can say everything there is to say on a subject, so you have selected as wisely as you could based upon your audience analysis, and you have put together the most appropriate speech you could. Therefore, keep the closing upbeat and positive in tone. No apologies should be necessary if you have done your speech preparation conscientiously.

Another common mistake student speakers typically make is to conclude by "hoping"—as in the phrase, "So today, I hope I've told you something you didn't know about *X*." Don't "hope" you've done something for your audience. This is a weak form of covert apology. Prepare a conclusion that has greater concluding power and that leaves the audience with a better feeling about your efforts.

Don't ramble on until you run out of energy for the act of speaking. In other words, prepare a definite conclusion. Don't leave yourself in the position of having to search for a way of concluding until you simply run out of energy and say, "Well, that's about it . . . uhhh . . . Are there any questions?" There is no sense of internal, organic integrity with this "method" of concluding, and no sense of closure to induce the spontaneous applause that usually follows a speech.

Don't introduce new points in your conclusion. A conclusion is just that—a conclusion or ending to what has already been said. It is not the place to mention thoughts you couldn't fit in the main body of your speech, or to add things you intended to say during your speech's body but forgot. Such thoughts, additions, and new points are not prepared for and are, therefore, inorganic inclusions in an otherwise living speech. Furthermore, they help destroy the expectations for closure you already established when you started your conclusion. Your conclusion marker—"In conclusion" "To sum up then"—creates an expectation of impending closure that the intrusion of new information serves to frustrate. The expectation of closure goes unfulfilled, and the natural, organic arc of tension holding the speech together as a living whole is shattered. The audience feels deceived. Consider how you feel when a teacher ends a lecture early, and all the students begin closing up books, putting away pencils, and shuffling papers preparing to leave. If the instructor then discovers that 10 more minutes are left, think about how you feel as you begin reopening your books, finding your place in your notes, and looking for a sharp pencil. In most cases, the instructor loses more than is gained by such a powerful frustration of student expectations. Apply this principle to your own audience, and you will see why it is so dangerous to add new points in a portion of the speech that has already prepared the audience for closure and leave-taking.

Don't close up shop prematurely. Gathering up your speech notes is a *post*speech activity having nothing to do with the speech itself, or with the impact you are trying to have on your audience. As a postspeech act, it should be delayed until after the entire speech is completed. It is distracting to have the speaker fidgeting with notes, as if he or she were planning an early escape, while otherwise trying to conclude the speech. Quite simply, conclude the speech effectively, accept your audience's response graciously, answer any questions willingly, and *then* gather up your materials.

Don't continue speaking as you leave the lectern. Sitting down is yet another act that should occur only after your speech has concluded. It should not begin before the speech is completed—that is, not during the final words of the conclusion. You've seen the equivalent of this in old movies—where the comic hero begins inching toward the door while he is still talking to the villain, trying to divert the villain's attention while the hero prepares his impromptu escape. The habit of concluding while moving back to one's seat is a result of an impulse for an impromptu escape rather than for a well-planned conclusion.

*T*ransitions

Every boundary between parts of a speech—whether the parts are introduction, body, and conclusion; point 1, point 2, and point 3; or examples one, two, and three—must serve both to close off one section and to open up the next. These boundaries that also serve as connectives are called **transitions;** and your speech must be held together as a single organic whole by dozens of them—even in a short speech of five to seven minutes. In fact, far more art goes into transitions than you might previously have expected. For they contribute very heavily to accomplishing the five principles being developed in this book: internal preparation, forward motion, growth, climax, and closure.

Functions of Transitions

Transitions have several functions to perform in a speech, depending upon the level of organization at which they are functioning. The most important of these are the following:

To Prepare the Way for a Point You Will Be Making Just as your speech as a whole needs an introduction that prepares the audience for what is to follow, the major points within a speech must also be prepared for—only on a much smaller scale. So, by way of preparatory transition, you might say: "Turning now to my first point . . ." This lets the audience know that the introduction is completed and that we are moving on to the body. These **preparatory transitions** are needed because, even though you have announced in your introduction the main destinations within your speech, the audience will not always know when you have actually arrived at each of them. The preparatory transitions get your audience ready for what is to follow by announcing the next phase in the progression of your speech.

To Let the Audience Know Where You Are in Your Speech As an audience listens to the details in your speech, it can easily forget where the ideas it is presently hearing fit into your overall structural progression. The audience needs an occasional reminder about where you are in your speech—some indication of the relation of the parts to the whole. These part-to-whole transitions might be called **milestone transitions** because they mark the stages of progress throughout the speech. A typical milestone transition might sound like this: "Now that you know what items you need to purchase, we are ready to look at how you begin to assemble them into . . ." Here, the speaker not only prepares the audience for the next point, but also indicates the relation of one part of the speech (the one just completed) to another (the next to come).

To Indicate You Are Going to Take a Side Trip from Your Main Theme Although more often than not your speech will be a fairly direct and predictable progression from idea to idea, there will also be many times when you will want to add a comment that is only tangentially related to the main theme or direction of your speech. This is quite normal, but you must prepare your audience for the side trip. Otherwise, the inertia of their train of thought will lead them off the track, and they will become confused. Thus, if you are going to add tangential or supplementary material, use a **parenthetical transition** such as "In passing, it is interesting to note that . . ." or, "Let me just add that . . ." Your audience will appreciate your thoughtfulness.

To Add Emphasis Since not all ideas in your speech will be equally important, it is useful to occasionally note for your audience when an especially significant point, observation, or argument is about to be made. Such **emphatic transitions** might sound like this: "As you are preparing your backswing, it is especially important to remember to . . ." This extra emphasis nudges the audience's consciousness and urges your listeners to pay special attention to the point to follow.

To Add Material In most speeches you will have the opportunity to do more than just outline a main structure of points. You will also be developing those points with all of the forms of supporting material presented in Chapter 8. When you move from a specific point to one or more forms of supporting material, that material should be organically incorporated into the body of the speech by a clearly worded **additive transition.** For example, you might say, "One instance of this point is . . ."or "According to . . ."

To Subordinate and Coordinate Subpoints and Supporting Material Because everything you say during the course of a speech is not of equal significance, you will probably need a liberal sprinkling of coordinate and subordinate transitions. **Coordinate transitions** are those that help to indicate that two points are of equal importance, that is, that they are coordinate or equivalent. Thus, for example, when you say, "My second main point is that . . ." you are indicating that you have reached a second portion of your speech that is approximately equal to the previous main portion. **Subordinate transitions** are those that help to indicate that two related points are not equal; rather, one fits under the other in some manner. For example, if you were to say, "We can divide this point into three components, (a) . . . (b) . . . (c) . . ." you would be using a subordinate transition to mark the relation of the three subpoints to the main point of which they are a division.

To Give the Speech a Sense of Rhythm Transitions are a major source of a speech's sense of living rhythm since they perform the task of motivating the subsequent phases of the speech at the very same time they are closing off a previous phase of the speech. To see this dual rhythmic function of closing off one phase of a process while simultaneously opening up the next, remember the example of the hourglass; the narrowing is the transition between the upper and lower halves. **Rhythmic transitions** perform exactly this same function of ending one section while at the same time opening up the next section. This preparation of a new act during the closing phases of a previous one is the source of organic, rhythmic unity in public speeches.

Suggestions for Effective, Organic Transitions

In closing the discussion of transitions, it is worth noting several small precautions concerning transitions that can help your speech *seem* as organized as it really is. These precautions may be summarized as three very specific suggestions.

Use more transitions rather than less. All things being equal, it is better to err on the side of using too many transitions than to use too few and thereby allow your audience to get lost, sidetracked, or confused. Since the audience hears the speech only once, and cannot rerun it to see where they went astray, give them as much help as possible by weaving an ample amount of transitional phrasing into your speech.

Vary your transitions. Since transitions serve many functions in your speech, you should use a variety of transitional types to make sure that your speech holds together in as many ways, and at as many levels, as possible. You should also plan to use a variety of transitional phrases even when you are serving the same function repeatedly. For example, do not restrict yourself to *moreover* as an additive transition. Use *in addition to* or any of the others. Too many repetitions of exactly the same transitional phrase can make it harder, rather than easier, for your audience to follow the organization of your speech.

Avoid "shopping list" transitions. Some transitional words are almost inherently vague when used too frequently within a speech, making a speech sound like a disorganized string of ideas that haphazardly follow one another. These transitions may be called **shopping list transitions** because they provide your speech with all the organization of a typical shopping list. Consider how a shopping list is usually prepared. You jot down the things you need in whatever order they happen to come to mind—perhaps a food item first, then a bathroom item, then two more food items, followed by a new plant for your living area, and so on. There is no system to your list because the supermarket has its own system of organization, which it imposes on you and your list. Aisle after aisle, you go up and down looking for and picking up items in the order the store has arranged them. The order on your list is irrelevant to the order in which you actually pick up items. You simply cross them off as you find them.

Shopping list transitions make your speech sound randomly organized and make you dependent upon the organizational skills of your audience to put your speech together into a coherent whole. Such transitions make it sound as if you had merely jotted down your speech ideas in whatever order they happened to come to mind. Three of the worst offenders are *and, then,* and *next you.* To see their effect, listen to yourself the next time you go shopping and see if you don't hear yourself saying something like this: "I need one of those *and* those *and* these *and* those . . . *and* . . . *and* . . . *and*." Or perhaps, *"Then* I need . . . *then* . . . some of this, *then* some of that . . . , *then* . . . *then* . . . *then."* And finally, *"Next* I . . . *next* . . . , *next."*

Such transitions fail to reveal the internal structure of the speech because, as coordinating transitions, they make every item they join together equal to all others. When used extensively, they hide rather than reveal your organizational plan. Not every sentence of your speech is equal in importance to every other; surely, you intended to subordinate some ideas to others. Shopping list transitions will not accomplish this; they can only coordinate—making your speech sound like a random list of ideas about your topic.

Conclusion

To be as lifelike as possible, your speech as a whole must follow the organic principles explained in Chapter 3. The introduction functions like the speech's impulse phase, and the principle of internal preparation is especially important here. Your introduction must prepare the audience for the main body of the speech. Similarly, your conclusion functions like the speech's cadence and must be constructed so as to fulfill the principle of closure. Finally, the skill with which you use transitional phrases determines whether or not your speech achieves a sense of forward motion, growth, and climax, or if it merely seems like a loosely related string of sentences. Give ample attention to your introduction, transitions, and conclusion and your audience will give greater attention to your speech and its main ideas.

Questions for Review

1. What are the major functions of a good speech introduction? A good conclusion? Why are transitions necessary to good speech construction?

2. List three techniques you can use to give your speech's conclusion a strong sense of closure.

3. What are the major functions of transitions?

Questions for Discussion

1. Why do questions have such a powerful effect on capturing the audience's attention?

2. What are the advantages of telling a story or anecdote to begin a speech?

3. How can you use transitions most effectively as you try to implement the principles of effective public speaking?

Things to Try

1. Prepare three or more alternate introductions to the same speech body. Try different techniques for fulfilling each of the major introductory functions.

2. Prepare three or more alternate conclusions to the same speech. Again, try different techniques for fulfilling each of the major concluding functions.

Bibliography

Burke, Kenneth. *Counter–Statement.* London: Cambridge University Press, 1931.

Nofsinger, Robert E., Jr. "The Demand Ticket: A Conversational Device for Getting the Floor." *Communication Monographs* 42 (1975), 1–9.

Smith, Barbara H. *Poetic Closure: A Study of How Poems End.* Chicago: University of Chicago Press, 1968.

CHAPTER 11

Projecting Your Ideas Visually

*O*ne of the most useful forms of supporting material for developing public speeches is the visual aid. It is such an important speech resource that it is being given its own chapter. And yet you may wonder why so much attention is being given to a form of supporting material that is not *spoken* at all. As you will soon discover, visual aids can help you express many ideas that words alone either cannot express at all, or cannot express as efficiently without the visual aid.

The reason visual aids require their own entire chapter stems from the concept presented in Chapter 2: logical projection. There are many different ways of projecting your ideas in order to make them available to others. Visual aids, at least many of them, work on a very different principle of projection than do spoken sentences. Sentences line up many words *one after another* so that they are heard in a sequential order. This orderly progression of words expresses your ideas, asserting a specific statement about the topic of discussion. Understanding occurs when the listener is able to decode your sequence of words and convert it back into the idea you intended to transmit. In contrast, most visual aids show something *all at once;* but they do not make any actual *statements* about what they are showing. Most visual aids assert nothing. But they allow you to show, in a brief moment, some aspect of an idea you want to express. In this way visual aids permit you to use your words to explain only the elements that need propositional commentary.

Since visual modes of projecting your ideas are sometimes better than the verbal mode alone in helping accomplish your speech's goals, it is important to know as much about visual aids as you can. Armed with such information, you can more thoughtfully choose the method of projecting your ideas that best serves your speech's purposes. Because most visual aids work on the principle of *simultaneous presentation* rather than the principle of *serial progression,* you need to consider them carefully before you can use them effectively. The purpose of this chapter is to explain how and when to use visual aids in your speeches.

*T*he Functions of Visual Aids

Visual aids can serve many functions. Before turning to the practical questions of what kinds of visual aids you might use and how to use them well, it is important to understand what a good visual aid can help you accomplish. Three of the most important functions of visual aids may be stated as follows:

1. Visual aids *enhance* audience attention.

2. Visual aids *reinforce* the spoken word.

3. Visual aids help *clarify* complex ideas.

Let's look at each of these functions—enhancing, reinforcing, and clarifying—a little more closely.

Visual Aids Enhance Audience Attention

Because paying attention to a speech is a mental act an audience performs, your audience's attention will have peaks and valleys that parallel the rise and decline of the four phases of all acts. This ebb and flow of audience attention is an inevitable consequence of the way people think. Since audience members cannot understand and remember a speech's key ideas if they are not paying attention at the time those ideas are being expressed, it is important to build a variety of attention-inducing materials into your speech. The goal is to try to guide the audience's peaks and valleys of attention to serve your speech's needs.

Because visual aids are usually quite different from sentences, revealing a visual aid at an important moment in your speech (or turning to use a previously revealed visual aid) can enhance your audience's attention. For example, if your speech is discussing an abstract principle of economics such as depreciation, using a chart that shows a five-year depreciation curve, and returning to the aid periodically throughout your discussion as you make points about the trend of the curve, should both recapture and refocus the audience's attention. As their heads turn and their eyes focus away from you, toward what you are pointing out, their attention will be restimulated.

Since you cannot eliminate the natural lapses in an audience's attention, you should try to serve as a pacemaker for their attention rhythm. Try to build your speech so that you guide the audience's attention—inattention rhythm. In this way, the audience members will be most fully attending when you are presenting your most important ideas. Using visual aids effectively can pique (and peak) faltering audience interest when and where you want it—by serving as a new center of attention. Moving from uninterrupted speech to a visual aid creates motion, and motion usually captures attention. Working to and from your visual aids should be a helpful resource in guiding your audience's periods of attention.

Visual Aids Reinforce the Spoken Word

Not only do visual aids enhance audience attention; they also help reinforce the spoken word. The spoken word is ephemeral, evanescent, fleeting. The words you say disappear almost as quickly as you speak them. If the ideas carried by your words are not understood as you speak them, the audience has no second chance—unless you happen to repeat them.

Most visual aids are more permanent than the spoken word. They can be left in view for an extended period of time. They can be referred to again and

Figure 11-1 Speaker Using Key Word Sequence on Posterboard

again throughout the speech. Audience members have time to build up their understanding of the ideas you are explaining by looking at the aids as frequently and lengthily as they need to. Furthermore, the audience has help in remembering the central ideas you are trying to convey if you leave some visible representation of those ideas for them to see. Therefore, a second function of visual aids is to help you reinforce your audience's understanding and memory of your key ideas by keeping those ideas visually in front of them as long as necessary.

Figure 11-1 demonstrates the use of a very simple visual aid to accomplish the reinforcement function. It is a straightforward poster listing the main points of the speech as a **key word sequence.** Such an aid could be revealed during your speech's introduction and left in view throughout the speech for occasional reference at transition points.

Another way to use a simple visual aid to reinforce your ideas, and to create a sense of forward movement as well, is to vary the simple key word sequence slightly. This time, instead of revealing all your main points at the same time, you will place the poster itself in view, but have the key words covered with some sort of easily removed masking material. Then, as you move from topic to topic within your speech, you can **progressively reveal the key words** by removing their masks. This creates some suspense (and therefore anticipation), provides additional movement to your speech, and still serves to reinforce the points of your speech after they have been made—since the key words for each of your points will remain in view. Figure 11-2 illustrates this technique.

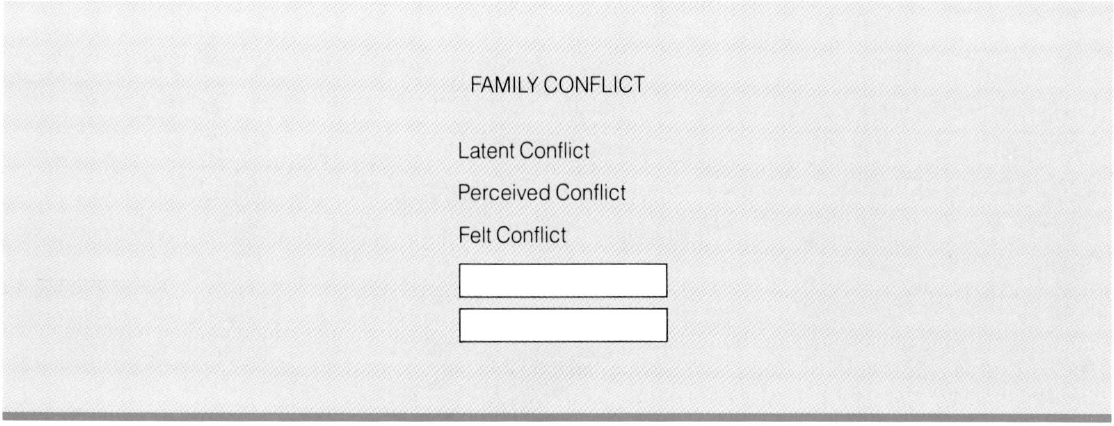

FAMILY CONFLICT

Latent Conflict

Perceived Conflict

Felt Conflict

Figure 11-2   Key Word Poster with Some Words Hidden

Visual Aids Help Clarify Complex Ideas

Some ideas are so complex that it is difficult for the audience to keep all the necessary components in mind at the same time. Your speech is given as a long sequence of words, but the idea those words represent is something that is a simultaneous whole. When an idea is so complex that it is hard to hold onto the earliest words long enough to make sense of the later ones, the audience needs the help a visual aid can provide. The relative permanence and stability of the visual aid gives the audience additional time to build up their understanding of how all the parts relate to the complex whole you are trying to explain.

There are several types of complex ideas for which visual aids are especially helpful. Visual aids should probably be used whenever you are trying to accomplish the following goals:

Clarify Numerical Relationships Many speeches require you to compare and contrast quantities or magnitudes of one thing, attribute, or quality with those of another. Since it is difficult for most audiences to keep the verbal expression of large numbers in mind long enough for you to develop your point, visualize the quantitative comparisons you are making at the same time you are talking about them. For example, a **pie graph** can be used to dramatize the percentage that one individual portion represents of some larger whole. In Figure 11-3, the pie graph supports the speaker's claim that caring for a house pet is a major responsibility, not to be undertaken lightly. It does so by showing the large percentage of a family's income a pet can often consume.

Chart Trends A trend is not a thing; it is an activity that occurs over time: Birth rates increase or decrease, new car sales progress or regress, the company's

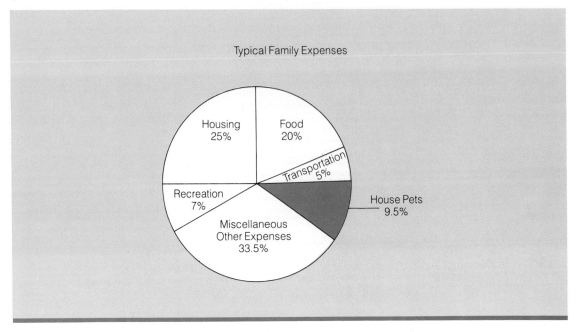

Figure 11-3   Pie Graph Used to Dramatize Percentages

economic growth improves or worsens. **Line graphs** are especially helpful in charting trends because they naturally lead the eye to follow the progression of the trend. Figure 11-4 uses a simple line graph to chart a two-year trend in the sales of a bathing suit manufacturer. The graph shows both the seasonal nature of such a business and the company's improved sales from one year to the next.

Illustrate and Dramatize Numerical Comparisons Visual aids may also be used to dramatize relative magnitudes, especially when a disparity between two or more magnitudes is important. Figure 11-5 use a **bar graph** to illustrate the large disparity among the sizes of the standing armies of some of the world's major military powers. It is a dramatic reminder that the balance of military force throughout the world is indeed a precarious one. As you can see, bar graphs are especially useful in emphasizing relative magnitudes, due to the proportional lengths of their component elements, that is, the bars themselves. Line graphs emphasize direction; bar graphs emphasize bulk or size.

Reveal What Something Looks Like If you are talking about an object, or if an object plays an important role in your speech, you may want to show an example of the item to your audience. This is especially true if size, shape, and color are significant to understanding your point. Figure 11-6 illustrates the

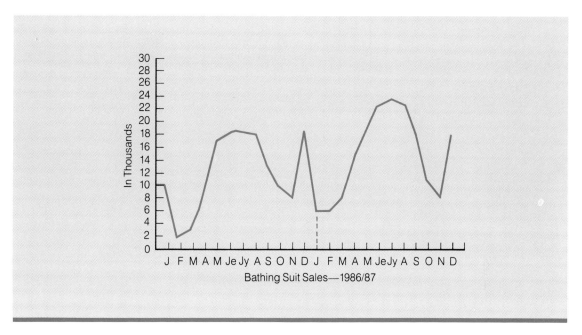

Figure 11-4   Line Graph Used to Chart a Trend over Time

function of visual aids in revealing what something looks like— in this case the different types of diamond cuts. In a speech on a topic such as this, the speaker would probably find it necessary to show a picture of each of the five most prominent diamond cuts side by side, so that the different shapes of the cuts could be compared and contrasted with one another. Without such an aid, it would be almost impossible to give this speech effectively.

Reveal the Relationship of Parts to Some Whole In a speech discussing something that has two or more component parts, try visualizing the relationship of the parts to one another. Figures 11-7 and 11-8 illustrate visual aids depicting how the parts of some complex object relate to one another to produce the whole. Figure 11-7 shows the various components of the gold electrolysis process, making it easier for the speaker to talk about the steps in the process without having to waste time merely describing the structure of the component parts. Figure 11-8 shows the proper placement of the two notches that must be cut for properly felling a tree. These aids were each necessary to their respective speeches because of the difficulty of putting into words the relationship among parts which these aids so easily reveal.

Physical objects are not the only things that have many parts to illustrate. Sometimes when a complex subject is analyzed into its component parts, you will want to show how these components relate to one another. Figure 11-9 shows how such an aid might look. The speaker has illustrated the compo-

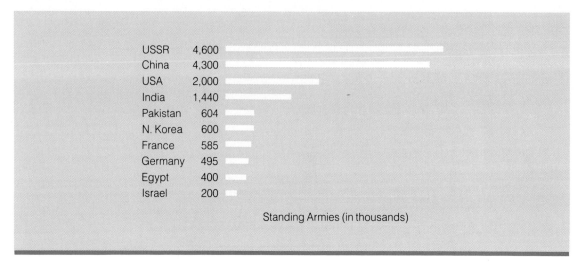

Figure 11-5   Bar Graph Used to Emphasize Relative Magnitudes

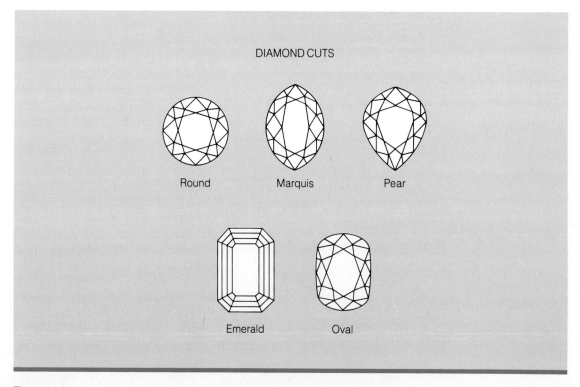

Figure 11-6   Visual Aid Used to Show What Something Looks Like

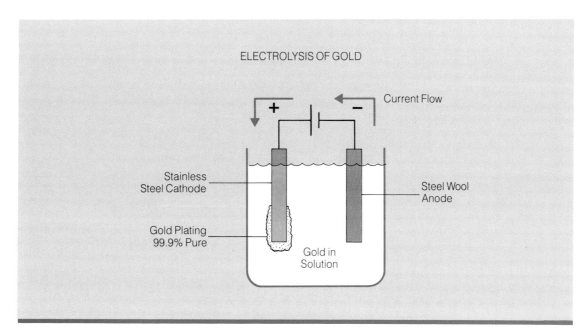

Figure 11-7   Visual Aid Showing the Relationship of Parts to One Another

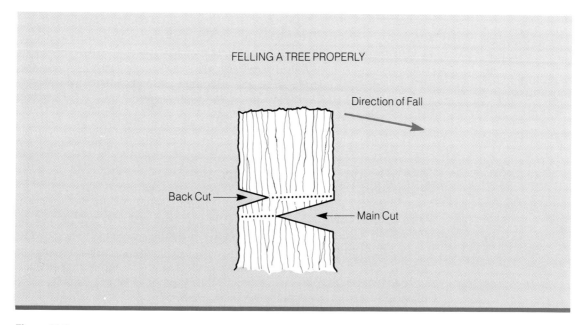

Figure 11-8   Visual Aid Showing the Relationship of Parts to One Another

(A)	Percentage of U.S. RDA		(B)	Nutritional Information per Serving	
	Protein	20		Serving Size	1 cup
	Vitamin A	10		Servings Per Container	8
	Vitamin C	4		Calories	100
	Thiamine	6		Carbohydrate	11 grams
	Riboflavin	25		Protein	8 grams
	Niacin	*		Fat Content	2 grams
	Calcium	30		Salt (Sodium, Potassium)	200 milligrams
	Iron	*			
	Vitamin D	25			

Figure 11-9   Visual Aid Showing How Labeled Components Relate to One Another

nents of a typical nutritional analysis on a package of processed food. The aid lists the elements of the two types of nutritional analysis and shows how they are organized to display the nutritional information they offer.

Make Process Relationships Clear If you are explaining the stages in some process, your audience may find a visual aid helpful in keeping the steps and their chronological order in mind. There are many forms of charts to help you accomplish this goal. Figure 11-10 shows a **flow chart** that employs only key words and arrows to show the direction of chronological flow. Figure 11-11 is more detailed in that it not only uses key words to name the stages of the process, but also illustrates each step with an appropriate drawing to serve as a visual reminder of the step. Although more difficult to prepare, this technique is more effective in helping the audience remember your points.

*T*ypes of Visual Aids

Many kinds of visual aids are available, and you will probably need to use all of them at one time or another. The purpose of this section is to review the types of aids you might use. One of the most fundamental distinctions among types of visual aids is that between electrically enhanced and nonelectrically enhanced visual aids. Because the decision whether or not to use electrical enhancement to project your ideas is an important one, this distinction will be used to organize the discussion of the types of visual aids.

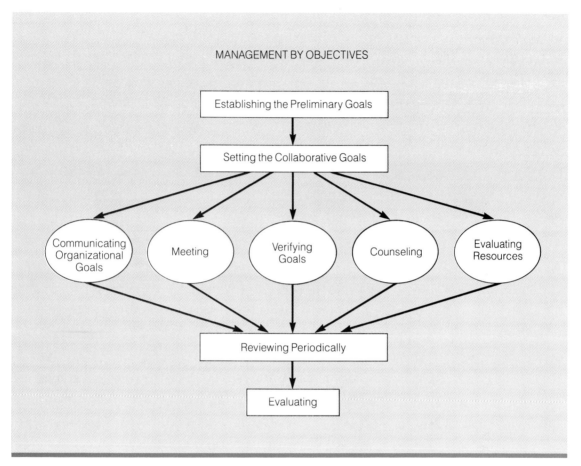

Figure 11-10	Flow Chart Using Words Only

Electrically Enhanced Visual Aids

Electrically enhanced visual aids include all those aids requiring electricity and some sort of projection hardware for their operation. Such aids most commonly include the following specific types: (1) films/videos, (2) slides, (3) overhead transparencies, (4) opaque projections, and (5) audio equipment (such as phonographs and tape recorders). Each of these aids has its own special advantages, but there are also some potential disadvantages to be aware of.

Films and Videos Films and videos are especially helpful if you want to show movement or changes over time. A speech about the stages of a plant's flow-

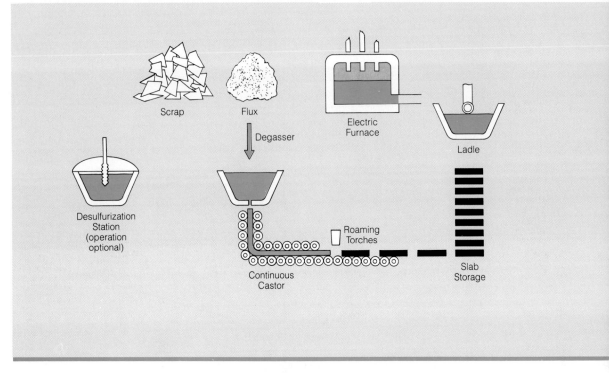

Scrap

Flux

Degasser

Electric
Furnace

Ladle

Desulfurization
Station
(operation
optional)

Roaming
Torches

Continuous
Castor

Slab
Storage

Figure 11-11   Flow Chart Using Words and Pictures

ering or about some activity that cannot be shown live before your audience (such as riding a bull or learning a figure skating maneuver) might employ a brief movie as part of its visual aid package. Another way a film might be employed is to provide a focus for a discussion. For example, at a panel discussion concerning the attempts to teach a chimpanzee to use American Sign Language, the panel moderator began the program with a film showing the trainers and their chimpanzee at work so that the audience would have a common point of reference as they listened to the speeches on this topic.

Slides   Although a series of slides cannot reveal the same sense of progressive movement that a movie can, slides have the advantage that they can stop action for detailed observation. Furthermore, slides can, if well planned, focus audience attention exactly where you want it. Slides are especially helpful when what you want your audience to see is too large or too small to be seen live during your speech.

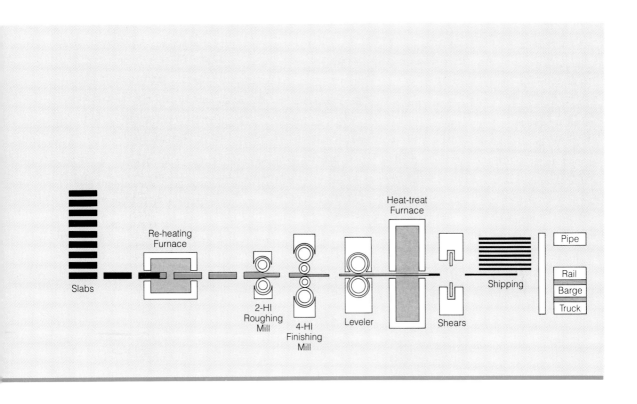

Slabs

Re-heating
Furnace

2-HI
Roughing
Mill

4-HI
Finishing
Mill

Leveler

Heat-treat
Furnace

Shears

Shipping

Pipe

Rail

Barge

Truck

Overhead Transparencies Overhead transparencies work by allowing you to write or draw on a piece of plastic film. Light shines through the film and whatever you have written on it is projected onto a screen. Overhead projectors are especially useful when you have many aids to show during the course of a long presentation, or when the room is too large for a posterboard aid to be easily seen.

Opaque Projections Opaque projectors permit you to show a picture from a book, magazine, or whatever to a large audience at the same time. Rather than shining light through the picture, as slides and overhead projectors do, the opaque projector reflects light off the original source and through a lens to the screen. The major disadvantages of opaque projectors are that they are generally bulky to handle, and they require the room to be be very dark in order for the image to be seen. Under most circumstances, you would be better off making slides of the pictures you wish to show and then using a slide projector to show your aids.

This is a fast-food outlet in Japan. Do you know how to cook foods from other countries? What ethnic groups make up your community? How have they affected the community?

Audio Equipment Although phonographs and tape players are not literally *visual* aids, they can perform some of the same functions—especially enhancing audience attention and clarifying a complex idea. If, for example, your speech is about the development of a particular musician's work throughout her career, your audience might find it especially helpful if you played samples of the artist's music taken from the various periods of development. Similarly, if you are talking about types of birdcalls heard in your local community, your audience would want to hear samples of what these sound like.

In spite of their usefulness as speech aids, there are several problems common to all of these devices, problems that you should consider as you think about using them. First, whatever can go wrong will. Three-pronged plugs will require adapters at the least opportune moments; projection bulbs will burn out without a replacement in sight; and the film or video tape will break right in the middle of the point you most want to illustrate. So, if you are using such aids, it is important to have backup supplies ready and waiting whenever possible.

Second, such aids tend to take over your speech and dominate it. Slides are especially wily and seductive in this regard. If you are not careful, your speech will degenerate into a disorganized commentary on your pretty slides. Remember, the slides are supposed to aid your previously prepared speech text. They should not become a moment-by-moment inspiration for your words. If you've ever been subjected to a friend's vacation slides, you know the problem. Your friends ramble on and on about their vacation. They certainly did not prepare a speech for the occasion—and you go to sleep. The point is, you must prepare your speech first, and then choose your aids *to help you make the points you had already planned to make.* You should not start with a series of slides you simply want to show and then hope to spontaneously fabricate a speech that ties them all together.

Nonelectrically Enhanced Visual Aids

Nonelectrically enhanced visual aids include all those things you bring with you to show the audience that do not require electricity in order to magnify images or sounds. We will consider five types: (1) the speaker, (2) actual objects, (3) models of actual objects, (4) representations of actual objects, and (5) representations of conceptual data.

The Speaker Sometimes you can be your own best visual aid. Over and above your normal animation and clothing, there are three special ways you can be a visual aid during your speech.

Use descriptive gestures. If you are describing the size of something, show with your hands or fingers how big it is; if you are talking about the shape of something, perhaps you can draw the shape in the air or form it with your hands. If something is five feet tall, relate that height to your own height by marking shoulder height or head height with your hands held at that level. All of these gestures will help the audience get a better mental picture of the size and shape of what you are verbally describing.

Model appropriate postures and movements. The second way you may be your own best visual aid is to demonstrate specific postures and movements. If you are teaching golf or skiing, for example, the audience must be able to see the appropriate stance in order to get started. Model it for them. They must also be able to perform a complex pattern of movement if they are to succeed in learning the skill. Show that to them as well.

Wear appropriate clothing. Most public speaking situations require you to dress up for the occasion. But "dressing up" does not necessarily mean wearing a suit and tie if you are a male, or a skirt and blazer if you are a female. Many subjects and situations allow you to dress appropriately for the topic. There are at least two ways to do this. The first is simply to wear clothing that sets the tone or mood for your speech. For example, a student giving a speech about The Society for Creative Anachronisms might come dressed in Renaissance-style clothing; a student speaking about day hiking in the mountains might come dressed in hiking boots and shorts. In each case, the clothing establishes the mood for the topic and sets the tone for the speech.

A second way to use clothing requires you to go beyond creating a mood and to actually integrate the clothing into the speech. One especially popular way to use clothing is to either add or remove pieces of clothing to help make a point. For example, if your speech were about how to use your clothing to save yourself from drowning in a boating accident, you might want to demonstrate how to remove your pants, tie them off, and inflate them as a life preserver. If, on the other hand, you wanted to reveal the differences between "drugstore" cowboys and working cowboys, you might come dressed as a typical drugstore variety, and show your audience by a sequence of clothing changes how to transform yourself into a working cowboy. There are numerous variations on this theme which you yourself might try.

Actual Objects You may have thought you left Show and Tell behind when you were graduated from first grade. But not so. Show and Tell was surprisingly good practice for many of the speaking experiences you will have as an adult. Speakers can often integrate actual objects into their speeches. If you are talking about your hobby of carving wood figures, for example, then bring some of your work to show. Most topics that involve the use of actual objects can be enhanced if you bring one or more examples to share with your audience.

Models of Actual Objects Many times the subject of your speech requires you to talk about an object that is too large or small to be seen conveniently by your audience. When this happens, your best bet may be to bring a model of

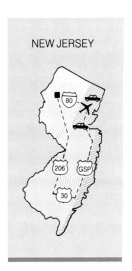

NEW JERSEY

Figure 11-12

Map Drawn to Highlight
a Speech Purpose

the object. For example, if you are talking about genetic engineering, you can hardly show an actual gene. But you *can* bring a plastic model of a gene and show the audience what scientists are presently trying to do in the realm of gene splicing.

Representations of Actual Objects If a model is not convenient to obtain or to work with, your next best visual aid is a pictorial representation of the actual object. Show your audience a photograph, a literal drawing, or an abstracted, schematic sketch of the object you are talking about. These serve much the same purpose as do models and objects, but they are often more convenient to prepare and easier to use with larger audiences. When your audience gets to be large in size, you may find that preparing slides of your pictorial representations will become necessary.

Representations of Conceptual Data Not every topic you will be talking about necessarily involves physical objects. Sometimes you must help your audience understand complex conceptual data. There are four types of visual aids that are especially helpful when you are trying to explain difficult conceptual data: flow charts, maps, graphs, and diagrams.

Flow charts are drawings of the various stages in a chronological sequence. The simplest kind of flow chart merely uses boxed key word names for the stages in the sequence being explained. Figure 11-10 (p. 211) illustrates this type of flow chart. A more detailed type of flow chart includes schematic drawings of each of the steps, labeled with descriptive words. Figure 11-11 illustrates this approach. The drawings aid memory by linking the pictures with the words.

Maps describe a space and show how all the components of the space relate to one another. When using maps, keep the map as simple and focused as you can given the use you will be making of it. Figure 11-12 illustrates a typical map that might be used in a speech. In this speech, the speaker's goal was to talk about the four major areas for tourism in New Jersey. Notice that the map was redrawn and simplified to focus upon just that purpose. It contains the outline of the state, a division of the state into those four portions, and a single road tracing a circular route from one area to the next in sequence. No extraneous details were included. Even the figure of the car was mobile, so that it could be placed within the quadrant of the map the speaker was currently discussing.

Graphs are pictures of numerical relations. There are several types of graphs, and each type is able to feature certain kinds of information especially well. Pie graphs, line graphs, and bar graphs have all been described and illustrated above (see Figures 11-3, 11-4, and 11-5).

Diagrams are drawings representing the configuration of any set of elements. They show how the elements relate to one another in space. Figure 11-7 is a diagram showing the relationship of parts that are required for the process of extracting pure gold from a mineral solution.

Avoiding Ineffective Visual Aids

So far this chapter has emphasized the functions of visual aids, the various type of visual aids available, and the ways of using them. Before closing, we must discuss briefly how you can avoid some of the most common pitfalls in using visual aids. There are at least eight commonsense guidelines for successfully using visual aids. Follow these guidelines and your aids will actually *aid* your speech; ignore them and your aids may turn into visual distractions.

Prepare your visual aids before you deliver your speech. Many types of visual aids can be spontaneously produced during your speech if you have access to a chalkboard or sketch pad. In spite of the apparent ease of producing such aids, there are good reasons to avoid the spontaneously inspired visual aid. To prepare your aid on the spur of the moment invites you to make too many of the most fundamental errors you should guard against in visual aid preparation. Such aids may take too much time to draw—as you correct and modify them. Because you are concentrating on drawing, you are likely to stop talking, which means that the speech comes to a screeching halt. Furthermore, because you are drawing on the board, you are likely to have your back to the audience for long periods of time, thereby losing contact with them. Therefore, unless there is a good reason for the audience to see you actually preparing the aid in their presence—for example, a demonstration of how to do something—it is best to prepare your visual aids in advance.

Make the visual aids large enough to be seen without strain. How large should your visual aids be? Ask yourself: "How large is the room I will be speaking in?" "How far away will people be seated?" These questions will help determine how large your visual aids must be in order to be seen without straining the audience. Aids that are too small distract the audience's attention away from what you are saying— they are busy trying to figure out what the aid looks like or what it says. The lettering on most posters, for example, should be from two to four inches high depending upon the size of the room and the type of aid you are using. If four-inch lettering is too small for the typical audience member to read, you may need to use electronically enhanced aids such as slides and overhead transparencies to magnify the image.

Make the visual aid simple enough to be understood at a glance. Keep your visual aids simple. Do not clutter them with extraneous information. A visual aid should be no more complex than the ideas it is designed to convey. For example, do not add more labels than you actually intend to discuss. While you must talk about the aid during the course of your speech, once you have finished discussing it, there should be nothing about the aid that still requires commentary. The information on the aid should thereafter be transparent to your audience. This will not be the case if you have made the aid more complex than minimally necessary to do the job.

When an aid seems to require numerous components, it is often better to make two or more aids, each with only part of the information featured, rather than to try to squeeze too much information onto a single aid. If you spread your information out over two or more aids, you can move from one aid to the next as you need to focus on specific aspects of your topic. Spreading the information over two or more aids has the dual advantage of maintaining audience attention as you change from the old aid to the new one and of focusing that attention on only those features of the aid you are actually talking about at the time.

Use color and contrast selectively to project your ideas. Closely related to the goal of making your visual aids large enough to be seen without strain is the need to give the visual aids enough color and contrast so that what you are trying to show clearly stands out from the background. For most purposes, heavy white posterboard with thick black lettering works best. Trying to add a lot of color when that color serves no specific communicative purpose is neither necessary nor helpful.

Talk **about** *your visual aid, but talk* **to** *your audience.* Two closely related pieces of advice are embedded in this guideline. First, talk *about* your visual aid. A single picture may be worth a thousand words, but it cannot by itself say a thousand words. Your visual aids will never truly "speak for themselves." They depend upon you to speak for them, since they themselves are stony silent. Whenever you use a visual aid, you will still need to discuss the information on the visual aid. You must make clear what the aid means and why you have included this particular aid in your speech. Merely leaving it in view is not enough.

Second, talk *to* your audience. Because you are talking about your visual aid, it is easy for you to become distracted and begin talking *to* to the visual aid instead of to your audience. But your visual aid is not only stony silent; it is also stony deaf. Only your audience needs to hear your speech. Only they can act upon it. Darting your eyes frequently to your aid, or gazing at it for long, uninterrupted periods of time, prevents you from keeping contact with the audience throughout your speech. Visual aids need to be talked about whenever appropriate, but remember that you are talking about them to your audience.

Don't block the audience's view of the visual aid. Once you have gone to the effort to make a good visual aid, be sure to place it where everyone can readily see it. Often speakers will display an aid beside or behind themselves and thereby cut off the line of vision for part of their audience. A good way to position the visual aid is on an easel or tripod, to your right (if you are right-handed), and slightly in front of your lectern.

Once you have the aid positioned where you want it, try pointing toward it with the hand nearest the aid so that you keep an open stance. Crossing your body with your arm (as you would be likely to do if you are right-handed and are pointing to an aid to your left) forces you (a) to step in front of your aid (thereby cutting off some of your audience) and (b) to turn your back on a large portion of your audience so that you lose contact with them in the process.

Reveal your aids only while you are using them. Whenever you display a visual aid, your audience assumes that you intend for the aid to be seen, and they begin wondering what you will do with it. To avoid this kind of distraction, don't display your aids until they are serving their intended *enhancing, reinforcing,* and *clarifying* functions. This guideline has two simple corollaries:

1. Don't reveal your aids too early.

2. Remove your aids when you are done with them.

If you use your aids to serve the three functions, and avoid the seven most common pitfalls in visual aid use, your speeches should be both more memorable and more enjoyable. But you can go beyond these negative warnings and try to bring your visual aids to life.

Create motion in your visual aids. Although most visual aids are literally static, you can create the life-giving illusion of motion in several ways. First, you can use the progressive revelation of a key word sequence, which was mentioned earlier (Figure 11-2). This animates the aid by tracing a pattern from top to bottom. Second, you can use arrows to direct the eye from point to point in the illustration. This leads the eye in the direction of the arrows, thereby creating motion. Third, you can create motion by pointing to features of the aid as you refer to them during your speech. The literal motion of your hand or a pointer imbues the aid with an added sense of virtual motion. But, whatever technique you use, creating a sense of motion in your aids will make them seem more vivid and alive, and will thereby enhance the overall organic qualities of your speech.

Conclusion

Communication, in the most literal sense of the term, always occurs within a complex welter of other closely related activities, both visual and auditory. Our eyes supplement our ears as we try to make sense of the speech we are hearing. Because our eyes participate in so many aspects of the total speech communication situation, visual aids can often enrich the speech itself. Visual aids perform three functions: enhancing your audience's general level of attention, reinforcing the spoken presentation of your ideas, and clarifying complex ideas by revealing their many interrelations all at once. Although not every speech will require visual aids as a supplement, most speeches can benefit from the additional impact or clarity provided by well-chosen visual aids.

Questions for Review

1. What major functions can visual aids perform for a public speaker?

2. What are the major types of electrically enhanced visual aids? When would you benefit from using each of these types?

3. What are the major types of nonelectrically enhanced visual aids? When would you benefit from using each of these types?

4. When is an electrically enhanced visual aid preferable to a nonelectrically enhanced visual aid?

Questions for Discussion

1. How does speech differ in mode of projection from the manner of presentation used by most visual aids?

2. Chapter 9 presents several examples of statistics. Which types of visual aids would be most useful in reinforcing or clarifying each of those statistics?

3. Examine the other types of supporting material presented in Chapter 9. Decide how you might use a visual aid to give these verbal materials greater impact and memorability.

Things to Try

1. Select a complex process from some area of interest to you and prepare a series of visual aids that presents the process in a clear and systematic progression.

2. Examine the visual aids in several of your textbooks (including this one). Determine what types of aids are used and evaluate how well they contribute to enhancing your attention, reinforcing the ideas being presented, and clarifying complex ideas. Do some of the books accomplish these functions better than others? Which subject matters seem to require the greatest number and variety of visual aids?

Preparing a Diagnostic Outline

Principles of Outline Preparation

Techniques for Outline Preparation

Sample Completed Outlines

Conclusion

Most people have gone to a physician for a routine checkup. The doctor administers a battery of tests to see if all of your organic functions are operating as they should be: heart rate, blood pressure, respiration, and digestion are all systematically checked out. If some problem is discovered, a corrective course of action is recommended: a change in diet, additional exercise, or reduced smoking and drinking. In some cases a prescription for medicine may be issued. In serious cases, emergency surgery may be called for. Whatever the doctor's recommendation, the whole process begins with a routine diagnostic checkup before you have a chance to feel the most acute symptoms.

Preparing a detailed analytical outline of your speech serves the same purpose as the physician's battery of diagnostic tests. The outline should catch any major problems with the speech's "organic functions" before you experience serious symptoms—for example, at the time you are presenting the speech to your audience. The purpose of this chapter is to explain how to conduct a detailed diagnostic outline of your speech's vital signs so that you can analyze the condition of your speech **before you deliver it.** Although no physical examination procedure can guarantee that you will catch every problem, the one described here is quite systematic and formal in its procedures and should identify any major problems with your speech. Furthermore, even though accidents can happen to even the healthiest speech, your best bet is to begin the public speaking experience with as fit a speech as possible. Since a diagnostic outline is far more detailed than the outline you will typically use when you actually deliver your speech, the final section of the chapter will explain how to adapt your diagnostic outline for use in preparing a performance or presentation outline.

There are many ways to visually design your outline, but the method recommended in this chapter is especially useful in helping you evaluate the organic qualities of your speech. Outlining follows several standardized procedures that have been worked out over the years for ease in the process of diagnostic testing.

An outline is a visual projection of the structure of your speech. Every major aspect of speech preparation discussed in earlier chapters will be expressed in the final form of the diagnostic outline. The diagnostic outline, therefore, is indeed a detailed tool. All of the techniques that follow are designed to help you test the quality of your preparation by having you project the results of that preparation into a visual form. The process is much like an X-ray or CAT-scan, both of which project the three-dimensional structure of your body into a two-dimensional picture for your doctor to see and evaluate. The outline is a two-dimensional projection of your multidimensional, full-bodied speech.

Principles of Outline Preparation

In preparing your outline, there are several principles to keep in mind that will help the diagnostic process serve its intended purpose. These principles will all be employed in the section on techniques for the diagnostic outline and will be illustrated there.

Project All Major Aspects of the Speech A speech is like a complex organism, with many functioning systems, and all of these deserve to be systematically checked out during your diagnostic exam. So plan to project *all* major structural aspects of your speech preparation in your analytical outline. This includes everything from the title of your speech and the speech's specific purpose, to the precise details of your introduction, body, and conclusion. Even brief summaries of your supporting material should be part of your diagnostic outline.

Use Spatial Relations to Project Ideational Relations A speech's ideational structure unfolds in time, but an outline can only project that structure as a pattern in space. Take advantage of the special characteristics of the spatial projection (especially its temporal permanence) by using spatial relations to indicate ideational relations—especially such relations as subordination and coordination of ideas. The example presented under the following principle concerning symbols demonstrates how spatial relations may be used to project conceptual or ideational relations. In it, each level of subordination is not only given a different symbol; it is also more deeply inset in order to show the subordination visually. Furthermore, when a sentence is too long to be completed on a single line, the visual projection of the subordination is preserved by maintaining the indentation. The sentence does not continue all the way back to the left, but follows the indentation above, which helps maintain the visual projection of the ideational relations.

Use a Consistent Pattern of Symbols A pattern of symbols has been developed for outlining that is both explicit in its meaning and consistent in its usage. It alternates between numbers and letters, and is usually ordered as follows:

I. Roman numerals are used for the main headings.
   A. Upper-case letters are used for the 1st level of subordinate headings.
      1. Arabic numbers are used for the 2nd level of subordinate headings.
         a. Lower-case letters are used for the 3rd level of subordinate headings.
            (1) Arabic numbers enclosed in parentheses are used for the 4th level of subordinate headings.
               (a) Lower-case letters enclosed in parentheses are used for the 5th level of subordinate headings.

The purpose of this system is to help you visually display the relationships among ideas that you have built into your speech, and to test whether or not ideas that have been subdivided have been divided in an appropriate manner.

Use Complete Sentences The purpose of your outline is to help you think through your speech as thoroughly as possible. The minimum unit for formulating a complex thought is the assertion, not the isolated word. Assertions are most often projected into complete sentences. A key word outline can only tell you what topics you intend to cover; it cannot reveal what assertions you intend to make about that topic. Although you may want to deliver your actual speech from a key word outline—and many instructors recommend this as the best way—your diagnostic outline serves a different purpose, and you must use complete sentences in order to project your assertions for diagnostic scrutiny. When you subsequently prepare your speaker's outline, you can use whatever form works best for you. As previously noted, the final portion of this chapter explains how to adapt your diagnostic outline for use as a presentation outline.

Revise Freely Your first attempt to outline your speech will probably include numerous flaws that need some corrective attention: organizational patterns that are inconsistently followed, ideas that don't belong in this particular speech, and examples that aren't really on the point you are trying to make. Also, you may find that you have omitted things that should be included: a point that is inadequately developed or supported, a redundancy of types of supporting material you hadn't intended, inadequate transitions between points, or a failure to provide enough explanatory elaboration where it is needed. Now is the time to catch these problems and correct them. The procedures presented below are designed exactly for this purpose, and so you should revise freely if your diagnostic tests reveal problems with your speech. The diagnostic outline is one of your final opportunities to shape your speech into the organic whole you are trying to make it. So revise, revise, revise, wherever necessary to make your speech even better.

Develop a Rage for Order Although the day-to-day business of living can get pretty messy and disorderly at times, the living organism itself is a highly ordered event in both space and time, and cannot afford to become internally disordered. To an organism, disorganization is death. In addition to the techniques developed below for displaying the orderliness of your speech, the physical presentation of your outline should be orderly as well. Outlines should be typed, or very neatly printed, on one side of a sheet of paper. If you hand print your outline, do not write the outline on spiral-bound notebook paper and rip it out. The ragged edges and the absence of a sense of visual completeness are too distracting. Quality diagnostic work demands quality tools and technique. So develop a rage for order in *all* aspects of your speech preparation work, including your diagnostic outline.

Techniques for Outline Preparation

Based on the principles presented above, as well as on what you've learned in the previous chapters about the organic principles of speech preparation, let's now take a step-by-step approach to preparing a complete diagnostic speech outline. While not every instructor will require all the detail presented here, the more completely you follow these techniques, the more alive your final speech is likely to be. Starting with a blank sheet of paper:

Give your speech a short, appropriate, but imaginative title. Near the top of your paper, write the title of your speech, giving the speech a short, appropriate title that imaginatively captures some important aspect of your speech. Since the title of your speech will often be announced at the time you are introduced to your audience, it is important that the title spark your audience's curiosity. The title helps establish the audience's initial expectations concerning your specific speech, and you want those expectations to prepare the way for attentive listening—not for a "Ho, Hum" response. The "Ho, Hum" response simply creates more static inertia for you to overcome as you try to establish a sense of forward motion in your speech. The difference between titles that merely give the speech a name and those that try to break through the audience's inertia, may be seen in the comparisons below:

"Ho, Hum" Titles	*"Oh Ho?" Titles*
How to Make a Terrarium	Gardening under Glass
Capital Punishment	An Eye for an Eye?
Grading Policies in High Schools	"Wadja Get?"
Facts about the Great Pyramid	Unsolved Mysteries of the Great Pyramid of Cheops

Put all of the identifying information in block form below the title and to the right of center. As shown in the sample outline at the end of the chapter, the diagnostic outline should identify the essentials of the speech's situation: speaker, audience, date, and so forth. Since your outline will probably be turned in to your instructor for evaluation, it is important to include the standard identifying information in block form on your outline. This usually includes the following information:

Your name

Course title, number, and section

Date due

Instructor's name

Since you will eventually be speaking to audiences outside the classroom, the same information, adapted to other social and professional speaking situations, can be included on every speech outline you prepare, as a reminder of the occasion for which the speech was originally prepared.

Your name

Group or organization before which the speech was delivered

Date the speech was given

Place the speech was given

Write out a clear and complete specific purpose statement for your speech. By the time you prepare your diagnostic outline, you should be able to formulate a clear, straightforward, and detailed specific purpose statement that serves as your guide in preparing the rest of the outline. Everything else you do should reflect the impulse represented by this specific purpose statement. For example, you might write:

Specific Purpose: To explain the three steps in making a terrarium

Specific Purpose: To present the four reasons why members of this class should sign an organ donor's card

In phrasing your specific purpose, be as explicit and complete as you can, while limiting your statement to a single, simple declarative sentence. As noted in Chapter 6 statements of purpose like the following provide your speech with very little focus:

Specific Purpose: To discuss the Equal Rights Amendment

Specific Purpose: To tell the audience a few of the reasons we need the MX Missile

Specific purposes such as the ones below are rambling and suggest two or more purposes rather than a single, overall purpose with several main points:

Specific Purpose: To examine the problem of obtaining an advanced college degree and, in part, to observe the growing necessity for doing so. This is related mainly to the problems of getting admitted to college.

Specific Purpose: To inform my fellow students, classmates, and perhaps consumers, that a type of advertisement exists that manipulates the subconscious mind and inhibits a person from making a conscious choice

Although the following specific purpose statement suggests more than one purpose, it has the advantage of being specific and to the point.

Specific Purpose: To explain the process of fish filleting, the materials necessary to fillet a fish, and the advantages of filleting over conventional cleaning

The sample outline shows how to place your specific purpose statement on the diagnostic outline.

Outline the introduction, body, and conclusion as three separate units. Speech outlines should reflect as closely as possible the structural relations that the parts of the speech have to one another. Of the three patterns of outlining shown below, Form A best reflects both the relations of the three main speech parts to one another and the relations of the points within each part to one another. Form A requires you to label each part separately and to begin your numbering over again within each part. See if you can tell why Forms B and C are less accurate representations of the relations of the parts of the speech to the whole.

LIKE THIS: Form A	NOT LIKE THIS: Form B	NOT LIKE THIS: Form C
Introduction	I. *Introduction*	*Introduction*
I.	A.	I.
II.	B.	II.
Body	II. *Body*	*Body*
I.	A.	III.
II.	B.	IV.
III.	C.	V.
	D.	
Conclusion	III. *Conclusion*	*Conclusion*
I.	A.	VI.
II.	B.	VII.

Although the differences among these three outline forms may seem trivial, Form A is preferred because it better projects the fact that the introduction, body, and conclusion each have a different set of functions to perform, and each have their own principles of internal organization to play out during the speech. Form B blurs these facts since, by labeling each speech subunit with a separate Roman numeral, it implies that each unit is coordinate with the other. Since that is not the case, Form B's outline method projects a false notion about the speech's structure. Similarly, Form C falsely suggests that the speech is simply a sequence of points and that the labels *introduction, body,* and *conclusion* are merely arbitrary points along the way. As you remember from earlier chapters, such a conclusion would not be true.

Outline your complete introduction, indicating in substantial detail how your introduction will fulfill each of the major introductory functions. By using a separate Roman numeral for each function wherever reasonably possible, outline your introduction. When necessary, combine functions, but indicate in parentheses in the margins which functions you are performing (as a way of checking whether all the necessary functions are being performed). Write out a complete version of what you might actually say. Do not write notes to the instructor, such as "I will capture attention by asking a series of questions about ..." Write out the attention-getting questions as a series under Roman I. The example below indicates how the introduction should be outlined.

INTRODUCTION

(attention getter)
    I. Are you listening? I mean, are you really listening? Not just to me. But to your friends and co-workers?

(relate to audience)
    II. Or, have you ever been telling a friend a problem and you felt that your friend just wasn't hearing you or really listening?

(announce subject)
    III. Today, I want to show you that there are some simple do's and don'ts to help make you a better listener.

(preview structure)
    IV. There are five simple things that you can do—or stop doing—to make yourself a better listener.
        A. Don't give unwanted advice.
        B. Don't rain on the speaker's parade.
        C. Allow the speaker time without interruptions.
        D. Don't give less than your undivided attention.
        E. Listen to the *words*, but not *just* the words.

(transition)
    V. Listen carefully and I'll give you more insight into each of these points.

Outline the body of your speech, in complete, simple declarative sentences. Your next step is to outline the body of the speech. Fill in the main headings (that is, the Roman numeral level), utilizing whatever pattern of organization you have previously decided upon (chronological, spatial, topical, and so on). Make sure each heading and subheading is worded as an assertion in a simple declarative sentence. Although your actual speech may use a rhetorical question, or other technique, to prepare for one or more of your main points (for example, "Why should you put a specified amount of your pay-check into savings every month?"), the question itself is not a main point in your speech—your *answer* is.

What your outline is testing at this point is whether or not you have a clearly articulated pattern of major assertions. Wording your main points as questions to be answered will not reveal whether or not you have a clearly worded assertion prepared to answer the question. The question is simply not as helpful as the declarative sentence assertion would be. Show the entire structure of the speech—both the main headings and all subordinate headings as well. Finally, use active verbs for your assertions if at all possible. They help give your speech a sense of forward motion. "Is" constructions are more static. In your actual speech you will combine active and static verbs to create rhythm between movement and rest, a rhythm that is characteristic of life itself. But the statements formulating your main points should be actively formulated if at all possible, since it is your main points that propel your speech forward at periodic intervals. Chapter 9 presented an example of how to convert main points using an "is" construction to points worded with active verbs.

Fill in your supporting material. Once you have outlined the structure of the speech, fill in summaries of the supporting material you intend to use. While you need not write out all of your supporting material word for word, you should include enough detail so that both you and your instructor know what types of developmental material you are planning to include to support the main and subordinate points of your speech. In parentheses in the left-hand margin, label each piece of supporting material according to its type (for example: definition, example, statistics, visual aids). This will allow you to see whether you are using a wide enough variety of supporting materials and whether you are adequately supporting each of the points you are making. The sample outline at the end of the chapter illustrates how your supporting material should be filled in to complete the standard outline form.

Indicate the transitions you intend to use. Because transitions are vital to the overall rhythm and organic quality of a speech, it is important to indicate the transitions you will be using. Since transitions are an integral part of your speech, they are usually placed inside of parentheses within the main framework of your speech outline (see sample Outline A). This placement contrasts with the placement of the names of the types of developmental material and introductory functions, which are also placed in parentheses, but which are located in the margins outside of the main framework of the outline. This is another instance of using spatial relations to project ideational relations.

Outline the conclusion. As you did with the introduction, write out the complete conclusion. Since the conclusion is so brief in relation to the rest of the speech, and has only two major functions to perform, you may find that you have only two or three main headings in this section and little or no substructure to show. The following is an example of how a conclusion might be outlined.

CONCLUSION

I. To sum up, any good swimmer can stay up more or less indefinitely in pools, using all kinds of improvised procedures. But, in rough waters with no land in sight, such as at a lake, or in the ocean, staying afloat long enough to be found and rescued is a very different sort of problem.

II. So, if you are a person who enjoys water activities such as skiing, boating, surfing, or just plain swimming in lakes and oceans, it is important for you to remember these five easy steps for staying afloat indefinitely: (1) rest periodically below the surface, (2) ready yourself to resurface, (3) respire appropriately, (4) recline horizontally on the surface, and (5) repeat the process.

III. Once you have mastered these five steps, you too will be able to survive in just about any water situation where you must remain afloat.

Check the outline for the speech's organic qualities; revise as necessary. You have now completed the first draft of the diagnostic outline. Before you type the final copy, take time to check the speech's subtler organic qualities, and revise the outline as necessary to make the speech more lifelike. If you have been preparing your speech by following the principles suggested in the previous chapters, your speech should be in quite healthy condition and major revision should be unnecessary at this point. The organic qualities to check for, once again, are internal preparation, forward motion, growth, climax, and closure. The following suggestions may help you improve the quality of your speech.

Word your main points so that the speech projects a single, consistent thought pattern. In the chapter on speech organization (Chapter 9), the concept of pattern was emphasized. Pattern in a speech establishes forward motion—as the mind moves from unit to unit within the pattern, anticipating the next unit. Breaks in the pattern, unless they are intentional and their effects specifically prepared for, interfere with audience attention by introducing competing impulses, which must be resolved by a process of figuring out what the speaker is attempting to do. The audience automatically looks for a pattern even if there is none. You must first check to see whether your main heads project only a single, overall pattern of organization, or instead drift inorganically from parts of one pattern of organization to another.

Example A mixes patterns of organization inconsistently, following only a vague central theme. In contrast, Example B projects a single, consistent pattern of organization, arising from a clearly worded specific purpose.

EXAMPLE A

Specific Purpose: To tell the students about the University Art Exhibits.

   I. The University Art Exhibits is a project of the Student Union Director.

  II. The themes of past exhibits have appealed to many students' interests.

 III. This semester appears to have that kind of fun, too.

  IV. Now you may be saying, "I don't like art so why do I need to know about the University Art Exhibits?"

EXAMPLE B

Specific Purpose: To explain four reasons students should consider attending the University Art Exhibits

   I. The University Art Exhibits are supported by your student services fees.

  II. The University Art Exhibits provide a nonclassroom opportunity to enhance your education.

 III. The themes of previous University Art Exhibits have appealed to a wide variety of student interests.

  IV. This year's University Art Exhibits are also very diverse.

The same process may be used in checking your subpoints under each main head, since they too should project a consistent pattern of thought if at all possible.

    Phrase your main points in parallel grammatical form. See if it is possible to word your main heads in a parallel grammatical form. As you know from the chapters on organization and language, grammatical parallelism is an important technique for adding to the living qualities of your speech. It creates forward motion, as your audience meets a familiar pattern at various points within the speech; it creates a sense of internal preparation and growth, as the grammatical form prepares the audience for the content that the form contains; and it helps create a sense of climax and closure. Examples I_1 through III_1 can be improved simply by working for greater parallelism— as revealed in Examples I_2 through III_2. In this speech the student was talking about how to act if you are in a boat that overturns. His three main points were originally worded as follows:

These kids are watching Saturday morning cartoons on television. Do children want what they see on television? How do you think TV violence affects children? Should children spend as much time reading as they do watching TV?

I.₁ Act quickly.

II.₁ Properly position yourself in and out of the water.

III.₁ Communicate with your sailing partner, if you have one with you.

These three points can easily be reworded in parallel grammatical form by simply making points 2 and 3 match the grammatical pattern of the first point, which uses a verb–adverb pattern to assert a directive to the audience. For example, these three main points could be made parallel as follows:

I.$_2$ Act quickly.

II.$_2$ Position yourself properly.

III.$_2$ Communicate effectively.

Look again at the examples in Chapter 9 to see how you can work for greater parallel structure in your main heads.

Make sure the main heads seem to arise directly from the specific purpose statement. Your specific purpose statement was designed to be the guiding impulse for the rest of your speech preparation. Has it worked out that way? Or have you drifted from it? The next check you will use on your speech outline is whether or not the wording of the main headings still reflects the specific purpose as you have formulated it. The speech should seem to grow from your specific purpose statement, as if by a process of individuation and involvement. If your speech's specific purpose statement no longer reflects the directions the speech has taken, modify the specific purpose so that it does reflect what the speech has become, or revise the main heads so that they reflect your specific purpose as you have stated it.

Similarly, make sure the subpoints under each main head derive from and support the main headings to which they are subordinated. Don't include material under a subpoint just because "it has to go somewhere," as a student once said. If the material absolutely *has* to go somewhere, then there is an organically appropriate place for it to go, and the speech outline should help you find that place. So make sure you know why the material has to go where you decide to put it.

Adapt your diagnostic outline to the speaking situation. The diagnostic outline is a specialized tool to help you determine the organic quality of your speech preparation. Because of its specialized purpose, the diagnostic outline generally contains far more information than you will need in order to deliver your speech in an extemporaneous manner. Because it is so complete, the diagnostic outline can tempt you to read from it word for word—almost as if it were a manuscript. Since your goal as a public speaker is to deliver your speech in a way that looks spontaneous, and that allows you to maintain maximum eye contact with your audience, you will want to edit your diagnostic outline down to the minimum amount of notes you can—and still be able to present the speech **as you have planned it.** For some speakers, it will be necessary to retain almost all of the detail developed in the diagnostic outline in order to present an adequate, organic speech. For others, all you will need is a mere outline of the topics you intend to cover, and you will be able to give the speech as you have planned and practiced it.

As you begin the process of preparing the set of notes you will use when you actually present your speech, many of the principles and practices developed earlier in the chapter will still apply. When compiling your speaking notes, remember the following:

1. Preserve only as much of your diagnostic outline as you absolutely need in order to deliver your speech as you have planned and practiced it.

2. Use spatial relations to project ideational relations.

3. Use a consistent pattern of symbols.

4. Outline the introduction, body, and conclusion separately and label the parts accordingly.

5. Outline your introduction in the greatest detail, since you are the most anxious at the beginning of your speech.

6. Indicate the supporting material you will use—briefly.

7. Use bold highlighting in a contrasting color to mark your outline with any reminders you may need.

Sample Completed Outlines

Outline A shows a complete diagnostic outline that follows all of the principles developed in the first portion of the chapter. It is not as complete as an entire manuscript would be, and certainly could be used to deliver your speech from. But Outline A contains far more information than you would typically need if you were to use it for your speech's actual presentation. For presentation purposes, you would delete all of the marginal labels in order to make room for any special reminders you might want to add. Typically, you would also mark the outline with a bold highlighter to identify key words that you need to find as you look down to use your notes. Such highlighting helps draw your eye quickly to the information you need on the page.

Outline A
HOW TO GET FIRED

Roger W. Student
SCOM 403, Section 508
March 12, 1985
Dr. Powers

Specific Purpose: To explain the three main steps required for getting fired from a job

INTRODUCTION

(attention getter) I. Have you ever been fired from a job? Probably not, I would guess.

(relate to audience) II. All of you are intelligent, hard-working people—you couldn't stay at this university if you weren't. But if you *wanted* to be fired from a job some-day, would you know how to do it? It's not as easy as it sounds.

(background) III. Over the years, I have worked as a busboy in several restaurants, and I recently spent several months as an engineering trainee at the NASA Johnson Space Center in Houston. During all of this time, I have seen several co-workers do one or two dumb things while on the job, dam-aging their careers somewhat. But I have never worked with anyone who actually successfully got fired.

(announce subject) IV. I was surprised to find a lack of available published guidelines on the subject of getting fired. I found no universally accepted systematic pro-cedure on how to be fired from any job.

(credibility) A. So I discussed this fact with my boss at NASA last summer, and we constructed our own systematic procedure for implementing career-damaging activities guaranteed to help get you fired from your un-wanted job.

(purpose) B. I have recently revised and perfected these procedures and would like to present them to you today.

(preview structure) V. My purpose today, then, is to share with you the three main steps you must take if you hope to get fired from your job. These are:
A. Become a nonproductive employee.
B. Develop a bad relationship with your boss.
C. Destroy your personal integrity.

(transition) VI. Please keep in mind as we examine these three steps that this is a very systematic procedure and that every step counts. To begin your journey to the unemployment office, you must first discontinue your productive work. So the first step in the process of losing your job is to become a nonproductive employee.

BODY

I. Become a nonproductive employee.
A. Waste time constantly.
1. Waste time by falling asleep on the job.

(anecdote) a. For example, last summer I worked with an engineer at NASA who always seemed to fall asleep after lunch for about a half-hour.
2. Waste time by often calling in sick.

(example) a. For example, you might try calling in sick every other Monday or every other Friday.
3. Waste time by arriving late and leaving early.

(examples)

B. Make excuses constantly.

[Some sample excuses you can use for arriving late to the job are the following:]

1. "My car wouldn't start."
2. "My alarm clock didn't go off."
3. "I was in a car wreck."

C. Complain constantly to co-workers.

1. Complain about work assignments.

(examples)

a. "My job is too hard."
b. "My job is too easy."
c. "My job is too boring."

2. Complain about your salary.

(anecdote)

a. [This is a very popular complaint.] At NASA last summer, I worked with a 23-year-old engineer who went out of his way to make sure that everyone in the office knew how much money he could be making with other companies. This, incidentally, was the same one who always fell asleep after lunch!

3. Complain about your boss.

(examples)

a. "My boss is unfair to me."
b. "My boss picks on me."

(transition)

[In fact, the boss is a key figure in our endeavor, because he or she will most likely be the one who will fire you. So the boss deserves special attention. This is why I have dedicated the entire second step to alienating your boss. So let's look at the specific things you can do in order to help you accomplish the second phase of the process of getting fired.]

II. Develop a bad relationship with your boss.

A. Don't request things, demand them.

(examples)

1. Demand better work assignments or a higher salary.
2. Let your boss know, in no uncertain terms, how privileged he or she is to have you working there.

B. Bad-mouth your boss within hearing distance.

(examples)

[Here are some sample things to tell your co-workers:]

1. "My boss is a dirty SOB."
2. "My boss is a real jerk."
3. "My boss acts like a spoiled child."

(transition)

[We'll assume at this point that you have faithfully followed all the methods of the previous two steps. You are now a consistent procrastinator who doesn't get along with your boss. You would probably be fired at this point, but why take any chances? Proceed now to the third and final step to guarantee being fired.]

III. Destroy your integrity completely.

(visual aid)

A. Steal from the company.

1. Steal equipment from the company.

(examples)

　　　　　　　　　　　　　　　　　　a. Steal small things like paper clips and pens.
　　　　　　　　　　　　　　　　　　b. Steal big things like typewriters, chairs, and desks.
　　　　　　　　　　　　　　　　2. Steal money from the company.
　　　　　　　　　　　　　　　　3. Steal articles from the company's vending machines.

(anecdote)

　　　　　　　　　　　　　　　　　　a. I've worked with people at restaurants who were notorious for robbing Coke machines—dismantling them, kicking them, stealing their master keys, and so on.

(visual aid)
(example)

　　　　　　　　　　　　　B. Drink your way to alcoholism.
　　　　　　　　　　　　　　　　1. Drink after leaving work each day.
　　　　　　　　　　　　　　　　　　[By doing this, you will arrive at work each morning with a hangover.]

(example)

　　　　　　　　　　　　　　　　2. Drink before arriving at work each day.
　　　　　　　　　　　　　　　　　　[With a couple of stiff belts each morning, you can arrive at work fairly drunk.]

(example)

　　　　　　　　　　　　　　　　3. Drink at work each day.
　　　　　　　　　　　　　　　　　　[Keep some hard liquor in your desk, for example. Not only will you be drunk at work, you will probably be in illegal possession of alcohol on the job.]
　　　　　　　　　　　　　C. Lie about everything.
　　　　　　　　　　　　　　　　[This is the culmination of your efforts toward getting fired. If it hasn't happened already, your boss will accuse you of performing the aforementioned career-damaging methods. This gives you the chance to lie to your boss by saying:]
　　　　　　　　　　　　　　　　1. "I do not lie."
　　　　　　　　　　　　　　　　2. "I do not drink."
　　　　　　　　　　　　　　　　3. "I do not steal."
　　　　　　　　　　　　　　　　4. "I do not bad-mouth my boss."
　　　　　　　　　　　　　　　　5. "I do not make demands."
　　　　　　　　　　　　　　　　6. "I do not complain constantly."
　　　　　　　　　　　　　　　　7. "I do not make excuses constantly."
　　　　　　　　　　　　　　　　8. "I do not waste time constantly."

(transition)

　　　　　　　　　　　["If it sounds as though you've now reached the point of no return, you're right. This is where the axe will definitely fall.]

CONCLUSION

　　I. In my introduction, I stated that getting fired from a job was not an easy task. The systematic procedures I have presented might actually seem a little demanding. But if followed properly, I think you will agree that they will work.

　　II. To review, let me repeat in closing the three main steps to follow to successfully get fired from your job:
　　A. Become a nonproductive employee.

      B. Develop a bad relationship with your boss.

      C. Destroy your integrity completely.

  III. I promise that these steps will one day lead you to a red-faced boss who will look you straight in the eye and yell, "You're fired!"

Outline B shows a severely cut outline of the same speech. Here only key words and phrases are preserved, along with a few sentences. Notice, for example, that the main points are still worded as shortened sentences. These could have been reduced further, to mere key words; for many speakers, the strictly topical outline will be the outline of choice when you actually present your speech.

Outline B

HOW TO GET FIRED

INTRODUCTION

    I. Have you ever been <u>fired from a job?</u>

   II. Would you know how to do it? It's <u>not as easy</u> as it sounds.

  III. I have seen several co-workers do dumb things while on the job, damaging their careers.

  IV. There is a <u>lack of available published guidelines</u> on the subject of getting fired—no universally accepted systematic procedure on how to be fired.

      A. My boss at NASA and I <u>constructed our own</u> systematic procedure for implementing career-damaging activities guaranteed to help get you fired from your unwanted job.

      B. I have recently revised and perfected these procedures and would like to <u>present them to you today</u>

   V. Purpose: To share the <u>three main steps</u> to get fired from your job:

      A. Become a nonproductive employee

      B. Develop a bad relationship with your boss.

      C. Destroy your personal integrity.

  VI. This is a very systematic procedure, and every step counts. The first step in the process of losing your job is to <u>become a nonproductive employee.</u>

BODY

    I. Become a <u>nonproductive</u> employee.

      A. Waste time.

        1. Fall asleep on the job.

          a. Engineer at NASA—always fell asleep after lunch.

        2. Call in sick.
           a. Try every other Monday or every other Friday.
        3. Arrive late and leave early.
     B. Make excuses constantly.
         [Sample excuses:]
        1. "My car wouldn't start."
        2. "My alarm clock didn't go off."
        3. "I was in a car wreck."
     C. Complain constantly to co-workers.
        1. Complain about work assignments.
           a. "My job is too hard."
           b. "My job is too easy."
           c. "My job is too boring."
        2. Complain about your salary.
        3. Complain about your boss.
           a. "My boss is unfair to me."
           b. "My boss picks on me."

 II. Develop a bad relationship with your boss.
     A. Don't request things, demand them.
        1. Demand better work assignments.
        2. Demand public recognition.
     B. Bad-mouth your boss.
        1. "My boss is a dirty SOB."
        2. "My boss is a real jerk."
        3. "My boss acts like a spoiled child."

III. Destroy your integrity completely.
     A. Steal from the company.
        1. Steal equipment.
        2. Steal money.
        3. Steal articles from vending machines.
     B. Drink your way to alcoholism.
        1. Drink after leaving work.
        2. Drink before arriving.
        3. Drink at work.
     C. Lie about everything.
        1. "I do not lie."
        2. "I do not drink."
        3. "I do not steal."
        4. "I do not bad-mouth my boss."
        5. "I do not make demands."
        6. "I do not complain constantly."
        7. "I do not make excuses constantly."
        8. "I do not waste time constantly."

CONCLUSION

I. These systematic procedures will seem demanding, but they will work.

II. <u>Summarize</u> the three main steps:
    A. Become a nonproductive employee.
    B. Develop a bad relationship with your boss.
    C. Destroy your integrity completely.

III. Boss will yell, "You're fired!"

Conclusion

This chapter has explained and demonstrated the diagnostic outline—a very important tool to help you make your speeches as lifelike as possible. You were introduced to five general principles of outline construction, and then were taken step by step through the procedures for constructing a detailed and useful diagnostic outline. Finally, the chapter explained how to adapt the detail contained in the diagnostic outline to the far more brief outline you will probably want to use as actual speaking notes. If you apply the principles of outlining presented in the first part of the chapter, and employ the techniques for outlining suggested in the second, the speech you finally deliver should be alive and creative.

Questions for Review

1. Why should you prepare a detailed outline for your speech—even if you plan to use only a sentence or topical outline for your actual presentation?

2. Why should you use spatial relations to project ideational relations?

Questions for Discussion

1. What are the advantages and disadvantages of using complete sentences as you outline your speech?

2. Review an outline you have prepared for a speech before you studied this chapter. How many of the principles presented here did you intuitively use? Which principles did you fail to employ? Based on your experience delivering that speech, which principles seem most fundamental in helping you improve your future speeches?

Things to Try

1. Prepare a detailed outline for one of your speeches using the diagnostic principles outlined in this chapter.

2. Adapt your detailed diagnostic outline for use in delivering your actual speech, marking your notes in whatever manner you feel best serves your needs.

CHAPTER 13

Choosing Your Language: Bringing Your Speech to Life through Words and Phrases

Whenever you speak you must phrase your ideas into words. Without words it would be almost impossible to project your ideas to others. But *which* words will you use? Ideas may be expressed in many ways. Will any words that spontaneously come to mind be OK? Or should you give special consideration to *how* you phrase your ideas?

Up to this point in your speech preparation you have been primarily concerned with decisions about which ideas you will present, in what order you will present them, and in what ways you can best support those ideas. But, if your goal is a high quality speech that your audience readily understands, enjoys, and remembers, then you must also give special thought to how you phrase your ideas into words. For often, the difference between a speech that merely "gets the job done" and one that really lives—making an impact on the audience—is the care you have put into phrasing your ideas.

Formulating your ideas into memorable verbal units—units that live in your audience's memory—increases the chance that those ideas will subsequently be acted upon. The purpose of this chapter is to explain the qualities of good oral style and to explore the language resources available to you as you try to bring your speech to life for your audience.

Qualities of Good Oral Style

After you have organized the basic framework of your speech well enough to begin rehearsing it, you must decide how you will actually phrase your ideas. As you begin working out your speech's final wording, there are four qualities you should strive for: precision, clarity, appropriateness, and vividness.

Precision

The goal of language precision focuses on you as a communicator. Precision in language means that your words must be true to the idea you intend to express. *Your language is* **precise** *when the words and phrases you choose express your exact intended meaning*, not some meaning that is merely approximate or convenient. Your language should be precise at the individual word-choice level and at the sentence-structure level. We will consider both levels in this chapter.

Precision at the Word-Choice Level Language precision at the word-choice level has two important aspects, traditionally called **denotation** and **connotation.**

Denotative Precision. Your language is denotatively precise when your words and phrases refer to what you intend them to refer to. When your words are definitely *not* what you intend, they are called **malapropisms,** after the character in Sheridan's play, *The Rivals* (1775), Mrs. Malaprop. In the following examples can you figure out what Mrs. Malaprop should have said?

"Illiterate him, I say, quite from your memory."

"As headstrong as an allegory on the banks of the Nile."

"You're our envoy; lead the way, and we'll precede."

Although these malapropisms are relatively obvious—the kind comedian Norm Crosby has made famous—there are more subtle misuses of words that may cause your audience to wince as they listen to you. For example, do you know the difference between:

adverse and *averse*

affect and *effect*

accept and *except*

Many students mistakenly use one word when they intend to use the other. If you are unsure of the conventional meaning of a word, look in the dictionary to see if you are using the word in a commonly accepted (not *excepted*) manner.

In addition to imprecision caused by misuse of words (*wrong* reference), there are at least two additional forms of inaccurate word choice: *vague* reference and *ambiguous* reference.

Vague reference occurs when you use words and phrases whose boundaries or limitations are not precisely known. Words such as *very, many, few,* and *some* are quantitatively vague—your audience does not know to how many you refer. The extension of the word (see Chapter 8) is unclear. Words such as *patriotism, democracy,* and *freedom* are also vague in many circumstances because the audience does not know what conditions you have imposed on their use (that is, their intension is not clear). If, therefore, you are going to use a potentially vague word, it is best to supply a brief definition to help make the word more precise.

Vagueness may be overcome by using **specific, concrete, sensory** words. For example, if you were to mention food, be explicit about what kind. Was it a delicacy, an appetizer, a soup, or a stew? A soup you say? Then was it broth, gazpacho, bisque, borscht, won ton, gumbo, minestrone, or chowder? Perhaps a stew? Goulash or mulligan? A pastry for dessert? A tart, a torte, a creampuff, or an eclair? The point is, many of the words you use do not pin down the exact referent you intend to talk about. The speech remains a little vague and lacks the interest generated by just the right detail. As you work through your speech to revise it, look to see where you can eliminate vagueness with a crisp, precise detail.

Ambiguous reference occurs when you use words that have several possible meanings, and you fail to be precise about which of those meanings you intend to apply. For example, if you say:

I went to the bank yesterday.

there are at least two possible referents of *bank* that you might intend: (1) a place where money is deposited and withdrawn, and (2) the shore of a river. Ambiguity differs from vagueness in that vagueness results when the word you choose lacks a precise boundary for a single meaning of the word; ambiguity results when there are two equally definite yet different meanings of the same word, and it is unclear which of these you intend.

Connotative Precision. Words not only refer to objects and qualities, processes and relations in the world; they also suggest your feelings about the things to which you make reference. A word's **connotation** is the feeling it suggests about the thing to which it refers. Two words may have the same reference (that is, denotation, extension) and yet have very different suggested feelings (that is, connotations).

Several series of words are listed below. In each series, the words all have roughly similar denotations, but they range from more positive feelings about the thing or quality denoted to more negative feelings. Under what circumstances would you be likely to use each of these words to denote the thing referred to?

1. Slow, retarded, dumb, stupid, moronic

2. Scholar, intellectual, bookworm, grind, egghead

3. Individual, eccentric, odd, goofy, crazy, weird

4. Alcoholic beverage, cocktail, drink, booze, rotgut

5. Gorgeous, lovely, pretty, good-looking, cute

6. Thrifty, frugal, cheap, stingy, miserly, niggardly

Similarly, what difference does it make how you report the following unfortunate event?

Jill *died.*

   or

Jack *killed* Jill.

And if Jack is in fact responsible for Jill's death, what difference does it make which verb you use to report it?

Jack *murdered* Jill.

Jack *slew* Jill.

Jack *slaughtered* Jill.

Jack *poisoned* Jill.

Jack *exterminated* Jill.

Jack *dispatched* Jill.

Jack *assassinated* Jill.

Jack *liquidated* Jill.

Jack *rubbed* Jill out.

Jack *bumped* Jill off.

Jack *put* Jill *to death*.

Jack *put* Jill *to sleep*.

Jack *sent* Jill *to her just reward*.

We speak of **connotative precision,** then, when the words and phrases you select express not only the denotative reference you intend to project, but also the exact emotional shading you intend to suggest.

Under most circumstances you will want your speech to maintain a consistent connotational tone. Audiences develop expectations about your feelings based on the wordings you choose. To carelessly shift mid-sentence or mid-speech from one feeling to another betrays the expectational impulses you have established and prompts the audience to question what is going on with your speech.

The following examples illustrate the importance of maintaining a consistent connotational tone. In each sentence there is at least one word that is connotatively inconsistent with the rest of the sentence. See if you can identify the inconsistent word, decide upon a better replacement, and explain why you made the choices you made.

Although she was middle-aged, there was a childish quality in her voice that delighted everyone.

Handle this Ming vase with extreme care. It's very brittle.

After thinking carefully about my question, he stated his retort in his usual quiet, almost hesitant, manner.

He was quite attracted to her nicely skinny figure.

Precision at the Sentence-Structure Level Single words aren't the only place you risk denotative and connotative imprecision. Sometimes an entire sentence may be confusing. Precision, therefore, also means that you select the most accurate syntactical or grammatical pattern for formulating your ideas into words. When the reference of an entire sentence is ambiguous, this is called **amphiboly.** The following widely cited examples are amphibolous sentences published from the files of the Veteran's Administration.

"Both sides of my parents are poor, and I can't expect nothing from them, as my mother has been in bed for one year with the same doctor and won't change."

"Please send me a letter and tell me if my husband has made application for a wife and baby."

"I can't get any pay, I has 6 children. Can you tell me why this is?"

"I am forwarding to you my marriage certificate and my two children. One is a mistake as you can plainly see."

"My husband had his project cut off two weeks ago and I haven't had any relief since."

Such sentences may seem humorous when taken out of the serious context of their authors' needs and fears. They are also misleading. Although careless use of your own sentences may never result in your being laughed at, you may mislead your audience about your intended meaning. In rehearsals for your speech, listen to yourself to see if your sentences can reasonably be misunderstood concerning what you intend to be saying.

Clarity

Being precise does not by itself make your speech either understandable or memorable. Precision in your word choices is a relatively self-centered language virtue. It focuses attention on you as a communicator. When you are concerned with precision, you are concerned with selecting words and phrases that express what *you* intend to express. You are putting *your* ideas into words, and you want those words to reflect *your* ideas as precisely as possible. But what about your audience? They need clarity as well as precision.

The quality of clarity takes into account your listeners' needs instead of your own. Words are like windows to your ideas—and the clearer you make them, the better your audience will be able to "see" what you are getting at. To be clear is to be "transparent"—to have your audience be able to see your ideas through your words, without significant distortion, confusion, or gaps. *Your language is **clear** when the words and phrases you select are instantly intelligible to your listeners, or can be made so by a brief definition.* Precision that ignores the audience's ability to understand your words is not a virtue.

As you can see, clarity focuses attention on your listeners. What may be precisely expressed may not be clearly understood. For example, the following is language from a contract for a group medical plan. It is written in precise, traditional legal language. But it is not immediately clear to the layperson. It begins innocently enough:

> You may elect to insure your eligible dependents. If you elect to insure any of your eligible dependents, you must insure all of them. Your eligible dependents include:
>
> (a) your spouse,

But then the confusion begins:

> (b) each of your unmarried children (including any stepchildren, adopted children or foster children) who rely on you for their principal support and maintenance and who are less than 25 years of age, except that this maximum age limit does not apply to a child, insured as your dependent on the Company's group medical plan, who is mentally or physically incapable of earning a living on the date the child attains this age as long as such incapacity continues, if initial due proof of such incapacity is received by the Insurer within 31 days of the date the child attains such maximum age and if due proof of the continuance of such incapacity is furnished the Insurer as it may reasonably require, but not more frequently than annually after the two year period following the date the child attains the maximum age.

If you had trouble following this paragraph, you will have no trouble understanding why an audience expects clarity as well as precision. For an audience to be able to instantly understand your speech four things are usually required:

1. A **simpler vocabulary** than is typically used in writing

2. A more **conversational sentence structure,** filled with active verbs

3. An abundance of **specific examples, anecdotes,** and **facts** to help make your generalizations more comprehensible

4. A **spoken** rather than a **written rhythm**

Each of these suggestions arises because your audience hears your speech only once, and they must understand it as it is actually being given—in real time—or the point will be lost. There is no time for long reflection as they listen to a speech, so your speech must be clear as you say it.

Appropriateness

Language that is precise and clear may still fail to be appropriate. *Your language is* **appropriate** *when it is adapted (1) to your own personality, (2) to your audience, and (3) to the occasion or speech situation.* Since the next major section of the chapter focuses on several techniques for consciously achieving greater precision, clarity, and vividness, it is important to understand how you can choose the most appropriate techniques for your speech from among the language options available to you.

Appropriateness to Your Own Personality Your natural, spontaneous verbal choices express quite a lot about your personality. Perhaps you have a large vocabulary and always "sound educated." Or perhaps you love supporting your main points with folksy stories and anecdotes. Whatever you actually say about some "topic," you will almost always also reveal something interesting or important about yourself at the same time. The purpose of explaining desirable language qualities, and some of the techniques for achieving them, is not to insist that you change your personality, or that you use artificial expressions that "sound good" but that do not fit your personality. Instead, it is to recognize that most people have a wide range of natural verbal expression—from informal to formal—and to survey the options you have for expressing your ideas *within your own personality range*. Try all the different techniques described later in the chapter. Stretch your language resources to the fullest extent your personality allows. Don't restrict yourself to the familiar, comfortable—and often moribund—language of everyday use. But, if a particular technique does not feel comfortable, then perhaps you should avoid it since it may sound artificial when you use it. These language resources are available to serve your communicative purposes, and not vice versa.

Appropriateness to Your Audience Different audiences are not all equally able to accommodate all word choices. It is, therefore, important to gauge your audience's general sophistication relative to your topic, and to make your language choices accordingly. Sometimes you may need to sacrifice precision for clarity—if, for example, your topic is so new to your audience that they lack the preparation needed for a more accurate presentation. For instance, in an anatomy course I once took, the professor prefaced many of his remarks early in the semester with a statement like: "What I'm about to say is generally true, but when you learn more, you will understand why it isn't *exactly* true." Then he would proceed to lecture in a less precise vocabulary than the subject matter of anatomy typically demands. By the end of the semester, the class had gradually built up enough background understanding of anatomical concepts that the professor's compromises with precision were no longer necessary. To accomplish his overall goal of introducing the details of human anatomy, he had appropriately gauged his audience's prior knowledge and had adapted his level of language in order to help the class get launched in understanding anatomy.

Appropriateness to the Occasion Different occasions often call for different types of speech. Some situations invite an informal and chatty style; others call for a highly elevated level of speech. Just as you have a range of clothing options that express the mood or feeling of various occasions—from cutoffs for a stroll along the beach, to a navy blue suit for an important business meeting—so too do you have an extensive repertoire of speech styles that can express the mood of different situations. And just as you must choose the

Alliteration repeats the initial sounds of words. For example, in an earlier chapter you learned that alliteration could be used to name the key word names of the main points of your speech, as in the "Three *C*'s of Credit": *C*ash, *C*ollateral, and *C*haracter.

If you cannot get credit, perhaps you will have to

rob *P*eter to *p*ay *P*aul.

And if that is the case, maybe you should have studied harder on the "Three *R*'s":

*r*eadin', *wr*itin', and *r*ithmetic

Rhyme repeats the final vowel and consonant sounds of words. Many commercial jingles and cultural maxims use rhyme as a way of imprinting their message on the listener's mind. For example, the following maxims use rhyme to emphasize their meaning and to make them more memorable:

Birds of a *feather* flock to*gether*.

A friend in *need* is a friend in*deed*.

As *snug* as a *bug* in a *rug*.

Might makes *right*.

Rhyme is especially useful when you are trying to create a jingle to help your audience remember a key point, or as a mnemonic device to remember a series of points.

Assonance repeats the central vowel sound in successive or nearby words:

H*o*ly R*o*man Empire

E.T. ph*o*ne h*o*me.

Out of s*i*ght, out of m*i*nd.

Repetition of Words You can use word repetition several ways in your speech. For example, you can use the same word more than once in a single sentence:

We must do this for the sake of our *children* and our *children's children*.

Or, you may use the same word in a succession of sentences. For example, in his very quotable address to the Democratic National Convention on July 17, 1984, Jesse Jackson emphasized the role of leadership in the production of social change with the following succession of sentences:

There is the call of conscience: redemption, expansion, healing, and unity. *Leadership* must heed the call of conscience, redemption, expansion, healing, and unity, for they are the key to achieving our mission.

Time is neutral and does not change things.

With courage and initiative, *leaders* change things. No generation can choose the age or circumstances in which it is born, but through *leadership* it can choose to make the age in which it is born an age of enlightenment—an age of jobs, and peace, and justice.

Only *leadership*—that intangible combination of gifts, discipline, information, circumstance, courage, timing, will, and divine inspiration—can lead us out of the crisis in which we find ourselves.

Leadership can mitigate the misery of our nation. *Leadership* can part the waters and lead our nation in the direction of the Promised Land. *Leadership* can lift the boats stuck at the bottom.

Finally, you may choose to use a key word throughout an entire speech in order to keep your audience's attention focused upon it. The following longer selections from a speech by Joseph M. Gaydos, U.S. Congressman from Pennsylvania, suggests how this repetition of words might be used effectively.

Mr. Gaydos's speech is entitled "From the Invisible Hand, a Gesture of Contempt: the Steel Industry." The image conveyed by the invisible hand mentioned in the title is repeated as a motif throughout Mr. Gaydos's speech on the free marketplace and protectionism in the U.S. steel industry. The speech to the U.S. House of Representatives opens as follows:

Mr. Speaker, I do believe in the invisible *hand* of the market, even as it pertains to steel; but having watched world commerce, I know that all *hands* have *fingers*, particularly as they have affected steel since we adjourned the first session.

Fingers may point in blame, beckon or show direction; they can be used to test the weather or they can be sticky. A *finger* to the lips asks silence in a conspiracy, and one to the temple in a circular motion signals lunacy.

In our culture, the *finger* of a divinely inspired hand wrote the future on a palace wall, and it also engraved the commandments brought down from the mount. *Fingers* drawn inward make a fist of the hand, and this is a sign of the intent to strike.

Mr. Gaydos later continues:

Hands and *fingers*, and the understanding of their language, are a mainstay of human communication even today amid the marvels of electronics. They show direction. . . .

Mr. Speaker, a 15 percent quota would have four times 4.4 million tons of imports into this market in a good year. We took almost four times 4.4 million tons in 1983, and it was a bad one. The *finger* would have to move a long way down our list of trading partners to get to one who sent only 300,000 tons.

> What the European *hand* pushes away will find a resting place, and this is the only open market in the world; and at 15 percent, it would remain the most open.
>
> Is this the infinite wisdom of the invisible *hand?* Or is it merely a *finger* of the *hand* raised in the universal gesture of contempt and disdain?

Finally, Mr. Gaydos concludes his speech with these words:

> So I invite all in this body who are concerned about the future of America and all of its industries to review all of the record and to consider co-sponsoring the bill.
>
> It would be an act of even-*hand*edness that is called for by the times; and it would be a gesture of steady-*hand*edness that cannot be misinterpreted, not even by our friend, Sir Roy.
>
> And finally, it would put a *finger* on a big part of the problem.

As you can see, repetition of a single word-image may be meaningfully carried through and developed throughout an entire speech without going overboard—at least when carefully and thoughtfully executed.

Repetition of Phrases Words tend to cluster together into larger units called phrases. Like words, phrases may be repeated to good effect. For example, in Benjamin Franklin's *Poor Richard's Almanac,* we find phrase repetition used effectively.

> A little neglect may breed mischief: *for want of a* nail the shoe was lost; *for want of a* shoe the horse was lost; *for want of a* horse, the rider was lost.

Such repetition may even be used as a **refrain** throughout an entire speech or throughout some important portion of it. For example, in the speech quoted previously, Jesse Jackson concludes with the following succession of repeated words and phrases, working together to culminate as a powerful refrain. His conclusion begins with word repetition and builds to phrase repetition, as follows:

> . . . I just want young America to do me one favor.
>
> Exercise the right to *dream*. You must face reality—that which is. But then *dream* of the reality that ought to be, that must be. Live beyond the pain of reality with the *dream* of a bright tomorrow. Use hope and imagination as weapons of survival and progress. Use love to motivate you and obligate you to serve the human family.
>
> Young America, *dream*. Choose the human race over the nuclear race. Bury the weapons and don't burn the people. *Dream* of a new value system. Teachers, who teach for life, and not just for a living, teach because they can't help it. *Dream* of lawyers more concerned with justice than a judgeship. *Dream* of doctors more concerned with public health than personal wealth.

Dream [of] preachers and priests who will prophesy and not just profiteer. Preach and *dream*. <u>Our time has come.</u>

<u>Our time has come.</u> Suffering breeds character. Character breeds faith. And in the end, faith will not disappoint.

<u>Our time has come.</u> Our faith, hope and *dreams* will prevail. <u>Our time has come.</u> Weeping has endured for the night. And, now joy cometh in the morning.

<u>Our time has come.</u> No graves can hold our body down.

<u>Our time has come.</u> No lie can live forever.

<u>Our time has come.</u> We must leave racial battleground and come to economic common ground and moral higher ground. America, <u>our time has come.</u>

We've come from disgrace to Amazing Grace, <u>our time has come.</u>

Give me your tired, give me your poor, your huddled masses who yearn to breathe free and come November, there will be a change because <u>our time has come.</u>

Repetition of Grammatical Patterns Repeating a grammatical construction is another technique that may be used at multiple levels within your speech. You've already seen that grammatical repetition may be used to organize and emphasize the main structure of your speech—formulating the main points in parallel grammatical form (Chapter 9). This may be done with key words that all have the same form, with phrases that use the same pattern, and even with complete sentences. But there are additional uses of grammatical repetition as well.

For example, you may use **parallel structure** within a single sentence. Parallel structure is created whenever a sentence has two or more important phrases or clauses, and each one uses the same grammatical pattern to express an idea.

It is easier <u>for a</u> camel <u>to</u> pass through <u>the</u> eye <u>of</u> a needle,
than <u>for a</u> rich man <u>to</u> enter <u>the</u> kingdom <u>of</u> heaven.

Antithesis is a special form of grammatical repetition in which the two halves of the sentence present either opposing or contrasting ideas. When the antithesis is based upon opposing ideas, it will typically employ a negative marker in one half of the grammatical unit. One of the most famous antitheses comes from John F. Kennedy's Inaugural Address, when Kennedy said:

Ask *not* what your country can do for you,
ask what you can do for your country.

As you can see, when opposition is used, both parts of the antithesis express a similar idea: one formulating it as a positive, the other as a negative. Simple contrasts build the antithesis slightly differently, since they do not use a negative particle, nor do they express the same idea in both halves of the structure. Simple contrast was expressed in Neil Armstrong's first words on the moon:

> One small step for a man; one giant leap for mankind.

Here, the contrast is between the smallness of Armstrong's own personal step and the magnitude of the act for the future direction of the human race.

Parallel constructions and antitheses are not only some of the most powerful grammatical devices for creating forward motion in your speeches, but they are also some of the easiest to accomplish with only a little extra thought. If you listen to yourself and your friends in normal conversation, you will hear these two techniques being used quite frequently in animated interaction. Although it may not be dramatically memorable, the following is just such a spontaneous antithesis: "I'm not going to the movie; I'm going to stay home tonight."

Another way to establish forward motion by the use of grammatical repetition is by using **correlative conjunctions.** Conjunctions are words that join other words together. Words such as *and, or,* and the like are conjunctions. Correlative conjunctions are pairs of words that must be used together within a sentence in order to join the two parts. In English, the correlative conjunctions are: *either . . . or, neither . . . nor, both . . . and, not only . . . but also.* Closely related is the pair, *if . . . then.*

Because correlative conjunctions require parallel grammatical forms in the phrases or clauses they coordinate, they establish a memorable pattern based upon grammatical repetition. Correlative conjunction constructions create forward motion by establishing an expectation of things to come. The first half of the correlative pair creates a feeling of incompleteness, and a strong expectation of the nature of the second half to follow. The following examples illustrate these forms:

> *Neither* a borrower *nor* a lender be.

> *If* nominated [*then*], I will not run; *if* elected, [*then*], I will not serve. [Original quote: I will not accept if nominated, and will not serve if elected.]

Such constructions enhance both internal preparation and forward motion, as well as aiding audience memory concerning the point you are making.

In closing this discussion of repetition, let's look at one final example. In announcing his candidacy for the presidency, Jesse Jackson used several forms of repetition. Can you identify them?

> [If] we move to get another 3 million on the books by next November, [then] we will have changed Democratic options in the primaries.
>
> I want to help again measure greatness by how we treat children in the dawn of life, how we treat poor people in the pit of life, and how we treat old folk in the sunset of life.

Images

A second powerful way to breathe life into your language is to use images. Your audience's imagination is an almost boundless source of animating energy for bringing your speech to life. Images are a spontaneous product of human mental activity—all you have to do is close your eyes and you can bring images flooding to mind. The verbal evocation of such images through well-chosen words can help make your speech seem similarly alive.

To use an image is to paint a brief word-picture of some idea for your audience. If, for example, you tell your audience that using a modern word processor is "easy," you have expressed your general belief concerning the use of word processors. But you have not given your idea much vitality or impact; your idea does not seem particularly alive or vivid. If, on the other hand, you embed your belief within a simple image, the idea gains considerably in staying power. For example, if you say that operating a contemporary word processor is "as simple as tying your shoes," your audience gets the concrete mental picture of tying shoelaces, which has the definite idea of ease. How easy is it? As easy as tying your shoes. Using images, then, to give life to your speech can be as simple as mentioning a concrete embodiment for your more abstract ideas. The selections earlier in the chapter from Congressman Gaydos's speech use not only the word *hand* repeatedly, but also the image of fingers and hands in motion doing things. These images serve as a way of giving his main thesis greater concreteness and more action; these images served as a general motif for his speech and made it seem especially vivid.

In general, images may be divided into two broad categories: comparative and noncomparative. We will consider comparative images first.

Comparative Images As the name suggests, comparative images require that the image be used as a part of some sort of comparison. Whenever you use comparative images, you will need to mention, or at least imply, two elements—one to be explained, and the other to be used to help with the explanation of the first. There are at least three types of comparative images you may wish to try as you develop your speech: metaphors, similes, and personifications.

Metaphors are images that make a comparison indirectly and implicitly, by implying an equivalence between two things that are not literally equivalent. For example, in trying to make more vivid the weakness of our national defense when he came into office, President Reagan often spoke of a "window of vulnerability." This is metaphorical language because there is no literal window involved. He wished to emphasize the comparison between the literal weakness of a window in an otherwise strong wall, and the relative weakness of some aspects of our otherwise strong national defense. Similarly, when President Reagan wished to emphasize that the changes he wanted in Social Security would not prevent it from continuing to serve its intended functions, he spoke of there being a "social safety net" for those in need. These comparisons are not explicitly stated, and therefore they are metaphors in the strict sense—implied comparisons between two things that are not literally comparable. Well-crafted metaphors give an idea staying power in the audience's memory long after the other details of the speech have faded.

Similes are comparative images that make the comparison directly and explicitly—usually using the words *like* or *as*, or their equivalent. For example, many people believe that the following comparison is helpful in understanding the brain: "The brain is like a very powerful digital computer." Here the comparative image is explicitly expressed. In his "I Have a Dream" speech, Martin Luther King, Jr. used the following similes: "No, we are not satisfied, and we will not be satisfied until justice rolls down *like waters* and righteousness *like a mighty stream*."

Personifications are specific types of metaphors and similes in which the comparison is between some human quality or attribute and something that is not itself literally human. That is, the item to be explained is endowed with human qualities as a way of trying to help the audience imagine or experience its nature. For example, in his acceptance speech for renomination, August 23, 1984, President Reagan noted that his first term had "eliminated unnecessary regulations which had been *strangling* business and industry." Later in the speech he said that "America is *on the move* again." Although subtle, these are personifications. For, regulations cannot literally *strangle*, nor can America *move*. But to picture them as doing these human deeds subtly gives the underlying business and economic facts a vividness and power they otherwise would not have. Giving dry, lifeless facts a sense of animation and movement is the purpose of personification in your speeches.

Noncomparative Images Not everything you ask your audience to imagine depends upon a comparison to bring it to life. You will often evoke an image with just a few descriptive words, or by mentioning a familiar experience shared with your audience. Noncomparative images can be divided into six types: (1) sensory images, (2) sensory descriptions, (3) scenarios, (4) archetypal images, (5) allusions, and (6) metonymies.

Sensory images are words or phrases that appeal to one or more of the five major, and a host of minor, human senses. They are used to give both precision and life to any sense experiences to which you might be trying to appeal during your speech. For example, visual images would include such sensory aspects as color, shape, size, and movement. Gustatory images concern tastes such as saltiness, sweetness, and bitterness. Olfactory images would create mental pictures of various odors—everything from muskiness to rose, from garlic to onion. Auditory images concern the character of specific sounds. And tactile images picture such aspects of touch as surface texture, shape, pressure, heat, and cold.

In addition to words relating to the five major senses, there are several less celebrated senses that also have words to name their peculiar ways of feeling. For example, Alfred Hitchcock selected a striking word related to the sense of balance for a memorable movie title, "Vertigo." The word alone creates an ominous image, launching the viewer's impression of the movie. Similarly, well-selected sensory images can add to the power and vitality of your speech.

Sensory descriptions are more extended attempts to create a sensory impression of something for your audience. In these, one or more full sentences are put together to build up the desired impression. The following paragraph, taken from a speech by Larry Elwell, presents a powerful sensory description of the sources of noise pollution that are damaging Americans' hearing at an alarming rate. According to Professor Elwell,

> This cacophony of noise takes many forms: the screaming of jet engines at 142 decibels; the machine-gun-like pounding of jackhammers; the piercing rhythms of rivet guns; and the shattering whine of motorcycles. And in our homes washing machines, hair dryers, food blenders, and vacuum cleaners add to the cumulative attacks upon our sensitive hearing apparatus. Moreover, consumers seem not only to tolerate but to expect and even demand higher noise levels. Enthusiasts of snowmobile sports do not protest the sixfold increase in noise output of these machines over the past couple of decades even though snowmobiles are now considered the No. 1 cause of recreational noise exposure.

Scenarios are verbal pictures of an action or an activity, rather than of a thing or setting. They create an image of people and things in action. Because of this, they are often excellent for adding a living quality to your speech—readily drawing your audience into the inherent action of the narrative you are presenting (see Chapter 10 for examples).

Archetypal images are literally pictures of an ancient form or pattern. Their operation depends upon the fact that the most significant formal elements of many images are shared by virtually all people everywhere in the world, and have an almost universal significance from culture to culture as well. Images of such things as the sea or ocean, fire, darkness, and the family are virtually universally human. According to Michael Osborn (1977), there are at least eleven such archetypes that can call up ancient and universal associations when properly used in your speeches. These are "water and the sea, light and darkness, the human body, war, structures [that is, the human act of building or constructing objects], animals, the family, above and below, forward and backward, mountains, and sexuality." Thus, for example, when Abraham Lincoln opens the Gettysburg Address with the words, "Four score and seven years ago our *fathers* . . ." he is using the familial archetype of father–children relationships in order to give his speech greater power with his audience (Adams, 1983). The nation's founders were not merely individual persons who are now relatively obscure to us; they are *our fathers*, and we have a special responsibility to them. It is in this role as fathers that Lincoln invokes them in his speech. Similarly, if you call a seductive opponent a wolf in sheep's clothing, in order to make the point that the audience should be especially wary of his or her motives, you are using an animal archetype to rouse the audience's expected strong suspicions about wolves.

To use an archetypal image, you will most often make a casual reference to the image you are using, without calling overt attention to the fact that you are using such an image. The point is, you are using the almost inherent power of the image to serve in energizing your own ideas in your audience's mind.

Allusions are similar to archetypal images in that they require you to conjure up an image or memory you share with your audience. But they differ from archetypal images in that allusions depend upon some sort of specifically shared speaker–audience experience rather than universal human experience. Like archetypal images, allusions are accomplished obliquely rather than directly. To allude to something is to make an indirect reference to something that both the speaker and listener know in common. Moreover, such indirect reference is expected to induce a commonly shared feeling about the object alluded to, which is why the allusion is used. Thus, for example, when Stephen Joel Trachtenberg named his speech "Building Bricks without Straw: Education Excellence in a Time of Austerity," he was using allusion to try to generate a sympathetic hearing for his speech. He assumed that his audience would be familiar with the biblical story of the pharaoh who forced the Israelites to make bricks without giving them the straw necessary to do so, and that the audience would also put that knowledge together with his subtitle, giving his contemporary purpose an enriched meaning: Higher education will have to be as resourceful as the Israelites if it is to accomplish its charge in these austere times.

Similarly, Colorado Representative Pat Schroeder's speech "Great Expectations: From Abigail Adams to the White House" alludes to Charles Dickens's novel; the title of the speech is meant to call up the associations the audience has with the social conditions portrayed in the Dickens novel, and to identify those conditions with the situation of contemporary women. If the allusion works as intended, the indignation felt upon reading the novel is transferred to the audience's sense of the contemporary political condition of women in America, which is what Schroeder's speech is actually about. To be successful, an allusion must indirectly call to mind some experience shared by both the speaker and the listener. Without the shared experience from which to draw animation, there is no enriched meaning. The allusion is a failure. But, when there *is* a shared fund of experience brought to mind by the allusion, the allusion can be a powerful, vivid device. Successful allusions unite an audience around a shared experience that merely needs to be indirectly invoked to unleash its power.

Metonymy is another very common form of indirect reference, which almost everyone uses spontaneously in conversations. Metonymy evokes an image not by mentioning the thing itself, but by referring to some closely associated thing or idea that you use to substitute for the original thing you have in mind. Many metonymies create an image by mentioning a part of something that you use to stand for the whole. When metonymy is used in this way, the part selected for actual mention is usually the part that is most relevant to the subject being discussed. Thus, if you are talking about *thinking*, then two *heads* are better than one; but if you are talking about *picking apples*, then you want as many *hands* as possible. Metonymy gains its animating power by focusing attention on the aspect of your subject that is the most significant to the point you are making.

In closing this section on images, it is important to note that, as some of the above examples demonstrate, many of these language resources may be combined with repetition in order to form a motif in your speech. A **motif** is a recurrent element in a speech—such as a word, phrase, or image—that captures and expresses the speech's central theme or point. A motif to which you return throughout your presentation can give your speech great animation and organic feeling.

*C*onclusion

A speech is primarily a fabric of words—words you select to express your ideas as precisely, clearly, appropriately, and vividly as possible. Because a public speech is a premeditated act, you have time to consider your words more carefully than you do in spontaneous conversation. You can try out several alternative formulations of your thoughts, experiment with a variety of language techniques, to give your ideas greater staying power, making them live in your audience's memory. Although you cannot, of course, be expected to use all of these techniques in every speech, you can use many of them in each of your speeches, if only you will take the time to try them. Try them and see if they do not enhance the response you get to your next speech.

Questions for Review

1. What are the four qualities that effective language in public speeches should display?

2. How does the quality of precision differ from that of clarity?

Questions for Discussion

1. Why is it possible to be precise, clear, and even vivid without being appropriate?

2. Under what conditions (if any) is vulgar or obscene language justified in a speech?

Things to Try

1. Review a speech you have presented earlier in the course and revise it according to the suggestions in this chapter. Be as playfully bold as you can in using the devices—even if you create a text that goes far beyond what you feel you could appropriately deliver to your class. The goal is to try the techniques on a topic of your own choosing to see what you can accomplish with your language.

2. Select an effective speech from *Vital Speeches* to analyze its use of language. On a photocopy of the speech, mark examples of as many of the forms of repetition and types of images as you can discover.

3. Select another, less effective, speech from *Vital Speeches* and identify any passages that could have been improved by minor modifications of its wording. Prepare a list of alternate wordings that would have enhanced the organic qualities of the speech.

4. Listen carefully to the next round of speeches in your class to determine what special language techniques the speakers have tried and to offer suggestions for improving the organic qualities of the speeches you hear. Where, for example, would phrase repetition have been effective? Or what comparative images could the speaker have used?

Bibliography

Adams, John. "The Familial Image in Rhetoric." *Communication Quarterly* 31 (Winter 1983), 56–61.

Elwell, Larry. "Hearing: Safeguarding an Endangered Resource." *Vital Speeches* 50 (Sept. 15, 1984), 715–718.

Gaydos, Joseph M. "From the Invisible Hand, A Gesture of Contempt." *Vital Speeches* 50 (March 1, 1984), 296–298.

Jackson, Jesse. "The Rainbow Coalition: Young America, Dream." *Vital Speeches* 51 (Nov. 15, 1984), 77–81.

Kennedy, John F. "Inaugural Address." Delivered January 20, 1961.

Osborn, Michael M. "The Evolution of the Archetypal Sea in Rhetoric and Poetic." *Quarterly Journal of Speech* 63 (December 1977), 347–363.

Schroeder, Pat. "Great Expectations: From Abigail Adams to the White House." *Vital Speeches* 50 (May 15, 1984), 472–474.

Trachtenberg, Stephen Joel. "Building Bricks without Straw: Education Excellence in a Time of Austerity." *Vital Speeches* 50 (April 1, 1984), 361–364.

CHAPTER 14

Delivery: Bringing Your Speech to Life through Voice and Movement

*U*p to this point in your speech preparation you have been working to prepare a speech text that will seem organic, that will seem like a living creature. Now it is time to breathe actual life into your speech by preparing your speech's delivery. **Delivery** is the oral and physical presentation of your speech to your intended audience. Through your delivery, you empower your ideas, projecting them in a way that best expresses the organic qualities you have been consciously building into your speech text. A living speech text demands a lively speaker.

The principles of effective speech delivery are the same organic principles that have been applied at every previous stage of your speech preparation: internal preparation, forward motion, growth, climax, and closure. But, with speech delivery, you are concerned with *actual* acts—acts that have their own natural phases of impulse, rise, climax, and fall. Yet, the fact that delivering a speech is literally an organic process does not by itself guarantee that your delivery will be organically artful. Delivering a public speech is not the same as engaging in everyday conversational speech. The differences between the two speech situations arise mainly from the increased formality (Skopec, 1979) and greater physical energy required from public speaking delivery. Delivery requires you to speak more loudly, gesture more expansively, and project your ideas more broadly than you usually do in casual conversation.

The difference between the demands of conversation and the demands of public speech may be compared to the difference between looking at vacation slides through an individual viewer and projecting them onto a screen to show a group of friends. A good slide projector requires a far more powerful energy source to project the same image than does a private viewer. But, just because the power is increased, it does not mean that the image on the screen will be a distortion of the image on the slide. Similarly, public speaking requires you to project your message with much greater power than you are used to, but it does not require you to distort your personality, or to pretend to be something you are not. Good delivery is not acting, even though the projection skills used by the actor are similar to those you use in public speaking. As a public speaker, you will remain your natural self; you will just be a much larger, more forceful self than you are usually.

Because you will need to project your speech expansively, learning to deliver a speech—at least at first—is a more self-conscious act than normal conversation. You must practice becoming "larger than life" in order to be perceived as being a normal, living speaker. You must learn to "fill the screen" represented by your more extended public audience. Your ideas must be projected many times larger than they naturally are in spontaneous conversation. The purpose of this chapter is to introduce you to the functions, elements, and principles of effective, organic speech delivery.

The Functions of Delivery

Even though your speech is primarily a pattern of words used to project your ideas, without an effective delivery to empower those ideas, the impact of your speech might be lost. A misplaced emphasis or a distracting mannerism may confuse or annoy your audience every bit as much as a vague word or an inaccurate detail. We will look at six important functions of speech delivery in projecting your ideas to your audience.

To Empower the Ideas You Wish to Communicate

Without the physical act of delivery, there is no speech. Without the actual presentation of your ideas through the power of speech, there is only think-ing; there is no communication at all. So the first, and most obvious, function of delivery is to supply the physical energy needed to make your ideas avail-able to others. Since your listeners will be much further from you during a public speech than during a normal conversation, you will have to project your words much further than you are accustomed to projecting them. Be-cause filling an entire room with your speech represents a new challenge, you will need to rehearse speaking more loudly, and learn to do it without becoming strained and strident.

To Indicate the Structure of Your Speech

Your speech is not merely a series of words; it is also a structure of words. In addition to the **verbal** transitional phrases and internal summaries that you accomplish with words, you can use **vocal** and **physical** aspects of delivery to help mark the units of thought within your speech. For example, taking a step forward or backward while you pause between ideas suggests a transi-tion in your train of thought from one idea to the next. Similarly, raising your voice pitch at the end of a sentence suggests that a question is being asked and that the audience is to briefly consider it before you continue.

Are such nonverbal indicators of the internal structure of your speech really necessary? All the evidence says yes. In a conversation, you are rarely "behaviorally silent"—even when you are a listener. As a speaker you are constantly punctuating the structure of your speech with your body motions. According to Albert Scheflen (1964), there are definite postural units accom-panying spoken conversation, and these postural units serve as indicators of the structure of ideas within your speech. Scheflen writes:

> When an American speaker uses a series of syntactic sentences in a conver-sation, he changes the position of his head and eyes every few sentences. He

may turn his head right or left, tilt it, cock it to one side or the other, or flex or extend his neck so as to look toward the floor or ceiling. Regardless of the kind of shift in head posture, the attitude is held for a few sentences, then shifted to another position. Each of these shifts I believe marks the end of a structural unit at the next higher level than the syntactic sentence. This unit I have tentatively named a "point" because it corresponds crudely to making a point in a discussion. The maintenance of head position indicates the duration of the point.

As Scheflen suggests, postural units may be of different durations—so that there are smaller postural units that fit within larger ones, just as words fit within sentences, and sentences fit within paragraphs. Scheflen identifies three levels of postural units that are larger than the sentence, calling them the *point* (mentioned in the selection quoted), the *position,* and the *presentation.* The names reflect the fact that a speaker will have an overall presentation to make, that the presentation will be composed of several major positions, and that each position will be composed of several specific points. All of these are marked behaviorally as well as verbally.

Not only do speakers spontaneously punctuate their conversations with point, position, and presentation postures and movements, listeners spontaneously and unconsciously use this nonverbal activity to help themselves understand the speaker's ideas. In a series of fascinating studies, William Condon and his colleagues (1969, 1974) have documented through slow-motion films that the precise timing of a listener's body movements closely mirrors the timing of the speaker's voice and body gestures. For example, Condon and Ogston (1971) write, "The body of a hearer moves in synchrony with the speaker like a parallel system—as the pattern of the one varies so also does the other. The interactants speed up and slow down together, and this appears to be related to stress and pitch variations."

What Condon's work suggests is that, as part of the overall act of listening, listeners spontaneously synchronize the timing of their own bodily activities to match those of the speaker. The rise and fall of the speaker's vocal and gestural acts serve as a pacemaker for the listener's listening acts. Thus, for example, the length of time it takes listeners to blink their eyes will change depending upon the ebb and flow of the voice and movement of the person to whom they are listening. This means that listeners depend upon the speaker's voice and body movement to help themselves organize the speaker's stream of words into meaningful units of ideas. Matching the timing of their own body motions with the vocal structure of the speaker's intonational pattern allows listeners to segment the speaker's verbal sequence into the same structure of ideas intended by the speaker. This spontaneous speaker–listener process is called **speaker–listener synchrony.**

Speaker–listener synchrony occurs at multiple levels of observation: from the individual speech sound all the way up to the presentation as a whole (Kendon, 1972). Without such vocal and behavioral cues to guide the listener, understanding the internal structure of a speech would be far more difficult, if not impossible. Listeners depend upon the speaker's vocal and bodily changes in order to guide their own understanding of the structure of the speaker's ideas.

Since most people spontaneously vary their voice and body movement during conversations, it is typically easy for conversational listeners to follow the speaker. The conversational speaker's normal vocal and physical micro-movements are usually powerful and varied enough to guide the listener's act of listening, that is, to help listeners follow the structure of the conversational speaker's ideas. But when an audience is further away than conversational distance, the normal amount of vocal variety and body motion cannot be easily distinguished, leaving the audience confused, or tired from straining to understand the speaker's ideas. In these situations, your delivery must compensate for the increased listener distance by employing larger gestures and movements, and by employing more extensive changes of vocal pitch, pause, and volume.

To Emphasize Key Points

An audience must be able to distinguish your main ideas from the supporting ideas. You have both vocal and physical resources for emphasizing key ideas. For example, you can raise your voice on a key word or sentence—to help lift it out from the other sentences that comprise its background. Or, you can lower your voice to a hush, in order to increase audience attention to a specific word or sentence. This latter technique dramatizes the point you are making because audience members suddenly have to listen especially hard to hear it. Thus, you can use your voice both to organize the relations of ideas to one another within your speech, and to dramatize those ideas you consider most important. Similarly, you can use bodily action for emphasis. Taking a step toward the audience, or using pointing gestures with your index finger, will help call special attention to whatever you are saying at that moment.

To Establish Contact with Your Audience

Human beings are a gregarious species. Most of us search out opportunities to be with others. Part of being together is making contact. We hug one another or shake hands when we greet; we hold hands or kiss when we feel affectionate; we pick up and hold babies when we want to rock them to sleep. Ashley Montague's book *Touching* (1971) documents both the need to make contact and the many ways we attempt to accomplish it.

One of the most important ways we keep in contact is through speech. We speak to one another almost incessantly: We discuss the weather, gossip, conduct business, and babble endlessly about sports. Talking is how we stay in touch with one another. This is because whenever people speak, they not only project their ideas and feelings, they also project their personalities to whomever may be listening. For most people, conversational contact is easy and spontaneous. We merely begin talking.

But contact is every bit as important in public speaking—where there are many more people with whom to make contact. Your audience needs to feel that you are reaching out to them, not merely presenting a monologue for your own benefit. Accordingly, you must appear to make contact with your audience through your delivery.

Audience contact is the result of projecting yourself toward your audience in a way that makes it clear that you care about them and their response to your speech. But audience contact demands more than simply making your delivery large enough and powerful enough to be heard. Many students can fill a room with their speech without ever establishing useful contact with their audience. Even when they are loud enough, they end up delivering their speech as a soliloquy, or a monologue to some "generalized other." They still ignore their particular audience. Effective audience contact is accomplished by the purposeful use of your eyes, voice, and body motion to try to involve your audience with yourself and your speech.

For example, good audience contact requires good eye contact. Rather than looking down at your notes, out the window, or over the audience's heads to the back of the room, you should look directly at your audience, engaging their eyes with your own. Since you cannot look at everyone at once, you will need to distribute your looks to all parts of the room at different times. Look to the left side of the audience for a sentence or two, then to the center, then to the back, and so forth, to all parts of the room. During the course of the speech, it will seem as if you have been in relatively continuous contact with all of the audience if you have frequently looked at specific, varied portions of it for short periods of time. In summary, then, your speech must seem to be directed toward each of your audience's members personally. Your delivery must create a sense of personal contact between yourself and your audience, between your mind and theirs.

To Enhance and Guide Audience Attention

Attending to a speech has its own peaks and valleys—rising and declining phases. No audience can maintain its attention in a steady state throughout an entire speech. Audience attention will ebb and flow. But an effective speech delivery can help you accomplish two important goals concerning audience attention.

First, an effective, animated delivery can help you establish more powerful listening impulses. Because an audience empathically falls in with your own mood and energy level (due to rhythmic synchrony, among other reasons), an energetic delivery helps create a higher level of general attention throughout your speech. Enthusiasm is generally contagious, so an animated delivery enhances the baseline level of audience attention.

In addition to strengthening your audience's impulse to listen, your delivery can also guide the audience's peaks and valleys of attention. Your voice and movement act as powerful pacemakers of audience involvement. Movement captures attention. Animated, active speakers tend to induce high levels of audience attention, and passive speakers, who slouch limply over the lectern, tend to induce boredom and inattention. This might be called audience *empathy* with a speaker. Since audiences cannot act upon ideas to which they are not attending, successful speakers use a varied and animated delivery to capture, enhance, and guide the audience's level of attention.

To Express How You Feel about Your Topic

However rational your ideas may be, they always come wrapped in a charge of your personal feelings. This cannot be avoided since simply having an idea is itself a form of human feeling. Although most audiences will reject conspicuous displays of emotion, audiences do want, even demand, to know that you feel deeply about your subject matter, that you care about what you are talking about. How will audiences know whether or not you care about your topic? They will feel it in your delivery—in your vocal and bodily manner as you speak. An audience spontaneously responds to your vocal and bodily mood by the processes of empathy and suggestibility. Because of these processes, it is important to recognize that your delivery also spontaneously expresses how you feel about your speech. And how you feel about your speech has a powerful effect on how your audience feels about your speech—and its verbal content.

The Elements of Delivery

Delivering a speech is a total bodily act. Every part of you must participate if your delivery is to be effective. Your legs must not only support you; they must also move you around in a manner that serves the best expression of your ideas. Your arms must do more than merely dangle unobtrusively at your sides; they must gesture meaningfully. Your voice must do more than merely empower your words; it must energize them and bring them to life. To see how your delivery can help animate your ideas, it is important to understand the basic elements of speech delivery. For convenience, we will group these elements under two categories: (1) vocal elements and (2) bodily elements.

Projecting Your Ideas with Your Voice

Your voice is a multifaceted instrument. To understand the vocal elements over which you have a considerable measure of control, it is helpful to understand how you produce the speech sounds you make. To produce even the simplest speech sound involves four separate component processes: (1) respiration, (2) phonation, (3) resonation, and (4) articulation. Each component process affects how you deliver your speech.

Speech Production In order to speak you must first take in a supply of air. This is usually done in a short powerful inspiration—which you can feel for yourself if you stop reading for a moment and pretend as if you are about to speak to someone. Did you feel the gasp? Once the air is taken into the lungs, you will begin to release it back out in a controlled manner. This is the **respiratory** phase of speaking. The respiratory phase is where the power for driving your speech outward, away from yourself, comes from.

But quiet breathing does not result in speech. You must use the column of air you are releasing to produce a sound. This you accomplish by bringing your vocal folds (vocal cords) together so that the air passing between them causes the folds to vibrate. Now you have a sound. This process is called **phonation.**

Words don't all sound alike so you must rapidly and constantly modify the sound you are producing in order to make the specific sounds of your actual words. You make the various sounds of individual words by the processes of resonation and articulation. When your vocal cords vibrate, the sound is complex and filled with overtones. By selectively amplifying or damping various overtones, you can make the different vowel sounds of your language. This process of selectively modifying tones is called **resonation.** You unconsciously choose the overtones to be amplified or damped by changing the shape of your mouth cavity. To feel this process, try saying the *e* sound of the word *eat,* and then say the *ah* sound of the word *father.* Say them rapidly, one after another—*e ah e ah*—and you will experience the difference resonation makes in the sounds that come out of your mouth, as well as how you reshape your vocal cavity to produce the different vowel sounds.

The final process of speech production is articulation. The speech stream is not produced by just a continuous shifting of resonation positions. The flow of air is often interfered with, and even stopped entirely, in order to produce the individual speech sounds. Feel what happens to the speech stream as your mouth changes positions to make sounds such as the *s* in sea and the *sh* in shore: *sea–sh*ore *sea–sh*ore. Breaking the flow of the air stream and then letting it flow again is **articulation,** which is done primarily with the teeth and tongue. Figure 14–1 presents a diagram of the vocal tract. Notice how the air must be driven upward from the lungs through the vocal cords, and past the tongue, lips, and nose before it emerges as a coded sound wave empowering your ideas for transmission to others.

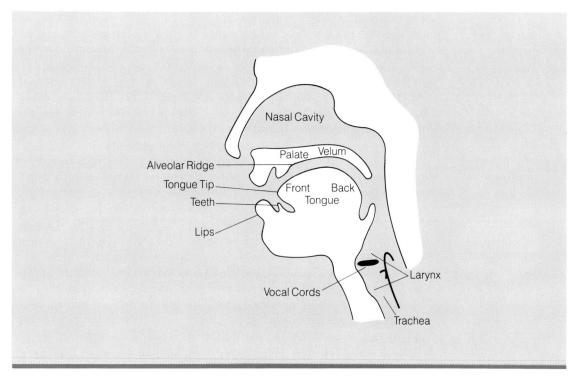

Figure 14-1   Diagram of the Vocal Tract

Vocal Elements of Delivery Control over these four processes gives you control over the many vocal characteristics that determine the effectiveness of your speech delivery. The most important vocal elements for you to work on as you improve your speech delivery are your volume, rate, pause, duration, pitch, stress, and climax.

Volume. Whenever you speak, you must speak with a certain degree of power. The air you take in during the respiratory phase is systematically expelled from your lungs and through your larynx with a measurable degree of force. This degree of force creates the quality of volume or loudness. Variations in your volume are responsible for carrying all the other vocal qualities to your audience.

Concerning volume, there are two things to note. First, your overall volume must be substantially increased in the public speaking situation, in order to have the same impact on your audience as your normal voice has in conversational settings. You are further away, and the power is progressively diminished the further it moves from the source. In addition, your volume must have substantial variety in order to carry the meanings you intend to convey. The further you are from your audience, the less noticeable are the subtle power differences that are sufficient for normal conversation. So, not only will you need to generate a greater general volume during a public speech, you will also need to use a far greater range of volume. Otherwise, there will simply not be enough contrast as the sound wave travels further and further away from you and loses its power. You will probably need to use greater contrasts in your maximum and minimum volume in order to convey to your audience a feeling of normal contrasts in volume. If you do not use slightly exaggerated contrasts in your volume, your audience will tend to feel that your speech lacks variety. Normal conversational loudness lacks the carrying power needed to give your speech a feeling of conversational variety.

Rate. Your rate of speaking is also very important in determining whether an audience will be able to listen easily and effectively to your speech. Whenever you speak, you articulate a certain number of words per minute. The number of words you say per minute (wpm) is your speech rate. The average wpm is between 120 and 180, but there is no ideal rate for public speakers. What is more important than absolute rate is your ability to vary your average rate for emphasis. Appropriate changes in rate of delivery will make your speech seem more natural. To speak at a relatively constant rate de-emphasizes the actual ebb and flow of spontaneous conversation and makes it hard for your audience to follow your speech. As we discussed earlier, your audience depends upon the sound differences to enhance their ability to follow your speech. You must make these differences slightly larger than normal when you speak in public. That is, you must make larger changes in your rate of speaking if you are to help your audience understand the structure of your speech. What will seem to your own ear to be slightly exaggerated changes in rate will seem quite normal and desirable to an audience that is listening to you at some distance.

Pause. One way of varying the rate of delivery is to use pause in your speech—that is, to stop talking for a moment. For example, if you have just presented a key idea, you may want to pause briefly to allow your audience time to take in the idea. Pause is especially important if you ask a rhetorical question, since the audience needs time both to understand the question and to think of the answer. Similarly, you may wish to pause after announcing that an important idea is coming, before you actually deliver it. This type of pause builds anticipation and focuses audience attention on the ideas to come. Such pauses also help suggest the internal structure of your speech. Don't feel you must race through the speech without taking time for meaningful pauses. An overly deliberate speech will tire an audience, but thoughtful pauses sprinkled throughout the speech help to punctuate it and help convey its meaning and structure.

In contrast to pauses used meaningfully—that is, pauses to suggest structure or to build anticipation—hesitation pauses, especially when filled with meaningless vocalization, can be damaging to your overall effectiveness. These pauses build anticipation at all the wrong times. They are unrelated to the inherent structure of your speech and therefore throw the audience off track. Since these pauses often come at the wrong time, the audience wants you to get on with it—to finish your thought. Hesitation pauses can be as brief as an "uhh" or "ah," or as long as an "okay" or a "you know." But, however long these vocalized pauses may be, they break the flow of the audience's listening act and force them to start over, rebuilding the impulse for listening to a particular sentence and idea. As well as being tedious, these frequent breaks make the audience start over many times, as they use up their energy for listening. So, practice your speech enough times that you do not require frequent, wasteful stops while you think of your next word, phrase, or idea.

Duration. Duration is the length of time it takes you to say any particular sound, syllable, or word within your speech. In conversation, the various sounds of words are not all spoken with the same duration. The beginnings and endings of words take more time than the middles (Condon, 1982). Furthermore, some sounds will be slowed down or speeded up for special emphasis, or to express a particular feeling you may have. In fact, you can say a word or sentence very abruptly to convey one feeling, and more slowly to convey something entirely different—even the opposite. Duration has a powerful impact on the meaning and feeling the audience receives. For example, if you say the following sentence abruptly, spitting out the words in short bursts of almost equal duration on every syllable, the feeling you convey might be anger:

Oh! I didn't know that!

But, if you extend the syllables of the various words, as emphasized below by the repeated letters, the effect (and affect) is quite different.

Oooooh . . . Iiii diidn't knoow thaaat!

Since you have a large measure of control over the duration of any particular sound whenever you speak, you can help guide the audience's feeling about your ideas, and their general understanding of your speech, by varying the duration of words to express your feelings. Again, don't rush through your speech. Be sure to give each syllable the duration it requires in order to convey the feeling you wish to convey.

Pitch. Because most speech sounds are produced by vibrations of the vocal cords at a certain frequency, your voice has a general pitch level. Pitch is the relative height of your voice on the musical scale. You take note of variations in general vocal pitch when you notice that females typically have a higher voice than males, and that boys' voices change—dropping in pitch—when they go through puberty. But as you also know from your own experience, you can vary the pitch of your voice within a certain range in order to accomplish various communication-related goals. These pitch changes are used in speech to alter the impact of your words on a listener. For example, when you raise the pitch at the end of a sentence you are typically asking a question.

Some of the most generally used types of pitch changes in conversational and public speaking are: (1) the slide upward, as at the end of a question, (2)

This egg farm has 2 million chickens. Discuss the growth of agribusiness and the demise of the family farm. What are some new techniques in farm management and food production? Would you like to live on a small farm?

the slide downward, as at the end of a simple declarative sentence, (3) the abrupt upward movement, as in calling a wayward child home to eat

(Hen^{RY}), (4) downward movement, as in shaming the same child (**HEN**_{ry!}

HOW **could you do it?**), and (5) waves, which are either down-up-down or up-down-up pitch movements on a single syllable.

All of these pitches are illustrated in the following examples. In each case, the single word *Oh* is to be said while expressing a wide variety of feelings, which are indicated in the words that follow the *Oh*. Try saying each of these with the meaning indicated, and see how the pitch changes from one to the next. Notice how the duration of the sounds changes, as well.

Oh (What did you say?)

Oh (I don't believe that.)

Oh (Now, I understand.)

Oh (You scared me.)

Oh (What a pity.)

Oh (You don't say.)

Oh (What a cute puppy.)

Oh (What a mess.)

Oh (zero.)

Oh (You can't fool me.)

Stress. Volume and stress are not quite the same thing. Volume refers to the overall power with which you deliver your speech. With volume, the major question is whether or not you can be comfortably heard by all members of your audience. But volume is never really constant. Some words are spoken with far greater power than average, and others are spoken with far less power than the baseline of volume you are using. **Stress** is the degree of power you selectively apply to a particular syllable, word, phrase, or sentence in order to make it stand out from the others. In this way the stressed unit is given special importance. Making some syllable or word stand out by giving it additional stress gives it **emphasis.** In fact, stress for emphasis is often illustrated by the intentional misuse of stress, in the sentence:

You've got the em**PHA**sis on the wrong syl**LA**ble.

Putting the emphasis on the wrong syllable is, of course, not the largest problem for most beginning speakers. Rather, it is that they don't put *enough* stress on the *right* syllable. They do not make the most important words stand out from the crowd of other words. All their words sound about the same when they speak in public. People who typically have no trouble having their intended emphases understood in normal conversation forget to add the extra power needed to make normal conversational stress differences noticeable at the extra distance required by public speech. This is what people often mean when they say that a speaker speaks with a monotone voice. Tone, per se, may not be the problem. Mono*stress* may be the real culprit. To see the difference in meaning that is carried by the appropriate stress, say the following sentences aloud with the stress indicated. What differences in meaning do you hear based on these changes in stress?

WHAT are you doing?

What **ARE** you doing?

What are **YOU** doing?

What are you **DO**ing?

If your audience cannot tell the difference in the stress levels of your various words, you will need to work on adding enough extra power to make these differences noticeable to your audience.

Climax. The aspect of vocal delivery that most contributes to making your speech like a living creature is **climax**—the feeling that your speech is building up to something special. Progressively increasing the volume, rate, pitch, or stress on a series of words contributes to a sense of vocal climax and enhances the overall organic quality of your speech. Climax is illustrated visually in the example below:

We must not *give in*. No! We **must NEVER** *give* in.

Notice that there is a building of stress and emphasis toward the word *never*. But notice also that there is a descending level of emphasis after the climactic word of the sentence. When using vocal climax, there must be both building up and ebbing away.

Projecting Your Ideas with Your Body

Audiences not only hear your speech; they also see you present it. Therefore, you must consider how you will *look* as well as how you will sound. There are at least four bodily elements of delivery that deserve special considerations: movement, posture, gesture, and eye contact.

Bodily Elements of Delivery Movement. Because you are trying to give your speech a living quality, your movements before, during, and after the speech should be energetic, enthusiastic, and emphatic. Audiences empathically catch your mood from the moment they first catch sight of you. Furthermore, they are guided in their moment-to-moment feeling about you in large measure by your movement to, from, and on the platform. Is it strong and vigorous, or weak and nervous?

How important is movement in your audience's assessment of you? Although this has not been tested directly, there is a fascinating indirect demonstration of the significance of your movements in influencing another's judgments about you. In a film study of people walking in New York City, one researcher found that police watching the films could predict which people would be the most likely targets of street crimes; moreover, people recently convicted of such crimes rated the relative "muggability" of the people in the films in the same rank order. When the films were analyzed, it was found that both the police and the convicts were picking up subtle cues in the rhythm of the way various people were walking. These movement cues determined whether those people would seem to be easy targets or not. Thus, even in films of strangers, people's movements reveal to others their confidence and preparedness for action. If the muggers and police can feel how vulnerable an innocent pedestrian is, merely by seeing the person in films, certainly your audience, which is paying close attention to your movements, will spontaneously respond to those movements and determine how you feel about what you are doing. So, how should you move?

If you must sit within your audience's view before speaking, sit up and look quietly alert and ready to speak. When it comes time to speak, move briskly to the lectern or podium, suggesting poise and a desire to communicate. These first impressions are lasting, and they are conveyed by the way you move in the first few moments in front of your audience. Once you are at the lectern, your movements should continue to be definite and purposeful. Unless you are confined by a microphone because of the size of the room, move away from the lectern. Take definite steps when you move, but do not pace randomly. When leaving the lectern, do not slink away like someone defeated.

Posture. Although you may think that your posture is a "steady state," characterized by an absence of movement, nothing could be further from the truth. Good posture or bad, your posture is maintained by a continuous pattern of muscular activity—with antagonistic muscles balancing their contractions against one another to create the pattern of bodily position known as your posture. Because posture is maintained by this continuous pattern of muscular activity, your audience responds to it just as strongly as they do to more overt types of physical movement. They feel as if they are swaying from side to side if you are swaying back and forth. If you are leaning limply and tiredly on the lectern for physical support, their muscle tone is likely to become flaccid, and their attention will soon begin to wander. If you are stiff and rigid, their bodies will become tense and uncomfortable. Accordingly, your posture must be one that helps the audience to feel at ease as they listen to you speak. In particular, this means that your posture should be erect without being stiff, comfortable without being overly relaxed and slouchy. Furthermore, your posture should make it easy for you to move from side to side; and, finally, it should support you upright so that you can gesture freely.

Gesture. What should you do with your hands during your speech? Gesture as freely and unself-consciously as you do during conversation with friends. Gestures are a routine and spontaneous part of conversational speech, and to give a public speech without the normal complement of gestures seems unnatural. In fact, you may tongue-tie yourself if you do not allow your hands to move freely. For most of us the impulse to gesture and the impulse to speak are formed virtually simultaneously (Kendon, 1980). Occasionally some students gesture too much or develop gestural **mannerisms**—which are distracting repeated movements. But for the most part, excess movement is unlikely to become a problem, and it is relatively easy to overcome. Most students go to the other extreme, gesturing far too little. Since in spontaneous conversations most of us talk with our hands, it is unnatural to inhibit such impulses in the public speaking situation. If you gesture too much or in a distracting manner, your instructor can help you take note of this and correct it. Otherwise, do not try to stop yourself from making definite, forceful, and abundant gestures. The audience will appreciate your effort.

Eye Contact. Eyes are amazingly expressive of our inner states and feelings. Subtle muscular changes in focus, pupil dilation, or direction of gaze convey where your attention is directed and what you feel about what you see. Audiences are incredibly sensitive to eye movements, even at a considerable distance from you. If your eyes are darting aimlessly around the room, above the audience's heads, or out the window, your audience will wonder why, and maybe even begin to look there themselves. If your eyes are buried in your notes, your audience will feel cut off from you and wish that you'd come back and rejoin them. It is toward your audience that your speech is directed, and it is toward them that your eye focus should be concentrated. As noted earlier, since you cannot look at everyone at once, your best bet is to look at various clusters of people in your audience—shifting the focus of your gaze every few seconds. Everyone wants to feel included, so move your focus from side to side and from front to back as you select clusters of people to look at for brief periods of time. This distributed form of eye contact works out quite well since, even in normal conversations, you rarely gaze at your listeners continuously. In fact, at any particular moment, you may very well be talking while looking slightly away from your conversational partner. In public speaking, there is no harm in selecting groups to look at for brief periods, but make sure you return to each of the clusters at intervals during your speech.

The Principles of Effective Delivery

Based on the previous background discussion, we can now summarize some of the basic principles of effective speech delivery. These are:

Effective Delivery Is Conversational without Being Commonplace What should your speech's delivery be like? In 1915, James Winans introduced an image of good delivery that has been the standard ever since (see Chapter 1). According to Winans, a speech's delivery should be like an enlarged conversation (1917). In other words, a speech's delivery should exemplify the best qualities of your best conversations, and those qualities should be enlarged so that they may be projected to the entire audience rather than to merely one or two others—as they are in our more conventional conversations. Winans came to this image of delivery by way of a short parable that is worth recalling here as you consider the best way to deliver your own speeches. In setting up his parable, Winans asks his readers to imagine that all memory of previous speech making has suddenly been blotted out. He writes:

> Is this the end of speech-making? Here comes a man who has seen a great race, or has been in a great battle, or is on fire with enthusiasm for a cause. He begins to talk with a friend he meets on the street; others gather, twenty, fifty, a hundred. Interest grows intense; he lifts his voice that all may hear. But the crowd wishes to hear and see the speaker better. "Get upon this cart!" they cry; and he mounts the cart and goes on with his story or his plea (p. 20).

Winans makes the point of his story clear when he notes that "a private conversation has become a speech" and then asks the key question: "When does the talker or converser become a speech maker? When ten persons gather? Fifty? Or is it when he gets on the cart? Is there any real change in the nature or the spirit of the act?" Finally, he asks, "Is it not essentially the same throughout, a conversation adapted to the growing number of his hearers as the talker proceeds?"

Indeed, in many ways a speech's delivery is exactly like an enlarged conversation and should have exactly the same qualities as your best conversations. According to Sarett and Foster (1936), some of the conversational qualities good public speaking should retain are a communicative attitude, close contact, spontaneity, and effortlessness. In other words, Sarett and Foster think (1) that you should seem eager rather than reticent to communicate— that is, you should seem enthusiastic at the prospect of sharing your ideas; (2) that you should seek to maintain the sense of physical closeness common in normal conversation; (3) that you should maintain a "disarming informality"—that is, you should not seem stuffy and pompous merely because you happen to be the featured speaker; and finally (4) that you should seem spontaneous rather than studied, forced, formal, or self-conscious.

Does conceiving of speech delivery as enlarged conversation mean that you can afford to ignore delivery and concern yourself exclusively with verbal content? Definitely not. Much of our conversational interaction is commonplace and not very good. As Sarett and Foster point out: "Some of the traits of ordinary conversation are bad: often the range of the voice is too narrow; the rate too rapid and too uniform; effective pauses are too few; language is too informal, and articulation too slovenly" (pp. 88–89). So it is the quality of conversation when conversation is at its *best* that you should seek to create during your speech.

Effective Delivery Springs from Spontaneous Impulses For your long-term success as a speaker, you must rehearse your speeches before you deliver them. But it is also important that your delivery seem to spring from spontaneous impulses generated at the moment of actual utterance. Although it may seem contradictory, your goal is to rehearse your speech in such a way that the final presentation seems to be spontaneous. How can you be both rehearsed and spontaneous at the same time?

Each of us has a fairly extensive repertoire of spontaneous gestures, postures, bodily movements, facial expressions, eye behaviors, and vocal elements that we routinely draw upon during our normal conversational speech. When you rehearse your speech you will spontaneously draw upon this repertoire of bodily and vocal acts from moment to moment. Each time you practice the speech it will come out a little differently—both in terms of the exact words you use and in terms of the accompanying nonverbal expressions you use. Concerning delivery, when you are rehearsing you are not planning the exact movements you will be making at particular points in the speech. **What**

you are rehearsing is your ability to draw spontaneously upon your natural repertoire of nonverbal expressions as the impulse of the moment moves you. What you are learning is how to be less inhibited in your range and number of supporting bodily movements. Rehearsing for a speech is somewhat like practicing for a tennis match. You can isolate all of the separate components of the game for special attention: serves, baseline shots, net shots, lobs, and backhands. But you cannot practice ahead of time the order in which you will use them—because the game situation itself dictates this. You must select your shots based on the ebb and flow of the game— from the repertoire of shots you have rehearsed. Similarly, you will select your gestures, postures, and vocal elements at the moment of utterance, in response to the ebb and flow of audience attention and behavior. But you will have rehearsed your repertoire of delivery skills relative to this particular speech several times.

Effective Delivery Actively Involves the Audience An active, animated enthusiastic delivery is contagious; it physically involves your audience with you, with your speech, and with your point of view. Because your individual listeners tend to synchronize their superficial body rhythms with the peaks and valleys of your voice and gestures, good delivery helps bind the individual listeners into something that can genuinely be called an audience. Your delivery provides them all with common, shared experience—your speech as an event. Thus, a good delivery not only involves your audience with you; it involves them with one another, helping make them into a more cohesive unit. This active involvement of your audience with the complex multilayered temporal structure of your speech, and the mutually shared speaker–audience feeling this involvement evokes, is called **empathy.** Good delivery results in an empathic response to your speech, as well as a cognitive, intellectual response.

Effective Delivery Complements Your Ideas There is no substitute for the clear verbal presentation of your ideas, but your delivery should complement and enhance your verbal presentation. Delivery can complement your ideas in several ways. First, delivery must be appropriate to the ideas you are trying to express. If, for example, you are trying to express difficult or weighty ideas, you should probably slow down and allow the force and gravity of your voice to suggest the importance you attach to those ideas. If, on the other hand, your ideas are readily comprehensible, or do not require great seriousness, then a quicker delivery pace will be appropriate. Normally, a speech will be composed of ideas of varying complexity and importance, and will therefore require a variable, flexible delivery to complement that shifting pattern of ideas. Second, your delivery must suit the feeling you are trying to create. Since you not only have ideas to express, but also have a feeling about those ideas—for instance, whether you consider them urgent, important, fun, or exciting—your voice and bodily manner should convey this feeling. Finally, your delivery must not conflict with your message. If you say that you are "pleased to be here," you should sound and look pleased—not bored, disinterested, or resentful. Your delivery is the support system for your entire speech, and it must complement, not compete with, your verbal message.

Effective Delivery Employs All of Your Bodily Resources Speaking is a total bodily act in which all of your muscles are mobilized to participate. Our acts of speaking serve as a temporal pacemaker for all of our other bodily acts. Because the speaking act involves all of one's bodily activities, all of your bodily resources may be used to help convey your ideas to your audience. Thus, to lock your hands at your side or onto the sides of the lectern and thereby fail to use them during your speech is to deny yourself an expressive resource, and to cut your audience off from one more avenue for understanding your ideas. To speak in a monotone or with an inanimate face, or to stand rigidly at attention throughout your speech, is to hold something back and to undermine the potential influence your ideas might have had with your audience. Try to use all of the bodily resources available to you—expansive gestures, movements from side to side, illustrative and spontaneous structural postures, pauses and stress changes for effect. Practice your entire bodily repertoire, and use it as necessary for a particular speech on a particular occasion.

Effective Delivery Responds to Audience Reactions Communication is a jointly engendered act. Without audience understanding, there is no literal communication. Where no idea goes across and becomes shared, there is only mutual interaction. Because the audience must actively participate in your speech if the shared act of communication is to begin and to continue, you must continually monitor your audience's reactions and modify the content or delivery of your speech if you discover signs that your audience is unwilling or unable to participate in the communication act. Good eye contact allows you to determine if your audience is following your train of thought and gives you an opportunity to modify what you are saying or doing. Because you have many options for how you deliver your speech, being responsive to your audience's reactions is a helpful guide concerning which content and delivery options to exercise on a particular occasion.

Effective Delivery Creates Feeling without Uncontrolled Emotional Display One of the most important features of delivery is its ability to elicit and guide audience feeling about yourself as a speaker, your topic, your speech, and your point of view on the subject. Although we often restrict the concept of feeling to emotional display, feeling includes much more. It is also the quiet warmth that infuses you as you talk about a favorite subject, the chill you experience when you report on a friend who has moved or died, the sympathy that arises when telling about a family that has lost its home, and the exhilaration that comes over you when you talk about your triumphs against all odds. Of course, feelings of anger and outrage due to some personal or social injustice motivate many speeches; but your feeling of personal competence when you are explaining, for example, how to fix a leaky faucet, can also motivate a speech. Good delivery shares your feeling for your topic and, by the process of empathy, helps induce a similar feeling in your listeners. Good delivery does not hide your feelings, making you sound like an impersonal automaton reciting the words of others. Thus, just as conversational speaking is infused with personal feeling, so too should public speaking express the warmth of human feeling—at least as long as that feeling does not degenerate into uncontrolled emotional display. A speaker out of control is rarely something audiences enjoy listening to for long.

Effective Delivery Avoids Obvious Weaknesses Speaking in public is such a novel experience for most students that they may fall into delivery habits that are not merely useless in serving their ideas, but that are positively harmful to their overall effectiveness. A brief discussion follows of some of the most common delivery mistakes students typically make. The first two concern vocal aspects of your delivery; the third concerns bodily elements of delivery.

Avoid vocal clutter. Vocal clutter includes all noncontent related vocalizations. These are typically uttered to avoid silence when you are thinking about what to say next, or are looking for a specific word. There are two types of vocal clutter to avoid. **Vocalized pauses** are sounds that have no dictionary meanings, such as *uh, um, heh,* and so on. When you use such sounds your speech sounds like this: "I . . . uh . . . don't know . . . uh . . . what the actual facts on this are, but . . . uh . . . I do think that . . ." When we hear a speaker like this, we know that the speaker has not prepared either the content or the delivery of the speech; the vocalized pauses are a sure sign that something is wrong. **Verbal fillers** are recognizable words that have approximately the same effect as do vocalized pauses. These include such words as *okay* and *you know.* These sound like this: "Today I want to talk about, you know, how digital watches work. Okay. . . . Well, the first thing, you know, that I want to talk about is . . ." The problem with all such fillers is that they break up the flow of ideas from the speaker to the listener and require the listener to stop listening to the ideas, to respond to the intrusion, and then to start listening again as the speaker continues the train of thought that was suspended while the filler intruded. Most listeners prefer silence during the speaker's suspended act because they can use the time themselves for processing what they have previously heard. The vocalized clutter intrudes on what is otherwise a valuable moment of silence.

Avoid mispronunciations and misarticulations. The final two phases in the speech production process are resonation and articulation. Many an embarrassing moment will be created if you fail to carry out these two processes in the manner typically expected by your audience. Two of the most troublesome problems for speakers are mispronunciation of words or syllables and misarticulation of sounds.

To articulate is to divide the speech stream into the individual sounds that compose the words you are using. To *mis*articulate, then, is to fail to form the sounds of your words properly. For example, if you habitually slur your sounds together so that your listeners have a difficult time telling one sound from another, you have an articulation problem to work on. To say "Jeetchet" for "Did you eat yet?" is to slur your sounds together. A second commonplace type of misarticulation is to drop a significant sound at the beginnings or endings of your words: "I don' wan' uh go" for "I don't want to go." Such articulation problems are habitual and typically need only a minimum of guided practice to be overcome. Ask your instructor for help if either of these articulation problems affects the acceptability of your speech.

In contrast to misarticulation, mispronunciation forms all of the individual sounds of your words in a recognizable way—but they are the *wrong* sounds. For example, in an informative speech, a student insisted on calling recently re-elected president "President R*ee*gan" and not "President R*ay*gan." He simply had the wrong vowel sound in the first syllable of the president's name, and after the speech, several audience members promptly called this fact to the student's attention. One of the greatest sources of mispronunciation comes from trying to use words in your speeches that you have only seen in print but have never heard properly pronounced. The fact is, many words do not sound exactly like they look in writing. The president's name is one of them (Reagan). A second source of mispronunciations is the mispronunciations of others—from whom you learn your own erroneous pronunciation. For example, you hear the coach talking about "ath*uh*letes," and you say it that way instead of "athlete." There is no *uh* in the middle of *athlete*. While it is hard to know that you've mispronounced a word until someone embarrassingly corrects you, check out words that sound funny to your ear. You may be the one in error! If you are the least bit uncertain about a word's pronunciation, check a regular dictionary or Kenyon and Knott's *Pronouncing Dictionary of American English* for guidance.

Avoid distracting movements, postures, and mannerisms. Because audiences become empathically involved in your speech, and subconsciously imitate your bodily activity, it is important to avoid movements, postures, and gestural mannerisms that call attention to themselves and thereby distract attention from the ideas you are trying to communicate.

Movements that distract audience attention include such things as nervous pacing like a caged animal, and sudden unmotivated movement at nonemphatic or nontransitional moments within the speech. Nondistracting movement is characterized by the fact that it occurs at useful times and by the fact that you stay perched in one place for a period of time once you have landed.

Postures distract when they are either too erect and rigid, too limp and flaccid, or too unbalanced or S-curved. The most useful posture is alert and energetic looking—as if you are ready for action. A rigid posture makes your audience tired due to the absence of ease; a limp posture lulls your audience into relaxing too much, thereby inducing inattention; an unbalanced posture—with one leg straight, the other bent, with your weight supported by your arms as you lean on the lectern—induces your audience to try to compensate, by body English, so as to straighten you out; and an S-curve posture, produced by a slightly unbalanced muscle tone in one leg, with knees slightly bent, induces your audience to slouch as well.

A mannerism is a gesture that is repeated whether or not it helps serve the expression of your ideas. Playing with a pen, your hair, or eye glasses is a mannerism. Jiggling change in your pockets, scratching your arm or nose, or playing with your notes is a mannerism. Poking repeatedly into the air with your index finger or a pen can become a mannerism. In fact, any repeated activity that calls attention to itself rather than to your ideas is a gestural mannerism and should be avoided.

Conclusion

Standing up and orally delivering a speech is what most differentiates a public speech from a written essay. In public speaking you not only encode your ideas into words, you also empower them so that they leave you as sound waves. Furthermore, you usually are also seen by your audience at the very same time you are delivering your speech. Because of this, successful public speaking involves more than the precise, clear, appropriate, and vivid encoding of your ideas into words and phrases. It also involves careful attention to the vocal and visual details of your actual presentation. Practice making your voice and physical manner as large as the room demands and as varied as your topic requires, and you will go a long way toward making your delivery serve, rather than compete with, your ideas for your audience's attention.

Questions for Review

1. What are the six functions of speech delivery?

2. How can you use your delivery to emphasize the major ideas of your speech and to reach out and establish contact with your audience?

3. What are the four major phases of the speech production process? Which specific vocal elements of delivery does each phase of speech production most help control?

4. Name six of the most important principles of effective delivery.

Questions for Discussion

1. When asked what the three most important elements of effective speaking are, the Greek orator Demosthenes is said to have responded "Delivery, delivery, delivery." Do you agree? If so, why? If you disagree, what other elements are more important?

2. Why is it that a faulty delivery can have such a powerful negative effect on the audience's reception of an otherwise well-prepared speech?

3. Can an especially effective delivery compensate for flaws in other areas of your speech preparation? Why or why not?

4. Under what circumstances (if any) is a less polished delivery preferable to a more highly polished one?

Things to Try

1. If the facilities are available, record your next speech on video tape. Then analyze your speech delivery. Did you have a good strong voice with ample variety in volume, pitch, and rate? Did you move effectively—gesturing with full gestures, moving with definite steps for greater emphasis?

2. Practice delivering your next speech with a friend as an audience. Have your friend monitor your delivery habits—perhaps signaling to you if you need greater volume or greater vocal or gestural variety. Practice making eye contact and reaching out with your voice as your friend moves around the room.

Bibliography

Condon, William S. "Cultural Microrhythms." In: *Interaction Rhythms: Periodicity in Communicative Behaviors.* (Ed.) Martha Davis. New York: Human Sciences Press, 1982, 53–67.

Condon, William S., William D. Ogston, and Larry V. Pacoe. "Three Faces of Eve Revisited: A Study of Transient Microstrabismus." *Journal of Abnormal Psychology* 74 (1969), 618–620.

Condon, William S., and Louis W. Sander. "Neonate Movement Is Synchronized with Adult Speech: Interactional Participation and Language Acquisition." *Science* 183 (Jan. 11, 1974), 99–101.

Condon, William S., and W. D. Ogston. "Speech and Body Motion Synchrony of the Speaker-Hearer." In: *The Perception of Language.* (Eds.) David L.

Horton and James J. Jenkins. Columbus, OH: Charles E. Merrill, 1971, 150–173.

Kendon, Adam. "Some Relationships Between Body Motion and Speech: An Analysis of an Example." In: *Studies in Dyadic Communication.* (Eds.) Aron Wolfe Siegman and Benjamin Pope. New York: Pergamon Press, 1972, 177–210.

Kendon, Adam. "Gesticulation and Speech: Two Aspects of the Process of Utterance." In: *The Relationship of Verbal and Nonverbal Communication.* (Ed.) Mary Ritchie Key. The Hague: Mouton, 1980, 207–228.

Kenyon, John S., and Thomas A. Knott. *A Pronouncing Dictionary of American English,* 3rd ed. Springfield, MA: G. and C. Merriam, 1951.

Montague, Ashley. *Touching: The Human Significance of the Skin.* New York: Columbia University Press, 1971.

Sarett, Lew, and William Trufant Foster. *Basic Principles of Speech.* Boston: Houghton Mifflin, 1936.

Scheflen, Albert. "The Significance of Posture in Communication Systems." *Psychiatry* 27 (1964), 316–331.

Skopec, Eric William. "Formality in Rhetorical Delivery." In: *Rhetoric 78: Proceedings of Theory of Rhetoric: An Interdisciplinary Conference.* (Eds.) Robert L. Brown, Jr., and Martin Steinmann, Jr. Minneapolis: University of Minnesota Center for Advanced Studies in Language, Style, and Literary Theory, 1979.

Winans, James Albert. *Public Speaking,* rev. ed. New York: The Century Company, 1917.

Principles of Persuasive Speaking

CHAPTER 15

Introduction to Persuasive Speaking

*T*he Impulse to Persuade

We are constantly trying to persuade others to believe as we believe. We try to influence the opinions of our friends and associates—sometimes by rational argumentation, sometimes by teasing and cajoling, and sometimes by pulling rank or producing convincing evidence. But persuasion works both ways. We are ourselves frequently bombarded by messages from people who want us to accept their ideas, buy their products, or do their bidding. The fact is, we are all constantly formulating ideas about our world, and are encouraging others to see the world as we have seen and formulated it. Deciding what is true and what to do almost always involves argumentation and persuasion.

To see just how pervasive the persuasive impulse is in everyday life, imagine the following scenario. Your parents have come to visit you on homecoming weekend. As you walk around campus, your father says, "The school sure has changed since I was a student here." Since that's a bold claim, you ask: "Why do you say that?" "Well," he answers, "there are several reasons. First, there have been a lot of new buildings put up since I was here—like the library there. Also, nearly all the teachers are new. I've only seen one face I remember from my days here. Finally, there are so many more students on campus now. When I was here the school was so small. The student body has nearly doubled in size. Yes, indeed, the old college sure has changed."

If you have ever participated in a dialogue such as this, you have been subjected to a persuasive speech. For the speaker has fulfilled the minimum essentials for a persuasive speech. First, he has made a **claim** ("The school sure has changed"), and he has supported it with **reasons** (the buildings, teachers, and the students). Suppose you had subsequently countered his arguments by saying, "Yes, but what are buildings, specific teachers, and a few more students? The school hasn't *really* changed. Its commitment to excellence, its concern for its students as individuals, and its goal of presenting a variety of extracurricular experiences are just as strong today as they were when you were a student here." Then, you too would be presenting a persuasive speech. For you too would have made a claim, and would have supported it with reasons. And both "speeches" would have taken little more than a minute or two—together!

What, then, is a persuasive speech? It is the attempt to influence the beliefs or behaviors of another person through the spoken word. A *belief* is a proposition or statement to which one gives assent or with which one agrees. Although you will typically employ all the verbal and nonverbal resources available to you whenever you try to persuade someone, the minimum essential components of a persuasive speech are a claim about the truth of some statement you are making, and one or more reasons for believing that claim. So, even though there is much more involved in effective persuasive speaking than simply advancing a claim and supplying good reasons for believing it, without a claim and reasons there is no chance for a persuasive impulse to get started.

As you can see from the sample scenario, persuasion is a commonplace activity that we often engage in. Much of our persuasive activity has no more long-term importance than the sample conversation above. It is a minor persuasive ripple on a larger sea of interpersonal interactions. In such circumstances, it probably doesn't matter whether you are a skilled persuader or not. What matters is the shared interaction and the human involvement it creates. But all of that changes when you decide to stand up and speak out in the public setting. When the City Council decides to annex *your* property, or the boss decides to reduce *your* department's budget, and you decide to try to persuade them to change their minds, then it matters, and matters deeply, whether or not you are a skilled persuader.

Because it matters in the public domain whether or not you are an effective advocate for your ideas, the purpose of the next two chapters is to help you learn to present your ideas in as persuasive a manner as possible. These two chapters cannot tell you how to make poorly conceived ideas or weakly supported arguments seem better than they are, but they can help you formulate your ideas and beliefs in such a way that those ideas gain all the persuasive power they rightfully deserve.

Preparing your persuasive speech involves special consideration of five aspects of general speech preparation: selecting an appropriate topic for your persuasive speech, phrasing a specific persuasive proposition, selecting the issues upon which you will base your persuasive case, organizing your individual arguments into an organically structured persuasive pattern, and adding appropriate motivational appeals. The purpose of this chapter is to introduce you to the first three of these aspects of persuasive speaking. Chapter 16 will then build upon these preliminary considerations by introducing you to the options you have available to you as you argue your case and by suggesting ways of giving your ideas their most persuasive impact.

Topics for Persuasive Speeches

Topics for persuasive speeches usually come to us spontaneously during the give and take of daily conversations—someone says something, someone else disagrees, and everyone is off to the persuasive races. As with informative speeches, topics may not come as easily when you must "make a persuasive speech." So, before going further, we need to look more closely at the question of topics for persuasive speeches.

In his *Rhetoric,* Aristotle suggested that persuasive impulses arise from three broad areas of conflict in our community life. These he called the (1) political or deliberative, (2) forensic or judicial, and (3) the ceremonial or epideictic divisions of persuasive speaking. These are a good starting point for our discussion of topics for persuasive speeches.

Deliberative Subjects

According to Aristotle, political speaking is *future* oriented. It treats subjects related to what the community *should* do in the future. What are these future-related speech subjects? In Aristotle's words, "The main matters on which all men deliberate and on which political speakers make speeches are some five in number: (1) ways and means, (2) war and peace, (3) national defense, (4) imports and exports, and (5) legislation" (1359,[b] 18–22). Not much has changed since Aristotle's observation—as a look at any weekly news magazine would reveal. You will find in virtually every issue articles about (1) American monetary policy, recession or recovery, and national debt ("ways and means"), (2) wars all over the globe, (3) our own defense policy, and that of our allies and adversaries, (4) international trade policies ("imports and exports"), and (5) laws currently being debated by local, state, and national governing bodies. Topics for your persuasive speeches may come from any and all of these important areas of our political, deliberative life. Should we raise the debt ceiling another trillion? Be more militarily active in the Middle East? Spend more money on bombers, missiles, and submarines? Impose trade sanctions on the Japanese auto manufacturers? Restrict freedom of access to small caliber firearms? These and thousands more deliberative subjects are excellent candidates for your own persuasive speeches.

Judicial Subjects

Subjects for persuasive speeches may also come from the forensic or judicial area of community life as well. Judicial speaking is *past* oriented. "One man accuses the other, and the other defends himself, with reference to things already done" (1385,[b] 16–18). If you select a judicial proposition for your speech, you will be claiming that some person, group, or organization is either guilty or innocent of committing some specific act. For example:

> The Interior Department during the first Reagan Administration allowed forest land to be destroyed for the monetary gain of a few rather than for the welfare of the general public at large.

In judicial or forensic persuasion, you may either *attack* or *defend*. Thus, in the case of the Interior Department, you might just as easily have claimed the opposite:

> The Interior Department during the first Reagan Administration did not allow forest land to be destroyed for the monetary gain of a few rather than for the welfare of the general public at large.

To summarize, judicial speaking treats propositions of accusation and defense concerning the past actions of some agent.

Epideictic Subjects

If you select an epideictic topic for your persuasive speech, you will be making claims of either *praise* or *blame*. That is, you will be making claims about a person or thing's essential goodness or badness. Epideictic is considered by Aristotle to be *present* oriented because the speaker is talking about a person, place, or thing's goodness or badness at a particular moment in time, generally the ongoing present. However, epideictic topics could be past oriented as in the case of a eulogy, which is a ceremonial speech of praise about someone who is no longer alive. Your persuasive claim, then, in an epideictic speech concerns the virtues or vices of a person, place, or thing. For example, if you were to give a speech at a graduation ceremony (an obviously ceremonial occasion), you might find yourself praising the virtues of the school, the graduating class members, their parents who raised them, and even the nation that supports and defends such schools—all as part of your epideictic speech.

Although Aristotle's list of persuasive subjects is not entirely complete—it applies directly only to persuasive propositions coming from our lives as citizens in a public community—it does suggest the range of topics available to you as you look for topics for your own persuasive speeches. With only minor adaptations, Aristotle's division and classification of persuasive subjects may also be applied to your professional and personal lives. The employers we work for and the families we live with must both make deliberative decisions about their future activities, factual judgments about the occurrence of past actions, and evaluative pronouncements on people's present character and worth. Accordingly, such decisions may be subject to deliberative, forensic, or epideictic rhetoric, and therefore may provide subjects for persuasive speeches. In any case, once you have selected a topic area, you must next evaluate its suitability for your own speech purposes.

Evaluating Your Persuasive Topic

As you can see, topics for persuasive speeches may come from any of the many worlds you care deeply about. In deciding whether a particular topic is suitable for a persuasive speech on a specific occasion, such as your speech class, you can use the following three test criteria.

The topic must be one upon which your audience can form an opinion. Persuasion represents a new general purpose for speaking. Up to this point, we have primarily focused on informative speaking, which has as its general purpose the goal of producing audience understanding of one's ideas. In contrast, the burden or goal of persuasive speaking is to produce a change in the audience's feelings or beliefs. An informative speech on taxes might focus on explaining the differences between a progressive and a regressive tax; a persuasive speech would advocate that the audience accept one type over another in a particular community situation.

An audience need not necessarily know anything about the topic before they hear your speech, nor do they need to have previously formed a definite opinion about it, but the topic must have *potential for controversy.* There must be at least two sides (often there are many more than two) to the question—one of which you are advocating. Therefore, your audience must be able to reasonably disagree with your opinion if the topic is to be a good one for a persuasive speech. So, even if your audience were unfamiliar with the subject of your speech before hearing it, you may use the topic for a persuasive speech if it is possible for your audience to form an opinion contrary to the one you are advocating. It is this potential for reasonable controversy that distinguishes the purposes of persuasive speeches from informative speeches. Informative speeches do not intrinsically take sides on controversial issues.

The topic must be one upon which you can make a clear claim and provide good reasons. Persuasive speeches are erected on a foundation of a definite claim and reasons that support that claim. Therefore, your topic must permit you to do these two things. A properly worded claim or proposition should be formulated as a simple declarative sentence with which the audience can either agree or disagree. If you cannot encode the belief you want your audience to share as a clearly worded proposition—that is, as a declarative statement—then the speech has little chance of success. Furthermore, if you cannot formulate your reasons for believing the claim as plainly as you do the claim itself, then you have little chance of positively influencing your audience. For, why should they believe what you want them to believe if you cannot tell them why? Sometimes there are strategic reasons for not wording your persuasive claim as directly as you are capable of, but you should at least *be able* to create clear and definite statements of both the claim and the reasons supporting it. Moreover, the more clearly you formulate your claim, the more likely it is that you yourself will understand what you are proposing and how you might best defend your belief to others. The following examples are poorly worded major claims for persuasive speeches.

To change the views of the class about federal subsidies for daycare centers

To convince the class that they should take better care of their health

To explain the controversies of the grading system, leading the audience away from its usage to a more effective system

To convince the audience that the 55 m.p.h. speed limit is a farce

To persuade the audience that federal and state statutes concerning cocaine should be changed

To illustrate the need for the United States to improve its world image and reassess its military goals

These persuasive propositions are vague, and a speaker would have a very difficult time devising a coherent strategy for convincing an audience to accept them. In contrast, the following specific purposes are simply and directly stated. They help guide a speaker's research, and suggest by their wording what kinds of evidence and reasoning it would take to support them.

To persuade the audience that women's athletics should be funded equally with men's athletics

To persuade the audience that passive restraint systems should be required in all cars

To persuade the audience that the electoral college should be replaced by direct popular election

To persuade the audience that boxing should be abolished

To persuade the audience that a modified flat tax system should be adopted

To persuade the audience that high schools should initiate mandatory human nutrition classes as a requirement for graduation

The topic must be one upon which you are willing to become something of an expert. Persuasive speaking routinely takes place in an extremely complex world. Audiences are not interested in your uninformed opinions and unsupported reasoning. They have enough of those already. Nor are they likely to be impressed by a rehash of old issues with which they are already familiar. If you are to be successful in presenting your case, you must bring new evidence and reasoning to bear on your audience's decision-making processes. Therefore, as you select your topic, plan to do some solid research—

so that you can generate fresh insights and new understandings into the issues involved. Demonstrated expertise on your topic is especially important if you are going to tackle such traditional and significant controversies as the following:

Abortion

Equal rights for women

Gun control

Compulsory national service for all persons

Euthanasia

U.S. tax, defense, or social policies

These are longstanding problems with rich histories. To treat them in a superficial way is to miss the mark and to insult your audience. In most cases it is also to fail in your persuasive purpose.

Persuasive Purposes

Persuasion is, of course, one of the three traditional purposes of public speaking, along with speaking to inform and speaking to entertain. But within the general persuasive purpose, there are several more specific purposes you might try to accomplish. Now that you have selected a general topic area for your persuasive speech, you must decide on your more specific persuasive goal. Four of the most common types of persuasive goals are (1) replacing an old belief with a new one, (2) changing the intensity of a currently held belief, (3) establishing a new belief, and (4) changing a behavior.

Replacing an Old Belief

The first specific persuasive purpose you might have is to try to replace a belief currently held by your audience. To replace a person's old belief is to try to persuade the person to accept a proposition other than the one he or she currently holds. If, for example, your target audience believes in capital punishment for selected crimes, and you believe that capital punishment should be universally abolished, your speech would be aimed at getting the audience to give up its old belief in the selected use of capital punishment and adopting a new one—abandonment of capital punishment.

A persuasive speech designed to replace an old belief assumes that the audience has already formed some opinion on the topic and that you must induce them to doubt the wisdom of that belief and to accept your alternative. Therefore, as a persuader trying to replace an old belief, you really have a two-step process to accomplish. First, you must reduce the audience's commitment to their currently held belief, giving them reasons to doubt its truth or wisdom, and you must also defend the value or truth of the new belief. Thus, whenever the speech situation indicates that the audience has already formed an opinion on your topic, you must be prepared to explain the weaknesses in that opinion as well as the strengths in your newly proposed opinion.

One further note. The capital punishment example may inadvertently suggest that replacing an old belief is simply a matter of replacing it with its opposite. The audience believes in X and you believe in non-X—as if all controversial topics could be balanced against one another as pairs of direct opposites. But in the real world of ongoing controversies, this is not typically the case. Rather than changing an audience's present belief to its opposite, you will typically be asking them to select a different option among several available alternatives. That is, you will be changing where their belief falls on a range of possible beliefs about your subject. Even on the subject of capital punishment there are more than "two sides to the question." For example, you may wish to increase or decrease the range of capital offenses, or you may wish to limit the appeals process, or control the methods of execution, and so on. The range of possible beliefs concerning capital punishment may be illustrated as in Figure 15–1, with the pro–capital punishment options ranged on the positive side of the scale, and the anti–capital punishment positions ranged on the negative side of the scale.

Changing a Belief's Intensity

Specific beliefs on a particular topic not only have a place on a range of beliefs concerning that topic, they also have varying degrees of audience intensity

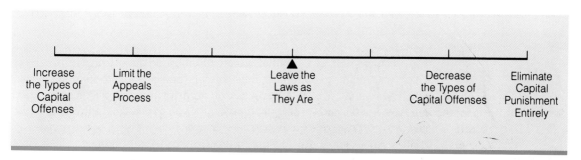

Figure 15-1   The Range of Beliefs on Capital Punishment

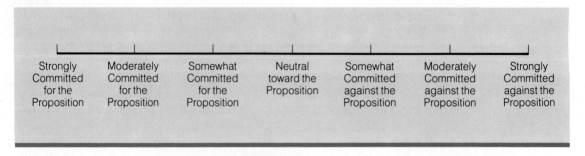

| Strongly Committed for the Proposition | Moderately Committed for the Proposition | Somewhat Committed for the Proposition | Neutral toward the Proposition | Somewhat Committed against the Proposition | Moderately Committed against the Proposition | Strongly Committed against the Proposition |

Figure 15-2   The Range of a Belief's Intensity

or commitment to a particular belief. Your audience can feel deeply or superficially about some belief they may have. This range may be illustrated as in Figure 15-2.

If the audience members feel strongly committed to their belief, you may find it difficult, and in some cases even counterproductive, to try to replace their old belief at all. In such a situation you may simply want to reduce the degree to which the audience is committed to the belief they hold. Thus, rather than claiming that your audience should switch from Belief A to Belief B, your claim might be that there are some good reasons for at least questioning Belief A. Belief B may not even be mentioned. Your only claim might be that Belief A can legitimately be questioned—that it is not 100 percent certain. If you take this approach to your speech, your persuasive purpose will be to try to reduce the intensity of your audience's belief in A. On the other hand, perhaps you will want to increase the intensity of your audience's belief in A. Every four years, the major political parties host national conventions in which the keynote speaker tries to rekindle the membership's loyalty to the party's ideas, and to increase their activity in support of those ideas. To try to increase the intensity of a currently held belief is to try to make it more salient or active in influencing your audience's current behavior, or to have it more strongly influence other beliefs to which it might be significantly related.

Establishing a New Belief

Not everyone will have a belief already established about every topic upon which you might speak. Sometimes you will be speaking about a subject to which your audience has given little or no prior thought. Accordingly, they will have formulated no specific opinion for you to change. In this case, your speech's purpose will be to establish a new belief where none previously existed. For example, if you were to give a speech to your college classmates on why toy and cereal commercials should be banned on Saturday morning, prime time television, you could reasonably expect few of your classmates to care about the subject. Child rearing and Saturday morning cartoons are still a few years away. But since now is the time to act if they are to protect their future children from intrusive children's advertising, you might try to establish a new belief by giving a speech on the disadvantages of commercials aimed at preschool and elementary school children. In such a speech you would try to show the audience why the topic is important to them and why they should adopt your position on the topic.

Changing a Behavior

Behavior often arises from specific beliefs about how one ought to behave, but it is not always easy to relate actual behaviors back to some well-considered opinion. Thus, the fourth purpose is inducing an audience to change its behavior in some specific and immediate manner—to give blood to a local blood bank or to sign an organ donor's card that is always carried. This type of persuasion does not necessarily entail a clearly formulated belief about how one ought to behave in general; it focuses on a one-time and immediate behavior. Similarly, you may be addressing an audience that already has an appropriate belief, but that has not yet seen fit to act upon it. If your purpose is to persuade the audience to take some sort of immediate action on a belief, you will be giving what is often called "the speech to actuate."

Formulating a Specific Proposition

Having selected your topic area, and considered your specific persuasive purpose, you must next carefully formulate the specific proposition you will actually defend. A **proposition** is a declarative sentence that states a claim. The following sentences present highly controversial propositions.

Private ownership of handguns by individuals should be outlawed.

The United States should support abortion clinics in poverty areas.

Topics for persuasive speeches are always stated as propositions—declarative sentences that take a stand on some issue or question, and that can either be agreed or disagreed with. Propositions are made in both persuasive and informative speeches. To be suitable for a persuasive speech your proposition must be worded as a declarative sentence to which an audience could reasonably respond: "I don't agree with that." An informative proposition is a declarative sentence to which one most properly responds: "I didn't know that."

Types of Persuasive Propositions

Four of the most common types of arguable propositions that provide good subjects for persuasive speeches are fact, value, policy, and definition claims. Since each type of proposition places somewhat different demands upon you as a persuader, we need to give each one its own special attention.

Propositions of Fact

Propositions of fact are controversial statements about how things really *are, were,* or *will be;* that is, they are statements about what has happened, is happening, or will happen. Fact propositions make claims about actual states of affairs in either the past, present, or future.

It may at first seem that fact claims are not good candidates for argumentation and persuasion. After all, if it's a fact claim, can we not "look it up"? Isn't it "in the book"? Can't we just go out and see for ourselves? In many cases we cannot. What makes a claim factual is not its present certainty, nor even its actual truth or falsity. "The moon is made of green cheese" is a fact claim—even though we know it certainly to be false. What makes a claim factual is that (1) the claim is about a past, present, or future state of affairs, and (2) the absolute truth or falsity of the claim is, was, or will be knowable for certain under specific ideal conditions. That is, the truth of the claim is at least ideally determinable by objective means—even if it is not presently known.

Much of our entire legal system rests on disputes over controversial factual claims: "Did John Doe commit the crime of which he is accused?" "Where were YOU on the night of October 7, 1977?" During the Watergate hearings, Senator Howard Baker made two factual questions nationally prominent by his insistent repetition: "What did the President know, and when did he know it?" In each case the claim is about a particular state of affairs at a specified moment in time, and the absolute truth would have been knowable if we were to have the ideal conditions—namely, a witness to the events in question.

You will probably recognize these factual questions as the same type that dominate Aristotle's classification of judicial rhetoric. But factual controversies are not restricted to legal disputes. Science, business, and the humanities all have their own disputes over important facts: How was the earth formed? Is our company's profit margin going up or down after our new advertising campaign? Did Emily Dickinson have a failed romance that subsequently affected her poetry? Are conversations governed by specific rules?

The following are examples of factual controversies that might make good topics for your persuasive speeches. Remember, they are fact claims even though their actual truth is presently unknown for certain, and their truth may never be known, due to the passage of time and degeneration of evidence, among other reasons.

Propositions Concerning Past Fact

James Earl Ray's assassination of Martin Luther King, Jr., was part of a much larger conspiracy to attack America's prominent black leaders.

Galileo was innocent of the crimes of which he was accused by the Catholic Church.

The dinosaurs became extinct because the earth passed through a cloud of cosmic dust that destroyed their food chain.

Human speech first became possible about 350,000–400,000 years ago.

Propositions Concerning Present Fact

Ready-to-eat cereal manufacturers subtly mislead consumers about the nutritional value, natural qualities, and sugar contents of their products.

Nuclear power generation is both ecologically safe and economically efficient when operated according to government regulations.

Left-handed people are systematically discriminated against in today's right-handed world.

The death penalty is an effective deterrent to violent crimes.

Propositions Concerning Future Fact

Laetril will soon be proven both safe and effective as a treatment for cancer.

By the year 2000, the majority of all electrical power will be generated by nonfossil fuel means.

High deficit spending by the government will bring about a strong recession.

Legalization of gambling will provide our state with ample money for improved educational facilities.

Propositions of Value

Propositions of value are controversial statements concerning the *relative merits* of something as measured on some subjective scale or set of criteria. Often value claims state or imply a comparison between two or more things on the same value scale. For example, "*E.T.* is a better movie than *Poltergeist*" states a value claim comparison based on a commonly shared value scale applied by the speaker to movies. In contrast, the statement "*E.T.* is a good

This is a cell in a city jail. Are prisons effective in rehabilitating criminals? What are some alternatives to prisons? For what crimes should there be mandatory prison sentences?

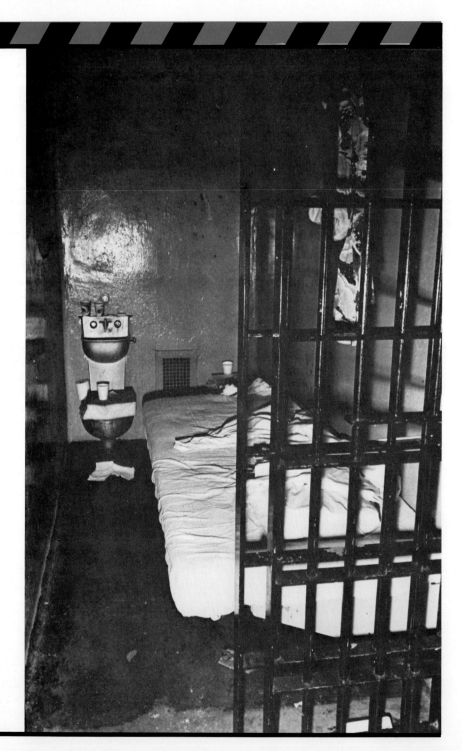

movie" does not make an explicit comparison. Yet, both propositions are value claims since both seek to rank something on a subjective scale of relative virtues or vices.

Unlike factual propositions, value claims are not theoretically decidable in some absolute sense. Because the bases for evaluative judgments differ from person to person, value claims are not absolutely determinable empirically, now or in the future. There is no absolute basis for such a choice. Two people may simply use different standards when they make their value judgments.

Are value claims arguable? Of course. We argue about values all the time. But if they are subjective—"mere matters of taste," as some might call them— are value claims worth arguing about? Or are they merely idle disputes about personal preferences? Value claims are often very worth arguing about. Our values have far-reaching implications for how we subsequently behave. And such behavioral choices have consequences for others. Everything from which movies we attend to which method of government we prefer is based upon one or another of our values. For example, the following value claim is a national commitment and guides our very way of life: "Capitalism is a better economic system than communism." As you can see, many significant topics for persuasion rest squarely upon value claims.

As was the case with factual claims, not all value claims are alike. Milton Rokeach (1973) suggests that our values may be divided into two distinct types: instrumental and terminal values. According to Rokeach, **instrumental values** are beliefs concerning the most desirable ways of conducting one's life. He divides instrumental values into two types: *moral* values (those relating to ways of behaving in our interpersonal interactions with others) and *competence* values (those having to do with how one chooses to actualize one's best self). Presented alphabetically, Rokeach lists the following 18 instrumental values (p. 361).

1. Ambitious	7. Forgiving	13. Logical
2. Broadminded	8. Helpful	14. Loving
3. Capable	9. Honest	15. Obedient
4. Cheerful	10. Imaginative	16. Polite
5. Clean	11. Independent	17. Responsible
6. Courageous	12. Intellectual	18. Self-Controlled

What does this list have to do with persuasion and persuasive propositions? Although these are all positive values, they are not all mutually attainable under all circumstances. Sometimes we must choose from among our values those that are the most important. We may not always be able to be both honest and polite, or obedient and ambitious, for example. Because differing values frequently come into conflict—either with one's own values or with the values held by other people—value claims involve much opportunity for conflict and persuasion. The following are several examples of general propositions related to someone's instrumental values:

Propositions Concerning Instrumental Values

It is more important to be cheerful and go along with the majority than to assert your independence and be seen as uncooperative.

It is better to be logical and reasonable than to be spontaneous and take risks.

Honesty is the best policy.

Obedience to your parents' wishes is very important.

In contrast to instrumental values, **terminal values** are beliefs concerning the most desirable end-states of existence. That is, they are beliefs about what life's most desirable long-term goals should be—about the ideal life condition, or what you are trying to accomplish with your life. Rokeach divides terminal values into two subgroups—personal and social terminal values—depending upon whether the focus is primarily upon the final goals of the individual or on the goals of the larger society of which the individual is a member. Paralleling his list of instrumental values, Rokeach lists 18 terminal values (p. 359).

1. A comfortable life
2. An exciting life
3. A sense of accomplishment
4. A world at peace
5. A world of beauty
6. Equality
7. Family security
8. Freedom
9. Happiness
10. Inner harmony
11. Mature love
12. National security
13. Pleasure
14. Salvation
15. Self-Respect
16. Social recognition
17. True friendship
18. Wisdom

As we noted with instrumental values, these terminal values may be thrown into jarring personal or community conflict—especially given the flux of circumstances in which we find ourselves from day to day. The following are examples of propositions arising from conflicts over a person's terminal values:

Propositions Concerning Terminal Values

National security is more important than the life, rights, or privacy of any individual citizen.

Personal harmony is more valuable than social recognition.

It is better to sacrifice personal freedom in hiring decisions than to withhold social equality from all citizens.

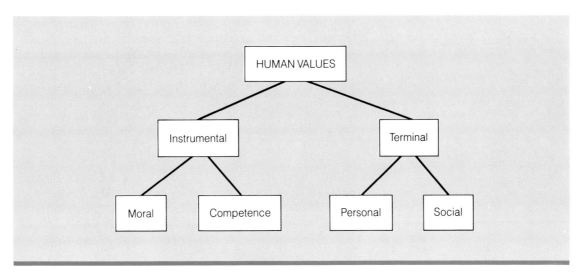

HUMAN VALUES

Instrumental

Terminal

Moral

Competence

Personal

Social

Figure 15-3   Taxonomy of Human Values

Personal accomplishment for all family members is more important than creating and maintaining a traditional family structure with the wife at home and the husband as the breadwinner.

Figure 15-3 illustrates Rokeach's taxonomy of the structure of human values.

As you can see, value claims can offer ample opportunity for disagreement and therefore for persuasion. But, given the earlier definition of value claims as statements about the relative merits of something as measured on some subjective scale, Rokeach's two-fold distinction clearly does not cover all of the types of value claims one might make. His structure is directed at the most fundamental values people have, the ones that really make an abiding difference in how individuals behave in the long term. Accordingly, we might add a third, catchall category to encompass the kinds of value claims we more routinely make. These shall be called **commonplace values,** to distinguish them from the more central values labeled by Rokeach with his terms instrumental and terminal values. The following propositions are examples of some of these more commonplace value claims.

Propositions Concerning Commonplace Values

Ligustrums are better decorative shrubs than are photinias.

Cats make better house pets than puppies do.

Trivial Pursuit is a great party game.

The East Coast is a better place to live than the Midwest.

Each of these propositions fulfills the basic definitional criteria for value claims, and yet none is as important as those listed by Rokeach. Although your public speeches are more likely to arise from clashes concerning instrumental or terminal values, they may also come from conflicts among commonplace values—especially since commonplace values are often significantly related to instrumental and terminal values. In any case, the important point is that these value propositions may serve as the major claim for your persuasive speeches.

Propositions of Policy

Propositions of policy are controversial statements about the relative merits of two or more *courses of action,* one of which *must* be taken. Policy propositions are usually formulated so as to advocate some change in present policy (a policy that will continue in force unless there is some specific reason to change it). Because propositions of policy always advocate that a particular course of action be taken by some person or some collection of persons, they always contain a word such as *should* or *ought.* The following typical propositions of policy are worded as they might be for a persuasive speech. You will recognize propositions of policy as being the sources of what Aristotle identified as deliberative rhetoric.

Propositions Concerning Personal Courses of Action

All physically able people should exercise vigorously at least 30 minutes three times a week.

Class members should reduce or eliminate meat consumption from their diets.

All class members should take a course in CPR.

You should set at least 10 percent of your annual net salary aside for savings or investment purposes.

You should use synthetic rather than petrochemical oil to lubricate your car.

Propositions Concerning State and Local Courses of Action

Patients should be allowed to keep pets in state-supported nursing homes.

Nutritional education should be a part of the state's high school curriculum.

Physicians should be permitted to advertise their services competitively.

The hunting season for deer should be extended by two weeks.

Propositions Concerning National Courses of Action

The United States should adopt a flat-rate income tax structure.

The United States should restrict its military activities to situations in which its own national boundaries, or those of its treaty allies, are in direct jeopardy.

Women should be included in any future military draft.

Air bags should be mandated for all automobiles by 1990.

Propositions Concerning Business and Professional Courses of Action

Our company should expand its sales territory to cover the three neighboring states.

Our company should delete its marginally profitable products in favor of concentrating its resources on those yielding the largest profit margin.

Our company should hire 15 new people in office support positions during the next 12 months.

Our profession should establish a licensing and certification program to screen all potential practitioners.

Propositions of Definition

Propositions of definition are controversial statements about how a particular word or phrase *should* be defined. Definitions of words become controversial whenever a word is centrally important to a universe of discourse but different people use the word in quite incompatible ways. *Communication* is just such a word. Almost all social scientific scholars agree that communication is important—but there is very little agreement on exactly what the word means. Many articles have been written about how to define the term *communication,* and many arguments and counterarguments have been advanced. Similarly, you may find yourself advancing claims about how certain words in your business or professional world should most usefully be defined. For example, safety engineers have offered many competing definitions of the word *safety,* and the legal profession is concerned with definitions of words such as *pornography.* Then, you might dedicate all or part of a persuasive speech to defending a particular definition of some key word.

The previous section discussed four types of propositions that can serve as the major claim in your persuasive speech. Your goal as a persuasive speaker is to construct the most convincing case you can in defense of your proposition. But how do you decide what constitutes a persuasive case on any particular proposition? The final section of this chapter will introduce you to the concept of issues and help you determine the relevant issues you need to try to address as you prepare to put together your persuasive speech.

Issues and the Four Types of Propositions

Whenever two people disagree, they must disagree about some specific point. The point over which they disagree is called an **issue.** For example, if Jack says that requiring firearm registration will reduce violent crimes and Jill contends it won't, then the issue is whether a particular policy (firearm registration) will *work.* To persuade an audience to accept your major claim, you must first discover the relevant issues over which there is disagreement, and then give reasons why you have chosen the side you have taken on each of those individual issues. Your reasons on these individual issues combine to form your overall case in support of your proposition. Every specific source of controversy has its own unique set of issues to resolve, but there is also enough similarity from controversy to controversy that a set of stock issues can be identified for each of the different major types of controversies. These stock issues represent major starting points for arguing various types of controversial propositions. Although there will be some repetition from type to type, each will also have its own unique issues to resolve, issues that distinguish it from each of the others.

Issues in Fact Claims

A fact claim is a statement about how things are in the present, were in the past, or will be in the future. Fact claims present propositions concerning actual states of affairs at some particular moment in time. What makes a fact claim arguable is that we presently have no direct way of establishing whether or not the situation is (was, or will be) as we claim it to be. Some crucial piece of evidence is missing that might establish absolutely whether the claim is true or false. In the absence of such crucial evidence, you must put together a case that establishes that your claim is probably true, or at least more likely true than false. What, then, are the issues you must answer satisfactorily if you are to establish your fact claim as probably true? These may be listed as a series of critical questions.

1. Are there any vague terms in the proposition that contribute to our uncertainty about the facts?

2. What other facts do we already agree to?

3. What signs point to the existence of the proposed situation?

4. What causal forces might have been working to bring the proposed situation into being?

5. What additional circumstances might have contributed to bringing such a situation into being?

6. What similar circumstances in the past have brought a situation into being like the present controversial one?

Notice the nature and order of these questions. They begin by trying to establish the exact character of the proposition being asserted (definitional issue) by the two parties. Perhaps the two parties disagree on the nature of the facts because they differ in their understanding of what is being claimed.

Having established the exact nature of the proposition being advocated, the issue moves to questions about supporting facts. As a speaker, your case is always strengthened if you can find a common ground or starting point of agreement with your audience. In fact claims, this means you may want to try to show that other, commonly agreed upon, facts support your contention in the present case.

From these commonly agreed upon facts, you next look for signs—indirect indicators that a particular situation exists. Most events leave a trail of evidence indicating their occurrence. This is precisely what detectives like Sherlock Holmes are famous for—discovering the signs of a past or present event. Even predictions concerning future events depend upon interpretations of patterns of signs. For all impending or developing fact situations depend upon preparatory events or conditions to bring them about. The existence of such preparatory events or conditions can then function as signs that the predicted event will soon follow.

Since events typically have identifiable direct and indirect causes, the next issue to raise is whether or not such causes were evident at the time in question. Similarly, you will want to note what indirect causes or supporting circumstances were in place that could have enhanced the likelihood that such an event took place, is taking place, or will take place.

Finally, it is important to address the issue of whether or not there are parallel cases to consider—cases that lend support to the claim that the present situation would be as we claim it to be. By successfully addressing issues such as these, you will immeasurably enhance the probability that you will persuade your audience concerning your fact claim.

Issues in Value Claims

A value claim is a statement concerning the relative merits of something as measured on some subjective scale or set of criteria. What makes a value claim arguable is that different people may disagree on the value scales or sets of criteria that are most appropriately used to evaluate a particular item, such as a movie, a form of government, or a style of living. Thus, to argue in defense of a value claim involves (1) offering a value scale or set of criteria for consideration, (2) defending that set of criteria as the most legitimate, and (3) showing how proper application of the criteria offered justifies the value claim that is made. The typical issues involved in arguing a value claim are as follows:

1. How is the value term used in making the claim defined?

2. What criteria properly apply in the area of values covered by the specific proposition?

3. How should the criteria be ranked in importance relative to one another?

4. What are the facts about the specific item being evaluated?

5. Do the facts as presented justify the value claim, when those facts are compared with the agreed upon criteria?

You will notice that, like the fact claim, value claims begin with an issue of definition. Indeed, this is typically true for all types of claims. We must establish the precise nature of the claim being made before other issues can even make sense. In the case of value claims, the most important definition centers on the value term itself. Since value terms are remarkably subject to personalized meanings, it is especially important to establish exactly how you will be using the term in your speech.

The second major issue concerns the set of criteria that should be used in assessing the value claim. For example, in assessing the value of a university faculty member's contribution, most disputants would agree on three types of criteria: teaching, service to the academic community, and research resulting in new knowledge. Because of the longstanding agreement of these criteria, anyone wanting to use different criteria would have to present strong arguments on this issue. The criteria for other value judgments typically are less powerfully established. But even where the relevant criteria are firmly established, one may still need to defend a particular ordering of their priority or importance. For example, many prominent universities would rank research as the predominant evaluative criterion in rating faculty members; in contrast, many private four-year colleges might consider classroom teaching as their highest priority evaluative criterion. Thus, the very same faculty member might be evaluated quite differently at two different institutions, depending solely upon the relative ranking of the three traditional evaluative criteria.

Once the criteria and their rank ordering have been established, the next issue is to establish the relevant facts. What do we know, for example, about the faculty member's teaching? Have student opinions been systematically polled? Have peers been in the classroom? Have complaints been received? Such facts must first be established, then matched against the evaluative criteria to show how they justify the value claim being made. That is, you must show how the facts fulfill the criteria previously established and thereby support the value claim in question.

Issues in Policy Claims

A policy claim is a statement concerning the relative merits of two or more courses of action, one of which must be taken. What makes a policy claim arguable is that people and institutions must act, even if they are not 100 percent certain that they are taking the proper course of action. Some critical moment comes and a decision must be made. Thus, to argue in defense of a policy claim is to say that, *given everything we know at the present time,* it is best to act in the way proposed rather than in some alternative fashion. To defend a policy claim entails a complex set of issues that may be listed as follows:

1. What is the present situation?

2. How did that situation come into being in the first place?

3. Is there a compelling need to change that situation?

4. What specific plan of action is called for given the situation?

5. Will the proposed plan or policy solve the problems created by the present policy?

6. Will the proposed policy avoid creating new problems of its own?

7. Is the proposed policy better than any competing policy?

Assuming that issues of definition have been resolved, policy claims always begin by establishing the relevant facts. So, the first issue turns on the nature of the present situation. What is there about the way things are now that calls for a policy decision at this time? Frequently, it is important to establish how things came to be as they are. This is because causes of problems often dictate what solutions will seem most reasonable. If the causes are not eliminated as a part of the new policy, then the situation is likely to recur. If, for example, the problem of beach erosion is due to the inherent instability of the waterfront land, then building a breakwater may not by itself be a useful policy. The plan would need other elements, or it would fail.

In policy claims, the disputants are likely to disagree over the issue of degree—contesting whether or not the problem is sufficiently troublesome to merit a policy decision at this time. Having argued that the problem merits attention, the question becomes one of what specific kind of attention is needed? That is, you must advocate a policy or course of action to solve the problem. With your plan on the table, you must establish two further issues in your favor: (1) that the plan will work to solve the problem as you have explained it, and (2) that it will not create any additional problems of its own. Thus, for example, if you argue that women's sports should be given exactly equal funding as men's sports, because that would solve sexism at your school, you would have to show that equal funding would indeed address the issue of sexism, and that such a policy would not produce other problems.

Finally, if there are competing policies being offered to solve the same problem, you must establish that your policy is the best policy. Since this is a value claim embedded within the overall policy nature of your speech proposition, the issues for value claims would be used to establish your side on this particular issue.

Issues in Definition Claims

A definition claim is a statement concerning how a particular word or phrase should be defined in a particular context or domain of inquiry. What makes a definition arguable is that different people use the same word in incompatible ways, and thereby make incompatible claims (fact claims, for example) based on their special ways of using the word. Thus, two people might make incompatible fact claims because they differ fundamentally in their definitions of a key term, such as *communication* as in the examples that follow: "Animals communicate" (influence one another via spontaneous signs); "Animals do not communicate" (exchange information via a syntactically structured symbol system). This is what happens when we give up on an argument in frustration, crying, "*It's only a matter of semantics!*" as if this somehow solves the problem. It does not; such definition claims are often of the most fundamental significance. Are definition disputes decidable? Yes. The following are some of the important questions that help raise the significant definitional issues.

1. Precisely what conditions control the proper use of each of the competing definitions of the term?

2. Which authorities use, suggest, or defend the definition offered?

3. What positive results will be brought about by accepting the definition proposed?

4. What negative results will be avoided by employing the definition proposed?

As you know from Chapter 8, words are controlled by a list of criteria or attributes, called the word's **intension.** So the first issue in definition claims is to identify clearly the intensional conditions that control the competing definitions of the term. Having specified your criteria for using the word, you can begin addressing the issues that permit you to defend your definition. Sometimes, it matters *who* uses the term the way you propose. So, if possible, in definition claims, marshal the support given by other authorities. But argument by authority is hardly enough. Authorities not only disagree among themselves at times, but you may also actually find yourself in disagreement with those authorities. Because definitions have conceptual consequences, you must then show the gains that can be made by adopting your definition. Often these gains are such things as greater clarity, or more precision, or even greater coherence with other related concepts. Conversely, it often pays to show that certain negative conceptual results can be avoided if your definition is adopted. Among the more common reasons for adopting a new definition are that inconsistency and paradoxical formulations can be avoided.

Conclusion

The purpose of this chapter has been to introduce you to the fundamentals of the impulse phase of persuasive speaking. We have looked at the persuasive impulse itself, noting Aristotle's three most basic types of persuasive subject matters: deliberative topics, judicial topics, and epideictic topics. We then looked at the criteria for evaluating a topic to see whether it constitutes a good one for public persuasive speaking. Having examined the topics for persuasive speaking, we next investigated the four specific purposes for which persuasive speaking is most often performed: to replace an old belief, to change the intensity of a belief, to establish a new belief, and to change a behavior. Persuasion requires advocacy of a particular belief, which is stated clearly as a single proposition; the chapter then reviewed the types of propositions that are typically argued, showing how these were parallel in some cases to Aristotle's original list of subjects for persuasive speeches. Chapter 15 concluded by introducing the critical issues involved in arguing on each of the four major types of propositions. The final chapter will build upon this introduction by explaining how to argue a case in behalf of a persuasive proposition.

Questions for Review

1. What is a deliberative topic? How does it differ from a judicial topic and an epideictic topic?

2. What criteria must a good persuasive speech topic fulfill?

3. Under what conditions would your purpose be to replace an old belief with a new one?

4. What are *issues?* What role do issues play in preparing a persuasive speech?

Questions for Discussion

1. Is it possible to have a persuasive statement that mixes two or more types of persuasive purposes? Or are the four categories mutually exclusive? Under what circumstances (if any) might you want your speech to have two "subpurposes" that join together to form an overall persuasive strategy?

2. If your persuasive goal is to convince your audience that airports need more air traffic controllers, what would be some of the most relevant issues to develop?

Things to Try

1. Using your classmates as your intended audience, create three deliberative, three judicial, and three epideictic topics that would probably be of interest to the majority.

2. Create explicit specific purpose statements for each of the nine topics you prepared in exercise 1. Try to develop at least two propositions of fact, value, and policy, and one proposition of definition.

3. Determine, relative to your audience, whether your purpose statement constitutes replacing an old belief, changing the intensity of a currently held belief, establishing a new belief, or changing a specific behavior.

4. List two or more issues that would have to be addressed for each of the subjects and specific purpose statements you have created.

Bibliography

Aristotle. *Rhetoric.* (Tr.) Lane Cooper. Englewood Cliffs, NJ: Prentice-Hall, 1932.

Rokeach, Milton. *The Nature of Human Values.* New York: The Free Press, 1973.

CHAPTER 16

Preparing Your Persuasive Speech

Now that you know what issues are at stake for each of the major types of arguable propositions, you are ready to begin preparing your persuasive speech. In this chapter we will look at three aspects of preparing a persuasive speech. First, we will analyze the individual building blocks of the persuasive speech, units typically called **proofs.** Proofs present your reasoning and evidence concerning each of the issues outlined in Chapter 15. Second, we will discuss organizational patterns that are particularly useful for arranging the individual proof units of your persuasive speech, focusing on how to weave together your individual proof units to build an organically structured overall case. Finally, we will close by developing several principles that can help you add to the organic qualities of your persuasive speeches.

*U*nits of Proof: *Developing Individual Arguments*

Whenever you try to persuade someone to believe as you believe, you will be trying to move that person's mind from one relatively stable position (that is, the current belief) to another one (the belief you want the person to adopt). To accomplish the goal of moving a listener's mind from one position on a proposition to some other, you will usually have to lead your listener through a chain of smaller steps.

In persuasion, these individual steps are known as proofs, and the entire process is known as argumentation. **Argumentation** may be defined as a special form of communication in which you present a claim and supply one or more reasons for accepting that claim. Each such claim–reason(s) unit may be called a **proof unit,** because you are in each case trying to prove your point by employing each of these units of argument. A persuasive speech is composed of a series of such proof units, organized in such a way that if the listener accepts each of the smaller claims that provides the focus for each individual proof unit, he or she eventually arrives at the proposition that is the ultimate goal of your persuasive speech. Generally speaking, you will have at least as many individual proof units as you have issues to defend in your favor. Each issue will be worded as a subclaim that you will support with reasoning and evidence. The process of using proofs to move an audience through a series of issues may be roughly illustrated as in Figure 16-1.

To see how to use proof units in your speeches, we need to explore the concepts of reasoning and argument.

*R*easoning and Argument

Reasoning and argument are closely related but not identical concepts. They bear the same relationship to one another as do private thinking and making

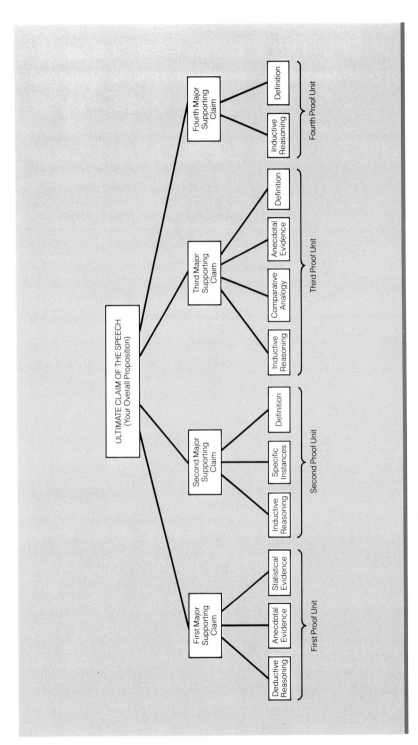

Figure 16-1   Process of Using Proofs in a Persuasive Speech

public assertions. Reasoning is a private mental process. **Reasoning** may be defined as the mental process of moving from one thought or idea to another one in a systematic fashion. Reasoning is typically how you come to believe most of the propositions you believe.

Argument is the public, communicative correlate to your private reasoning processes. Because reasoning is a private mental process, its systematic progression of steps and its final products are not available to others unless they are verbally communicated. Until you put your reasoning into words for others to hear, it can have no direct impact on your audience's opinions. The purpose, then, of putting together proof units (arguments) is to communicate an effective formulation of your reasoning about your topic.

Argument is the public projection of your private reasoning. Although argument is a communication skill, and reasoning is a thinking skill, the two go hand in hand because your best private reasoning about your topic is the basis for your public argument. Because skillful argument depends upon careful reasoning, it is useful to understand the reasoning process. After all, it is your reasoning that gets verbally encoded and publicly projected as your speech's arguments, or units of proof.

In general, reasoning may be described as "the process of building up insight into relations which are too complex to be grasped by direct inspection" (Langer, 1967, p. 146). That is, we reason our way to new beliefs when the things we are observing are too complex for us to figure out simply by looking at them. The process of reasoning may be divided into two basic types: induction and deduction.

Inductive Reasoning

When our minds move from *direct observations* about the world to the verbal formulation of a *summarizing statement* (that is, a proposition) about those observations, we are using inductive reasoning. For example, if you observe a race and see that Jack crossed the finish line first, and then subsequently formulate the proposition "Jack won today's race," you would be employing a relatively low form of induction, known as **classification.** This process constitutes induction because you have moved from a direct observation of an event (the race) to a summarizing proposition (in this case, a proposition classifying the event observed as "winning a race").

But inductive reasoning can go much further than mere classification of a single event. If, for example, you were to see a couple more races, and Jack wins those too, you might begin to formulate some considerably higher level inductions, such as the following progressively higher inductions:

Jack sure is a fast runner. (generalization)

Jack is likely to win next week's race at the Camelot Games. (prediction)

Jack is certain to win many more races this season. (generalized prediction)

These are all inductively reasoned statements because their direct immediate support is actual empirical evidence based upon one or more direct observations. The higher level inductions begin to look more like what we typically recognize as inductive reasoning because they are made on the basis of several observations, rather than just one. But the process is the same whether the inductive move is made from a single observation to a specific proposition, or from a set of observations to a more general proposition about that larger set of observations. These three propositions are considered higher level inductions than the original classification of crossing the finish line first as "winning the race" because they proceed from a set of empirical observations, and because they yield more general (that is, more widely applicable) propositions. The more inclusive the proposition formulated, the higher level the induction. The highest level inductions are all-inclusive statements based upon one or more specific instances. "[All] Americans behave boorishly when they go overseas" is a widely held induction about *all* American tourists, which is based on the directly observed behavior of only *some* American tourists.

Deductive Reasoning

In contrast to inductive reasoning, which moves from one or more direct observations to the formulation of a proposition, deductive reasoning moves from the truth (or, presumed truth) of one or more previously formulated propositions to the truth of some other systematically related proposition. In deductive reasoning, no new empirical evidence is required from the outside world to complete the reasoning process. This is possible because there are several strictly formal relations that exist among propositions based simply upon the way the language code itself operates. Among the most important of these formal relations among propositions are **implication** (also called **entailment**) and **preclusion.**

Statement A implies (entails) statement B if the truth of proposition A guarantees the truth of proposition B. Statement A precludes statement B if the truth of proposition A guarantees the falsity of proposition B. Thus, for example, if it is inductively true that (A) *Jack won today's race,* then you need no further empirical evidence to prove deductively that (B) *Jack did not lose today's race.* This is entailed or implied by proposition A. Further, the statement (C) *Bill won today's race* is deductively false because it is precluded by the truth of proposition (A). You can deduce the latter two propositions (B and C) simply by knowing the former (A). To say that someone "won" is to say by implication that they did not lose, and by preclusion that no one else won. Similarly, but with a little more complexity, if we accept the proposition that (A) Jack's house is north of Bill's, and that (B) Bill's house is north of Sam's, then at least two further propositions can be deduced by implication without resorting to any further empirical evidence:

(C) Jack's house is north of Sam's.

(D) Sam's house cannot be north of Jack's or Bill's.

That is, if we accept the inductively established truth of propositions A and B, then we need no further direct observations to confirm the deductive truth of propositions C and D. The way the English language works guarantees the truth of the final two claims.

The power of *in*ductive reasoning is that it allows you to bring together one or more individual observations in order to formulate higher and higher level propositions. The power of *de*ductive reasoning is that it allows you to use whatever "true" propositions you already have available to you to generate new propositions. By carefully chaining together a series of apparently independent, inductively derived propositions, the deductive reasoner can often generate new, and often surprising, propositions that are also true, and for which no empirical evidence was available to establish. The process will be illustrated in the following section.

Based on this preliminary introduction to inductive and deductive reasoning, we are now ready to explore how to use each of these two types of reasoning to develop individual proofs for the critical issues in your speeches. For every persuasive speech is created by a skillful weaving together of empirically supported inductive reasoning, and deductively arrived at conclusions generated using the results of the inductive process. We will begin by examining deductive reasoning in greater detail.

*D*eductive Reasoning and Proofs

Deduction allows you to produce new propositions by systematically manipulating the information that exists—but that is hidden or latent—in the propositions you already know. As noted earlier, the power of deduction lies in making one or more related, previously known, propositions yield one or more important new propositions, in the absence of new empirical data.

The classic type of deductive reasoning is known as the *categorical syllogism*. The categorical syllogism has only three parts: a *major premise* stating a general claim, a *minor premise* stating a specific claim that is related to the major claim, and a *conclusion* stating a specific claim on the basis of the deductive (in this case "categorical") relationship between the major premise and the minor premise. The standard example of the categorical syllogism runs as follows:

All men are mortal. (major premise)

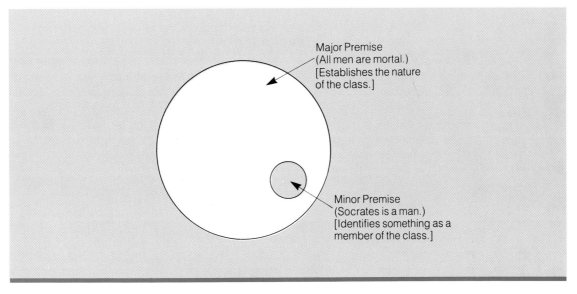

Major Premise
(All men are mortal.)
[Establishes the nature
of the class.]

Minor Premise
(Socrates is a man.)
[Identifies something as a
member of the class.]

Figure 16-2   The Categorical Syllogism

Socrates is a man. (minor premise)

[Therefore] ∴ Socrates is mortal. (conclusion)

The categorical syllogism's three parts may be illustrated in a way that explains why it is called a *categorical* syllogism. In Figure 16-2, the large circle stands for the major premise, which establishes a class or category and presents a proposition about all members of that class. That is, the major premise states the condition that establishes the class in the first place. In this case, the category is "all men," and the claim that is made about the class is that all members of the class share in the property of "being mortal." The second, smaller, circle represents the minor premise, which claims that some object (in this case, Socrates) is a member of the class. Based on these two claims, it is logical to deductively conclude that Socrates shares in the characteristic that defines the class and therefore to say that "Socrates is mortal." This final proposition is new, and is not based on any direct evidence. It is merely deductively latent (implied, entailed) in the information contained in the previous two inductively derived propositions.

In this form, deductive reasoning seems almost silly. Who, after all, would actually argue in such a labored way to such an obvious conclusion? Although the categorical syllogism is a cumbersome intellectual device, it can be far more subtle than the above example reveals, and may play a meaningful role in your persuasive speeches. It is particularly useful when you want to have the audience *feel* the obviousness or inevitability of your conclusion—when that proposition is categorically related to beliefs they already have. Even so, the categorical syllogism is indeed a limited form of deductive reasoning.

But the categorical syllogism is only the tip of the iceberg as far as deductive reasoning is concerned. The real strength of deductive reasoning comes from its ability to link a series of apparently independent (and seemingly unrelated) propositions together to generate nonobvious and significant novel propositions. To see how deduction can be used to create new information from apparently unrelated and even random facts, try to solve the following standard deduction puzzle. Based on the information given, you should be able to deduce the answer to the questions involved.

> Mr. Smith, Mr. Jones, and Mr. Robinson live in Chicago, Omaha, and Detroit, but not necessarily respectively. They are passengers on a train run by a three-man crew. The men on the crew are named Smith, Jones, and Robinson, and they are an engineer, a fireman, and a brakeman, but not necessarily respectively. The following additional facts are also known about these six men:
>
> 1. Mr. Robinson lives in Detroit.
>
> 2. Mr. Jones never studied algebra.
>
> 3. Smith beat the fireman at billards.
>
> 4. The passenger whose name is the same as the brakeman's lives in Chicago.
>
> 5. The brakeman lives in Omaha.
>
> 6. The brakeman's nearest neighbor, one of the passengers, is a mathematician.
>
> The problem: What positions do Smith, Jones, and Robinson hold on the crew?

In this puzzle, you have been given six apparently random pieces of information. And yet, on their basis alone, you should be able to deduce the answer to the problem. You should also be able to deduce which cities Mr. Smith, Mr. Jones, and Mr. Robinson hail from. (The solution is printed at the bottom of the page.)

To accomplish this task, you must manipulate the given propositions in various combinations. By putting the known facts together in various ways, you can generate new propositions. These new propositions can themselves then become premises for new arguments that yield further conclusions. In this way deductive reasoning becomes a powerful tool in arguing for your beliefs.

To use deductive reasoning in a speech, it is important to determine what relevant propositions your audience already subscribes to. Since these do not need to be established through argument, they may simply be used as premises for your deductive use. Then, you must show how these propositions—when combined with any other propositions you inductively or deductively establish during the course of your speech—lead to the conclusion or proposition you want them to accept.

Inductive Reasoning and Proofs

Unlike deductive reasoning, inductive reasoning cannot be formally systematized to yield valid conclusions based on true premises. Even so, inductive reasoning can be evaluated and criticized on several standard commonsense criteria. We will now look at the major types of inductive reasoning.

Types of Inductive Reasoning

Inductive reasoning proceeds from some sort of direct observation of a thing, process, or situation to the formulation of a proposition based on the observations made. Inductive reasoning may be divided into five basic types, distinguished from one another based upon the type of inductive movement the person makes in proceeding from the observation to the proposition formulated. The five most common types of inductive reasoning are: classification, sign, analogy, generalization, and causation.

Classification The simplest and yet most fundamentally important type of inductive reasoning is simple classification. In classification, one observes an event, assigns it to a class of events of which it is a member, and attaches an appropriate verbal label to the event. All of the following are examples of propositions based on the straightforward classification and verbal labeling of an event. In each case, the word labeling the relevant class is italicized to emphasize the class to which the event has been assigned.

That was a very *rude* thing to do.

Jack *won* the race.

War is *hell.*

In each proposition, some event has been classified and labeled. What makes classification significant as a form of inductive reasoning is that different people may observe essentially the same basic event and classify it quite differently—as signaled by the label they attach to the thing or event. For example one person might label a politician's voting record as that of a "wild-eyed liberal," but another person would see it as the record of a "socially conscious concerned citizen." The voting record remains the same, but the classification and the label do not. Since labels have profound repercussions for how persons respond to events and situations, a major part of your persuasive efforts often involves trying to convince the audience to change its classification of an act, and therefore to attach a different label to whatever it is they are judging. Classification is an essential act of inductive reasoning, and must be taken into consideration as you plan your persuasive strategy.

Signs A sign is anything that indicates the existence or presence of something else. Red spots are signs of measles; wet streets in the morning are a sign that it has rained in the night. In reasoning from signs, one observes various components of a complex event and reasons that something else exists, happened, or is also present. Since signs are always a part of whatever situation they are said to be signs of, sign reasoning may move from the sign to a meaning in either of two possible directions. Sometimes the movement is from the existence of one specific sign to the existence of another equally specific aspect of the total situation. That is, the movement is from a specific component to a proposition concerning some equally specific component. Thus, if a father discovers red spots, he will reason that there must also be fever and therefore check the child's temperature. At other times, the inductive movement is from the specific signs observed to a proposition concerning the existence of a total condition of which the sign is merely a part. In the father's case, the red spot will not only be a sign that another specific condition is present (that is, fever), but also that a total medical condition called measles exists. Thus, to move from a sign to predictive propositions concerning one or more additional signs, or to propositions concerning some total condition, is to reason inductively from signs.

Analogy Two things, processes, situations, or events are analogous when they have the same essential form. As you will recall from Chapter 2, a form consists of two parts: elements and relations among those elements. Two things, situations, or events are analogous when they share a common pattern of elements and relations among those elements. Reasoning by analogy occurs whenever one observes an event, discovers features of that event that have a pattern similar to some other event, and subsequently makes a proposition about the event being observed based on the formal similarities between the earlier event and the later. Reasoning by analogy is important in all areas of our lives since it is impossible for two situations ever to be absolutely identical. All any two situations can ever literally share in common is a pattern among their elements and relations. So reasoning from analogy will probably be used frequently in your persuasive speeches.

Generalization To generalize is a two-step process. First, you must discover a pattern in a number of specific examples; then, based on the pattern discovered, you must form a proposition that predicts that some future event will follow the same pattern. Thus, for example, if Jill received an *A* in all of the courses in her major during her first three semesters in school, you might generalize that she will probably get an *A* in her major courses this semester as well. That is, then, in reasoning by generalization, you are predicting that the feature or pattern you have discovered in the instances you have already inspected will carry over to apply to instances you have not been able to directly inspect.

Causation To cause something is to be responsible for its occurrence. You are reasoning causally when you say that factors in the currently observed situation are capable of and likely to bring about some subsequent situation. The inductively derived proposition one arrives at when arguing causally represents a prediction concerning a future situation based on the strength attributed to presently observed situational factors.

Putting a Case Together: Organizing the Persuasive Speech

A persuasive speech shares many attributes with an informative speech. Both should have a clear organic progression from introduction, to body, to conclusion. The introductions of each must capture and direct the audience's attention to the subject, reveal the speaker's source of expertise, and so forth; their bodies must be clearly organized to create forward motion, and must have an ample variety of supporting material to bring them most fully to life; their conclusions must both summarize the speech and provide a strong sense of closure for the audience. Such qualities are requisites of all good speeches. But the fact remains that persuasion is a different speech purpose and requires its own significant adaptations of the general principles of effective speaking if your speech is to succeed in its persuasive goal.

One of the most obvious places where persuasive speeches differ from informative ones is in the organization of their bodies. *Understanding of an idea,* not *acceptance of a proposition,* is the goal of informative speaking. The bodies of informative speeches are organized so as to help the audience systematically and progressively reconstruct the speaker's understanding of some subject. Each organizational pattern—chronological, spatial, topical, and so on—is designed as a convenient way of breaking down a subject matter into its component parts, and of arranging those parts in the best order for enhancing an audience's understanding.

Leading an audience **to accept a specific proposition** is a different type of goal. Because the goal is different, the specific organizational methods for achieving it are also different. To lead someone to accept a proposition requires a specially reasoned and argued sequence of steps. And that is exactly what the five patterns of organization described below are designed to do: to lead the audience **by a series of reasoned steps** from whatever they presently believe, to the proposition you wish them to accept. These five patterns of organizing the persuasive speech are:

1. Topical Reasons

2. Problem–Solution

3. Comparative Advantages

4. Criteria-Satisfaction

5. Elimination of Alternatives

We will look at each of these patterns in turn, emphasizing the characteristics of the pattern that might make it appropriate for you to use for a particular audience on a particular occasion.

Topical Reasons

Since every persuasive speech requires you to formulate a claim and to present reasons in support of the claim, one of the simplest and most useful patterns of organization is the straightforward presentation of a topically organized slate of independent reasons. The **topical reasons** pattern gets its name because each of the reasons you mention in support of your major claim functions almost like an independent topic (in this case, an independent proof unit). There is little attempt to systematically link the independent proof units into any larger pattern—as there is in each of the other patterns that follow. Each separate reason lends only its own individual support to your claim.

In actual practice, the topical reasons pattern calls on you to clearly announce your persuasive proposition early in your speech and to present a topically organized list of reasons for accepting the proposition. You will elaborate upon those reasons during the course of the body of your speech, but the main slate of reasons themselves provides the overall framework for your speech's body. Thus, as you perform your introductory functions, you will not only announce the speech's topic, but also the proposition, and the pattern of reasons you will use to support it. For example, an introduction to a topical reasons patterned speech might sound something like this:

> Ladies and gentlemen: It has recently come to my attention as president of the Flat Earth Society that many of you still believe the earth to be round. Today I would like to share with you four reasons the members of our society believe the earth to be flat.

In this introduction, the speaker has quickly performed the major introductory functions, established the proposition to be defended, and directly announced the topical reasons pattern of organization. This prepares the audience for what is to follow, and begins the speech's sense of forward motion. Then, as these major points are discussed and developed with supporting reasoning and evidence during the speech's body, the speech gains a strong sense of growth and movement. Having introduced the speech in this way, the speaker would then need to make sure that each main point of the speech's body corresponded with one of the four topically arranged reasons. That is, each of the Roman numeral level points in the outline would be one of the four main reasons previously announced. Thus, for example, Roman numeral I might be worded as: "The first of my four reasons is that *the earth actually looks flat.*"

Using the topical reasons pattern of organization is not as simple as announcing the proposition and the main reasons in the introduction, and repeating them in the speech's body. What if the reasons announced in the introduction are not self-evidently true? Then the speaker must support the main line of reasons with reasons to believe *them.* And if the reasons for one's reasons are not immediately and obviously true to the audience, then those reasons must also receive further support. Each of your main points must itself be supported with reasoning and evidence if it is to be believed. Although an infinite regression of "reasons for your reasons" is neither possible nor desirable, there may very well be several levels of reasoning in a topical reasons speech. In outline form, the body of the topical reasons patterned speech might look like this:

I. Main Reason #1
   A. 1st Subreason in support of Reason #1
      1. Evidence to support subreason A (definition)
      2. Evidence to support subreason A (statistics)
      3. Evidence to support subreason A (quote)
   B. 2nd Subreason in support of Reason #1
      1. Evidence to support subreason B (visual aid)
      2. Evidence to support subreason B (quote)
      3. Evidence to support subreason B (anecdote)
   C. 3rd Subreason in support of Reason #1
      1. Evidence to support subreason C (comparison)
      2. Evidence to support subreason C (quote)
      3. Evidence to support subreason C (examples)

II. Main Reason #2
   A. Etc.
   B. Etc.
   C. Etc.

These community volunteers are using straw to clean up a coastal oil spill. Who should pay for cleaning up oil spills and chemical disasters? Have you ever been involved with any environmental projects?

III. Main Reason #3

IV. Main Reason #4

The topical reasons pattern of organization is often used. For example, in a magazine ad advocating the factual proposition that "Coal gasification can make an important contribution to our nation's energy supplies before the end of the next decade," the American Gas Association used the topical reasons pattern of organization, with two levels of argument. The top of the ad announces the major claim of the argument:

FOUR REASONS FOR TURNING COAL INTO CLEAN GAS ENERGY

After a brief introduction stating the importance of finding economically sound and environmentally clean energy sources, the ad advocates coal gasification, listing four reasons:

1. It's extremely efficient in terms of capital investment.

2. It costs consumers less, too.

3. It's environmentally clean.

4. The pipeline system is there to deliver it.

Under each point, there is a brief paragraph giving reasons to believe each of these four claims. For example, under the claim that coal gasification is environmentally clean, the ad provides the following two reasons in support of the claim: "It releases little sulfer into the air . . . ; it uses only an eighth as much water as coal/electric systems do." Although a one-page ad cannot elaborate on its reasons as fully as a speaker with five or more minutes can, the principle used in the ad is the same as that in a speech. When using the topical reasons pattern, you will announce your reasons and support each of them with reasons to believe them. The arrows in the outline that follows illustrate the flow of reasoning involved as a speech progresses by way of the topical reasons pattern of organization.

Main Proposition to Be Supported

I. Main Reason #1
   A. 1st Subreason in support of Reason #1
      1. Evidence to support subreason A (definition)
      2. Evidence to support subreason A (statistics)
      3. Evidence to support subreason A (quote)
   B. 2nd Subreason in support of Reason #1
      1. Evidence to support subreason B (visual aid)
      2. Evidence to support subreason B (quote)
      3. Evidence to support subreason B (anecdote)
   C. 3rd Subreason in support of Reason #1
      1. Evidence to support subreason C (comparison)
      2. Evidence to support subreason C (quote)
      3. Evidence to support subreason C (examples)
II. Main Reason #2
   A. Etc.
   B. Etc.
   C. Etc.

III. Main Reason #3

IV. Main Reason #4

The topical reasons pattern of organization has many advantages: It is simple and direct to use; it gets to its point quickly, and begins its defense of the proposition almost from the beginning of the speech; it creates immediate forward motion toward the proposition you are defending; and it is extremely versatile—being useful for all types of propositions (fact, value, policy, and so on), and for all persuasive purposes (replacement of an old belief, changing a belief's intensity, and so on).

But, in spite of its many advantages, there are times when the topical reasons pattern is not the best choice for your persuasive speech. First, because its major points are relatively independent of one another, this pattern does not invite you to develop a complex overall persuasive strategy or argument. Each independent reason does it own independent persuasive work without any real help being given by the others. Furthermore, the very directness of the pattern is a potential source of problems. Because the topical reasons pattern launches so quickly into its defense of the proposition, it does very little to precondition the audience to be receptive to the proposition. Thus, if your audience needs to be more fully prepared for your claim and reasons, the topical reasons pattern may be less effective than some other pattern in leading your audience to accept your claim. If extensive audience preparation is necessary before they can be receptive to your proposal, or if a more complex argument structure needs to be developed than the topical reasons approach permits, then the problem-solution pattern is perhaps your better persuasive choice.

Problem–Solution

A fully developed problem–solution speech has at least four major, closely linked phases in creating its persuasive forward motion. You must establish that a problem exists, present an adequately detailed plan or solution to solve the problem, show that the solution you have proposed will actually work to solve the problem you have identified, and prove that your proposed solution does not create any new problems with its implementation. As you can see, in contrast to the topical reasons pattern, the four phases of the problem–solution pattern are closely linked and create a definite sense of progression from one specific issue to another. We will now look at each of these phases in more detail.

In the problem–solution pattern, the body of your speech has as its first major claim that some specific problem exists. Because establishing that a problem exists is the first major subpoint, this pattern is especially useful under two circumstances: (1) when the audience is essentially *unaware of the problem* before they hear your speech, or (2) when the audience *does not see the problem in the way you see it*. In the first case, your goal is a simple one of introducing your audience to a problem upon which they have no prior opinion. You merely need to formulate your portrayal of the problem in a sympathetic manner. In the second case, the audience is presumed to have already made a judgment about the essential nature of the problem— but their assessment differs in fundamental ways from your own. Perhaps, for example, a new road is to be built and two different routes are being considered. One view of the problem is purely economic: Which route is cheapest to build? In contrast, you might want the audience to see the problem as essentially ecological: Which route is the least harmful to the wildlife? Since your audience sees the decision about the road route as one type of problem (economic) and you see it as quite another (ecological), your persuasive goal would be to have your audience understand the essential nature of the problem differently—which would, of course lead to a different solution, demonstration of workability, and justification of the absence of additional problems than would be the case if the problem were seen as purely economic.

Whether your primary goal is to make an audience aware of a problem and its solution, or to change their minds about the essential nature of the problem, when using the problem–solution pattern of organization, your first task is to try to paint a vivid picture of the problem as *you* see it. Your goal is to create a need for a solution to the problem as you have imagined it. To create a need for your solution, your first main point should include subpoints concerning such things as (1) who is involved in the problem, (2) who gets harmed by the problem, (3) how much and what kinds of harms are caused by the problem, and (4) the causes of the problem. Having created a need to correct some ill, your next major subclaim is that a solution or remedy exists—one that you will describe in whatever detail is necessary to explain its operation. Sometimes this explanation is a simple description of an action to be taken; at other times the solution phase of your speech will require a detailed explanation of a complex plan, involving a series of actions. Whichever is the case, the third phase of a problem–solution patterned speech requires that you explain exactly how your solution/plan would eliminate the specific details of the problem *as you have described it*. For example, the following introduction to a typical problem–solution patterned persuasive speech might sound like this:

> Ladies and gentlemen: Imagine that you were in a movie theatre, and every 15 minutes a popcorn peddler came by yelling, "Popcorn, peanuts." What would you do? Get up and leave? Write to the management in protest?
>
> Well, your children are faced with this situation every day— when they watch prime time morning television. This "popcorn peddling" by toy and cereal manufacturers constitutes a serious problem that needs immediate attention and action.
>
> Today I'd like to tell you why advertising on children's prime time television constitutes a serious problem both to you and to your

children, and tell you some of the things you can do to protect your children from being taken in by the peddlers of the latest in social popcorn.

With such an introduction, the outline of the rest of the speech might look something like this:

I. There is a serious problem caused by advertising on children's prime time television.
   A. This advertising causes problems for parents.
      1. Type of harm to parents #1
         a. Evidence of harm #1
         b. Evidence of harm #1
      2. Extent of harm to parents #2
         a. Evidence of harm #2
         b. Evidence of harm #2
   B. This advertising causes problems for the children themselves.
      1. Type of harm to children #1
         a. Evidence of harm #1
         b. Evidence of harm #1
      2. Type of harm to children #2
         a. Evidence of harm #2
         b. Evidence of harm #2
   C. This advertising causes harm for society as a whole.
      1. Etc.
      2. Etc.

II. There is a solution to these problems.
   A. First, we must . . .
      1. Details
      2. Details
   B. Second, we must . . .
   C. Third, we must . . .

III. The solution will solve the problems.
   A. The solution will solve the parents' problems.
      1. First reason it will solve the parents' problems
         a. Evidence to support the 1st reason
         b. Evidence to support the 1st reason
      2. Second reason it will solve the parent's problems
   B. The solution will solve the children's problems.
   C. The solution will solve society's problems.

IV. The solution will cause no new problems of its own.
   A. The solution is inexpensive to implement.

    B. The solution does not infringe on advertisers' constitutional rights.
    C. Etc.

The problem–solution pattern may be used successfully with neutral and uninformed audiences since the problem phase of this organizational pattern emphasizes the presentation of information about the problem. It may also be used well with informed and strongly committed audiences because it allows you to paint a particular picture of the problem that they may not have previously imagined. For as you now realize, if you intend to picture the problem differently than your audience currently envisions it, the problem–solution pattern is a good method to accomplish this restructuring of the audience's vision of the problem. This feature of the problem–solution pattern is among its most important, because it is often necessary to change the audience's picture of the situation before you can get them to act on the solution you wish to propose.

Comparative Advantages

Not every proposition you wish to advocate requires that there be some serious problem to remedy. Sometimes you merely wish to make things even better than they presently are. Under such circumstances, you may find the comparative advantages pattern of organization useful. The comparative advantages pattern requires the speaker to compare two different possible propositions with one another, and argues that one of them has a set of advantages over the other. The comparative advantages pattern is usually employed when you are comparing two policies (courses of action), but it need not necessarily be restricted to propositions of policy. Any two competing propositions may be compared with one another, and the advantages of believing the one may be compared with those of believing the other.

    When using the comparative advantages pattern of organization, each main point of your outline will be worded in terms of an advantage that the proposition you are defending has over the competing proposition(s). For example, suppose a speech's introduction began as follows:

> Ladies and gentlemen: There is a clear choice between the belief that former President Kennedy was killed by a lone assassin and the claim that Lee Harvey Oswald was a minor figure in a much larger conspiracy. There are three advantages to believing that there was a larger conspiracy involved. For the conspiracy theory solves three main problems left by the lone gunman theory—problems that can be explained in no other way.

The outline for this speech might very well look like this:

  I. The first advantage of believing in the conspiracy theory is . . .
    A. The 1st subreason

    1. Evidence in support
    2. Evidence in support
  B. The 2nd subreason

II. The second advantage of believing in the conspiracy theory is ...

III. The third advantage of believing in the conspiracy theory is ...

The strength of the comparative advantage pattern of organization is that a speaker does not have to bear the burden of showing some major deficit in an opposing proposition. So the pattern has a smaller burden of proof and a generally more positive tone. Its major limitation is that it is useful for a narrower range of propositions.

Criteria-Satisfaction

Whenever we make a decision whether or not to accept some proposition, our decision will be based on some criterion or another. These are always standards of judgment to be applied to a particular case. The criteria-satisfaction pattern of organization works by helping the audience become consciously aware of the appropriate criteria for evaluating competing propositions. Often it does this by arguing in defense of a set of criteria. When employing the criteria-satisfaction pattern, the body of the speech is typically divided into two main parts. The first part, indicated by Roman numeral I in your outline, must establish the appropriateness and importance of the members of a set of criteria. The second part requires that you establish why your preferred proposition best meets those criteria that you established in the first part.

    The introduction to a criteria-satisfaction organized speech will first sketch some issue to which your most preferred proposition will be an answer. For example, a typical introduction to a criteria-satisfaction speech might go like this:

> Ladies and gentlemen of the Council: Today you must vote on whether or not to allow the Ace Trash Company to build its new garbage dump at the Rockport, Carter Road, or Zephel site. This decision can only be made by seeing which site best meets the criteria required for a satisfying solution. Today I would like to argue first that there are three criteria that must be satisfied for a solution to be satisfactory, and then to explain why the Rockport site best fulfills those criteria.

The following outline illustrates the criteria-satisfaction pattern of organization.

  I. There are three criteria which must be met.
    A. Defense of criterion #1

        1. Evidence in support
        2. Evidence in support
     B. Defense of criterion #2
        1. Etc.
        2. Etc.
     C. Defense of criterion #3

  II. The three sites may be evaluated against these criteria.
     A. Evaluation of the Carter site
        1. Evaluation against criterion #1
        2. Evaluation against criterion #2
        3. Evaluation against criterion #3
     B. Evaluation of the Zephel site
        1. Evaluation against criterion #1
        2. Evaluation against criterion #2
        3. Evaluation against criterion #3
     C. Evaluation of the Rockport site
        1. Evaluation against criterion #1
        2. Evaluation against criterion #2
        3. Evaluation against criterion #3

The strength of the criteria-satisfaction pattern is in its usefulness in arguing about value-based decisions—because this pattern forcefully reveals the value structure that should be applied in a controversial area. By making the values more overtly visible to your audience, you can more readily show why your proposition is the most satisfactory one among one or more competitors.

Elimination of Alternatives

The elimination of alternatives pattern involves the systematic discounting of less desirable alternative propositions, followed by a defense of the most desirable one. To see how this pattern works, compare its goal with the logic of the criteria-satisfaction pattern. In the criteria-satisfaction pattern, you will compare each of the several competing proposals against *the same set of criteria*—those established in the first part of your speech. Your goal is to eliminate the options you least prefer by showing how they fail to live up to a common set of criteria upon which they are all compared. In the elimination of alternatives pattern, the goal is the same—to eliminate the audience's options for belief. But rather than first establishing a common set of criteria to use for all competing beliefs, you make the claim that each competitor is unsatisfactory for its own individual set of reasons. There is no requirement that these reasons be parallel to one another, as there is in the criteria-satisfaction pattern. In the elimination of alternatives pattern, each main point works to eliminate one of the competing beliefs by showing its inadequacy on whatever criteria seem most appropriate.

In the elimination of alternatives pattern, your introduction will briefly allude to some problem the audience is aware of, and will mention all the currently discussed solutions. Then your first main point will discuss the flaws you find in the first solution. The substructure of the point will be composed of a discussion of the reasons you find the solution to be problematic. After you have shown that each of the major competing positions is inadequate, and your most preferred position is the only one left, the final major point of your speech explains why your preferred position does not have any of the flaws of the other solutions, nor any other ones of its own that would keep it from being the best of the possible alternatives.

The body of a typical elimination of alternatives pattern of organization might look like this:

I. The first alternative is not satisfactory for three reasons.
    A. Reason #1
    B. Reason #2
    C. Reason #3

II. The second alternative is not satisfactory for two reasons.
    A. Reason #1
    B. Reason #2

III. The third alternative is not satisfactory for four reasons.
    A. Reason #1
    B. Reason #2
    C. Reason #3
    D. Reason #4

IV. The fourth alternative *is* satisfactory for two reasons.
    A. It is not subject to the weaknesses of the previous solutions.
       1. Evidence for claim
       2. Evidence for claim
    B. It has several positive qualities to recommend it.
       1. Positive quality #1
       2. Positive quality #2
       3. Etc.

*P*rinciples of Persuasive Speaking

Effective persuasive speaking depends upon having a clearly worded proposition to defend, a detailed analysis of the relevant issues, careful reasoning on each of the specific points you wish to make, and thoughtful organization of your pattern of points into an overall case. Having put together an overall case that is thoroughly supported with evidence and is well organized with cogent arguments should go a long way toward making you a persuasive speaker. But you can refine and enhance your persuasive power by applying a small handful of additional principles to your persuasive efforts. This final section will develop four principles of persuasive speaking that should make your persuasive efforts more successful.

Use forces already at work in the audience's mind to promote persuasion. The source of all persuasion is in the minds of the audience. No speaker can ever make an audience believe a proposition. Like all communication, persuasive communication requires the listeners to take an active part in completing the act. Without your audience's cooperation in the process, your persuasive message cannot directly cause the audience to believe or act as you advocate. As a speaker, all you can reasonably do is to prepare a message and to deliver it with personal conviction and enthusiasm. Your audience must then use your message to persuade themselves to believe.

As a persuader, then, you can only determine what message is given to your audience; the listeners will determine what ideas are taken away, and what they will actually do with those ideas in the future. But the fact that you cannot directly cause listeners to accept your ideas does not mean that you are completely at the mercy of your audience's listening and conceptual whims. Listeners' minds are filled with ideas, values, hopes, and beliefs, and these are active forces you can marshal in the service of your own persuasive message. If you plan your persuasive message appropriately, you can take advantage of the forces already at work in your listeners' minds and increase your chances of having your persuasive message accepted. Think of your task in this way: In your persuasive speech, you are trying to create the message conditions in which your audience is most likely to persuade itself to accept your proposition.

Taking advantage of the forces already working in the listeners' minds can be accomplished in two important ways.

First, *use audience involvements to support your case.* As you learned in Chapter 7, audiences are involved with one another in many different ways: demographically, socially, and conceptually. Depending upon the nature of your specific proposition, most of these involvements can have quite direct implications for your persuasive strategy if you will only look for them. Thus, for example, if your speech is being given before the Chamber of Commerce, your audience is probably involved with one another through their common interest in the business and general economic climate of your community. Their social involvement in the Chamber tells you that. So, you would try to link your proposal to the community's economic well-being; this would take advantage of the audience's general involvement that brings them together in the first place.

Second, *use audience values to support your case.* Values are a central source of persuasive power. What people value they will usually act upon.

Chapter 15 treated values in considerable detail, listing several instrumental and terminal values that people typically have. These values may be used in at least two different ways: by identification and by opposition.

Value Identification. Whenever possible, you should seek to identify your proposal with the known values of the audience. If the audience sees your proposal as merely an instance of something they already believe in, your proposal will be likely to be caught up in the tide of energy they already give to this particular value. In this way your proposal becomes easier to accept. Thus, for example, if you are talking to an audience known to value "community improvement," then you should emphasize how your proposal to rezone a controversial plot of land would contribute to the value they cherish. Thus, you might argue that, "Allowing this land to be rezoned for light commercial use would improve our community in at least four ways. . . ."

Value Opposition. In actual practice, many values we have lead us to contrary judgments when we are confronted with concrete situations requiring specific actions. One value says to "be a good sport" and go to the beach with the group; another value says "be a good student" and stay home to study for an important test. Because our ideal values often come into conflict within ourselves when applied in practical situations, we often have to prioritize our values into some sort of order of importance. While we may not consciously put it this way, we organize our values in an all things being equal arrangement: "All other things being equal, I consider this more important at this time." So, you may say, "If I didn't have something else to do, of course I would go to the beach today. But I've got to start studying for my test, so I'll catch you next time." This is a decision based on a ranking of values.

Since values often come into conflict, you can take advantage of this by putting the relevant values into opposition in your speech, and arguing that the value that supports your proposition is the more important or the more fundamental one. For example, in an issue such as whether or not legal abortions should remain readily available to all women, both sides place competing values into direct opposition—with the pro-choice advocates arguing that the rights of the woman to choose whether or not to have a child are more important than continuing the development of the unwanted fetus, and the pro-life advocates arguing that the rights of the unborn child to live are more important than the personal desires of the reluctant mother.

Similarly, two values can be placed into conflict in all sorts of environmental conflicts where "progress" as a value is often placed into conflict with values such as "preservation" and "protection." Effectively bringing such value conflicts into the open, and developing arguments for one value as being more important or more fundamental than the opposed value, should energize your persuasive impact.

Use audience motives (pathos) to support your case. Audiences are not logical automatons. They are living, breathing people with their own personal reasons for believing the things they believe. Their fullest humanity, not just their ideal reasonableness, must be taken into account as you seek to influence their beliefs. Aristotle recognized the importance of an audience's own motives for believing as they do, and sought to account for these motives in his approach to persuasion. He called the mode of appeal that links a speaker's proposal to the audience's motives pathos.

Pathos is sometimes called the appeal to emotions. But pathos is really more than just emotion. **Pathos** is the appeal to the audience's own motives for belief. Some of these motives are indeed emotional in the strict sense of being passionate. But most are not. Simply put, most audiences listening to a persuasive speech have some personal stake in the issues involved. Because the issues make a difference to them, they do not listen like disinterested judges. They listen with their own interests acting as a persuasive filter. Pathos, then, covers all those persuasive elements built into a speech that try to relate the speaker's proposition to the audience's self-interests in some personal way. Pathos-based appeals attempt to reveal the nature and importance of the audience's personal benefit in adopting the speaker's proposition. A speech on handgun control, for example, might emphasize the greater safety the audience will feel if they are each encouraged to own and operate a handgun. Since audiences have a personal stake in being safe from harm, such an appeal reflects the appeal to pathos. To go further, and to offer an anecdote about a neighbor who recently protected herself from an intruder by skillfully using a handgun, would be to drive the "emotional" appeal home even more forcefully. Some principles of pathos that you should try to apply in your speeches include the following:

1. Throughout the speech, explain how the audience is involved in the proposition.

2. Use connotatively powerful language (see Chapter 13) to suggest specific feelings about the claims you are making.

3. Use scenarios and vivid images to draw the audience's own imagination into the persuasive process.

The goal of each of these techniques is to induce a personal response that energizes your proposition in your audience's mind.

As you can tell from the previous discussion, the concept of audience motives differs slightly from that of audience values. An audience's values are relatively conscious, and they relate to choices people make about what is comparatively important in life. The notion of motives comes from a different tradition in psychology, and assumes that people have certain fundamental needs that they will seek to fulfill by taking various sorts of actions. That is, the needs motivate people to take actions that seek to satisfy those needs.

Your goal as a persuader from this point of view is to show how adopting your proposal will help the audience fulfill one or more of its fundamental needs. The most widely known list of such needs was mentioned in Chapter 7, Abraham Maslow's hierarchy of human needs. According to Maslow, all humans face five classes of needs that they are motivated to fulfill: (1) physiological needs, for the minimum organic essentials to sustain life (such as food and water); (2) safety needs, for protection from external harm (such as shelter from predators and the weather); (3) social needs, for interaction with other people; (4) self-esteem needs, for a feeling of one's own competence and worth; and (5) self-actualization needs, for becoming the most complete and enriched person one can become.

As illustrated in Figure 7-1, Maslow ranges these human needs in a hierarchy of importance. For example, one must have the essential physiological needs cared for before it makes sense to pursue safety needs. Because the motives for pursuing one's needs are hierarchically arranged, the same two strategies that applied to values apply equally well to motives. Your first goal should be to simply identify your proposition with one of the basic needs and to show how adopting your proposition would fulfill a basic audience need. This was illustrated in the handgun proposition above. If there are conflicting needs involved, then bring the conflict into the open and show how your proposition either serves a more "basic" need, or a "higher" need. The hierarchy of needs can be used both ways! This is because, in either case, you are revealing to the audience what is in the proposal for them if they accept it.

Use your own personal characteristics (ethos) to influence your audience. Ethos, or credibility, is the audience's perception of the speaker's positive or negative personal attributes. Positive ethos is characterized by the audience's belief that the speaker (1) knows what he or she is talking about, (2) will honestly and fully present that knowledge during the speech, and (3) will not try to mislead the audience concerning their own best interests in terms of the proposition under consideration. To gain credibility with an audience, a speaker must demonstrate knowledge of the subject matter, honesty in presenting the persuasive case, and sincerity in caring for the well-being of the audience (see Chapter 4).

It is important to remember that it is not enough to *be* knowledgeable, honest, and sincere. You must also consciously project these qualities to the audience during the speech. For example, you might suggest your knowledge on the topic by the amount of facts and figures you cite, and the other detailed information your speech contains. Quoting experts or citing information from personally conducted interviews also contributes to the audience's sense of your expertise on the subject. It is more difficult to describe how to project honesty and sincerity, but if you hope to be successful, the audience must feel these qualities emanating from you—before, during, and after your speech. Personal animation, minimal reliance on your notes for help, and good eye contact will all contribute to the audience's sense that you are honest and sincere.

Some additional guidelines for gaining personal ethos in the audience's eyes may be briefly listed.

1. Allude to the sources of your expertise. (personal experiences you've had, interviews you've conducted, relevant formal training you've undergone, and so forth)

2. Quote respected sources. (who has the audience heard of whose opinion can be used in support of your proposition?)

3. Be animated throughout your speech.

4. Gain contact with your audience. (not your text)

5. Seem sincere and enthusiastic in your delivery.

6. Develop a goodwill bond in the speech's introduction.

Doing these six things should help you to use your own personal characteristics to increase your audience's susceptibility to your persuasive message.

Use the organic principles of internal preparation, forward motion, growth, climax, and closure to enhance your persuasive effect. A persuasive speech is designed to change an audience's mind in some specific way—either by replacing an old belief with a new one, changing the intensity of a currently held belief, establishing a new belief where none previously existed, or inducing a specific behavior. Such change entails movement. Since even relatively stable, long-term beliefs are continuously sustained from moment to moment by mental activity, to induce changes in audience beliefs you must create mental motion. Your speech must begin where the audience's mind presently is and then induce that mind to move in a progressive fashion to where you want it to be. The arguments in your speech must clear the mental path of objections that impede the audience's movement from where it currently is to where you are trying to take it. Like a guide through a jungle, your arguments must seem to lead progressively toward a goal. Because of this your persuasive speech must constantly be seen as preparing the way for a small series of yes-responses to your arguments on each of your points. Each of these points to which the audience gives its assent moves the audience one step closer to accepting your proposition.

Within the speech, each proof unit is just such a motion-building step. You present a reason and support it with evidence. The audience believes each of these minor claims, and in each case, they have taken a step toward accepting your overall claim. Similarly, the overall speech represents a large chain of such steps. One after another you have cleared the path of objections (obstructions) to your persuasive goal. Such path clearing cannot guarantee that the audience will stay at the goal (after all, a cleared path can be walked both ways), but without a feeling of progressive motion toward a final conclusion, the audience will tend to remain where it is in its beliefs, and will not move on its own.

So your goal must be to use the techniques developed elsewhere in this book (1) to prepare your audience for movement, both during your introduction, and as you proceed from point to point within your speech; (2) to create a sense of forward motion as your argument moves from issue to issue; (3) to create a sense of growth and climax as you build toward the final persuasive goal; and (4) to create a sense of satisfying closure as you and your audience reach the end of your argument's journey, and they have been led to accept a new belief. The principles and techniques developed throughout this book are as important in persuasive speaking as they are in informative speaking.

In summary, then, *use all aspects of the speech situation to increase your persuasive impact.* All aspects of the speech situation may influence your speech's success or failure with the audience. Accordingly, all aspects of your public expression should be given consideration. Thus, in addition to your actual inductive and deductive arguments, you should build in factors that enhance your personal credibility. For example, rehearse your speech so that you can present your ideas without faltering, and dress appropriately for the occasion. The impressions such little secondary activities make on the audience can often tip the balance in your favor in a closely contested persuasive contest.

Conclusion

This concludes our discussion of persuasive speaking, as well as the discussion of the general principles of effective public speaking. During the course of this book, we have covered considerable territory, and there has been a considerable amount of material to remember, and a large quantity of skills to master. And yet, if you have been doing speech exercises right along with your reading, and focusing upon the basic principles, you should by now have a definite feeling of accomplishment and confidence about your public speaking ability. Keep practicing—you are now more than able to merely "hit the ball over the net." Although you may not yet be producing masterpieces, you are considerably more accomplished than you might have ever thought you could be. Remember the organic principles that have been emphasized throughout, and use the organic metaphor to guide your speech practices. If you work on giving your speeches a sense of internal preparation, forward motion, growth, climax, and closure, your speeches will be more alive than you ever thought possible.

Questions for Review

1. What are the major features of deductive and inductive reasoning?

2. What types of inductive reasoning are typically used in developing persuasive speaking?

3. List the five types of patterns for organizing a persuasive speech. What are the distinguishing characteristics of each?

Questions for Discussion

1. Under what circumstances is inductive reasoning preferable to deductive reasoning as a strategy for your persuasive speeches? Similarly, when is deductive reasoning preferable?

2. When would you be likely to use each of the five patterns of organization? Be sure to consider factors such as the type of subject (deliberative, judicial, or epideictic), the type of persuasive purpose, the type of proposition (fact, value, policy, definition), the relevant audience involvements, and the nature of the relevant issues in your evaluation of the five most useful patterns of organization for persuasive speeches on a particular occasion.

Things to Try

1. Select an issue relevant to a persuasive topic of your choice and develop a detailed argument to support your claim on the issue.

2. Develop and present a persuasive speech to your class that shows that you have thoughtfully matched your arguments and issues to your audience's involvements.

Bibliography

Langer, Susanne K. *Mind: An Essay on Human Feeling,* Vol. 1. Baltimore: Johns Hopkins University Press, 1967.

Researching Your Speech

*I*n order to develop your speech as fully and appropriately as you can with the types of materials described in Chapter 8, you will usually need to look beyond what you already know and spend some time researching your speech. Speech research usually means investigating the library, interviewing the experts, and exploring for yourself. Since the library often seems like a foreign land—with its own native customs, language, and special ways of doing things—this appendix on speech research focuses primarily on how to get the most out of the time you spend in library research.

Using the library effectively is simple once you know the basic steps in the research process. The purpose of Appendix A is to survey the six most important steps in researching a speech.

1. Become familiar with your library early.

2. Develop your research plan carefully.

3. Read your resources selectively.

4. Record your research purposefully.

5. Document your discoveries fully.

6. Supplement your library work adequately.

*B*ecome Familiar with Your Library Early

Every library is organized according to some master plan designed to make finding the materials you need as easy as possible. Accordingly, your first research step should be to meet the person who knows how your particular library is organized—usually your librarian—so that you can ask some important questions. You will need several types of reference materials from the library, so you will need to ask your librarian where the various materials are located. Among the most important library tools are those listed below.

The Major Types of Library Resources

The card catalogue—a master list of all the books and major reference works in the library. The card catalogue is organized alphabetically using three different and separate classification schemes: by author, by title, and by subject matter headings. Using this three-way classification, you should be able to find the major works you need by going either to the author catalogue (if you know who wrote the book), the title catalogue (if you know an exact title), or the subject catalogue (if you know only the general subject area you wish to research).

The periodical catalogue—a master list of all the magazines and professional journals the library currently holds. The periodical catalogue typically lists the periodicals only alphabetically by the title of the journal. Because it is organized by title rather than by subject matter, you must generally know the name of the journal you are trying to find. Once you know the title of an article you wish to find, and the magazine or journal in which it is found, you will be ready to turn to the periodical catalogue to locate it within the library.

General and specialized encyclopedias—collections of articles summarizing the general knowledge concerning some area of study. The articles are arranged alphabetically by topic. General encyclopedias survey important topics drawn from all areas of human knowledge, and specialized encyclopedias go into greater depth within some narrower specialty area. *The Encyclopaedia Britannica* is an excellent example of a general encyclopedia; the *Encyclopedia of Philosophy* is typical of specialized encyclopedias. Below is a list of some additional general and specialized encyclopedias you might find useful in your research:

General Encyclopedias
Collier's Encyclopedia
Encyclopedia Americana
New Columbia Encyclopedia

Specialized Encyclopedias
Encyclopedia of World Art
Encyclopedia of Banking and Finance
The Encyclopedia of Education
An Encyclopedia of World History
Encyclopedia of World Literature in the 20th Century
Encyclopedia of Popular Music

Encyclopedias are excellent ways to get oriented to a new area of study, and to discover general facts that are not subject to sudden or yearly changes. But for most topics they are merely the beginning of your research. You will quickly exhaust their usefulness and need to locate specialized articles that go into greater depth on more specific aspects of your topic. For this work you will need indexes and abstracts.

General and specialized indexes and abstracts—lists of recent magazine and journal articles, organized alphabetically by subject matter and author. Although encyclopedias are excellent for general background, they are far less useful in areas of study where the facts or theories change rapidly, and where up-to-the-minute data are necessary, such as in the physical and social sciences. These discoveries are reported and discussed in countless professional journals and popular magazines that pour into the library daily. To help you keep up with the resources you need, most libraries subscribe to numerous general and specialized index and abstract services. Index services list the titles of all the articles in the periodicals they cover, organizing the article titles by the topics of the articles. General indexes survey primarily popular magazines that contain articles having broad appeal—such as *Harper's* and *Atlantic Monthly.* The most widely known general index to popular magazines is *The Reader's Guide to Periodical Literature.* Using whatever subject category you are researching as your starting point, you will look up the subject in the *Reader's Guide,* and the *Guide* will list all the recent articles on that topic and tell you in which magazines to find them. Specialized indexes work on a similar principle, but are much more focused since they list articles appearing only in professional journals for the discipline covered by the index. Every major discipline has one or more indexes covering its primary subject matter. For example, the following are just a few of the specialized indexes for the humanities and social sciences:

Humanities Index

Psychological Abstracts

Sociological Abstracts

Communication Abstracts

Once you have prepared a list of articles you want to read by using the general and specialized indexes, you will be ready to go to the periodical catalogue mentioned earlier to find the various magazines and journals you will need.

Bibliographies—lists of articles, chapters, and books on highly specialized or widely studied topics. Some areas of study are so specialized, yet so widely studied, that hundreds or thousands of articles have already been written about them. To facilitate research in these areas, detailed bibliographies (lists of articles) have been compiled and published. These bibliographies save hours of research time, which you might otherwise have spent leafing through individual indexes and abstracts—because someone else has already done this before you. Some typical bibliographies in, for example, speech communication research are *Frye's Index to Nonverbal Data* and Mary Ritchie Key's *Nonverbal Communication: A Research Guide and Bibliography.* There are now so many bibliographies available that there is actually a book entitled *A World Bibliography of Bibliographies* and an index called *The Bibliographic*

Index to help you find the most appropriate bibliography for your research work and interests. Such is the complex nature of contemporary knowledge.

Computerized search services—automated bibliographic research aids. With the explosion in scholarly and popular publication, the amount of physical labor and time spent looking through indexes, abstracts, and even bibliographies can be both frustrating and wasteful. In recent years, more and more libraries have offered computerized search services that are capable of using a key subject matter word as a guide for performing a computer search of all the published indexes in various fields. Although typically some personal expense is involved in using the system, the cost is surprisingly small considering the countless hours saved. Thus, if you need to generate an extensive and relatively complete bibliography on a narrowly definable topic, a computerized search of the relevant subject matter indexes is often your best, most economical, and time efficient option. Ask your librarian which computerized search services your library subscribes to and how you can use them.

Almanacs and yearbooks—summaries of statistical and general facts, typically published yearly because of the rapidly changing nature of the subject areas they cover. Many topics require you to know the most up-to-date facts on some aspect of a topic you are researching. General almanacs such as the *Information Please Almanac,* and yearbooks published by encyclopedia manufacturers, among others, are ideal sources. Below are a few additional examples.

Britannica Book of the Year

Catholic Almanac

Statistical Abstract of the United States

Whitaker's Almanack

Biographical collections—brief biographies of notable persons. Because researchers often need to find information about important people in public and private life, there are a variety of resources for learning about individual people. Some of the most important of these include the following:

Who's Who in America

Current Biography

Dictionary of National Biography

International Who's Who

Index to Women

Biography Index

Dictionary of American Biography

Special collections unique to a particular library. Many libraries have unique collections of materials not duplicated in any other library. Three works that list libraries having special collections that you may use to research your speeches are the *American Library Directory, Subject Collections,* and the *Directory of Special Libraries and Information Centers.*

Miscellaneous other research and reference materials. The above list does not come close to exhausting the types of special materials libraries offer to make your research work easier and more comprehensive. Not listed in any of the major categories above are the following additional special materials: atlases, pamphlets, audio-visual materials, microforms, government publications, ERIC documents (Educational Resources Information Clearinghouse), and newspaper indexes. Ask your librarian how to find these, and many more, resources in your particular library. More guidance in using a library's resources is available in Jean Key Gates's *Guide to the Use of Books and Libraries,* and Alden Todd's *Finding Facts Fast.* The latter book is also helpful with the second step of the research process, developing your research plan.

As you can tell, the library is not only filled with useful information, it is also well stocked with related materials designed to make your research task as easy as reasonably possible. If you are not sure if your library has what you need in order to conduct your research, ask your librarian for help—especially for help in finding the supporting materials you need, such as indexes, which can help you locate what you are looking for.

Develop Your Research Plan Carefully

Knowing what resources are available is one thing; using them in an efficient and systematic manner is another. Once you have learned where the major research tools you need are located, you must begin to use them systematically to find the best materials you can. Good research is always a time-consuming task—even under the most ideal conditions. After all, you must decide what items you want to look at, go to the shelves to get them, read them when you find them (or wait for them to be returned if someone else has them checked out), and process what you learn in a useful way once you have read them. Typically, this means taking a formal set of notes on 4 × 6 cards. So, the next step is probably *not* a quick raid on the library's shelves to find the first source you located on the first card catalogue or index entry you discovered. Instead, your next step should be to develop a general research plan for your overall work. Developing an explicit research plan for a particular project is especially important since different research goals require different amounts of detail. Your plan should match your goal.

Under most circumstances your best strategy is to begin by preparing a bibliography of many items, working from the more general treatments of your topic to the more specific. A bibliography is a master list of items you intend to look at during the course of your research. Thus, step one in your research plan might be to go to the subject section of the card catalogue and look up your topic to see what, if any, book-length items have been written about it. In chronological order, you might pursue the following research plan, designed to help you develop a comprehensive bibliography for your research.

1. Card catalogue subject listings

2. General periodical listings

3. Specialized indexes and abstracts

4. General and specialized encyclopedias

5. And so on

Once you have prepared such a list, you may then proceed to systematically prepare a list of specific items to look at, and to begin locating them for your actual research.

For each item you plan to look at, prepare an individual bibliography card, using a 3 × 5 index card for each entry. For each bibliographic entry, write on the card the author's name, the work's complete title, and the standard publication data: place of publication, publisher, and date of publication. At the bottom of the card, place the library call number for permanent reference in case you need to locate the material a second time. Figure A-1 illustrates how to complete a bibliography card for your use. One final note: Using separate cards for each bibliographic item, rather than writing several citations on a single sheet of paper, may seem wasteful at first, but it is far more efficient in the long run. It allows you to reorganize your search in many different ways, to make your work easier. Being able to conveniently shuffle standard-sized cards into piles for different purposes as your research needs change throughout your work will quickly repay any additional costs in time and paper. Furthermore, using cards will allow you to quickly alphabetize your final bibliography for the speech.

*R*ead Your Resources Selectively

Having developed a thorough bibliography on your subject, you must locate and read the materials. For most topics your bibliography will have many more items on it than you can hope to read for a particular speech. Therefore, you must learn to read selectively. As with your bibliography development, you should develop a reading plan to guide your research. Again, depending upon how new the topic is to you, and your purpose for researching it, you

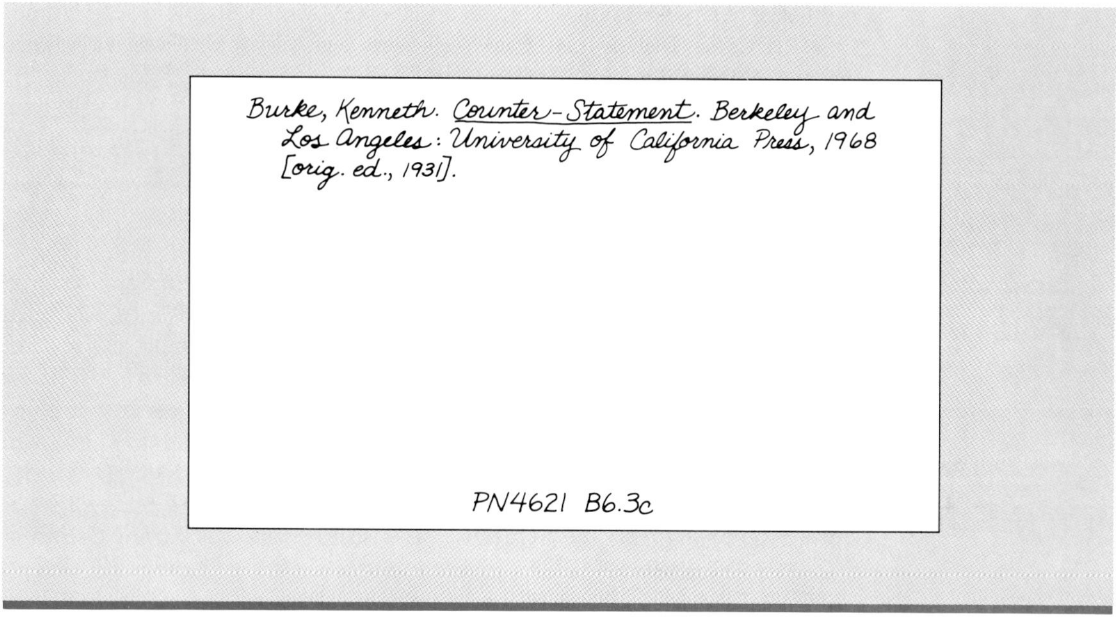

Burke, Kenneth. *Counter-Statement*. Berkeley and Los Angeles: University of California Press, 1968 [orig. ed., 1931].

PN4621 B6.3c

Figure A-1   Bibliography Card for a Book

should arrange your reading from the general to the specific. Begin by reading one or more survey articles or books. This will help orient you to the area, and help you discover how the experts have organized the subject matter. Then, as you focus upon more specific aspects of your topic, you can begin looking at more specific articles. For example, if your subject for an informative speech is "nonverbal expression," you might begin by reading Mark Knapp's *Nonverbal Communication in Human Interaction* (1978), which is an excellent introductory survey of the basic areas of nonverbal research.

But reading selectively means more than merely planning a specific order for your reading. It also means evaluating the items on your bibliographic list to see if they are going to be useful, and omitting those that are not. Just because you checked out a book from the library, you do not have to use it if you discover that it is not really appropriate. Nor does it mean that you have to read the whole thing cover to cover if only a portion of it is helpful. Many students are intimidated by library research because they feel they must read entire works rather than only relevant selected portions. As Francis Bacon observed, "Some books are to be tasted, others to be swallowed, and some few to be chewed and digested." Although you must read enough to determine whether the book is to be merely tasted, hastily swallowed, or slowly chewed, you should first evaluate the book by inspecting its table of contents, index, chapter heads, and so on before deciding to read it first page to last. If you have trouble reading selectively and thereby waste valuable research time reading things that do not repay the effort, you may find Mortimer Adler's *How to Read a Book* (1972) quite helpful.

Record Your Research Carefully

Reading without retaining what you have read is little better than not reading at all. Because few of us are blessed with photographic memories, we must make notes about what we have read. Thus, as you read, you must also record what you are learning in a systematic and purposeful manner.

There are at least three types of purposeful recording: exact word-for-word quotes, paraphrases and summaries of long passages into your own words, and abstracts of entire books and articles into your own words. Whichever type of recording you decide to do, there are three key phases to the process: (1) selecting the materials you wish to retain, (2) writing them on 4 × 6 note cards, and (3) filling in the supporting data, including (a) an identifying key word or phrase header, for use in classifying and organizing what is on a specific card, (b) bibliographic information that identifies the source of the quote, and (c) any necessary comments you wish to make about the quote or to provide a context for it. Figure A-2 shows a properly filled out note card.

Document Your Discoveries Fully

Not only must you know what was said, you must also know who said it and when. Quoting properly from your sources not only gives credit to those who deserve it, it also enhances your personal credibility with your audience, since such quotes imply that you've done your research. Therefore, as you record what you are learning from your resources, you must also fully document your discoveries. This process involves noting the author's name, the title of the source, the place and date of publication, the publisher of the source if known, and the page within the source from which your information was taken. You need this information even if you do not use all of it when you cite your source within the body of your speech.

There are several ways to ensure that you have all the necessary information for documenting your discoveries. The simplest and easiest is to prepare a complete bibliography card for every item you look at, and then to record only the author's last name, the date and pages cited from each work, on each note card. This method relieves the tedium of recording the complete bibliographic citation on every single note card taken from a particular

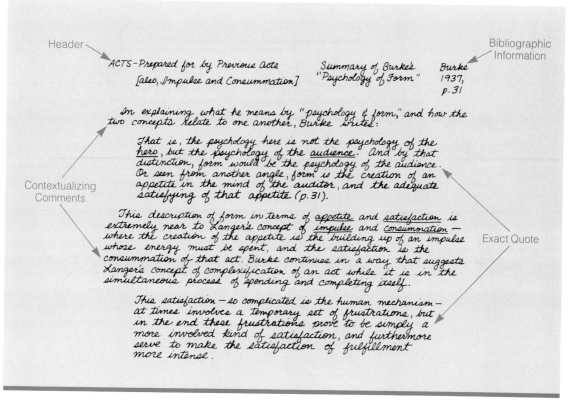

Header

Bibliographic Information

ACTS – Prepared for by Previous Acts
[also, Impulse and Consummation]

Summary of Burke's
"Psychology of Form"

Burke
1937,
p. 31

In explaining what he means by "psychology of form," and how the two concepts relate to one another, Burke writes:

That is, the psychology here is not the psychology of the hero, but the psychology of the audience. And by that distinction, form would be the psychology of the audience. Or seen from another angle, form is the creation of an appetite in the mind of the auditor, and the adequate satisfying of that appetite (p. 31).

This description of form in terms of appetite and satisfaction is extremely near to Langer's concept of impulse and consummation — where the creation of the appetite is the building up of an impulse whose energy must be spent, and the satisfaction is the consummation of that act. Burke continues in a way that suggests Langer's concept of complexification of an act while it is in the simultaneous process of spending and completing itself.

This satisfaction — so complicated is the human mechanism — at times involves a temporary set of frustrations, but in the end these frustrations prove to be simply a more involved kind of satisfaction, and furthermore serve to make the satisfaction of fulfillment more intense.

Contextualizing Comments

Exact Quote

Figure A-2   Typical Note Card for Speech Research

source. Figure A-1 above presents an example of a properly filled out bibliography card for the note card in Figure A-2.

Supplement Your Library Work Adequately

The library is an irreplaceable source of knowledge. Without the written word, the best of human thought and investigation would be lost to memory and future use. But a library is not your only source of developmental speech materials. Three additional sources of materials for your speeches are your own experiences relative to the topic, the opinions of experts currently researching the field, and your own fieldwork on the topic. To take advantage of these three resources, you must (1) inventory your own knowledge and experiences with the subject matter, (2) interview available experts to gather their knowledge for your own use, and (3) investigate the subject yourself.

Inventory Your Own Knowledge and Experience However tedious and impersonal your library research may have been, your speech itself should not seem tedious and impersonal. It should not "smell of the lamp," as Pythias is recorded to have said of the speeches of the Greek orator Demosthenes. In fact, however impersonal the research you do, your speech is always seen as a personal statement. After all, it is *your* understanding of the topic you are sharing; it is your interpretation of the facts you are presenting; it is your selection and synthesis of the available materials you are advocating; and it is your expression of ideas your audience hears delivered on a particular occasion.

Because a speech is always taken to be the speaker's individual statement of a point of view, your speech materials should be percolated through the filter of your own prior knowledge and experiences. Now that you've learned what the experts say, what do *you* think? What experiences have you had that can be drawn upon to support what you found in the library? For example, if you have researched budgetary cuts in federal poverty aid, do not stop with the impersonal statistical facts you found in the demographic almanacs; tell your audience about the old man in your neighborhood who could not pay his rent and was evicted after his supplemental income was slashed. This makes the impersonal research into a personal and powerful individualized statement only you could make. Since most speaking situations call upon you to speak about things you already care about, you probably have some relevant personal experiences that can help you individualize your research.

Interview Others to Gather Knowledge Knowledge gets into books and articles only because people put it there. There is nothing magical about the process by which ideas get stored permanently. Knowledge is stored by people. Therefore, after you have read what people have committed to writing in various library resources, talk to others to find out what's not in the books. On any college campus there are hundreds of experts available to you if you will only take the time to ask for their help. Most of these people will help you quite willingly if you are thoughtful enough to prepare ahead of time for an information-gathering interview. The guidelines for successful interviewing are relatively simple. The following outline represents the most important steps and principles for conducting an information-gathering interview once the expert you have chosen agrees to the meeting.

I. Prepare for the interview adequately.
   A. Research the topic. (So that you do not go into the interview ignorant of the basic facts. An interview is not a fishing trip.)
   B. Prepare a series of questions to be asked. (Don't depend upon divine inspiration to help you conduct the interview meaningfully. Plan ahead.)
   C. Find out what you can about the interviewee. (This will help you anticipate what is likely to happen during the interview.)

      D. Set an appointment time and date. (Then keep it promptly.)

  II. Conduct the interview systematically.
      A. Explain the purpose of the interview.
      B. Ask your prepared questions.
      C. Ask any follow-up or clarification questions you feel are necessary.
      D. End the interview by the agreed upon time.

 III. Conclude the interview process properly.
      A. Thank the interviewee orally.
      B. Send a written thank-you note.
      C. Forward any agreed upon results based upon the interview.

Investigate the Subject Directly Everything we know, we know because someone—either ourselves or others—has gone out exploring the situation for themselves. Everything you learned in your library work and your interviewing was originally learned by a direct wrestling with the subject matter itself in order to find out what is true and false. Somebody had to go out and "count the horse's teeth" so the rest of us could know. You can be that somebody. If the issue, for example, is the lack of student housing off campus, go to the office of the board of realtors and find out why no new housing units have been built recently. Look at the records in City Hall. Call the president of the local builders' association. You can be the primary investigator for your speech; you do not need to be dependent upon the facts and opinions generated by others.

    To sum up then, when you are researching your speech, use the library, interview experts, and look within your own present fund of knowledge. But do not deny yourself the opportunity to explore the topic directly for yourself—to become an expert in the subject. Your speech will be far better for all the research efforts you have put into it, whether those efforts were in the library, in interviewing experts, in your own experience, or in the field.

Explaining Processes

In Chapter 9 you learned six patterns for organizing the bodies of informative speeches. One of those six patterns is so widely used in informative speaking that it deserves some additional specialized consideration. That pattern is chronological order.

The reason chronological order is so widely used is that speakers are always explaining how to do something or how something works. In fact, Americans have always been strongly motivated to improve their individual ability—in everything from cooking to canoeing, from competing in sports to cooling their homes. There are how-to books covering everything from how to *Dress for Success* (Molloy, 1975) to *How to Read a Person Like a Book* (Nierenberg and Calero, 1971), from *How to Consult the I Ching* (Douglas, 1972) to *How to Buy Your Own House When You Don't Have Enough Money* (Gabriel, 1982). In performing most of these skills there is a definite chronological order to follow.

Because of the special importance of chronologically ordered speeches—especially those of the how-to variety—Appendix B treats in greater detail how to do a chronologically ordered process speech. Preparing speeches that explain chronologically ordered processes (the process speech, for short) requires you to give special attention to three of the major stages in speech preparation with which you are already familiar: (a) selecting the topic appropriately, (2) organizing the speech carefully, and (c) developing the speech fully. Let's begin by looking at the nature of topics that are especially appropriate for the chronological order typical of process speeches.

Selecting an Appropriate Topic

When you are considering topics for process speeches, you must make sure you are really talking about a process. A **process** is any activity occurring over time and having a definite beginning, middle, and end. If your speech topic meets the key elements of this definition, then your speech will be a process speech, and chronological order is required.

Many kinds of processes fit this definition. We can divide processes into at least six types: (1) how something natural happens, (2) how something mechanical works, (3) how something physical is made or manufactured, (4) how some human social process takes place, (5) how some historical situation came to be as it is, and (6) how some specific skill is performed or improved.

How some natural process happens. Our world is filled with naturally occurring processes that you may be qualified to explain to others. A few such natural processes include the following:

How a geyser works

How tornadoes and hurricanes are formed

How the nitrogen cycle operates

How caves are formed

How the human immune system functions

How alcohol affects the brain

How DDT travels in the food chain of an ecosystem

How something mechanical works. Not only is our natural world filled with processes that interest and fascinate us, so too is the world that people have made. A second type of process you may find worthy of explaining are the processes performed by the many mechanical wonders we humans have made. Among these processes are how any of the following things work:

How LED and LCD calculators and watches operate

How numerical control machining works

How an air conditioner produces cold air

How radar or sonar works

How a stereo speaker produces sound

How a computer's memory functions

How some physical object is made or manufactured. All of the objects made by humans were made by some personal or manufacturing process. The third type of process you might choose to talk about includes all those activities by which something is made. Samples of these processes include:

How hot dogs are made

How computer chips are manufactured

How beer is brewed

How penicillin is produced

How commercial candies are made

How gasahol is produced

How kosher meat is prepared

How phonograph records or tapes are mass produced

How shark meat is processed for consumption

How human social processes or institutions operate. Many of the most interesting processes you might talk about are related to the activities of social institutions and the people involved with them. That is, they are processes that people do. The fourth type of process that requires a chronologically ordered speech concerns the operation of our social transactions and institutions. A few of these processes include the following:

How your check gets back to you after you've written it

How an exorcism is performed

How the campus newspaper is produced

How livestock are judged

How a bill goes through Congress

How job interviews are conducted by the placement center

How some historical situation came to be as it is. Some processes occur only once, but they leave in their wake a relatively stable political situation or historical condition to be dealt with. We often want to know how the present circumstances came to be as they are. That is, we wish to know the process, the chronology, by which some current circumstance came into existence. A speech on historical process would explain such a chronology. Some examples of processes of this type include the following topics:

How the U.S. came to be involved in Central America

How the pyramids came to be built

How Ronald Reagan's political career developed

How the Cuban missile crisis of 1962 happened

How some skill is performed. Finally, there are the types of processes that we ourselves can perform and improve at. These are the source and fundamental motivation of the how-to speech. The following is a very small sample of the possible topics:

How to select and evaluate wines in a restaurant

How to use directional lighting in photography

How to make an ant farm

How to buy your own fast food franchise

Organizing Your Speech Carefully

The second step in speech preparation that needs special attention with the process speech is speech organization. Two suggestions are especially important to keep in mind: (1) divide the process memorably and (2) arrange the steps organically.

Divide the Process Memorably

As you discover every time you study for a test, human memory is a fragile, fallible thing. But as a speaker—especially one trying to get an audience to remember the details of a process—you must try to enhance your audience's chances of remembering the sequential details of your speech. Dividing the topic into a relatively small number of meaningful units is the key to enhancing your audience's memory.

The secret of dividing a process memorably is to limit the number of major steps into which you divide it. As you remember from Chapter 9 on speech organization, this means dividing it into from three to five major steps (but never more than seven). Information arranged in a small set of organized units is easier to remember than is information arranged as a series of independent items. Thus, even though most processes occur continuously over time, you will need to divide your process into discrete units in order to explain it. But our span of immediate memory dictates that you "chunk" the information you wish to transmit into no more than five or so units.

Since you cannot omit steps in order to get your speech down to the maximum of five chunks or units, you must work hard to group the steps into clusters or phases of the process that seem closely related. In this way each major chunk will have its own set of substeps, but again, a maximum of five. What this means for your actual speech preparation is this: You will probably begin by dividing your process into a simple list of all the steps that go into making it up; then you will look for natural clusters of activity that go together into some sort of larger units; and then you will give each cluster a short memorable title for your audience to use in remembering the major steps. The following example is a simple list of steps used in making a routine sales call.

How to Make a Sales Call
Preliminary List of Steps

1. Look for potential customers.
2. Look for information about the prospect.
3. Call the customer.
4. Introduce yourself.
5. Begin the presentation.
6. Give a detailed explanation of the product.
7. Answer objections.
8. Use indirect denial.
9. Admit objections.
10. Use boomerang arguments.
11. Try direct denial.
12. Attempt to close inconspicuously.
13. Build customer rapport.
14. Ask for the order.
15. Offer personal services.
16. Thank customer for time.
17. Call the customer afterward.

Starting with a list like this, you will next look for natural clusters of related steps and begin the process of reorganizing it into larger, more memorable chunks. The following is an example of how the topics might be grouped in a preliminary fashion.

First Attempt at Reorganizing and Grouping of Steps

I. Prospecting

II. Preapproach

III. Approach

IV. Actual presentation

V. Answering objections

VI. Trial close

VII. Closing the sale

VIII. Follow up

This is an improvement. But, even here there are too many main steps. One more reorganization seems to be required. Using the act-structured principles of chronological order developed in Chapter 8, here is what the final reorganization might look like.

Second Reorganization

I. Preparing for the sales call
   A. Prospecting
   B. Pre-approach

II. Developing the sales call
   A. Approach
   B. Presentation
   C. Answer objections

III. Culminating the sales call
   A. Trial close
   B. Final close

IV. Following up on the sales call
   A. Call the customer
   B. Deliver the post-sale services

Arrange the Steps Organically

To help make your process speech more vivid and memorable, make it as organic as the topic and subject material will allow. That is, you want to arrange the events you are describing in such a way that the process seems to build to a high point of activity, and then comes to a conclusion. Studies of oral memory suggest that the sense of action, movement, and climax make the speech intrinsically more memorable (Havelock, 1963). In the example developed earlier, the actual attempt to close the sale is the high point of the process, and the final organization of the steps permits this fact to be emphasized. The follow-up call is the cadence of the overall sales act described in the process speech, and helps to build an appropriate sense of organic closure into the speech. The process comes to a logical and satisfying end. Virtually any process speech may be organized in this organic fashion.

*D*eveloping Your Speech Fully

Every speech must employ adequate and appropriate supporting material, but the how-to process speech requires some special types of supporting material. This section presents four suggestions for how to develop a how-to speech in the fullest manner possible.

Give Complete Details Most of the processes that you perform you understand well enough to take its steps for granted. Remember, though, that your audience does not take them for granted. Thus, although your speech will typically have only four *main* steps, your speech's finer structure cannot omit steps that seem obvious to you unless you believe that those steps will also seem obvious to your audience. If you do not adopt your audience's point of view as you plan your speech, you may end up making sense only to those in the audience who are already familiar with the process.

Define Special or Unfamiliar Terms If the process is genuinely unfamiliar to your audience, it probably also has a specialized vocabulary that has been developed to make communication among its practitioners easier. But that specialized vocabulary is a foreign language to your audience. You will need to use new vocabulary occasionally in your process speeches, so be sure to offer definitions of the terms when you do.

Provide Special Considerations All speaking must take the audience and its background into consideration, and the process speech is no exception. You must provide your audience with four special considerations that can help them understand your speech better and remember it longer.

Explain why you do certain steps. Since in how-to speeches you are explaining a sequence of steps to be performed, it is often very helpful to explain why certain critical steps are performed. We often understand better and remember longer those things for which we understand the "whys." For example, if you are telling an audience how to bone a fish, you might say something like, "Always work with the knife turned away from you—so that you won't cut yourself if it slips." Or, if the speech is on preparing a recipe, you might say, "Let the milk cool after scalding before adding the beaten eggs—or it will cook the eggs and make the mixture lumpy." In this way you will be setting the advice in a context that makes it more memorable.

Anticipate potential problems. Many processes have moments when something typically can go wrong. If you know this, you can save your audience frustration by helping them prepare for the possibilities ahead of time. For example, you might say, "This step needs your constant attention because . . ." or, "You'll need to wear old clothes because the paint will spatter."

Give negative directions. Closely related to helping your audience anticipate potential problems is helping them to anticipate what they should *not* do as they try to execute a process. If you can envision what audience members might do wrong, tell them what not to do. For example, if your speech is on orienteering, you might need to tell your audience, "Don't hold the compass too close to your belt buckle or it may fail to register properly."

Tell what to do if something goes wrong. In spite of your best intentions, some processes can still go astray in typical but salvageable ways. If this is true of the process you are explaining, tell your audience what to do if something that can routinely go wrong actually does. The following two examples are typical of the things you might say on such occasions: "If the pecan pie is not yet firm, reduce the heat to 250 degrees and cook 15 minutes longer." "If you can't remove the bolt with a regular wrench, get some liquid wrench at the hardware store and soak the rusty bolt for a few minutes."

Help Your Audience Because your audience only hears the speech once—and because they are expected to understand the process well enough to actually perform it after they hear your speech—you should build several types of audience aids into your speech. There are four such aids that are especially useful in your process speeches.

Use visual aids. Show your audience the process, don't just talk about it. This means either an actual demonstration or using a flow chart of some sort. But, in either case, visual aids are exceptionally helpful in process-oriented speeches.

Speak slowly at important points. Keeping in mind that audiences only hear the speech once, you need to give them time to process the critical ideas within your speech. One way of doing this is to speak more slowly as you present your most important ideas for consideration.

Repeat key ideas. For the very same reason—that your audience only hears the speech once—you should probably build a greater amount of repetition into your process speech (at least the how-to variety) than you might employ in other types of speeches. Your audience must *do* the process, and they will appreciate the extra aids to their memory. They will not usually think you are talking down to them if you repeat key ideas.

Encourage audience participation. There are two types of audience participation: actual and imaginative. Actual participation involves having the audience try to do something along with you as you demonstrate it. Thus, if you are teaching them macrame, and the audience is small enough, put some cord in their hands and let them try to make something. In other types of processes, imaginative participation is all that is either required or possible. Have the audience picture themselves doing something, or put the speech in the second person *you.* Audiences understand better and remember longer when they have been imaginatively involved in understanding.

Bibliography

Douglas, Alfred. *How to Consult the I Ching.* New York: Berkeley Medallion Books, 1972.

Gabriel, Richard F. *How to Buy Your Own House When You Don't Have Enough Money!* Engelwood Cliffs, NJ: Prentice-Hall, 1982.

Havelock, Eric. *Preface to Plato.* Cambridge, MA: Harvard University Press, 1963.

Miller, George A. "The Magical Number Seven, Plus or Minus Two: Some Limits on Our Capacity for Processing Information." In: *The Psychology of Communication: Seven Essays.* (Ed.) George A. Miller. Baltimore: Penguin Books, 1967.

Molloy, John T. *Dress for Success.* New York: Warner Books, 1975.

Nierenberg, George I., and Henry H. Calero. *How to Read a Person Like a Book*. New York: Hawthorne Books, 1971.

Sample Informative Speech

Date Rape

The Date, Act I, Scene I—Place: Back seat of Volkswagen.

Jill: *"Gee, Jack, I'm really glad you asked me out. You know, I really didn't think you would 'cause you're a football player and popular and everything."*

"Well Jack, I like you OK—but not that much."

"Now Jack, . . . stop please, I'm not really into that. I'm only 15."

"Jack stop it. I mean it! Unlock the door!"

"Stop it! No!"

[Fade to black.]

Acquaintance rape: the forceable sexual assault in which the victim knows the assailant either intimately or casually.

That was me four years ago. I was in a situation where I had to decide if I was going to be intimidated or if I was going to act. Fortunately, I had the sense and the guidance to act. However, not all girls are as fortunate as I was. Some of them are intimidated by men, and intimidated by their fear of men.

Acquaintance rape is appearing more and more frequently on college campuses. Being more frequent, it is also coming out of the closet. People are starting to acknowledge that it is a form of violence.

In the February '86 issue of *On Campus,* a publication of *Newsweek,* they describe date rape as a little known form of sexual aggression. The magazine says that suddenly the problem is coming out of the closet and women are realizing they do not have to be the object of a man's physical aggression; they feel that they should have a say in whether or not they participate in sexual acts.

Concern about this form of rape led to a conference on acquaintance rape in Louisiana. The conference attracted administrators, police, teachers, and students from 27 states. Ellen Daughtrey, a counselor who attended this

---

Printed by permission of Cheryl Clements, Texas A&M University.

seminar, calls date rape "the single largest problem on college campuses today."

Today I would like to tell you a little more about this form of rape. First of all, I'd like to tell you about the problem. Should we talk about it? Should we admit that it's there? Second, I would like to tell you the causes of this form of rape. Why would a man force a *friend* of his to have sex with him? Third, I would like to tell you something about the victims of date rape. What makes them vulnerable to this form of crime? Fourth, I would like to inform you about what type of person a date rape victim is. Are they women who aren't in control of their lives? Last, I would like to tell you what happens after the rape. Is the victim encouraged to get help? What exactly happens after the rape?

First of all, how much of a problem is date rape? Professor Mary Collins of Penn State University did a three-year study of over 6000 women on 33 campuses and found that 15 percent of these women had been raped. Of those, 84 percent knew their assailant. The statistics of her survey show that out of 1000 women, 103 have been raped. Only 5 percent of those went to the police, and virtually none of those who knew their assailant did anything about it.

Second, what causes young men to want to force intercourse with a friend of theirs? Psychology professor Barry Burkhart of Auburn said "Our culture tends to fuse together sexuality and aggression." It encourages young men to sow their wild oats while they're in college. They say, "Do this before you get married 'cause after you get married you can't do stuff like this any-more." So, they're misled. They are made to believe that college is their opportunity to do something like this. Another probable cause of date rape is the encouraged aggressiveness in single-sex groups, like dorms, athletic teams, and fraternities. *On Campus* said that at the University of Florida, a fraternity keeps a tally of how many beers it takes to get one of the affiliated Little Sisters into bed. Meg Davis, who told *On Campus* that she is a rape therapist, was herself a rape victim. She was raped repeatedly at a fraternity party at Penn State. The only action taken against that fraternity was that their charter was revoked from the national fraternity. None of them were put in jail, none of them were fined. Nothing happened, except that she was humiliated.

Meg Davis wasn't wearing a sign that said, "Rape me!" What made her a victim? What is a date-rape victim like? Most researchers of this problem say that college women are particularly vulnerable to this form of rape. Freshmen are obviously the most likely to be date-rape victims. They're leaving home for the first time. They're out the door. No parents and very few high school friends around. They want to be accepted. They want a new boyfriend—maybe a senior. What more could they want? Burkhart also found that women who are more sure of themselves are less likely to be victims of date rape. They tell themselves, "I don't have to put up with this." Women who are able to do that are less likely to be victims of date rape.

What happens after the rape? How much can the victim count on her family, the police, and the judiciary system to protect her? Well, Meg Davis told *On Campus* that her father said, while she was pressing charges against the fraternity, "I can't believe you could do this to me." That was her *father!* While Davis was trying to press charges, she had obscene phone calls and prank letters from students on campus. Eventually, she had to drop out of college. It ruined her chances for the career that she could have had with a college degree. People like Meg's father don't want to admit that there is a problem. Schools like Penn State don't want to press charges; they are afraid of the lawsuits that could occur if the accusations are false. Police are hampering the case even more by mixing up street rape and date rape. They think, "Well, you knew the guy. There's no way he could have raped you." A rapist does not have to jump out of the bushes with a ski mask on. The police are mixing up the forms of rape. The person who suffers the most is the victim. No one was convicted in Davis's case.

However, the colleges themselves are taking some action to try and solve the date-rape problem. The dorms and fraternities are starting fish bowl groups so that men and women can discuss what should happen when a woman says "N-o-o-o" or "NO!" Does she mean no! or yes? Things like the fish bowl groups are going to help solve the problem.

Look at the word *rape*. It doesn't look nice. It doesn't sound nice. It doesn't feel nice. Don't be fooled. Date rape can happen to you.

Sample Persuasive Speech

One Nuclear Bomb Can Ruin Your Whole Day

One nuclear bomb can ruin your whole day. The threat of a nuclear war is something that we all live with every day, so we need to be more aware of the policies concerning this threat. I would like to share with you some of the ideas I have found through extensive research on this subject.

There is a serious problem caused by today's policy of Mutual Assured Destruction (MAD). MAD is a policy based on the assumption that if the United States is attacked by nuclear weapons from the Soviet Union, we will have enough time to return fire with our own nuclear weapons. In theory, neither side can win a nuclear war because each is mutually assured of destruction.

This policy contains several flaws that need to be corrected. I would like to discuss three major flaws with this policy. I would then like to suggest a new policy that will alleviate many of these flaws. Let us begin by discussing the flaws with the present day policy of MAD.

MAD's first flaw is the assumption that if the United States is attacked from the Soviet Union, we will have time to retaliate. Today's technology can make detection of incoming missiles almost impossible until an attack is over. This problem could wipe out most ICBM [Intercontinental Ballistic Missile] sites. This problem could wipe out bomber bases. Accidents could happen where it was thought that we were under attack, and we could launch our forces against a nonexistent threat.

MAD's second flaw is the assumption that the Soviet Union will be our attacker. With Soviet backing, a second- or third-class power could launch a single nuclear missile against us. If this problem occurred, who would the United States retaliate against, especially if the Soviet Union promised to back up the smaller guilty power? Our government's hands would be tied because of the threat of total nuclear war if we retaliated because of one bomb. A single nuclear missile could be launched by a terrorist organization. Because MAD's defense is the assumption of a retaliatory offense, we do not have an effective defense against small terrorist organizations. We are vulnerable to terrorist attacks because of this lack of defense.

MAD's third and worst flaw is that the policy is based on the idea that no one can win a nuclear war; but this idea is fast becoming a myth in the Soviet Union. The Soviet Union has an active antiballistic missile system surrounding Moscow. Moscow now has the sense of security that they can survive a nuclear attack. The Soviet Union's system eliminates MAD's defense of Mutual Assured Destruction. The Soviet Union has a very sophisticated radar and tracking system that would be needed to make a total ballistic missile defense (BMD) system operational. Thus, they can complete a fully operational strategic defense system before us, eliminating our only deterrent from war. If the Soviets complete a strategic defense system before we do, we could be held as nuclear hostages.

There is a solution to the problems in MAD's present day policy. First, we must pull together all existing programs on BMD [ballistic missile defense] and decide on a system that can be implemented quickly and upgraded in the future. After deciding upon an upgraded system, our nation must decide what to defend. The BMD system can defend only our retaliatory missiles and bomber bases. The BMD system can give full umbrella defense coverage for the entire United States and allies. Last, we must implement this system as quickly as possible.

This solution will solve the present day problems found in the MAD policy our nation follows. This solution will solve the problem of the time restraint to launch a retaliatory strike. With better tracking facilities of the BMD system, we will know for sure if an attack is imminent. With a BMD system, we will not need to immediately attack when we are uncertain about a Soviet strike because the defense system will absorb the frontal assault. The solution will solve the problem of someone other than the Soviet Union attacking our nation because the missiles would not get through the strategic defense system. The solution will solve the problem of the Soviet Union acquiring a defense system and eliminating our MAD defense. If both sides have a strategic defense system then the threat of nuclear war will be downgraded. If war did break out between the United States and the Soviet Union, total nuclear annihilation of the world would not result because the defensive systems would eliminate most of the nuclear missiles before they exploded.

This solution will cause no new real problems. All the basic technology has already been developed. The Space Shuttle will be able to place the system in orbit cheaply. The Space Shuttle can also maintain the upkeep of the system. There may be political problems over what the system should actually protect, but at least we will have something to protect our nation from the threat of nuclear war.

As you can see, today's MAD policy has three flaws that need to be corrected if we are to be assured that *one nuclear bomb won't ruin our day.* The United States is under a time constraint to quickly launch a retaliatory strike if an attack is thought imminent. The United States may not be attacked by the

Soviet Union. The Soviet Union is acquiring a strategic defense system that could eliminate our MAD defense.

A solution to the problems presented by MAD is a strategic ballistic missile defense system. The BMD system will allow for more time before launching a retaliatory strike. The BMD system will not allow single missiles to penetrate our defenses, so that we will not need to worry about an attack from a second- or third-rate power. If both the Soviet Union and the United States acquire a BMD defense system, both nations will be on equal footing; thus neither power will be inclined to believe that it can win a nuclear war.

Therefore, the United States needs to change its defensive policy from MAD to one based on a strategic BMD system.

Sample Professional Speech

From the Invisible Hand, a Gesture
of Contempt

The Steel Industry

By Joseph M. Gaydos, United States Congressman from Pennsylvania
Delivered in the United States House of Representatives, Washington, D.C.,
February 6, 1984

Mr. Speaker, I do believe in the invisible hand of the market, even as it pertains to steel; but having watched world commerce, I know that all hands have
fingers, particularly as they have affected steel since we adjourned the first
session.

Fingers may point in blame, beckon or show direction; they can be used
to test the weather or they can be sticky. A finger to the lips asks silence in a
conspiracy and one to the temple in a circular motion signals lunacy.

In our culture, the finger of a divinely inspired hand wrote the future on
a palace wall, and it also engraved the commandments brought down from
the mount. Fingers drawn inward make a fist of the hand, and this is a sign of
the intent to strike.

Furthermore, there are lone hands, upper hands; heavy hands and hands
that wash one another, whether visible or invisible. There are right hands that
do not know what left hands are doing. Things can go hand in glove, and often
the hand is of iron and the glove of velvet.

Hands and fingers, and the understanding of their language, are a mainstay of human communication even today amid the marvels of electronics.
They show direction.

The Direction of World Steel
Since we adjourned the first session, event has piled rapidly on event in
world steel and the sum of these developments points toward more (and
more intense) raiding of the United States market.

Even an unskilled hand can retrace the route of the invisible hand once it has moved. You can't tell where a tornado will form; you can't miss where it has been; there is devastation where it has touched down. The question we should consider is whether it is due to the hand of man or to natural forces.

So let's start with December 27, 1982, when Bethlehem Steel closed about 20 percent of its capacity and fired 10,000 workers.

These were workers and plants that had been competitive but fell after an 18-month siege by massive amounts of dumped and subsidized steel. The dumping and subsidies were proved in unfair trade cases.

Nevertheless, the Europeans continued to subsidize their industry, and the heavy hand of government staved off the bankruptcies that the invisible hand might have directed. The Asians held the hand of government and leaned on policy. The developing nations added capacity and increased shipments in the snap of an invisible finger.

And this remained the only steel-producing nation in the world to maintain an open market; and it is the biggest market.

Then on December 27, 1983, United States Steel announced the closing of about 20 percent of its capacity and the firing of about 15,000 workers.

Again the cause was loss of market to dumped and subsidized steel, this time over the last 30 months. And once again trade findings are proving the case.

And still there is maneuvering in Europe, support in Asia and ambition in the developing world.

Left Hand Works, Right Slumbers

The Europeans are showing a uniqueness in their adjustment to world conditions—a unique hypocrisy.

For example, U.S. protectionism was condemned out of hand in December by the European community's man in Washington, Sir Roy Denman. He said it threatens to topple orderly world trade. He scolded American steelmakers for claiming their legal right to fair trade, for fighting subsidy and dumping.

And Sir Roy was particularly indignant over the Fair Trade in Steel Act and its 15 percent quota, which would be the most generous in the world.

Meantime, in Europe, almost as Sir Roy sermonized here, the European community began talks with a number of countries on a matter of great importance, according to *The Wall Street Journal*.

They began negotiations on steel.

They began negotiations on restraining steel imports from 15 nations, including Brazil, South Korea and Japan. The Europeans want quotas that will limit their imports from the 15 nations to 4.4 million tons a year; this is less than 300,000 tons per year per nation.

Mr. Speaker, a 15 percent quota would have four times 4.4 million tons of imports into this market in a good year. We took almost four times 4.4

million tons in 1983, and it was a bad one. The finger would have to move a long way down our list of trading partners to get to one who sent only 300,000 tons.

What the European hand pushes away will find a resting place, and this is the only open market in the world; and at 15 percent, it would remain the most open.

Is this the infinite wisdom of the invisible hand? Or is it merely a finger of the hand raised in the universal gesture of contempt and disdain?

European Hand Supports Prices

Among the things that caused Sir Roy to wring his hands was the corrupting effect that a successful exercise of the legal right to fair trade might have on American business. And he condemned the higher prices he saw falling on American consumers.

In Europe, the community has just completed arrangements for internal production quotas and a price-fixing plan. They are setting "minimum prices" to end what they view as cut-throat competition to restore some profitability to the market.

As the director of the German Iron and Steel Federation said, "it would be much better to have clear control of subsidies, but the second best choice is to control the quantities of steel traded; and it seems the community has got this point."

The Germans calculate subsidies of $75-to-$85 a ton for steelmakers in Britain, France, Belgium and Italy. They figure subsidies on coal products from Finsider (an Italian concern) at $137 a ton for items selling at $278. They complain of sharp price cutting meant to keep up output and employment.

Meantime, even our flinty-eyed American market analysts acknowledge that "cut-throat competition" from imports has destroyed profitability for U.S. companies. New records for losses are set each year.

Clearly the hand of the market wears a government designed velvet glove in Europe.

A Joining of Hands

In addition, there are telling combinations taking place within countries as well as between and among different countries, and the invisible finger signals that the goal is the only open market in the world.

In Sweden, almost as Sir Roy wagged his finger at us in the name of free trade, four big specialty steel firms announced they will merge to become one of the biggest in the world. They will be very efficient.

And one of the prime market strategies of the surviving steelmaker is penetration of the U.S. market through an American subsidiary, Ingersoll Steel.

The Wall Street Journal story on the merger said the Swedes look on Ingersoll as a "strategic beach-head." It is peculiar how often the language of war finds application in international trade.

Meantime, a major U.S. specialty company has had to lodge a complaint with his government on what seems to be a haphazard and ineffective monitoring of specialty imports. Specialty steel is monitored because the American industry fought and won a major case while under assault from massive subsidy and dumping.

Furthermore, in Germany, Krupp and another giant company (Kloeckner) have merged casting and processing operations for titanium steel, forged pieces and steel for railroads. They expect significant savings and higher productivity.

All of these firms compete directly with American workers and companies because this is the only open market in the world.

The striking thing about these mergers is that in none of them does the hand of government seem to have been raised on antitrust or any other grounds. In most cases the governments officiated at the marriage ceremony.

They do not worry overseas about things like competitive balance in the market because the only market in which they really compete is this one; and they get every kind of help and encouragement to do it.

Invisible hands can shake in agreement and work towards a common goal when they have secured profitability and there is an open market.

Hands Across the Oceans

The combinations are not restricted by national boundaries.

For example, American specialty steel companies recently initiated a trade case against a Spanish steelmaker. The allegation is that there has been a violation of fairly won specialty quotas.

The owners of the Scofflaw Company are a Spanish Bank—talk about access to capital—and a Japanese Company.

Also, in Europe, the governments of Belgium and Luxembourg have worked out a deal to save three steel companies in which they have social and business interests, the journal reports.

The company controlled by the government of Belgium and the one controlled by the government of Luxembourg will share their EC production quotas. The third one—the one they own jointly—will get a $250 million infusion of capital.

In addition, events in the developing world have kept pace with those in Europe. In Asia, the South Korean government is building another export mill. The government of Taiwan wants to expand its capacity.

And in Brazil, whose steel exports here were up 108 percent last year, the first heats have been run in a brand new $3 billion export mill. The first steel will arrive here this month.

This new plant is jointly owned by the Brazilian Government and two minority foreign partners.

The partners are Kawasaki of Japan and Finsider of Italy. Finsider is the firm willing to subsidize up to 50 percent of the price of a ton. It is 93 percent owned by the government of Italy. It lost $2 billion in the last two years and the announced plan is to put $3 billion more into it by the end of 1985.

As for Brazilian steel, the U.S. Department of Commerce recently returned yet another verdict; the hand was found to be deeply in the cookie jar. There was a finding of dumping margins of up to 179 percent on hot rolled sheet and up to 225 percent on hot rolled plate.

It seems that one invisible hand washes another in international commerce.

Furthermore, the Dutch will put an additional $315 million into keeping alive their big steel group; and the French are hard at work trying to keep their biggest company out of the death grip of the invisible hand, which we know as bankruptcy.

On the Other Hand

Meanwhile, there have been two developments in the United States, the only open market in the world, that we can compare to see who might emerge with the upper hand.

U.S. Steel's closings drew applause from market analysts; from another part of the financial community, the act drew a reduction in credit rating. The reason? The company's debt to equity ratio now is too high. The result: higher borrowing costs in hand-to-hand combat with competition that has low cost or no cost government financing. Debt accounts for more than 80 percent of capitalization in some steel industries.

And a merger between two big steel companies is pending in the United States. It has been pending since September. It has been delayed while the Justice Department tries to read the palm of our invisible hand to predict what might happen here if it is permitted.

And all we have heard from Justice in public comment in more than 120 days is a thinly veiled threat. The quota bill, a Justice spokesman said, might make the merger anti-competitive and, therefore, doomed.

Is the invisible finger pointed at our temple and moving in circles? Or is the swirling merely the winds coming together for another tornado?

Meantime, in the world, companies have merged within countries and countries have come together within companies. Feeding from the generous hand of government, they will compete with subsidies of 50 percent and dumping margins of 225 percent.

They speak of and they establish strategic beach-heads in the only open market in the world. They use the language of war; and the first law of war is that there are no laws.

They do business in ways not sanctioned by what we consider to be sound practice; and they do things forbidden by law to American companies, particularly as they gather capital. In addition, they combine in power concentrations that would be severely punished were they to take place here; they fix prices and they agree on who will make what and where it will go.

Is this the visible hand of the American market working its evolutionary magic? Or is it the gloved fist unclenching momentarily to render a mono-digital salute to some quaint and insular 19th century notions that blend the passion of theology with the novel findings of economics?

In short, is it creative destruction or simply destruction?

The Moving Finger

As the poet, Fitzgerald, so appropriately said, "The moving finger writes; and having writ, moves on; nor all your piety nor wit shall lure it back to cancel half a line, nor all your tears wash out a word of it."

It may be bad business to fix prices in the long run; I believe this, firmly.

It may be bad business for government to subsidize and to own in the long run; I believe this as well.

However, just as bad money drives out good, so does bad business make it impossible for good business to survive; neither can honest workmen pay their taxes nor meet their responsibilities nor make the contributions this society demands if they play the lone hand against foreign governments.

If you cannot survive the short run, there is no long run. The immediate future is being written today by the hands of foreign governments in languages we refuse to comprehend.

But neither pious belief in 19th century theo-nomics, nor tears, will stay execution of the warrant once it is served. We had execution on December 27, 1982, and again on December 27, 1983. We can expect something in the last week of the last quarter of the year on a regular basis until we understand that some invisible hands are heavy clenched fists.

When we understand this, we can take a tip from the Dutch. No law or command of man can turn back a rising tide, yet the Dutch reclaim land from the relentless North Sea. There would be no Netherlands without the cunning hand of their workmen.

Natural change cannot and should not be thwarted; but whatever is made by the hand of man (whether visible or hidden) may by the hand of man be overturned.

The 15 percent quotas proposed by the Fair Trade in Steel Act are four times more generous than those the Europeans are negotiating with 15 nations, who are themselves more stingy in their markets than the community. The quotas are temporary. They are designed to give the American industry time (five years) to do for itself at higher borrowing costs what every other nation does for its steel industry at low cost or no cost.

And remember, without these subsidies and this dumping the foreign steel that is coming here would be too high-priced to sell in this market, which is the only open market in the world. Without the helping hand of foreign governments, this steel could not compete here.

So I invite all in this body who are concerned about the future of America and all of its industries to review all of the record and to consider co-sponsoring the bill.

It would be an act of even-handedness that is called for by the times; and it would be a gesture of steady-handedness that cannot be misinterpreted, not even by our friend, Sir Roy.

And finally, it would put a finger on a big part of the problem.

Photograph Credits

Index

R

Reading
  as preparation for listening, 69–70
  of speech, 13
Reasoning
  argument and, 320–324
  deductive, 323–327
  defined, 322
  inductive, 322–323, 327–329
Reference materials, 349–353
Refrain, 257–258
Rehearsing, 14–16, 192–193
Religious preference of audience,
    115
Repetition, 253–259
  forward motion and, 49
  of grammatical patterns, 164, 233–235,
    258–259
  of phrases, 257–258
  of sounds, 168, 254–255
  of words, 165–166, 255–257
Research, 349–359
Resonation, 274
Respiratory phase of speaking, 274
Rhetoric, 5
Rhetorical question, 179
Rhyme, 255
Rhythmic transitions, 196
Rise, defined, 42
Rokeach, Milton, 307–309
Rousseau, G. S., 40

S

Sarett, Lew, 283
Scenarios, 183, 262
Scheflen, Albert, 269–270
Sensory descriptions, 262
Sensory images, 261–262
Sentences, precision of, 249–250
Sex of audience, 111
Sheehy, Gail, 110
Shopping list transitions, 197
Signs in inductive reasoning, 328
Similes, 261
Simple-to-complex order, 158–159,
    162
Situation as element of communication,
    31–32

Situation-generated expectations, 56,
    57–62
  about ethics, 61
  about listeners, 60
  about occasion, 59
  about preparation, 59–60
  about purpose, 58–59
  about speaker, 57–58
  about topic, 58
Skopec, Eric William, 268
Slides, 212
Smith, Barbara, 189
Social class of audience, 114
Social involvements, 113–115
Sounds
  articulation of, 274, 286–287
  repetition of, 168, 254–255
Spatial order, 154–155, 162
Speaker
  audience and, 33, 175
  code and, 33–34
  credibility of, 174, 344–346
  delivery style and, 34
  as element of communication, 27–28
  ethics of, 61
  expectations about, 57, 61
  idea and, 33
  as visual aid, 215–216
Speaker-generated expectations, 56,
    62–65
Speaker–listener synchrony, 270–271
Speech. See also Body of speech;
    Persuasive speech
  artistic aspect of, 19–20
  central idea of, 8–9
  climax of, 50–51
  closure in, 50–51
  developmental materials in, 10–11,
    124–145
  forward motion in, 48–49
  growth in, 49–50
  importance of, 5–6
  internal preparation for, 44–48
  main points in, 10, 190–191, 271
  preparation of, 7–16
  research for, 349–359
  spontaneous vs. prepared, 4
  systems of, 148–149
Speech duration, 277
Speech production, 274, 275
Speech rate, 276
Stage fright, 16–19